READING RESEARCH

Advances in Theory and Practice

Volume 5

READING RESEARCH

Advances in Theory and Practice

Volume 5

D. BESNER
T. GARY WALLER
G. E. MACKINNON

Department of Psychology
University of Waterloo
Waterloo, Ontario, Canada

ACADEMIC PRESS, INC. 1985
Harcourt Brace Jovanovich, Publishers

Orlando   San Diego   New York   Austin
London   Montreal   Sydney   Tokyo   Toronto

COPYRIGHT © 1985 BY ACADEMIC PRESS, INC.
ALL RIGHTS RESERVED.
NO PART OF THIS PUBLICATION MAY BE REPRODUCED OR
TRANSMITTED IN ANY FORM OR BY ANY MEANS, ELECTRONIC
OR MECHANICAL, INCLUDING PHOTOCOPY, RECORDING, OR
ANY INFORMATION STORAGE AND RETRIEVAL SYSTEM, WITHOUT
PERMISSION IN WRITING FROM THE PUBLISHER.

ACADEMIC PRESS, INC.
Orlando, Florida 32887

United Kingdom Edition published by
ACADEMIC PRESS INC. (LONDON) LTD.
24–28 Oval Road, London NW1 7DX

ISSN 0191−0914

ISBN 0−12−572305−9 (hardcover)
ISBN 0−12−570501−8 (paperback)

PRINTED IN THE UNITED STATES OF AMERICA

85 86 87 88   9 8 7 6 5 4 3 2 1

LB
1050.6
.R42
v.5

CONTENTS

RECOGNIZING PRINTED WORDS: A LOOK AT CURRENT MODELS
Thomas H. Carr and Alexander Pollatsek

THE DECODING OF WORDS IN LEXICAL ACCESS: A REVIEW OF THE MORPHOGRAPHIC APPROACH
Marcus Taft

WHAT DO WE REALLY KNOW ABOUT SEMANTIC CONTEXT EFFECTS DURING READING?
Curtis A. Becker

PHONOLOGY IN VISUAL WORD RECOGNITION: THEIR IS MORE TWO THIS THAN MEATS THE I
Ian Dennis, Derek Besner, and Eileen Davelaar

THE TIME COURSE OF INFORMATION ACTIVATION AND UTILIZATION IN VISUAL WORD RECOGNITION
Mark S. Seidenberg

ATTENTION, AUTOMATICITY, AND AUTONOMY IN VISUAL WORD PROCESSING
Glyn W. Humphreys

WORD RECOGNITION AND CONSCIOUSNESS
Jim Cheesman and Philip M. Merikle

CONTRIBUTORS

Numbers in parentheses indicate the pages on which the authors' contributions begin.

CURTIS A. BECKER (125), *AT&T Information Systems, Lincroft, New Jersey 07738*

DEREK BESNER (167), *Department of Psychology, University of Waterloo, Waterloo, Ontario, Canada N2L 3G1*

THOMAS H. CARR (1), *IBM Watson Research Center, and Department of Psychology, Michigan State University, East Lansing, Michigan 48824*

JIM CHEESMAN[1] (311), *Department of Psychology, University of Waterloo, Waterloo, Ontario, Canada N2L 3G1*

EILEEN DAVELAAR (167), *Department of Psychology, Wilfrid Laurier University, Waterloo, Ontario, Canada N2L 3C5*

IAN DENNIS (167), *Department of Psychology, Plymouth Polytechnic, Plymouth P14 8AB, England*

GLYN W. HUMPHREYS (253), *Department of Psychology, Birkbeck College, University of London, London WC1E 7HX, England*

PHILIP M. MERIKLE (311), *Department of Psychology, University of Waterloo, Waterloo, Ontario, Canada N2L 3G1*

ALEXANDER POLLATSEK (1), *Department of Psychology, University of Massachussetts, Amherst, Massachussetts 01003*

MARK S. SEIDENBERG (199), *Department of Psychology, McGill University, Montreal, Quebec, Canada H3A 1B1*

MARCUS TAFT (83), *School of Psychology, University of New South Wales, Kensington, New South Wales 2033, Australia*

[1] Present address: Department of Psychology, University of Saskatchewan, Saskatoon, Saskatchewan, Canada S7N 0W0.

PREFACE

The study of visual word recognition has given rise to a vast array of models, issues, and data. The present volume offers a number of views on topics in visual word recognition that are under active investigation. The intent is not to provide a consensus (it is surely too early for that) but rather to provide new data and reconceptualizations relevant to evolving debates, to provide summaries of current theoretical positions, and, in some cases, to juxtapose radically different views in a rapidly growing field. Our hope is that this volume will prove useful to those actively engaged in the study of word recognition processes in reading, as well as to those who have some interest in the issues covered here but whose research involves other aspects of reading.

Overview

In Chapter 1 Carr and Pollatsek give a remarkably broad yet detailed review of current theory and data in visual word recognition. They distinguish the major classes of models that are currently on the table and identify the unique properties of the individual models that are being most actively investigated. They also trace the empirical foundations of the array of models they describe, and in the process bring into sharp focus a set of issues that ought to be addressed by any model of the word recognition process. Their ultimate conclusion is that a Parallel Coding System model is at present more viable than a host of other models in terms of its ability to handle data from tachistoscopic recognition, pronunciation, lexical and semantic judgments, and context effects. The main features of the model are three parallel systems. Two of these are driven directly by the processes of visual code formation; one is a visual/orthographic pathway to whole word meaning, the other is a visual/orthographic pathway mediated by morphemic decomposition. The third is a pathway based upon phonological recoding; this has an internal structure consisting of parallel mechanisms, one working on paired-associate principles, the other working on grapheme-to-phoneme translation rules. While Carr and Pollatsek's preference is for the PCS model, they explicitly caution the reader that the chapter contains a complicated review of a complicated area; there are few succinct and unqualified summary statements which can be made. A final, extended postscript dealing with text processing raises problems for all the models.

Lexical Access: Morphology and the BOSS

In Chapter 2 Taft provides a critical review of the evidence for and against the involvement of morphemes and syllables in lexical access of visually presented words. Based in large part upon his own seminal work, Taft's position is that a word is recognized when its access code, which is a representation of the first syllable (orthographically defined) of its first morpheme, is located in the recognition device of the lexical system. When a word is to be read, any prefixes are identified and stripped off. The remaining stem of the word is then parsed in order for the access code to be isolated. Once a match has been successful within the recognition device, the full details of the lexical item which has been accessed become available. The issue(s) seem straightforward. Cognitive economy at one level (lexical representation of the morpheme rather than separate representations for all possible forms) serves to increase complexity at another level in the form of demands for machinery to do the stripping and parsing. If Taft is correct, then any serious model of word recognition will need to incorporate these mechanisms. At present, the majority of these models do not even recognize morphology as an issue.

Context and the Verification Model

A continuing and major issue concerns how context affects visual word recognition. It is a received idea that *single* word context affects the process of visual word recognition. Hotly debated is whether *sentential* context also affects ongoing word recognition, or whether, as some believe, word recognition is best described as an autonomous process with the effect of sentential context being relegated to a post-lexical integration process. In Chapter 3 Becker reviews these and related issues in the context of a verification model of word recognition developed almost a decade ago. Basically, the verification model views context as part and parcel of the word recognition process. Becker presents new data, using sentence context, which suggest that there is little difference in the way that single word and sentence context have their influence upon visual word recognition.

Phonological Recoding

Is phonological recoding ever used in any of the common laboratory tasks thought to tap reading processes? In Chapter 4 Dennis, Besner, and Davelaar restrict themselves to discussion and investigation of one manifestation of phonological recoding. They report a series of four experiments on the pseudohomophone effect in lexical decision. In this task a string of letters is displayed and the observer must indicate whether the string spells a real word or not. The pseudohomophone effect refers to the fact that responses to letter strings which sound like, but are not spelled like, a real word (e.g., *brane*) are slower and/or more error prone than responses to letter strings which neither spell nor sound like a real word (e.g., *frane*). The data reported by Dennis *et al.* suggest that the pseudohomophone effect in lexical decision is context sensitive in that its presence/absence is linked to the presence/absence of homophones in the list. Their results thus offer a basis for reconciling different results in the literature. Theoretical interest resides in their claim that differences in the magnitude of the pseudohomophone effect do not, as commonly assumed, reflect differences in the degree of reliance on a phonological code or in the ease of grapheme–phoneme translation. In this account the *absence* of a pseudohomophone effect is not to be taken as evidence that phonological coding is eschewed.

Modularity, Orthography, Phonology, and Context

In Chapter 5 Seidenberg examines a number of issues, but addresses most directly the questions of how sentential context affects word recognition, and when and how phonological recoding affects visual word recognition. Seidenberg's views stand in sharp contrast to the conclusions from some of the other chapters. He argues that sentential context has only a post-lexical locus, in contrast to simple associative priming between words which has a lexical component. This argument is driven by the *modularity assumption* which asserts that visual word recognition is autonomous. This conclusion is quite different from Becker's (Chapter 3) and can be seen as an instance of two differing theoretical stances in search of a proving ground. This particular theoretical disagreement arises from distinctions which are drawn in one model (lexical versus post-lexical) but not in the other. Frank disagreements such as these are to be encouraged; emphasizing differences between theories will surely lead to a vigorous search for experiments capable of adjudicating between these views. Seidenberg also takes issue with the traditional two route model (independent visual and phonological codes) which can give rise to lexical/ semantic access and pronunciation. On the one hand, two route proponents appeal to the notion of *control* over phonological recoding in order to explain differences between tasks such as naming and lexical decision. On the other hand, Seidenberg concludes that the idea that subjects can control initial decoding processes is simply unsupported by empirical evidence. If anything, he concludes that the reverse is true; given the presence of certain triggering conditions, phonological processes run off despite the fact that such processing is detrimental to performance. The conflict between Carr and Pollatsek on the one hand and Seidenberg on the other is partially due to the different literature to which they refer. Nonetheless, it is evident that little agreement currently exists on how to reliably distinguish the notion of *control* from that of "the presence of certain triggering conditions." Finally, Seidenberg suggests that the traditional "boxes and arrows" approach to word recognition as exemplified in Morton's logogen system suffers from a number of deficiencies which limit its usefulness. He opts instead for a framework in which word recognition is seen as a parallel distributed process. This framework, which owes much to McClelland and Rumelhart's seminal work but goes beyond it, offers an account of a wide range of phenomena. In particular, it appears to provide an account of phonological effects in word recognition across a number of tasks and differences in the use of phonology as a function of reading skill. It also provides a framework for predicting similarities in performance between orthographies organized along quite different principles.

Attention, Automaticity, and Autonomy

A common view is that age-related increases in word recognition speed reflect the transition from "controlled" to "automatic" processing. To a large extent this automatic–controlled distinction has dominated theoretical orientations to recent study of problems in "attention," and a number of explicit proposals have been made which lay out criteria (both single and conjoint) for determining membership in these mutually exclusive categories. In Chapter 6 Humphreys provides an alternative to this view. He reviews evidence indicating that there are dissociations between the various criteria which are currently thought to characterize automatic processing in word recognition and identification, and suggests that even some of the single criteria are inchoate. Humphrey concludes by suggesting that the notion of functional autonomy should replace the automatic–controlled distinction because it provides both a better account of existing data and a more useful heuristic for driving new research.

Unconscious Perceptual Processing

In the final chapter Cheesman and Merikle address the question of whether word recognition is possible in the absence of conscious perceptual processing. Their first claim is that all of the backward masking studies commonly believed to support the notion of unconscious perceptual processing are unconvincing because of serious methodological flaws. They then proceed to demonstrate that when brief, backward masked stimuli are at properly defined and assessed chance levels of detectability, these stimuli have *no* influence on decisions to other subsequently presented stimuli which are clearly visible to the subject. Cheesman and Merikle take this result as evidence that when an *objective* measure of awareness is defined as chance detectability, unconscious perceptual processing simply does not occur. They note, however, that as soon as detectability is above chance, priming effects begin to emerge despite the fact that *subjects claim not to see anything*. Cheesman and Merikle therefore suggest a revised definition of unconscious processing, one which relies upon *subjective* rather than *objective* thresholds. In order to avoid the problem of merely transferring the responsibility for operationally defining awareness from the investigator to the observer, they suggest an additional criterion; stimuli presented below a subjectively defined awareness threshold should show qualitatively different effects upon behaviour than stimuli presented above this threshold. An elegant experiment which fulfills this criterion is reported in the chapter. Their approach undoubtedly will stimulate new interest in unconscious processes.

The editors would like to thank Philip T. Smith of Reading University, England, who served as a consulting editor on this volume.

D. BESNER
T. GARY WALLER
G. E. MACKINNON

RECOGNIZING PRINTED WORDS: A LOOK AT CURRENT MODELS

THOMAS H. CARR* and ALEXANDER POLLATSEK†

*IBM Watson Research Center, and
Department of Psychology
Michigan State University
East Lansing, Michigan
and
Department of Psychology
†University of Massachusetts
Amherst, Massachusetts

For the last 25 years or so experimental studies of visual word and letter processing have appeared at a great rate. These investigations have amassed an enormous body of data on the relative perceptibility of strings of letters as a function of many, many different variables. As the body of data has grown, emphasis has shifted away from empirical explorations of the conditions that influence perceptibility toward attempts to reconstruct the cognitive system that does the perceiving. This article will examine the models of visual word recognition that have resulted from these attempts. While we will touch on developmental issues, the primary focus is on mature,

1

Copyright © 1985 by Academic Press, Inc.
All rights of reproduction in any form reserved.

experienced readers. Thus all the models apply to adult readers of average or above-average ability unless specific mention is made of other populations.

We have three goals in this discussion. First, we will distinguish two major classes of models that are currently available and, within these classes, identify the unique properties of the individual models that are being most actively investigated. Second, we will trace the empirical foundations of the array of models we have described and in the process establish a set of issues that ought to be addressed by any model of the word recognition process. These issues are organized around the major empirical phenomena that a model must be able to account for. Finally, we will comment on the relative viability of the various models.

I. CLASSES OF MODELS

In our view, the models of word recognition that are active and viable can be divided into two classes: the **lexical instance models** and the so-called "horse race" or "multiroute" models, which we will refer to as **parallel coding systems models**. The class of lexical instance models actually has quite a complicated internal structure. We will eventually break it into three subclasses, though more could be created if one made use of all of the many dimensions of difference among the models that are potentially important. Figure 1 portrays our classification scheme in a rough way.

A. The Basis of the Classification Scheme We Have Chosen

The division between lexical instance models and parallel coding systems models is based on the type of mechanism by which each achieves behavior that appears to embody generalizable rules. The particular rules of interest here are the ones contained in linguistic descriptions of the orthographic and phonological structure of words. This sort of issue is not unique to models of word recognition: capturing the underpinnings of apparently rule-governed behavior is a persistent and highly visible problem in cognitive psychology. It has received special attention in such varied areas of study as concept formation (Brooks, 1978; Smith & Medin, 1981), language acquisition (Brown, 1973; Gleitman, 1981), language production (Chomsky, 1957, 1965; Lachman, Lachman, & Butterfield, 1979, Chapters 3–4), and spatial navigation (Tolman, 1948) in addition to word recognition, and in each area it has sparked extended debate.

Traditionally, one of two different gambits has been taken in attacking the problem. Theoreticians have supposed either that people know rules

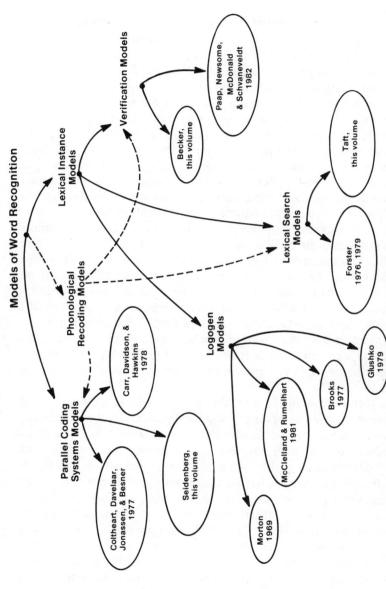

Fig. 1. Organizational diagram of the models of visual word recognition reviewed in this article. The two major categories, the lexical instance models and the parallel coding systems models, are indicated with solid arrows. The lexical instance models are divided into three subclasses, the logogen models, the lexical search models, and the verification models. Relationships between these models and a third major category, the phonological recoding models, are indicated with dotted arrows. For reasons described in the text, phonological recoding models no longer exist on their own, but they have influenced the course of modeling in general and the development of parallel coding systems models, lexical search models, and verification models in particular. These influences are discussed in the text.

directly, or that people know many instances or examples from a domain of activity that can be described by rules and use those instances in some way that mimics knowing the rules themselves. The study of word recognition is no exception to this tradition. Lexical instance models have attempted to mimic rules through clever use of instances, whereas parallel coding systems models have refused to burn any bridges in their quest for explanatory power—they employ both types of mechanisms, proposing that the mechanisms operate in parallel.

In order to better understand the difference between these two approaches, it will help to describe a third species of model that thrived in the early 1970s but is now nearly extinct (e.g., Gough, 1972; Rubenstein, Lewis, & Rubenstein, 1971; Spoehr & Smith, 1973). According to these **phonological recoding models** activation of the meaning of a printed word can only occur if the visually presented string of letters is mentally recoded into a phonological representation (essentially converting reading into a variant of listening). This representation is **prelexical,** meaning that it is constructed from knowledge of the generalizable rules that govern translation from graphemes or spelling patterns to phonemes or pronunciation patterns. The recoding process has no access to instance-based knowledge of particular words. Because of the rule governance of recoding, these models are capable of recognizing printed words that are in a perceiver's speaking vocabulary but have not been seen before (and also printed "pseudowords" that are orthographically well formed but are not actually words and therefore have been neither seen nor heard before, such as *nard* or *prisket*). This is an advantage in that it captures in a straightforward way the characteristics of word recognition that seem to demand an ability to follow rules.

However, such models run into trouble with the characteristics of word recognition that deviate from rule governance. Specifically, they are incapable of correctly processing words whose phonological recodings are irregular with respect to normative generalities, such as *one, two,* or *shoe,* and they are incapable of dealing with families of orthographically related words for which it is simply impossible to find a generality, such as the *ough* words (*rough, tough, enough, dough, though, bough, cough, bought, brought, sought, thought, drought*). Furthermore, they cannot distinguish between strings of letters that are spelled differently but pronounced the same, such as *there* and *their*—once recoded, such quite different words become identical. These are disadvantages that have laid strong forms of the phonological recoding position to rest. It is now generally agreed that visual codes can gain direct access to word meanings independently of phonological recoding (see, e.g., Barron & Baron, 1977; Bauer & Stanovich, 1980; Coltheart, 1978, 1980; Kleiman, 1975; McCusker, Hillinger, & Bias, 1981;

Patterson & Marcel, 1977; Singer, 1980; Stanovich & Bauer, 1978). However, the exact relation between visual and phonological access remains a matter for debate (e.g., Besner & Davelaar, 1982; Besner, Davies, & Daniels, 1981; Carr, in press; Coltheart, 1978; Singer, 1980; Bauer & Stanovich, 1980). The lexical instance models have chosen to drop phonological recoding as a prelexical encoding process, whereas the parallel coding systems models have chosen to retain it and add a complementary mechanism based on visual access to knowledge of instances. Let us turn to a more detailed description of these two classes of models.

B. The Lexical Instance Models

We said earlier that the category of lexical instance models has a complicated internal structure. We will now try to lay that structure out. The defining characteristic of the class as a whole is that its members depend on visual access to a memory system that represents individual words rather than using general rules in order to achieve recognition. In this respect lexical instance models are the opposite of phonological recoding models. The distinction between using instances and using rules gets blurred somewhat (as we will see) if one expands the meaning of "lexical instances" to include morphemes or other subword units that have been directly experienced (such as letter clusters). To simplify the discussion we will assume at the beginning that lexical instances are words and later consider the consequences of weakening that assumption.

A note on terminology that applies to all the lexical instance models should precede discussion of the three subclasses. Cognitive psychology is witnessing a rapid increase in the popularity of theories in which most of the work of perceptual recognition, categorization, and decision making—even very abstract processing that requires considerable generalization of established knowledge to new stimuli, situations, or events—depends on memory systems that represent **only** specific episodes of experience (e.g., Jacoby & Brooks, 1984; Whittlesea, 1983). These nonanalytic, antiabstractionist theories are sometimes referred to as "instance based" or "exemplar based" (Brooks, 1978; Hintzman & Ludlum, 1980). Our use of the term "instance," however, does not carry this implication. A **lexical instance model** is one in which, like the dictionary, each word has its own separate representation in a memory system, and that representation is responsible for recognizing all occurrences of the word in print, regardless of variations in typeface, ink color, letter spacing, or other stimulus properties that do not change the identity of the word. Thus the lexical instance models of word recognition operate at a level of abstraction a step higher than the newer, episode-based models. A "lexical instance" is a prototype of a word

(Posner & Keele, 1968; Rosch & Lloyd, 1978; Smith & Medin, 1981) rather than the episodic trace of a single encounter with the word in a specific text at a specific time and place. Though episode-based theories show considerable promise, their eventual standing relative to the more established notion of prototypic representation remains to be determined.

The three subclasses of prototype-based lexical instance models can be identified by taking into account how their internal representations get activated by input from the visual stimulus. **Logogen** or **word detector** models propose that sensory inputs are fed into a system of stored representations that function as threshold-type detection devices. Each detector responds to sensory inputs as if they were pieces of evidence either for or against the presence of a particular word represented by the detector. If a representation collects enough pieces of evidence to exceed a threshold of certainty that its word is in fact present, then it activates a code or set of codes containing information about the word and makes the information generally available to decision and response mechanisms that might act on it.

Because of a variety of empirical findings that the speed or accuracy of word processing often depends on the familiarity of the word (e.g., Broadbent, 1967; Broadbent & Broadbent, 1975; Scarborough, Cortese, & Scarborough, 1977; Solomon & Postman, 1952; Treisman, 1978; Theios & Muise, 1977), the system is biased as a whole toward easier recognition of words that are more familiar. This is accomplished by making the evidence requirements of the logogens vary with the frequency and recency of their past activations. The logogens of words that occur frequently and are encountered quite often while reading require less evidence for their activation than the logogens of words that occur only rarely.

Because sensory input has simultaneous access to all of the detectors in the lexicon and these detectors carry out their evidentiary computations in parallel, a given word stimulus may cause several detectors to become partially activated. As an example, the stimulus *horse* might cause considerable activation in the detectors for *house* or *hearse* or *hose* and smaller amounts of activation in the detectors for *force* or *louse* or *noise* in addition to activating the *horse* detector. As sensory evidence accumulates, detectors representing words that are visually quite similar to the stimulus approach their thresholds faster than detectors representing words that are less similar. The first detector to exceed its threshold wins the competition and announces its word to the rest of the information-processing system. One expects the winner to be the actual stimulus word on most occasions. The foregoing description characterizes the first creation of Morton (1969), who coined the term "logogen," as well as the "activation-synthesis" model of Glushko (1979) and the "interactive activation" model of McClelland and Rumelhart (1981).

Subsequent work by Morton (1979; Murrell & Morton, 1974; see also Kempley & Morton, 1982) has retained the detector concept of activation, but has turned from one-to-one mappings between logogens and words to a representational scheme in which each detector corresponds to a morpheme. The difference lies in how polymorphemic words such as *loving, decoded,* or *antidisestablishmentarianism* are represented. For words of a single morpheme such as *crowd, gentle,* or *seed* the morphemic representational scheme and the word scheme are the same. The need to decompose stimulus words that are polymorphemic into their constituent morphemes adds some steps to the recognition process that are not present in logogen models whose lexicons represent words instead of morphemes. While Morton has not pursued the processing implications of morphemic versus lexical representation in great detail, another group of researchers has focused quite directly on the special requirements of morphemic representation. That group is led by Forster (1976, 1979) and Taft (1979; this volume) and its product is called the **lexical search model.**

Many characteristics of lexical search distinguish it from the logogen approach. First, it works through serial matching of sensory input against the members of a list of candidate representations retrieved from the mental lexicon, as opposed to the logogen model's reliance on parallel access to the entire body of word detectors simultaneously. In order to achieve a bias toward familiar words, the candidate list is ordered by frequency of occurrence. One of the central concerns of the approach is to constrain the search process to avoid establishing the whole lexicon as the search set. This pruning of the lexicon is accomplished by postulating an "access code" consisting of a subset of the letters of the printed stimulus that has to be matched in order for a lexical entry to become a candidate in the search. Since the access code may be a subword unit—a morpheme or a letter cluster of some kind—the model must include processes that can decompose words into these units and map them onto the morphemes represented in the lexicon. A major part of the research program spawned by the lexical search model involves determining the nature of the access code in light of the constraints on orthography that can be described linguistically plus the kinds of decomposition processes that are required by the morphemic representation scheme (Lima & Pollatsek, 1983; Taft, this volume).

Together, these characteristics of the lexical search model make it seem quite different from the logogen model, and on this basis we give it a separate classification. There is yet another distinction between the lexical search and logogen models, however, that is not heavily emphasized but which seems to us to be very important. Forster and Taft, following a proposal of Rubenstein *et al.* (1971), envision the use of a top-down checking process in which sensory input from the stimulus is consulted by activated lexical codes before those codes make their information available to decision and response mechanisms. The checking process verifies that the word chosen in the initial search of the lexicon is in fact the word that is present as the stimulus. If verification fails, then other lexical candidates are tried until the right one is found. Again, this is an ordered process, with more frequently occurring candidates being verified ahead of less frequently occurring candidates.

Using a verification procedure to obtain independent confirmation of recognition decisions contrasts with the logogen model's reliance on internal competition among detectors within the lexical system itself to select a single code from a larger number of possible candidates. The mechanisms required to achieve this external confirmation are potentially quite complex and their operation could account for a considerable portion of the variance in the time course and accuracy of recognition. The lexical search model does not focus on this possibility, but other models do. Thus our third subclass of lexical instance models consists of those that give verification a central place in the recognition process and rely on its properties for a large part of their explanatory power. Two such **verification models** are currently active, one by Becker (1976, 1979, 1980) and one by Paap, Newsome, McDonald, and Schvaneveldt (1982).

C. The Parallel Coding Systems Models

The three types of lexical instance models all stand in contrast to models based on the notion of parallel coding systems, which we will refer to from now on by the initials PCS. In the PCS models there is a visually addressable lexicon whose job is to process words that have been entered into it as a result of past reading experience and a rule-based phonological recoder that can process visually unfamiliar words that do not have entries in the visual lexicon because they have not been read before. (Pseudowords, of course, are the ultimate in unfamiliar words.) The combination of mechanisms is intended to give the PCS approach the best of both worlds in trying to maximize the total resources available for the task of recognizing words.

An important question is the role of the phonological recoder in processing familiar words. This question arises because the parallel organization of the mechanisms can potentially cause difficulties, most notably with familiar words whose pronunciations are irregular with respect to the rules of phonological recoding (e.g., *women, sword, some*). For such words the two mechanisms will reach conflicting decisions about the appropriate pronunciation. To the extent that phonological recoding is involved in semantic access, they may arrive at conflicting decisions about the meaning of the word as a result. Since people are able to resolve such conflicts, so must the PCS models if they are to be viable.

Three different kinds of solutions to this problem are possible. The first is to assume that conflicts do not arise because the recoder never tries to process familiar words on which the lexicon can succeed and the lexicon never tries to process unfamiliar words or pseudowords. This ESP-like solution has been attributed to PCS models by some advocates of the lexical instance approach, including Glushko (1979) and Barron (1981), but it does not appear to be a solution that any of the PCS models has actually adopted.

A second possibility, proposed by Coltheart, Davelaar, Jonasson, and Besner (1977) and reiterated by Coltheart (1978, 1980), is to assume that conflicts can arise in principle, but that they are minimal in natural reading situations where most of the words are familiar. This is because the visual route to the lexicon is held to be much faster than the phonological recoder, meaning that for visually familiar words recognition is always completed before the prelexical phonological code becomes available (see Coltheart, Besner, Jonasson, & Davelaar, 1979). When conflicts do occur, they will be in situations where words are quite unfamiliar or in situations that require unpracticed decisions about the phonological structure, lexical status, or meaning of letter strings. Such unpracticed decisions may take so long to make that prelexical phonological recoding can catch up with visual access and create some competing activation in the lexicon that interferes with the evaluation process required by the decision. In this way Coltheart and colleagues relegate conflict between mechanisms to the status of a minor nuisance that mainly plagues laboratory tasks like lexical decision rather than real-world reading activities.

The third solution is to assume that both mechanisms may attempt to encode all types of letter strings, making conflicts possible, and that the processing rates of the two mechanisms can be sufficiently similar that recognition of a word may often—rather than only rarely—involve both mechanisms. This third solution, while attractively flexible, is also the most complicated because of the need to deal explicitly with how conflicts between the two mechanisms are handled. As a result it has seldom been worked out in detail by anyone who has raised it as a possibility, either in the present context of reconciling the outputs of visual access and phonological recoding (e.g., Carr, 1986; Coltheart, 1978; Meyer & Gutschera, 1975) or in the context of reconciling competing multiple activations caused by the visual route alone, as in the logogen models (e.g., Glushko, 1979; Larochelle, McClelland, & Rodriguez, 1980). Indeed, one of the reasons for the existence of the verification approach as an alternative to the logogen model is the difficulty of the problem of resolving competition among word detectors that are activated to similar levels (Allport, 1979; Becker,

1976). Progress has recently been made by McClelland and Rumelhart (1981) toward a solution for competitions arising within the lexicon, but to date no algorithmic solution has been proposed for competitions between the lexicon and the phonological recoder. The third solution to the conflict problem faced by PCS models would be worth implementing only if research were to demonstrate that the PCS approach is desirable but the two simpler solutions do not work. We will ultimately argue in this article that it is time to seriously attempt such an implementation.

II. THE EMPIRICAL FOUNDATIONS OF THE ARRAY OF MODELS

One has to wonder how a collection of models that ostensibly all pursue the same end could be so varied. It might seem that the task of choosing among the models would be straightforward: If they are so dissimilar they could not all be right. However, the study of word recognition is by no means a slow-moving business. The rapid accumulation of new data means that the phenomena to be explained and hence the characteristics of the models themselves are in a continual state of flux. As a result, the area is not very well ordered, despite the fact that by many criteria it is highly developed and quite sophisticated. When one is immersed in the daily work of the field, its flux and its sophistication are exciting and rewarding, but when one attempts to step back and conduct a survey as we are now doing, the same characteristics can create confusion.

There are several reasons for this state of affairs. First, the models do not share a standard definition of "word recognition" (and trying to get everyone to agree on one might cause the intellectual equivalent of a brawl). Second, the models arise out of several different task domains and do not all address the same data base. In part this is a direct consequence of the lack of a shared definition of word recognition and in part it is a matter of historical and methodological accident. Third, the models draw on different kinds of source metaphors for their inspiration, ranging from the physiological organization of nervous systems to the functional architecture of computer systems. This means that the models sometimes differ in their pretheoretical assumptions, making the differences that arise out of definitions and data bases more profound and more difficult to reconcile to everyone's satisfaction.

Given these sorts of contributions to word recognition's current theoretical state, we feel that it is necessary to try to capture the range of definitions, task domains, and data bases of the various models as well as their more formal conceptual properties in order to have a useful and accurate survey. For that reason we will now try to lay out in a brief and rather selective fashion the empirical foundations of the classes of models we have identified. Hopefully this device will provide a more concrete understanding of the models and also the raw materials for evaluating them. We want to obtain from our empirical odyssey a set of issues and phenomena that must all be comprehended in order to solve the problem of "word recognition" in a general way. In keeping with the manner in which models actually emerge from data we will take a substantially task-oriented perspective in this section. The discussion will begin with a consideration of tachistoscopic recognition, move on to pronunciation, and then consider tasks that involve semantic processing. Models will be introduced as we come to task domains and empirical phenomena that they have tried to address in central ways. We warn you in advance that the result is a complicated review that offers very few succinct and unqualified summary statements. This, however, mirrors the character of the area we are reviewing.

A. Tachistoscopic Recognition as a Testing Ground

A major body of data that most models of word recognition make an attempt to explain comes from tachistoscopic recognition experiments in which a string of letters (henceforth, the "target") is exposed for a very brief time, typically tens of milliseconds, and the perceiver is asked either to report as much of the stimulus string as possible (the "whole report" technique) or to choose the target from a set of response alternatives provided by the experimenter ("tachistoscopic forced choice recognition" or "the Reicher paradigm"). Tachistoscopic recognition was originally conceived as an attempt to simulate aspects of the conditions under which words must be recognized during natural reading: a brief exposure of a stimulus to the fovea that occurs during a single fixation of the eye on a particular point in the text followed by an eye movement that causes blurring and lowered information intake until a new fixation point is reached (see Section IV for a more detailed discussion of eye movements and information-processing conditions during reading of extended text).

Exemplars of all the types of models except one have been applied to tachistoscopic recognition performance at one time or another; only the lexical search models have not taken this data base as a major testing ground. Therefore we will begin with a discussion of tachistoscopic recognition, whose goal is to show the PCS, logogen, and verification models in action.

In 1886 Cattell, using the methodology of whole report, demonstrated that tachistoscopically presented words are identified more accurately than random letter strings of the same length. In 1969 Reicher replicated the advantage of words over random strings and also showed that words are identified more accurately than single letters. Especially in the context of the theories of serial letter-by-letter readout from iconic memory that prevailed at the time, it was quite remarkable to find that four letters could be identified easier than one letter if the four letters spelled a familiar, meaningful word.

A modification to Cattell's whole report technique enabled Reicher to argue that this striking "word superiority effect" was likely to have perceptual origins rather than arising from conscious tendencies to guess unperceived letters in ways that produce words (for an extended discussion of why one cannot distinguish these two possibilities using the whole report technique, which is highly susceptible to guessing strategies, see Smith & Spoehr, 1974). Instead of asking subjects to tell what they saw in whole report fashion, Reicher masked the target stimulus with visual noise and displayed two response alternatives for the subject to choose between. One alternative was the target and the other was a distractor of the same type. Word targets were paired with word distractors that differed by a single letter, such as *word* and *work* or *cane* and *cone,* random nonsense strings were paired with other nonsense strings, and single letters were paired with other single letters. This procedure was intended to eliminate a guessing strategy that could favor words: Since both alternatives were words when the target was a word, guessing that the string was a word would presumably be of no help in selecting the correct alternative. On this basis Reicher concluded that letters in words were **perceived** more accurately than a single letter presented alone.

1. Why Are Letters in Words Perceived More Accurately? The Unitized Code Hypothesis

A number of alternative accounts of Reicher's phenomenon ensued. Knowing which account is correct would place some constraints on a model of word recognition. The details of these accounts and the differences among them have been recited elsewhere (e.g., Baron, 1975, 1976; Carr, 1984; Henderson, 1982; Johnston, 1981; McClelland, 1980). For present purposes the gist will do.

First, Massaro (1973; Thompson & Massaro, 1973) argued that the phenomenon was not perceptual after all, but was the result of trying to guess the identity of the critical letter that distinguished the two alternatives given that some of the other letters in the word had been recognized but the critical letter had not. For example, if the subject had seen *wor#* in the word condition, then only *d, e, k, m, n,* and *t* could fit in as the last letter and still make a word, whereas if the subject had seen *owr#* in the nonsense condition or # in the letter condition then any of 26 alternatives would be equally likely. A guess, then, would be more likely to succeed on a chance basis in the word condition than in the nonsense condition, so that more accurate perception of the letter string would not necessarily have to occur in order to obtain a word superiority effect.

To test this hypothesis Massaro specified the alternative critical letters **in advance.** No matter whether the stimulus was a word, a nonsense string, or a single letter it would contain either a.g, c, r, or p. The subject's only job was to decide on each trial which of the four critical letters had occurred. Under this restriction subjects were no more accurate at recognition performance on the four words *age, ace, are,* and *ape* than on the four nonsense strings *vgh, vch, vrh,* and *vph*, and single letters were recognized more accurately than either type of multiletter string.

However, as you can tell from the stimulus list, the critical letter always appeared in the middle position of the display, right at the subject's fixation point. In addition, the stimulus strings were quite widely spaced (each three-letter string subtended 3° 20′ of visual angle). Therefore subjects may have focused their attention on the middle letter position to such an extent that the other letters in the multiletter strings went essentially unprocessed. If so, then Massaro's experiments were a poor test of the word superiority effect. Functionally speaking, words were not used as stimuli.

Three subsequent experiments supported this reinterpretation of Massaro's results. Carr, Lehmkuhle, Kottas, Astor-Stetson, and Arnold (1976) spaced their stimuli closely rather than widely (1° for each three-letter string) and allowed the critical letter to appear in any of the three display positions by adding more letter strings of each type to the stimulus pool. With these changes, the advance specification of a fixed set of critical letters failed to eliminate the word superiority effect. Purcell, Stanovich, and Spector (1978) then showed that a word advantage could even be obtained in Massaro's design, with the prespecified critical letters only occurring at the middle position of the display, so long as the stimuli were spaced closely enough to prevent subjects from excluding the other letters in the display from being processed by focusing on that position (0.53° for each three-letter string).

These two experiments came in the wake of Johnston and McClelland's (1974) demonstration that in the original Reicher task the word superiority effect could be made to appear or disappear by telling subjects how to focus their attention. When subjects were instructed to try to take in the whole display at once because the critical letter could occur at any position, a robust word superiority effect was found. When subjects were instructed to focus on one particular position because the critical letter would only occur there, the effect reversed and letters were actually perceived more accurately in nonsense strings than in words. The spacing used by Johnston and McClelland (slightly less than 2° for each four-letter word) was intermediate between the wide spacing used by Massaro and the close spacing used by Carr *et al.* (1976) and Purcell *et al.* (1978). Taken together, these experiments make it clear that the word superiority effect is not due to a postperceptual guessing strategy. If the effect is not magical, then the alternatives would seem to be either a process that treats the word as a whole Gestalt or a process that deals with some or all of the component letters in concert.

Two such processes have been proposed and tested. The first again involves guessing. According to the "sophisticated guessing" hypothesis, knowledge of the letters that can occur in particular words is combined with feature information from the stimulus as a fundamental part of the visual system's encoding operations, rather than being applied postperceptually as a consciously controlled strategy (Broadbent, 1967; Broadbent & Broadbent, 1975; Massaro, 1979). The combination of the two kinds of information determines the perceptual code that becomes active enough to control recognition.

Were the sophisticated guessing hypothesis correct, then words that severely constrain the letters that can occur at the critical target position ought to be perceived more accurately than words that allow many different letters to occur at the critical position. However, several experiments failed to obtain this result, making sophisticated guessing an unattractive explanation (Adams, 1979; Johnston, 1978; Johnston & McClelland, 1980; Purcell & Stanovich, 1982; Van Santen, 1979; see also Treisman, 1978).

The other possibility relies on the existence of higher order, nonvisual encoding mechanisms that can abstract information from the visual system and transform it into a code that is safe from masking and from memory loss long enough to support the decision processes that are required in the tachistoscopic recognition environment. The basic claim is that words benefit from the computation of codes that bundle all the available stimulus information together into one unit. Under many conditions these higher order "unitized codes" for words are activated automatically, though their formation can be disrupted by such manipulations as changing the ordinary spacing of letters or having subjects focus on a single letter and thus interfering with the usual tendency from reading experience to try to take in several letter positions at once.

Besides being consistent with the tachistoscopic recognition phenomena described so far, the unitized code hypothesis also accounts for data suggesting that the word superiority effect is more likely to occur when a visual mask is used than when the stimulus display is lower in energy or briefer but unmasked (Johnston & McClelland, 1973). This suggests that whatever causes the word superiority effect gives its largest benefits when visual input from the target stimulus is only available for a short time and is then rapidly and actively degraded to the point that it (and its iconic representation) can no longer be interrogated.

The unitized code hypothesis easily accommodates this suggestion. According to the theory random nonsense strings have no higher order structure that allows them to be encoded into a single nonvisual unit—for example, a phonological, semantic, or some other lexical level code—with any speed or accuracy. Therefore the recognition of random strings depends relatively more than the recognition of words on the quality of the available visual codes, and if masking disrupts visual codes, then random strings will be at a greater disadvantage.

The disadvantage of single letters relative to words is harder to explain from this perspective, since letters can be named quite readily and therefore ought to enjoy the same benefits of higher order nonvisual coding that are enjoyed by words. However, Mezrich (1973) showed that the superiority of words over single letters could be reduced or eliminated by instructing subjects to name each stimulus as rapidly as possible before the response alternatives appeared. He concluded that, for some unknown reason, people do not spontaneously try to take advantage of the nameability of letters, attempting to rely instead on visual information that is susceptible to masking. Mezrich's experiment suggests that the word superiority effect may typically occur because words are recoded into a nonvisual form whereas other types of stimuli are not. However, the reason for not recoding is different for nonsense strings and single letters: Nonsense strings are not recoded because they have no higher order structure to support a unitized code, whereas single letters tend not to be recoded because people fail to take spontaneous advantage of an association to a higher order code that does in fact exist.

Given the data currently available, the unitized code hypothesis is the only tenable explanation of the word superiority effect. Therefore a model of word processing that is going to take on the tachistoscopic recognition data must be able to explain them in terms of a unitized code. Mezrich's (1973) experiment suggests that such an explanation might be able to rely primarily on phonological recoding as the unitizing mechanism. This possibility is increased by some much more direct evidence that the unitized code supporting tachistoscopic recognition of words is ordinarily phonological.

2. The (Typically) Phonological Nature of the Unitized Code

The evidence that points toward phonological coding comes from a tachistoscopic forced choice recognition experiment by Hawkins, Reicher, Rogers, and Peterson (1976). Using only words as stimuli, Hawkins *et al.* varied the nature of the response alternatives. Usually the two alternatives differed from each other not only in visual appearance but in pronunciation and in meaning as well, such as the *word–work* example given earlier. Occasionally, though, the alternatives differed in meaning but were identical in pronunciation, as in *week* versus *weak* or *site* versus *cite*. Subjects were nearly at chance in choosing between these homophonic alternatives despite the fact that they performed well above chance on the standard, nonhomophonic alternatives. This finding indicates rather strongly that in the standard tachistoscopic task, subjects rely primarily on phonological codes to support their identification of the target stimuli, and that phonological codes are therefore the unitized representations that typically create the tachistoscopic word superiority effect. (Other types of codes may become activated during task activity, but they appear to contribute little to performance.)

While this conclusion may be correct for the standard version of tachistoscopic recognition, the picture is actually a bit more complicated. Both Hawkins *et al.* and Spoehr (1978) argue that while phonological coding may be the strategy of choice, the functionally important coding in tachistoscopic recognition is not **always** phonological. Hawkins *et al.* found that when the majority of pairs of response alternatives were homophonic rather than only a few, homophonic pairs were responded to about as accurately as nonhomophonic pairs and both were substantially superior to single letters. This result suggests that subjects switched away from reliance on phonological codes when such codes proved to be dysfunctional on most of the trials. Since the target stimuli were still being masked and visual information was therefore disrupted, the code to which subjects switched may have been semantic. Spoehr found that evidence of phonological recoding such as a dependence of performance on the number of syllables in the word (see Bock, 1982; Klapp, 1971; Spoehr & Smith, 1975) increased when the target stimuli were masked and subjects had to wait a relatively long time after target offset to see the response alternatives, but decreased when there was no mask or the response alternatives appeared with little delay.

Putting all this together, it seems that under conditions of rapid, masked presentation of target stimuli, perceivers ordinarily rely on phonological codes for tachistoscopic word recognition, especially if memory demands are significant. However, perceivers can switch attention to less preferred but still effective nonphonological codes (possibly semantic) if the phonological codes prove unable to support the decisions required by the task, as in Hawkins *et al.* (1976), or they can stick with visual codes and forego much of their reliance on recoding if the mask is removed and unitized codes become less necessary, as in the study by Spoehr (1978). Thus if models of word processing are to explain the word superiority effect that occurs in tachistoscopic recognition, they must be able to make distinctions between phonological and other recoding of visual letter strings and they must provide the perceiver with a certain amount of flexibility in choosing which kind of code to pay attention to.

3. The Pseudoword Superiority Effect

So far we have discussed three different kinds of stimuli in detail: words, random nonsense strings, and single letters. In tachistoscopic recognition tasks words exhibit special properties relative to the other two stimulus types. Because a word is an entity with which speakers and readers of the language are specifically familiar, these special properties could result from the kinds of paired associate processes that allow a visual stimulus to activate internal representations that have been laid down in memory through past experience with that particular stimulus. That is, the special properties that words exhibit could result from the operation of a lexical instance model, at least if one assumes that activation of a lexical entry produces either a phonological code or a phonological code and a semantic code that can be accessed separately by decision mechanisms.

It is quite clear, though, that alphabetic languages such as English allow people to pronounce or approximately pronounce strings of letters that they have **not** encountered before: orthographically regular but unfamiliar and meaningless pseudowords such as *nard* and *prisket*—our earlier examples— or *tup, noom, crundy,* and *flarben.* We will now consider some tachistoscopic recognition experiments that have included pseudowords as stimuli.

Gibson, Pick, Osser, and Hammond (1962) found that pseudowords were reported more accurately than random strings in Cattell's whole report procedure, and Baron and Thurston (1973) found the pseudowords were also recognized more accurately than random strings in Reicher's forced choice task. In fact, Baron and Thurston obtained no difference in accuracy between pseudowords and words, though subsequent research has more often found a small but not always statistically significant advantage in favor of words (e.g., Carr, Davidson, & Hawkins, 1978; Manelis, 1974; McClelland & Johnston, 1977; Spoehr & Smith, 1975). Thus one must entertain the possibility that paired associate principles might not be able to explain the entirety of tachistoscopic phenomena. Because perceivers have not usually encountered pseudowords before, they cannot have logogens or lexical representations already established in memory with which to encode them— yet pseudowords are still processed more efficiently than random nonsense strings.

How might pseudowords be encoded? Several linguists and psycholinguists have tried to formulate systems of spelling-to-sound or grapheme-to-phoneme translation rules that can map between strings of letters and pronunciations in a way that can capture people's ability to pronounce pseudowords (see Kavanagh & Venezky, 1980; van Wijk, 1966; Venezky, 1970, 1979), and educators have employed phonics rules as a part of reading instruction for a long time (see Gibson & Levin, 1975; Kavanagh & Venezky, 1980). These rule systems contain a description of the constraints that exist on letters and letter sequences as they occur in English spelling (the **orthography**) and a set of mapping rules for pronouncing the letters and letter sequences (the **spelling-to-sound translation rules, grapheme-to-phoneme translation rules,** or **correspondence rules**).

Though these rule systems were developed primarily as linguistic descriptions, they are ultimately based on observations of performance, and many investigators have taken them as hypotheses about the psychologically active knowledge by which readers actually achieve pronunciations for the words that they read. However, we have already seen in discussing the ill-fated phonological recoding models of word recognition that an internalized set of correspondence rules cannot succeed as the **only** kind of pronunciation knowledge available to a reader (unless the rules are so specific, applying to so few cases, as to be essentially equivalent to paired associate knowledge). Some of the correspondence rules proposed by linguists are highly algorithmic, holding without exception throughout the lexicon, but many are only heuristic, providing rules of thumb and best guesses about pronunciations that hold for some words but not for all. Depending on the estimate, anywhere from 5 to 50% of the lexicon is quite difficult to describe in terms of generalizable or logically defensible rules (Coltheart, 1978; Simon & Simon, 1973; Venezky, 1970). One might conclude, then, that two kinds of knowledge must be readily available if we are to explain tachistoscopic recognition performance in terms of the unitized phonological codes that the data seem to require (1) rule-based or alphabetic knowledge about orthography and grapheme-to-phoneme correspondence, plus (2) paired associate knowledge about specific words or lexical instances.

4. PCS Models and Expectancy Effects

The foregoing conclusion is essentially a claim that one must adopt the PCS approach in order to explain tachistoscopic recognition. Carr *et al.* (1978) attempted to test this claim by applying the principles of isolable subsystem analysis (Posner, 1978). If rule-based knowledge and word-specific knowledge are embodied in separate encoding mechanisms that both operate during tachistoscopic recognition, then one ought to be able to manipulate reliance on the two kinds of mechanisms independently. For example, one might be able to find conditions that affect the ability to recognize pseudowords but not the ability to recognize words, or vice versa.

If one cannot manipulate the two mechanisms independently, then it would be necessary to rethink the notion that rule-based and lexical instance knowledge are represented separately in the word recognition apparatus.

In two tachistoscopic forced choice recognition experiments, subjects were told either that they would see nothing but words, nothing but pseudo-words, or nothing but random nonsense strings. These expectations were met for 100 trials, but then target stimuli of an unexpected type were surreptitiously presented on a randomly selected 16 of the next 32 trials. The response alternatives throughout the experiment consisted only of the pair of critical letters rather than the entire letter strings so that presentation of the alternatives would not expose the subterfuge of the experiment. Table I shows performance on the expected and unexpected stimulus types during the final 32 trials.

Across the three expectation conditions letters in words were always recognized some 14–16% better than letters in random strings. Pseudoword processing, however, varied substantially with expectations. An advantage for letters in pseudowords over letters in random strings occurred when pseudowords were expected, but when the exclusive expectation was for words or for random strings, pseudoword superiority did not occur at all. These results led Carr *et al.* to argue that lexical or word-specific processing is relatively automatic in tachistoscopic recognition, but that rule-governed processing is much less automatic and, furthermore, it must be the responsibility of a mechanism that is separate from the lexicon—that is, that a

TABLE I

Word Recognition as a Function of Expectation[a]

Expectation	Target types			Difference scores	
	Words	Pseudowords	Random strings	Words–PW[b]	Words–RS[c]
For words	84.6	72.9	69.8	11.7	14.8
Pseudowords	78.6	74.2	63.5	4.4	15.1
Random strings	85.4	66.7	69.0	18.7	16.4

[a]Percentage correct tachistoscopic forced choice recognition of words, pseudowords, and random nonsense strings as a function of subject expectations that only words, only pseudowords, or only random letter strings would be presented. Words were always processed more accurately than nonsense, but pseudowords were only processed more accurately than nonsense when they were expected. This dissociation suggests that words and pseudowords may be processed by different mechanisms, and that the word mechanism operates relatively automatically whereas the pseudoword mechanism is under a greater degree of strategic control. (From Carr *et al.,* 1978.)

[b]Difference between words and pseudowords (PW): Varies with expectation.

[c]Difference between words and random strings (RS): Remains constant.

PCS model must be correct. If the same mechanism encoded both words and pseudowords, then recognition of the two kinds of stimuli should not have dissociated as completely as it did under the influence of absolute expectations. Figure 2 portrays the PCS view of phonological code formation.

5. An Alternative Explanation by a Logogen Model

Despite the intuitive appeal of the PCS account, however, parallel organization of independent encoding mechanisms is not the only way to accommodate the kind of dissociation between words and pseudowords observed by Carr *et al.* (1978). It would also be possible for such a dissociation to occur if a single mechanism that can encode both stimulus types has two distinct modes of operation, one conducive to high accuracy only on words and the other conducive to high accuracy on pseudowords as well. McClelland and Rumelhart (1981; Rumelhart & McClelland, 1982) have proposed a lexical instance model of the logogen type that appears to have this property.

In their "interactive activation" model, two levels of internal representation store codes for letters and codes for familiar words, respectively. Visual input goes to the letter codes, which in turn can activate word codes. Activation spreads from code to code within and between the two levels of representation along pathways such as those indicated by arrows in Fig. 3. Excitation is communicated between codes that are consistent with one another and inhibition is communicated between codes that are mutually ex-

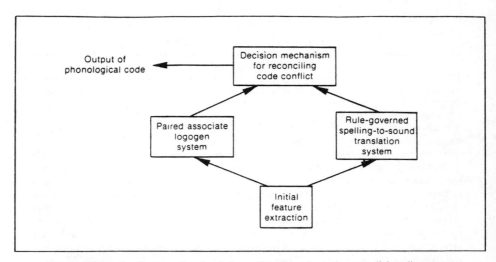

Fig. 2. Schematic diagram showing information flow through a parallel coding systems model that is capable of accounting for the existing empirical evidence on phonological recoding.

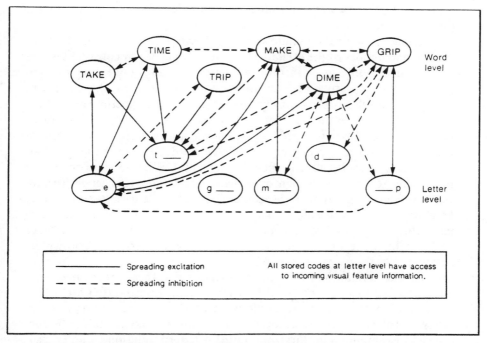

Fig. 3. Schematic diagram showing excitatory and inhibitory interconnections among representations in McClelland and Rumelhart's (1981) logogen-based "interactive activation" model of word recognition.

clusive. Each code's level of activation at any given time is the algebraic sum of the excitation and inhibition it is receiving from all sources in the system.

These patterns of excitation and inhibition do the work of perceptual recognition in the McClelland–Rumelhart model. The supposition for tachistoscopic tasks is that responses are computed by reading out activated codes from the letter level. Feedback to letter codes from activated word codes boosts and sustains their activation, producing better letter-level information about words than about either random strings or single letters, since neither of these stimulus types activate word-level codes to an appreciable extent. Strings of letters that are more similar to words can activate word codes, even if there is some mismatch, though never to as high a level as complete matches in which all of the letters of the word are actually present in the correct order in the stimulus. Thus pseudowords, which often differ from words by only one or two letters, can partially activate word codes, producing feedback to the letter level that supports a pseudoword

SAINT PETER'S COLLEGE LIBRARY
JERSEY CITY, NEW JERSEY 07306

superiority effect in addition to the word superiority effect that the model produces in a more obvious way.

The magnitude of the pseudoword superiority effect will depend on the relative magnitudes of the excitation sent to word codes by consistent letters and the inhibition sent by inconsistent letters. By allowing expectations to influence the magnitude of letter-to-word inhibition, then, the interactive activation model can perform like the subjects in the experiments of Carr *et al.* (1978). For example, a letter-to-word inhibition that is three times larger than the letter-to-word excitation will prevent four-letter pseudowords from ever activating any four-letter words (assuming that the patterned mask degrades all letter positions equally). With no word activation to provide feedback that reinforces letter activation, four-letter pseudowords will be perceived no more accurately than four-letter nonsense strings. Four-letter words will still be perceived quite well, though, because they match their word-level representations at all four-letter positions and hence do not inhibit the word-to-letter feedback on which word superiority depends.

Computer simulation of the model suggests that these procedures do in fact allow the logogen model of McClelland and Rumelhart (1981) to reproduce the influence of expectations on pseudoword recognition. There are two problems with the account that we can see, though neither is necessarily insurmountable. First, the ratio of letter inhibition to letter excitation that is required to turn off feedback for pseudowords depends critically on the number of letters in the pseudoword. As it stands, McClelland and Rumelhart's proposal would not work for anything but four-letter stimuli unless subjects are given simultaneous control over a separate inhibition-to-excitation ratio for each possible letter-string length in the lexicon. While the Carr *et al.* stimuli were all four letters in length, there is no a priori reason to believe that expectation effects would hold **only** for four-letter strings. Therefore McClelland and Rumelhart's model seems to require modification in a cumbersome direction. Furthermore, as Paap *et al.* (1982) have pointed out, it is not clear how the perceiver would gain access to such an obscure-sounding parameter of system operation.

Second, the model assumes that responses are computed solely on the basis of activation at the letter level, with word representations functioning only to provide feedback that modifies the operation of the letter codes. This assumption is inconsistent with the results of Hawkins *et al.* (1976) in which performance on homophonic response alternatives implicated phonological codes in tachistoscopic recognition performance: Homophony is defined at the word level rather than the letter level. We find it difficult to evaluate the extent to which the viability of McClelland and Rumelhart's model depends in general on the assumption of letter-level readout. (Indeed, for tasks other than tachistoscopic recognition they some-times allow readout from the word level. The rule by which they determine the level of readout for a given task is not explicit in the model.)

6. Relaxing the Assumption of Letter-Level Readout: An Explanation by a Verification Model

While the above criticisms of the McClelland–Rumelhart model are cause for concern, they are not obviously fatal. Even so, it would be interesting to see what would happen if the assumption of letter-level readout were relaxed so that both levels of representation could participate in response computation. Paap *et al.* (1982) have proposed an alternative to the inter-active activation approach that does this. Because it is a verification model rather than logogen-based, the work of Paap *et al.* will serve to round out our consideration of how the various categories of models have tried to explain tachistoscopic recognition.

Like McClelland and Rumelhart (1981), Paap *et al.* (1982) postulate a set of letter representations, called the "alphabetum," and a set of word representations called the lexicon. Also like McClelland and Rumelhart, visual input goes to the letter level which in turn feeds excitation to appro-priate codes at the word level. From this point the models diverge. Paap *et al.* do not rely on inhibitory interactions within and between levels of rep-resentation to identify the stimulus. Instead, all word representations that have surpassed a threshold degree of activation join a set of candidates for the next step in the recognition sequence, which is a verification process. The candidates are used one by one as probes in a top-down comparison that attempts to match the expected visual characteristics of each candidate against the actual visual characteristics of the stimulus. When a match is found the stimulus is identified as the candidate word that produced the match. Figure 4a illustrates this "activation-verification" model of word recognition.

Applying the activation-verification model to tachistoscopic recognition tasks requires an additional assumption, illustrated in Fig. 4b. Because the mask very quickly obscures visual input from the stimulus, Paap *et al.* as-sume that top-down verification is curtailed or precluded under tachisto-scopic conditions. This forces the perceiver to rely on bottom-up activation alone, or on bottom-up activation plus whatever contextual information may have already been processed, to compute a response. [For those in-terested in more detail, the plausibility of this assumption has been de-fended in an experiment by Schvaneveldt and McDonald (1981) that compared the influence of semantic priming on several different kinds of decisions about words made either under tachistoscopic conditions or under

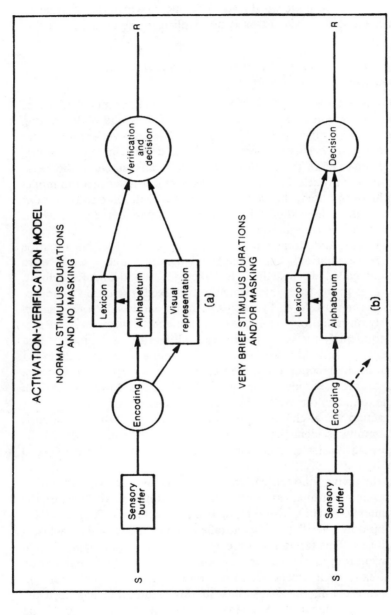

Fig. 4. Schematic diagrams showing information flow through the Paap *et al.* (1982) "activation-verification" model of word recognition under two different sets of conditions. The upper diagram (a) corresponds to the operation of the model under optimal visual conditions in the absence of masking or other visual disruption. The lower diagram (b) corresponds to the operation of the model under conditions in which the visual stimulus is only available for a brief time before being interfered with by some other event, such as the appearance of a pattern mask in tachistoscopic recognition.

speeded conditions in which verification could take place but subjects were under time pressure to make their decisions.]

Note that the process envisioned by Paap *et al.* for use under tachisto-scopic conditions resembles the operation of a logogen model such as McClelland and Rumelhart's, given that the verification half of the recognition cycle is disabled. However, there is one important difference. Rather than postulating mutually inhibitory connections among the representations in the lexicon, Paap *et al.* supply a different means of selecting a single representation among the several that become partially activated in response to a stimulus word. When attempting to compute responses without benefit of the verification process, the perceiver is assumed to supplement the candidate set chosen from the lexicon with readout directly from the alphabetum, thereby adding some constraining information that would not be necessary when verification is possible. Paap *et al.* give perceivers a degree of strategic control over how much each level of representation is emphasized in response computation, enabling the model to explain strategic flexibility such as that observed by Carr *et al.* (1978). When only words or nonwords are expected, people increase the criterion level of activation needed for a word-level code to enter the candidate set in an attempt to exclude erroneous word-level information from the response-relevant data base. When pseudowords are known to be a possibility, the criterion is lowered so that partial matches will enter words into the candidate set and give the perceiver a better basis for deciding what the stimulus might have been on trials in which it was a pseudoword.

The result of these criterion shifts is that the occurrence of a word will activate the appropriate lexical code and performance on words will be good regardless of expectations. The occurrence of a pseudoword, however, will not activate word codes sufficiently to give pseudowords any advantage over nonsense strings unless pseudowords are expected and the word-level activation criterion is lowered accordingly.

For present purposes we will not try to determine whether one should prefer the McClelland–Rumelhart logogen account or the Paap *et al.* verification account of expectation effects on the pseudoword superiority effect. There are two reasons for this decision. Because Paap *et al.* disable the verification process in their explanation of tachistoscopic recognition, the dissimilarities between the verification approach and the logogen approach are not sufficiently fundamental to warrant a concerted effort to distinguish them in this task domain. Furthermore, the recognition of isolated words, whether or not they are presented tachistoscopically, is not the best arena for displaying the special wares of the verification model. Its current incarnations were developed primarily to explain some effects of context on word processing with which logogen-based models have difficulty (see Becker, this volume; Seidenberg, this volume). We will discuss those context effects briefly later in the article (Section II,C,3) in order to take up the relative merits of logogen and verification models in a more serious way.

At this point, we will focus instead on the more general fact that regardless of which particular subclass eventually proves to be superior, the lexical instance models of word recognition can succeed remarkably well at explaining patterns of tachistoscopic recognition data that might seem at first glance to require a PCS approach. As we have noted, the interactive activation model seems slightly strained by expectation effects. In addition, it cannot easily account for the effect of homophony reported by Hawkins *et al.* (1976), since it restricts response computation to ouput from letter detectors and it takes no position one way or another as to whether word detectors produce phonological representations. The verification model also takes no position on the type of code produced at the word level, and it needs modification in order to account for the effects of word frequency so ubiquitous in tachistoscopic recognition. The model's explanation of frequency effects in other tasks involves the order in which lexical candidates are verified. This creates problems in explaining data from masked tachistoscopic presentation, since the verification process is assumed to be disabled under such conditions. Nevertheless, the overall performance of both of these lexical instance models is impressive.

B. Unitized Codes Reconsidered: Producing Overt Pronunciations

Ultimately, however, tachistoscopic recognition falls short of providing as demanding a test of the relative merits of lexical instance and PCS approaches as one might like to have. The major difficulty is that determining the kind of code that is functional in tachistoscopic recognition requires a highly inferential chain of reasoning. One must be able to say with a fair degree of confidence what kind of code is being used in order to interpret data from the tachistoscopic recognition task in a way that is analytic to differences between models. But as we have seen, a variety of options appear to be open to the subject concerning what code or codes to rely on. Though there is good evidence that subjects show systematic preferences among these options, they **are** options. This means that the experimenter must either be satisfied with a best guess about code utilization or be prepared to include special manipulations to determine it empirically, such as was done by Hawkins *et al.* (1976).

The problem of determining the functional code is compounded by the fact that tachistoscopic forced choice tasks are usually designed with each pair of response alternatives differing by a single letter. Therefore all one knows **for sure** from observed performance is how accurately that letter has been identified. This property of the task is exemplified in the letter-level readout assumption of McClelland and Rumelhart (1981), which is challenged in a direct way by only a small number of studies such as the one by Hawkins *et al*. We know, though, that readers of English are capable not just of identifying the individual letters of words and pseudowords, but also of producing complete phonological and articulatory representations of them. If a lexical instance model could successfully compute phonological or articulatory codes for specific words and pseudowords in a way that resembles the abilities of people to do so in a task such as overt pronunciation, then the case for the lexical instance approach would be considerably strengthened.

1. The Lexical Instance Approach to Pronunciation

The best-known attempt to do this is Glushko's (1979, 1981) "activation-synthesis model" of pronunciation, which is widely regarded as an existence proof of the sufficiency of the lexical instance approach to word recognition. This model is built around a system of stored detectors of the logogen type that represent (1) familiar words, (2) familiar letters, and (3) familiar letter clusters or spelling patterns, such as *sh-* or *-ave*. All three levels of codes are stored together in the same logogen system, and a letter string presented as a stimulus will activate any and all codes that are appropriate to its spelling regardless of the level of linguistic description of the code. In order to achieve a pronunciation, a decision mechanism takes the panoply of activated codes and synthesizes them into a single integrated phonological output that captures something like the central tendency of all the activated codes. This two-stage, detector-based system encodes letter strings of all types—the claim is that it can succeed as well on pseudowords it has never encountered before as it can on words with which it is familiar, though it may take more time on the pseudowords.

Such a model is similar in many respects to the models of McClelland and Rumelhart (1981) and Paap *et al*. (1982) discussed earlier, especially with respect to its exclusive dependence on logogen-like detectors rather than postulating any kind of rule-based mechanism. However, there are also two profound differences. First, the previously discussed models had detectors only for words and letters, whereas the activation-synthesis model opens up a broad vista of subword units that seem to correspond quite closely to the spelling patterns represented by rules in the PCS approach. Second, the levels of representation are not distinct in Glushko's model as they are in McClelland and Rumelhart's or that of Paap *et al*., and the interactions between levels of representation are not so well defined.

These two properties of the activation-synthesis model complicate its evaluation. If there are no clear a priori theoretical constraints on the nature of the representational units and no explicitly formulated procedures for adjudicating among the competing units that have been activated in order to synthesize a pronunciation, then it would be difficult to distinguish such a lexical instance model from the PCS approach. Similar vagueness about the details of operating characteristics on the part of PCS models exacerbates the problem. Saying only something as general as the letter cluster *cei-* activates the pronunciation *see* is little different from postulating that there are "rules" that say that *c* is pronounced *s* before *e* and that *-ei-* is pronounced *ee* after *c*. At present neither model is sufficiently specified to determine with certainty whether the metaphor of directly activatable subunits and the metaphor of rules suggest anything different about how performance should look in word-processing tasks.

However, there exists a simpler (and relatively unacknowledged) precursor to Glushko's model of pronunciation that keeps to the principle of representing words but not subword letter clusters yet still proves capable of handling many of the important empirical findings on pronunciation of words and pseudowords—including some of the results that led Glushko to propose the activation-synthesis formulation. We will describe this model, which was created by Brooks (1977; Brooks & Miller, 1979), and apply it to pronunciation findings in an attempt to discover whether it fails in ways that are serious enough to create a need for the more complex approaches taken by Glushko or the PCS models. We will then return to the question of whether the latter two approaches can be distinguished.

Brooks' model was devised in the context of a series of experiments on learning to pronounce strings of letters written in an artificial alphabet (Brooks, 1977). The phenomenon that triggered Brooks' thinking was that orthographic regularities that were built into strings constructed from the alphabet facilitated rapid naming of those strings even though subjects were not told that the regularities were present and showed no awareness of their nature. In response to this phenomenon Brooks proposed that a word or a pseudoword presented as a stimulus activates a candidate set of logogens representing words that are visually similar to the stimulus. Each member of the candidate set in turn activates its pronunciation, whose representation is parsed into phonological segments. There is then an accounting process or tally at each phoneme position across the activated pronunciations and the phoneme with the highest tally is selected to be pronounced. As in the models of McClelland and Rumelhart (1981) and Paap *et al.* (1982), the logogens vary in the level to which they become activated as a function of the degree of their similarity to the stimulus, and the phoneme tallies incorporate these differences so that the contributions of more highly activated logogens are given greater weight in computing the pronunciation.

Presumably, the number of highly activated phonemes at any particular position would influence the time taken to complete the computation.

Application of these principles allows Brooks' model to account for the two most basic empirical facts about pronunciation: pseudowords take longer to pronounce than words and exception words take longer to pronounce than regular words (Baron & Strawson, 1976; Forster & Chambers, 1973; Frederiksen & Kroll, 1976; Gough & Cosky, 1977; Perfetti & Hogaboam, 1975; Stanovich & Bauer, 1978; Theios & Muise, 1977). The difference between words and pseudowords can be explained by postulating a strong weighting for the logogen of the word itself which arises because that logogen is more similar to the stimulus than any other internally represented letter string. The result would be much greater consistency at all phoneme positions for word stimuli than would be the case for most pseudowords, which would tend to activate the logogens of several quite similar words to about the same intermediate level rather than activating a single logogen to a very high level.

The difference between regular and exception words is explained in the same spirit, but with slightly different particulars. All words, both regular and exception, can share spelling patterns with other words. For example, the regular word *coat* shares the spelling pattern *-oat* with *boat, goat, moat,* and of course *oat,* which is itself a word, while the exception word *have* shares the spelling pattern *-ave* with *cave, Dave, gave, pave, rave, save, shave,* and *wave.* These examples have been chosen rather carefully to provide an extreme illustration of an important point: Regular words (by definition) share spelling patterns largely with words in which those patterns are pronounced similarly, whereas exception words (again by definition) share spelling patterns largely with words in which those patterns are pronounced differently.

Suppose, then, that a word is presented as a stimulus and activates more than one logogen: its own and some others that are visually similar to it. Because the greatest part of visual similarity arises from shared spelling patterns, either a regular or an exception word will activate mostly logogens for words with similar spelling patterns. However, the majority of these erroneous activations will be pronounced similarly to the real stimulus word when the stimulus is a regular word, but the majority of the erroneous words will be pronounced differently from the real stimulus word when the stimulus is an exception word. Thus regular words will generally elicit greater consistency of activated phonemes than will exception words, and hence a pronunciation process such as Brooks' will take longer to complete its computations for the exception words.

Clearly, then, Brooks' model can accommodate the empirically established difference between pronouncing regular and exception words. We can force the model to make a further prediction by noting that the magnitude of the difference ought to depend on the extent to which the activation level of the correct logogen exceeds the activation levels of the similar but incorrect logogens. The greater the excess in favor of the correct logogen, the smaller will be the advantage of regular words, since the advantage depends for its existence on the occurrence of incorrect activations that are strong enough to compete with the correct activation. Therefore words which are very frequent in the printed language should be less susceptible to effects of regularity than words of lower frequency, given the bias toward familiar words that is a part of the logogen model's theoretical accoutrements. Seidenberg, Waters, Barnes, and Tanenhaus (1984) have shown that this is true. Subjects in their pronunciation task exhibited a much larger difference in pronunciation latency between regular and exception words of low frequency than between regular and exception words of high frequency.

Of course, PCS models can also account for these differences, but in a different way. Regular words enjoy a "redundancy gain" relative to pseudowords, and regular words also enjoy a redundancy gain relative to exception words, because in each case regular words are pronounced correctly by both of the phonological recoding mechanisms whereas the other type of stimulus is pronounced correctly by only one of the mechanisms. However, there are some additional findings on the pronunciation of words and pseudowords, obtained by Glushko (1979), that seem, at least at first, to pose a problem for PCS models—and which Brooks' model can accommodate quite easily. The first involves what Glushko called "exception pseudowords," constructed by changing the initial consonant of an exception word, such as *heaf* constructed from *deaf* or *bint* constructed from *pint*. In Glushko's experiments these stimuli took longer to pronounce and elicited more irregular pronunciations than did "regular pseudowords" such as *hean* constructed from *dean* or *bink* from *pink*. The second of Glushko's observations is essentially the same phenomenon in the domain of real words. He defined a class of stimuli called "regular/inconsistent words," which are regularly pronounced words that differ from an exception by only the initial consonant and hence share the exception word's irregularly pronounced spelling patterns. An example would be *wave*, which shares *-ave* with *have*. These stimuli took longer to pronounce than regular words that did not bear such similarity to an exception word, such as *wade* or *haze*.

If one assumes, as did Glushko in discussing the implications of these findings, that in a PCS model perceptual input from a pseudoword makes contact only with the grapheme-to-phoneme translation mechanism and does not induce partial activations or searches in the logogen system or lexicon, then the PCS model fails to account for the exception pseudoword

effect. Furthermore, if one assumes that perceptual input from a word produces activation only in the logogen that represents that word exactly and
does not produce partial activation in logogens representing other, similar
words, then the PCS model also fails to account for the regular/inconsis-
tent word effect. Clearly, though, a lexical instance model such as Brooks'
not only handles the occurrence of such effects, but demands them.

We have already seen, however, that extant PCS models do not make
the assumptions just described. The lexical instance mechanism of the PCS
approach looks much like the currently viable logogen models, such as
Brooks', in that both allow for partial activation by words (and pseudowords) that are similar but not identical to the word represented by a given
logogen, and both must therefore include decision processes to reconcile
patterns of multiple activation. The rule-governed, grapheme-to-phoneme
translation mechanism of the PCS approach cannot know in advance that
it is dealing with a real word rather than a pseudoword (or a real word with
which it is unfamiliar). Therefore its output will figure into the pronunciation process regardless of the stimulus type, and as Coltheart (1978) points
out, the extent of the measurable influences of the two mechanisms on the
pronunciation process will depend on the relative time courses of the lexical
instance and rule-governed mechanisms on any given encoding attempt.
Thus the raw ingredients of the exception pseudoword and regular/
inconsistent word effects are present in the PCS models as well as in Brooks'
logogen-type lexical instance model, and the PCS model's explanation of
the effects would be very similar to Brooks'. Indeed, the two explanations
might be so similar that they would prove exceedingly hard to distinguish
experimentally. At this point, then, we still have little empirical reason to
prefer one class of models over the other. However, matters get more complicated.

2. What Is the Need for Rules or Subword Logogens?

So far in our empirical review we have seen that a model that merely
postulates lexical entries for words and letters together with appropriate
combination rules for reconciling multiple activations can go quite far in
dealing with a wide variety of findings on the processing of both words and
pseudowords. Two such models (McClelland & Rumelhart, 1981; Papp *et
al.*, 1982) make good quantitative predictions about tachistoscopic recognition and another (Brooks, 1977) makes good qualitative predictions about
pronunciation. However, we believe that there **are** problems with such a
model, and those problems are sufficient to force the lexical instance approach to move in the direction of Glushko's (1979) more complicated
model. Unfortunately, that move, which involves postulating directly activatable subword logogens, makes the resulting lexical instance model

harder to distinguish from the equally complex and only slightly different PCS model. We will explain the problems that we see with the simpler lexical instance model and then discuss the chances of being able to choose between the more complicated lexical instance approach and the PCS model.

The major difficulty with the simple model is posed by the fluent ability of people to pronounce pseudowords such as *neev, huc,* or *joov* that have few "neighbors," or words that share spelling patterns with them (Coltheart, 1981). The absence of neighbors whose activation would feed information into the pronunciation process predicts, in the context of a model like Brooks', that pronunciation of such pseudowords should be problematic. According to the PCS approach, on the other hand, since *n, ee,* and *v* have relatively invariant pronunciations in the English language, the rule-governed mechanism would produce a pronunciation for the string rather easily. Thus the PCS model could account more gracefully for fluency with neighborless pseudowords than could the simple lexical instance model. For the first time, then, one class of models seems to have gained an edge over the other.

In order to recoup, the lexical instance approach might try to expand the definition of "neighbor" to include something like *Steve* as a neighbor of *neev* and *chuck* as a neighbor of *huc,* but that would require the formulation of a complex set of rules about how to "line up" logogens representing words of quite different lengths and how to trade off differences in length against differences in letter features in determining the degree of match between a stimulus and a logogen. This line of reasoning leads easily to a proposal such as Glushko's (1979) that word and letter logogens ought to be supplemented by logogens for subword units, each activating associated phonological or articulatory codes that are then reconciled in a more sophisticated synthesis process than the one envisioned by Brooks. Such a proposal allows the activation-synthesis approach to capture people's fluency with pseudowords more completely than Brooks' model and reduces the apparent disadvantage of the lexical instance model relative to the PCS approach. The score appears once again to be approximately even.

3. Activation-Synthesis versus PCS: Same or Different?

To this point we have argued, mainly on the need to account for pronunciation data, that the lexical instance model of word recognition must be expanded from the relatively simple and elegant conceptions of Brooks (1977), McClelland and Rumelhart (1981), or Paap *et al.* (1982) to a much more complex and unconstrained conception like that of Glushko (1979, 1981) in order to approximate the PCS model's explanatory power. The question must now be raised: Is such a "lexical instance" model any different, either in principle or in its empirical predictions, from a PCS model?

The principled difference, of course, is that the lexical instance model embodies all of its knowledge and processing in one mechanism whereas the PCS model divides its knowledge and processing between two mechanisms (perhaps with some degree of overlap between them). However, identifying empirical predictions that are unique to each model runs immediately into the difficulties associated with lack of specification to which we referred earlier. At present we see two areas of experimental investigation in which discriminating predictions may be achievable.

The first is individual differences in speeded pronunciation. A common hypothesis in the reading literature is that good readers are more facile at rule-governed translation from spelling to pronunciation than are poor readers. Indeed, some children who can learn to pronounce familiar words by paired associate techniques remain totally or almost totally incapable of pronouncing unfamiliar words or pseudowords (Boder, 1973; Carr, 1981; Gleitman & Rozin, 1977; Rozin, Poritsky, & Sotsky, 1971; Rozin & Gleitman, 1977). Barron (1981) has compared pronunciation latencies for regular and exception words among good and poor readers of elementary school age. Both groups pronounced regular words more rapidly than exception words. Barron then used statistical techniques to control for "neighborhood" effects created by other words with which the target words shared spelling patterns. Remember that the lexical instance approach derives the entirety of the difference in pronunciation latency between regular and exception words from such effects—regular words have a preponderance of neighbors with similar pronunciations whereas exception words have a preponderance of neighbors with different and therefore conflicting pronunciations. Instituting these statistical controls over neighborhood effects eliminated the regular–exception word difference among the poor readers, as would be expected on the lexical instance account, but good readers still showed a significant advantage on regular words after neighborhood effects were removed. The latter outcome is what the PCS model would predict, because of its reliance for obtaining regular–exception word differences on redundancy gains due to the two mechanisms agreeing on the pronunciation of regular words but disagreeing on the pronunciation of exception words. Because the PCS model also predicts that readers who are poor at using the rule-governed mechanism will not benefit from it very much and hence should not show much effect of it in their pronunciation data, these results would seem to favor the PCS conceptualization.

The second source of potentially discriminating data is the neuropsychological literature (for a variety of reviews, see Coltheart, Patterson, & Marshall, 1980; Ellis, 1981; Margolin, 1983). Clinical studies of dyslexia resulting from cortical lesions have identified a group of patients who cannot pronounce pseudowords at all, yet can still correctly pronounce many familiar words in an oral reading task and discriminate familiar words from pseudowords in a lexical decision task (Coltheart, 1980; Marshall, 1976; Marshall & Newcombe, 1973; Patterson & Marcel, 1977; Saffran & Marin, 1977). Furthermore, these patients have no trouble rejecting pseudowords that sound like words when pronounced according to the correspondence rules of English, such as *nerse, blume,* or *bote.* Normal, brain-intact readers often take longer to reject such "pseudohomophones" in the lexical decision task (Marcel & Patterson, 1978; Patterson & Marcel, 1977; see also Dennis, Besner, & Davelaar, this volume; Rubenstein *et al.,* 1971).

It appears from these neuropsychological studies that naturally occurring brain injuries can dissociate rule-governed knowledge from lexical instance-based knowledge in much the same way that strong absolute expectations did in the tachistoscopic recognition experiments of Carr *et al.* (1978) that were discussed earlier. In fact, one patient has been identified who could pronounce familiar words but showed little ability to comprehend their meanings (Schwartz, Saffran, & Marin, 1980). Thus the clinical data point specifically toward the existence of dissociable lexical and rule-governed mechanisms for achieving pronunciations that are **both** independent of semantics. Because the precipitating agent in the neuropsychological studies is the destruction of neural tissue rather than a temporary expectation, it is hard to argue that the results can be explained by a theory that relies on a single mechanism to store and use both kinds of knowledge (or to simulate storing and using both kinds of knowledge when in fact there is only instance-based knowledge). In terms of Glushko's (1979) activation-synthesis model, for example, how could damage be so selective as to destroy access **just** to stored codes that are smaller than whole words while sparing access to word codes, if all codes are stored together in the same mechanism and activated in the same fashion by incoming stimulus information? Though hardly watertight, this plausibility argument, like the analysis of individual differences presented above, would seem to favor the PCS approach over the lexical instance approach.

As is often the case in attempts to choose among competing models of psychological phenomena, this conclusion is in no way absolute. The lexical instance model might be able to account for the data we have been describing if suitably adjusted. One could argue, for example, that the relative weightings given to the output of the logogen representing a particular word versus the outputs of logogens representing similar but nonidentical words can be adjusted both between stimuli and between people. This might add power for explaining phenomena that vary with the type of word or the type of person under investigation.

However, such wholesale freedom to modify classes of connections within the lexicon on a post hoc basis seems to us to begin to violate the spirit of the lexical instance approach, which began as an attempt to get as far as possible toward an understanding of word recognition using only basic paired associate processes such as the frequency of occurrence of particular stimuli and the frequency of coactivation of nodes within the network that represents those stimuli (see Jacoby & Brooks, 1984). This impression leads us to consider in a more general fashion the implications of how one goes about explaining interindividual differences and intraindividual flexibility in word recognition performance.

On the one hand, the lexical instance model as it currently stands does not make clear which of its connections are easily modifiable and which are not, nor which changes must be made in concert for the whole lexicon, which can be made for some classes of words but not for others, what classes of words are distinguished to begin with, and which changes can be made for individual pathways. Thus, the explanations of flexibility effects that are proposed in lexical instance models often seem quite arbitrary even when they work very nicely. A good example is McClelland and Rumelhart's (1981) account of flexibility in the recognition of pseudowords. In contrast, the major thrust of the PCS model has been to highlight such distinctions. Relationships and connections within an encoding system are considered to be structural products of extended experience and relatively difficult to modify except through more extended experience, while relationships between systems, such as the relative weight given to the output of the phoneme-to-grapheme translation mechanism versus the output of the logogen system, are considered to be relatively easily modifiable and therefore potential objects of strategic control. Because the PCS model captures the observed patterns of flexibility and individual differences more effectively, we view it as the approach to be preferred at present.[1]

A word of qualification is in order. As we have already stated, the PCS approach is clear on the **existence** of a rule-governed encoding mechanism but it is very vague about what the rule system actually looks like. Specifying the details of the rule system's representation and operation is a major step that the PCS approach must take soon or forfeit its current advantage (see Coltheart, 1978; Henderson, 1982; Venezky, 1979). One possibility that would blur anew the distinction between PCS and lexical instance models is that the "rule system" might look much like Glushko's system of directly activable subword units, with word units stored in a separate lexicon rather

[1]Part of the development of the nonanalytic, episode-based theories of cognition mentioned in Section I,B has been predicated on arguments against the view that many properties of perceptual mechanisms are much more heavily determined by the invariants of extended experience than by the exigencies of momentary episodes (Jacoby & Brooks, 1984). To the extent that these arguments succeed, the notion of prototypic representation that underlies our position—and the positions of the models we are comparing—would be weakened.

than in the same mechanism as Glushko envisions. A proposal sort of like this has been made by Rosson (1982, 1984).

Similarly, the PCS approach, as we argued in Section I,C, must also elaborate the details of the decision process that reconciles conflicts between the lexical mechanism and the rule-governed translation mechanism (see Fig. 2). Proposals on this matter have commonly assumed that each mechanism produces a fully specified candidate. If the two candidates are the same, then no problem arises. If they are different, then further steps must be taken to decide which candidate should be the winner (e.g., Carr, 1984; Coltheart, 1978; Meyer & Gutschera, 1975). Since the nature of those steps has not yet been demonstrated, it might be useful to consider alternatives.

Suppose that instead of generating fully specified candidates (which it could do on demand), the rule-governed translation mechanism ordinarily produces only a partial specification of the pronunciation, perhaps emphasizing what might be called the "islands of reliability" in English correspondence rules—those letters and letter combinations, many of which are consonants or consonant clusters, whose grapheme-to-phoneme translations are invariant or nearly so across the words of the language. The contents of this partial or preliminary representation combine with activation in the lexical mechanism, serving mainly to reinforce that activation rather than compete or race with it as in some PCS accounts. Such a process has the potential, at least, for smoothly integrating the input from the two sources of phonologically relevant information. It might exact some cost in the case of exception words (though this is not certain), but the cost seems likely to be outweighed by the benefits of rule-governed reinforcement in the case of words that are regular or mostly regular. Whether the potential can be realized needs an ambitious simulation effort of the kind mounted by McClelland and Rumelhart (1981) or Paap et al. (1982).

The underlying premise of this proposal is that adding a relatively noisy information channel (the partially specified rule-governed translation) to a cleaner channel (the visually driven lexical route) will **improve** the overall performance of the system. Because this might seem to be a strange notion, we should provide some sort of evidence that it is reasonable. The evidence we would like to consider is the use of visual cues (mainly the configuration of the lips) as a supplemental input to sound in speech perception. It is well known that lip configurations are quite ambiguous input for decoding speech, yet it is also clear that having such input usually enhances recognition (try listening to a lecture with your eyes closed). Furthermore, recent data suggest that lip information may actually be **combined** with auditory input. For example, McGurk and McDonald (1976; Massaro & Cohen, 1983) showed that presenting a film of a person pronouncing /ga/ simultaneously with an auditory presentation of /ba/ results in perception of /da/. This outcome is hard to explain with a model in which each system puts forth a single candidate that competes with the other system's candidate. Instead, it seems that the two systems are working together to find a "best fit" to the combined information they have accumulated. In terms of our sum-of-activation idea, the visual /ga/ and the auditory /ba/ would both activate /da/ because of similarity, and the total activation of /da/ due to the two sources would exceed the total activation for either /ba/ or /ga/—hence, perception of /da/ as the stimulus. While our thoughts along these lines are just beginning to form, the analogy to speech perception makes it seem possible that such a combination process could explain how a lexical mechanism and a rule-governed translation mechanism could operate synergistically to achieve an efficient phonological recoding. Whatever the inner workings of the rule system and whatever the means of utilizing its output, however, the rule system appears on available evidence to be psychologically distinct (that is, isolable or dissociable) from the lexicon.

C. Tasks that Involve Semantic Processing

In the preceding sections we have considered data from two tasks that focus primarily on phonological recoding. Some readers of this article may be quite irritated by now—on the argument that the major goal of reading is to get the **meanings** of printed words, not the pronunciations, we have been wasting space that could have been devoted to tasks that involve semantic rather than phonological processing.

We did touch on such evidence at the end of the discussion of neuropsychological studies of word recognition (Section II,B,2). We cited a study by Patterson and Marcel (1977) in which brain-injured dyslexics who could not pronounce pseudowords were nevertheless able to carry out lexical decisions with nearly normal accuracy while suffering no interference from pseudohomophones. Given that these patients can also sometimes pronounce high frequency words, and that pronunciation is sometimes independent of the ability to comprehend the words (Schwartz et al., 1980), we argued that the neuropsychological data are consistent with the PCS view of phonological recoding. However, one could argue instead that these studies support the lexical instance models' claims that semantic access can be achieved by a direct visual route to semantic memory and that phonological recoding need not occur as a prelexical process. Pronunciations of high frequency words are retrieved from stored word-specific knowledge after that knowledge has been accessed via the direct visual route that supports lexical decision. This argument might require discounting or reinterpreting the data collected by Schwartz et al. (1980), but after all, those data came from but a single person.

A similar conclusion has been drawn from studies of neurologically intact college students (Kleiman, 1975) and normally progressing first grade readers (Barron & Baron, 1977) in which a secondary concurrent articulation task interfered substantially with rhyming judgments about pairs of familiar words but only minimally with synonym judgments. The secondary task, which was shadowing digits in Kleiman's study and continually repeating the word "double" in Barron and Baron's, was intended to occupy the speech mechanisms responsible for phonological recoding. With phonological recoding significantly impaired, evidence of normal or nearly normal performance of a semantic task like judgment of synonymy would be hard to explain except by appeal to a direct visual route to semantic memory.

Let us examine the more widely cited of these studies in greater detail. Kleiman (1975) used a visual comparison task (determining whether all but the first letter of two letter strings match, as in *break* and *freak*) as a base line against which to evaluate performance in the rhyming and synonym judgments. He found about 100 msec of interference due to concurrent articulation in the visual comparison task. Interference was also about 100 msec in the synonym judgment, but increased substantially to about 300 msec in the rhyming judgment. Assuming that the visual comparison task involved no phonological coding, Kleiman ascribed the 100-msec interference in that task to generalized competition for central processing capacity, and argued that because interference was of the same magnitude in the synonym judgment, the semantic activation and comparison required by that task did not involve phonological processing either. The much larger interference in the rhyming task reflected the kind of interference that ought to be observed in a task that does involve phonological processing.

When combined with the ability to recognize exception words, this type of argument delivered the death stroke to strict phonological recoding theories of word recognition, and promulgated even stronger theoretical claims that phonological recoding is **never** used for semantic access. It also contributed to pedagogical claims that grapheme-to-phoneme translation exercises such as those involved in phonics instruction are at best a waste of time and at worst an actively harmful influence on the development of skilled reading.

1. Reconsideration: A Case in Favor of Phonological Access to Meaning

Despite these theoretical and pedagogical claims, we still believe that semantic access is best understood as the result of a "horse race" (or more likely, a cooperative computation or mutual reinforcement) between visual and phonological codes. There are several reasons for our position.

Subsequent work by Besner (Besner & Davelaar, 1982; Besner, Davies, & Daniels, 1981; see also Baddeley & Lewis, 1981; Baddeley, Eldridge, & Lewis, 1981) has questioned the assumption that concurrent articulation tasks interfere with phonological recoding. Two types of results are important. First, Besner *et al.* (1981) found that concurrent articulation interfered much more with rhyming judgments (*blame-flame*) than with homophony judgments (*ail-ale*) and that concurrent articulation interfered only minimally with judgments that pseudowords sounded like real words when pronounced according to the rules of English (such as *brane* or *phocks,* the same type of "pseudohomophones" used by Patterson & Marcel, 1977). Sometimes, if concurrent articulation was slow enough, it did not interfere at all with the latter kind of judgment. Second, Besner and Davelaar (1982) found that in short-term memory tasks requiring ordered recall of subspan lists of pseudowords, concurrent articulation eliminated detrimental effects due to larger numbers of syllables in each list member's pronunciation. It also eliminated detrimental effects due to phonological/articulatory confusability between one list member and another. However, concurrent articulation did not eliminate the advantage that accrued when list members sounded like real words, as in the examples of *brane* and *phocks* just given.

Besner's argument from these results is that there are two speech-related codes involved in reading. Concurrent articulation interferes with a code that supports short-term memory but **not** with the code that is involved in semantic access. The code that supports short-term memory is probably an articulatory code of some kind; the code involved in semantic access is probably a phonological code per se.

This argument, which if correct would overturn the logic underlying the conclusions of Kleiman (1975) and Barron and Baron (1977) described above, is consistent with recent data on judgments about the sensibility of sentences. Doctor and Coltheart (1980) asked children aged 6-10 to decide whether each of a series of sentences made sense or not. Some of the sentences contained a single word or pseudoword that made them sound correct even though they were in fact nonsensical, as in "He ran threw the street" or "We swam in the see." Figure 5 shows that such nonsense sentences were hard to reject, especially for the younger children. Even the 10 year olds still had difficulty rejecting a sentence that sounded right because it contained a homophone, though they had largely overcome the tendency to accept pseudohomophones.

These data strongly implicate phonological recoding in computing the meaning of phrases or sentences, and suggest that among beginning readers it may even be a dominant influence. At higher levels of experience the influence appears to persist, though reduced in magnitude. Baron (1973) observed that college students showed susceptibility to homophone con-

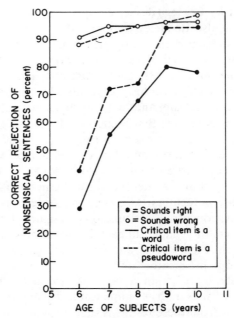

Fig. 5. Doctor and Coltheart's (1980) data on correct rejection of nonsensical sentences as a function of the type of word or pseudoword in each sentence that made it nonsensical. This critical letter string could be (1) a word that does not fit, making the sentence look wrong (the spelling corresponds to a word that does not fit) and sound wrong (the pronunciation corresponds to a word that does not fit), (2) a word that is a homophone of a word that *would* fit, making the sentence look wrong but sound right, (3) a pseudoword that looks wrong and sounds wrong, or (4) a pseudoword that is a homophone of a word that would fit, again making the sentence look wrong but sound right.

fusions in sensibility judgments that was much like that of Doctor and Coltheart's subjects. Baron's college students responded to sentences containing homophones just as rapidly as to sentences that did not, but the error rates suggested that they should have been less impetuous. The homophonic sentences were significantly more likely to be incorrectly classified as acceptable than the nonhomophonic sentences. Furthermore, Treiman, Freyd, and Baron (1983) showed that college students took longer to make sensibility judgments about sentences containing an exception word than sentences containing only words with regular spelling-to-sound translations. They also took longer to make sensibility judgments about sentences in which two words with the same spelling pattern were pronounced differently ("He made a nasty hasty remark") than sentences in which two words with the same spelling pattern were pronounced similarly. Even at relatively high

levels of experience and skill, then, it would appear that phonological recoding is utilized for semantic access.

However, one should not agree to this argument too readily. While it is
clear that the experiments just discussed have demonstrated an influence of
phonological recoding somewhere in the course of semantic processing, the
exact locus of the effect is not so clear. A variety of evidence in addition
to the work of Besner and Davelaar (much of it from the concurrent articulation paradigm described earlier) indicates that speech-based coding is
utilized as a short-term memory medium to support integrative comprehension processes that form propositions and add them to text representations (e.g., Baddeley *et al.*, 1981; Slowiaczek & Clifton, 1980; Kleiman,
1975; Levy, 1978). The tasks used by Doctor and Coltheart (1980), Baron
(1973), and Treiman *et al.* (1983) all required such integrative comprehension. Therefore it is possible to argue that the effects of phonological recoding could have occurred during postlexical memory storage and
proposition formation rather than during initial semantic activation of word
meanings. To counter this alternative, it would be helpful to have converging evidence from experimental paradigms, perhaps involving single
words rather than sentences, that are not susceptible to such a criticism.

We have already cited work showing that while certain types of brain-
injured dyslexics have no trouble rejecting pseudohomophones in lexical
decision, normal readers often do. Similar interference occurs in making
judgments of category membership. For example, in deciding whether the
referents of concrete nouns are fruits, it is harder to reject a phonologically
acceptable noninstance such as *pare* than a phonologically unacceptable
noninstance such as *pier* (Meyer & Gutschera, 1975). It would appear that
phonological recoding followed by phonological access of graphemically
inappropriate lexical entries is interfering with performance in these lexi-
cal/semantic tasks.

However, Coltheart (1978), in an analysis first cited in Section I,C, has
pointed out that since homophony interferes with the **negative** responses in
lexical decision and category membership, the interference may arise quite
late, during the decision process by which a response is selected, rather than
during the initial activation of semantic information on which word recognition is ordinarily based. Coltheart argues that negative responses usually take longer than positive responses in these tasks and that they might
be made by default. If no meaning gets activated, subjects eventually tire
of waiting and decide that the stimulus must not be a word, or if meanings
get activated but none is appropriate to the category being judged, the subject eventually decides that the stimulus must not be an instance. From these
suppositions Coltheart reasons that visual access to meaning could be uni-

formly faster than grapheme-to-phoneme translation followed by phonological access, yet pseudohomophonic or homophonic interference could still be observed in negative responses. The interference would arise because the time lag of negative responses allows the slowly produced phonological code to catch up with the faster visual code in semantic memory, creating activation that confuses the perceiver. Thus, as we discussed in establishing the classes of models, Coltheart's approach is nominally PCS, but in fact initial semantic access is virtually always achieved by the visual route.

To defeat such a view and maintain the stronger version of PCS, one would have to demonstrate phonological effects on the positive responses of lexical or semantic judgments. Several such demonstrations have been made. Meyer, Schvaneveldt, and Ruddy (1974) have shown that a word like *touch* is harder than usual to accept as a word in lexical decision when the subject has just finished processing *couch,* which is orthographically similar but phonologically different. This result—which was the basis for the experiment by Treiman *et al.* (1983) using sentences like "He made a nasty hasty remark"—is reminiscent of Glushko's (1979) regular/inconsistent word effect in pronunciation. It indicates that when phonological recoding is biased toward an incorrect reading of a word, that bias will slow semantic access as well as pronunciation. One might conclude that the same mechanism that achieves pronunciation contributes to semantic access.

Indications of phonological involvement also appear in positive lexical decisions reported by Davidson (1978). Subjects reading continuous text were occasionally interrupted by the occurrence of an underlined letter string that required lexical decision. Positive decisions were facilitated when the immediately preceding clause contained a word that rhymed with the target, suggesting that phonological priming aided target processing in a way that might be safe from Coltheart's criticism.

Another source of evidence comes from lexical decisions about regular words versus exception words. This evidence appears at first glance to be mixed, but in the end it tells a fairly coherent story. Coltheart *et al.* (1979) failed to obtain a difference between regular and exception words, supporting the position that initial semantic access is always achieved visually rather than phonologically. Other investigators, however, have reported an advantage for regular words, suggesting instead that the faster phonological recoding that is possible for regular words speeds semantic access as well as pronunciation (Bauer & Stanovich, 1980; Parkin, 1982; Parkin & Underwood, 1983). Why the discrepancy? Bauer and Stanovich (1980) investigated this question, and found that the word set used by Coltheart *et al.* (1977) included three different kinds of words: regular words, exception words, and—unbeknownst to Coltheart *et al.* because the concept had not yet been invented—a fairly large number of the words that Glushko (1979) called regular/inconsistent. When the three kinds of words were tested, Bauer and Stanovich discovered that regular words were accepted more rapidly than exception words whereas regular/inconsistent words were accepted more *slowly* than exception words. When regular and regular/inconsistent words were averaged together, as was done by Coltheart *et al.*, there was no difference between them and the exception words. Hence, the failure to obtain a regularity effect in lexical decision was due to a failure to distinguish between regular words that are truly regular and regular words that share spelling patterns with exception words. Thus the data turn out in the end to be consistent with a phonological contribution to semantic access.

We have already seen, though, that by themselves differences between the phonological effects of regular, regular/inconsistent, and exception words cannot determine whether one should prefer a PCS or a lexical instance account of the origins of the effects. A stronger case could be made if such effects depended on word frequency, with differences due to regularity of pronunciation more likely among lower frequency words. Such an outcome could be accommodated more easily by the PCS model than by any other approach. While Seidenberg *et al.* (1984) found an interaction between regularity and frequency in their pronunciation task, they failed to find such an interaction in lexical decision. Indeed, they found no significant effects of regularity at all. However, the subjects were adults. When Waters and Seidenberg (1983) tried the same experiment with children, lexical decision did produce a regularity by frequency interaction. A reasonable conclusion would be that, relative to children, the added reading experience of the adults speeds up the direct visual route to meaning sufficiently to obscure effects of the slower access routes that depend on phonological recoding. Among children, such effects in general, and effects due to differences in speed between the logogen-based and rule-governed phonological routes, become more prominent. This interpretation allows all of the above results to be encompassed comfortably by the PCS approach.

So far, then, despite a rather complicated body of data with a number of inconsistencies that remain to be worked out, the PCS account of semantic access is faring reasonably well. One more line of research, however, can be raised against it. Speed–accuracy trade-off studies by Singer (1980) and by Stanovich and Bauer (1978) found that lexical decision accuracy is better than chance even after evidence of phonological recoding has been completely eliminated from performance. Singer (1980) concluded only that phonological recoding is on the average slower than visual coding, but Stanovich and Bauer argued, like Coltheart, that phonological recoding plays no part in semantic access. In fact, Stanovich and Bauer went on to argue that phonological recoding is entirely postlexical, occurring as a **result** of activating lexical knowledge rather than serving as a means of producing such activation. Thus Stanovich and Bauer took their result to favor a lexical instance model. However, in both studies speeding performance decreased lexical decision accuracy as well as reducing evidence for phonological recoding. This is entirely consistent with the PCS account. The type of speed–accuracy trade-off result that would cause the PCS models trouble would be a large decrement in evidence for phonological recoding *before* lexical decision accuracy declined.

2. Comparing Words with Logographs and Pictures

These lexical decision experiments can be put in perspective by taking a look at studies that have compared words with logographs or pictures, two types of stimuli that are generally thought to enjoy very direct visual access to meaning. Treiman, Baron, and Luk (1981) asked readers of Chinese and readers of English to make sensibility judgments about simple sentences that—like the sentences used by Doctor and Coltheart (1980) in the study described in the previous section—sometimes contained homophones of words whose presence made the sentences sound sensible even though they were not. Readers of English showed interference much like that observed by Doctor and Coltheart, but readers of Chinese did not. Other studies have shown that readers of Chinese **do** use phonological or articulatory recoding as a means of supporting short-term memory (Tzeng, Hung, & Wang, 1977), so it seems reasonable to conclude that phonological recoding plays a part in semantic access for English words that it does not play for Chinese logographs. If this line of reasoning is correct, then one might be more comfortable attributing the homophone and pseudohomophone interference effects identified by Doctor and Coltheart to semantic access rather than to proposition formation and memory storage.

Another Stroop-type task has been used by Smith and Magee (1981) to compare words with pictures. Subjects saw pictures of common objects that had the names of either the same or different objects printed across them (see Rayner & Posnansky, 1978; Rosinski, Golinkoff, & Kukish, 1975). When subjects had to perform a semantic category membership judgment, conflicting pictures interfered with the classification of words but conflicting words did not interfere with the classification of pictures. When the task was changed to naming, the pattern of interference reversed. Words interfered with naming pictures but pictures did not interfere with pronouncing words. Smith and Magee concluded that semantic codes become activated more rapidly for pictures than for words whereas phonological codes become activated more rapidly for words than for pictures (see also Potter & Faulconer, 1975). Carr, McCauley, Sperber, and Parmelee (1982) reached a similar conclusion from patterns of facilitation in primed naming and categorization rather than from patterns of interference in the Stroop task. They argued that, on the average, the relatively direct relationship between spelling and sound makes phonological recoding faster and more automatic than semantic recoding when words are being read. Such a relationship would make it more likely that phonological recoding could aid semantic activation than the reverse. However, practice at semantic activation from visual stimuli ought to speed and automate that process, so that on the PCS account, higher frequency words should show less evidence of phonological recoding and greater evidence of direct visual access to meaning than lower frequency words—which they do, at least in lexical decision, as discussed earlier in the article.

3. Context Effects and the Case for the Verification Model

Where have we come to? We have considered a selection of evidence from the voluminous research on tachistoscopic recognition, pronunciation, and lexical decision, plus experiments using two other tasks that involve semantic processing: judgments of category membership and judgments of sentence sensibility. We have used that evidence to show the PCS, logogen, and verification models at work, and we have concluded from this demonstration that the PCS account is the strongest of the three. However, we have not yet examined the verification model in its area of strength, and therefore it has not had a fair chance to display its virtues. To remedy the problem, we turn now to a brief discussion of the effects of semantic context on word recognition.

a. The Logogen Model, the Two-Process Theory of Context Effects, and Some Problems. Because the verification model has been cast most often as a challenger to the more widely accepted two-process theory of context effects, we will begin with a description of two-process theory and its origins in the logogen model of word recognition.

One of the major attractions of Morton's (1969) first logogen model was its ability to account for the fact that words vary in recognizability depending on the context in which they are encountered. Suppose that each target word in a tachistoscopic recognition task is presented after one of three different kinds of antecedent events: a neutral warning signal (the standard procedure in tests of the recognition of isolated words), a sentence that the target word completes in an appropriate or predictable manner, and a sentence that the target word completes in an inappropriate or nonsensical manner. Relative to the first condition of context-free word recognition, the perceiver would be more likely to recognize the target correctly after the appropriate sentence and less likely to recognize it after the inappropriate sentence (Tulving & Gold, 1963; Tulving, Mandler, & Baumal, 1964). Thus appropriate contexts provide a benefit to recognition whereas inappropriate contexts exact a cost. Similar phenomena occur in lexical decision and pronunciation tasks, though the cost associated with an inappropriate context tends to be less in pronunciation than in either lexical decision or tachistoscopic recognition (Fishler & Bloom, 1979; Forster, 1981; Stanovich & West, 1979, 1981, 1983; West & Stanovich, 1982; Seidenberg, 1983).

The logogen model can accommodate the broad outlines of these phenomena by supposing that context sends inputs to logogens in much the same way as do visual stimuli. The logogens accept facilitatory and inhibitory inputs from visual feature analysis and from semantic sentence processing alike, combining them as equivalent sources of information. The result is that appropriate context reduces the amount of evidence that is needed from the visual stimulus to activate a logogen whereas inappropriate context increases the amount of evidence that is needed (in addition to Morton's work, see Schuberth & Eimas, 1977; Schuberth, Spoehr, & Lane, 1981).

A basic tenet of the original logogen model is that the visual and contextual inputs operate passively and automatically rather than strategically or consciously. However, Posner and Snyder (1975) demonstrated that the magnitude and time course of context effects vary substantially with the expectations and intentions of the perceiver. When the perceiver does not expect the context to be related to the target or to be helpful in carrying out the decisions required by the task, facilitation occurs from related or appropriate contexts and this facilitation appears very rapidly after the context's onset. Cost from unrelated contexts, though, does not occur unless the perceiver expects to be able to make use of contextual information to help with task performance. Under such circumstances cost does occur, but not on the same time course as facilitation. Whereas facilitation appears very rapidly, cost usually requires some 300–500 msec to develop to significant levels (though exceptions can be found; see Antos, 1979; Neely, Fisk, & Ross, 1983).

This dependence between perceivers' expectations and the effects of related versus unrelated contexts led Posner and Snyder to propose a two-process theory of context effects, consisting of the fast-acting, passive-automatic process of the logogen model plus a slower-acting, attended and strategically controlled process that utilizes context to make predictions about the upcoming target stimulus. When the automatic logogen-like or "pathway activation" process is operating by itself, related contexts produce facilitation but unrelated contexts exert no influence at all. When the pathway activation process is accompanied by attended predictions, then related contexts produce facilitation—and according to the theory, they ought to produce more facilitation than in the unattended situation, since the benefits of a correct prediction are combined with the benefits of automatic pathway activation—but unrelated contexts produce cost, since the attended predictions turn out to be wrong and lead the perceiver astray. Neely (1977) confirmed several predictions of the two-process theory using single words as contexts, and Stanovich and West (1979, 1981; Stanovich, 1980) elaborated the theory into a general statement about the role of context in reading and the relationship between context utilization and reading ability (see Carr, 1986, for a more detailed review).

Despite the appeal and power of the two-process conceptualization, however, details of the data in a number of experiments have proven to be troublesome. First, two-process theory predicts that the magnitude of benefit and the magnitude of cost should be positively correlated, because, as we have already seen, the conditions that produce cost when predictions are wrong also produce benefit when predictions are right. This component of benefit due to confirmed predictions enhances the facilitation that would have occurred anyway because of automatic pathway activation. But contrary to this requirement of two-process theory, the results of experiments by Becker (1980, 1982), Eisenberg and Becker (1982), and Stanovich and West (1981) showed that experimental conditions with large amounts of cost tended to produce **smaller** amounts of benefit relative to conditions with low cost.

Second, two-process theory predicts that the more constrained the target word is by the context, the larger should be the benefit when the constraints are met and the larger should be the cost when the constraints are violated and the perceiver is led down a garden path. Experiments like those of Fishler and Bloom (1979) in which inappropriate sentence contexts produced much larger costs than benefits when they caused the perceiver to entertain very strong expectations for a particular word have been taken as evidence that this aspect of two-process theory is correct. On the other hand, several experiments by Becker (1980) and Eisenberg and Becker (1982) have shown just the opposite effect, and have done so in a very analytic and informative fashion. To illustrate, consider a series of lexical decision trials in which each target is preceded by a single context word that the perceiver is told to use to try to prepare for the upcoming target. In one condition the related contexts are antonyms of the target, so that *black* primes *white* and *hot* primes *cold*. In another condition the primes are category names and the related targets are category members of moderate or low typicality, so that *fruit* primes *pear* or *tangerine* and *bird* primes *sparrow* or *owl*. The most likely outcome based on two-process theory would be that the antonym condition would produce large benefit on related trials and large cost on unrelated trials, because the perceiver can predict with great accuracy what a related target will be and commit processing resources quite specifically to that narrow prediction. The category condition, on the other hand, should produce smaller benefits and costs, because the perceiver cannot predict with any accuracy exactly what target will appear and must prepare for a broader spectrum of possibilities.

The results, however, showed a rather different pattern of costs and benefits. The antonym condition produced large benefits and almost no cost, whereas the category condition produced large cost and almost no benefit. How could this have happened? It is conceivable, of course, that subjects simply had to work harder to generate a list of expected targets in the category condition, and the greater mental workload elevated all times in the primed conditions relative to the neutral condition. Such generalized elevation would give the appearance of a shift toward less benefit and more cost. Alternatively, the data may indicate that context is utilized in a fundamentally different way than two-process theory supposes. Such has been Becker's contention in developing the verification model (1976, 1979, 1980, 1982; Becker & Killion, 1977).

   b. *The Verification Model.* Becker's model is a radical departure from the logogen and PCS models we have discussed. In essence, Becker does not allow bottom-up, stimulus-driven encoding mechanisms ever to recognize a word on their own. The knowledge-driven verification process must always have the final say in word recognition operations. Bottom-up visual feature analyzers construct a set of primitive sensory features that comprise a rough representation of the stimulus. This representation activates a set of candidate words in the lexicon whose visual appearance is generally consistent with that of the stimulus. The candidate words are then used one by one as probes in the verification process that actually determines what word is present.

The set of candidates established by bottom-up encoding is called the "sensory set." This set takes time to construct and once it is completed, it takes time to verify. Because of the serial nature of the process, verification takes longer for larger sets.

Context exerts an influence on word recognition by contributing a set of candidates to be verified in addition to the sensory set. The members of this contextual or "semantic set" are selected from the lexicon on the basis of semantic criteria established by the processing of preceding words or text rather than visual criteria established by feature analysis. Once entered into the verification queue, though, semantic set members are verified in the same way as sensory set members, by matching expected visual characteristics of each candidate against the actual visual characteristics of the stimulus.

In Becker's approach, the trick to obtaining facilitation from related or appropriate contexts and inhibition from unrelated contexts lies in the temporal priorities assigned to verifying semantic as opposed to sensory candidates. Becker assumes that because context precedes the stimulus word, a semantic set is selected and ready to go well before bottom-up processes can generate a sensory set. For efficiency's sake verification of the semantic set begins in parallel with selection of the sensory set. If context has accurately constrained the target, then a match is found in the semantic set. If semantic relatedness fails to produce a match, then members of the sensory set are verified. Given these assumptions, a related context could facilitate recognition relative to the case in which there is no context at all by producing an early match from the semantic set. An unrelated context could produce cost by delaying verification of the sensory set until the misleading semantic set has been rejected.

Here is the key to explaining the relations between cost and benefit that cause difficulty for two-process theory. When context can support very specific expectations about related targets, the semantic set will be small and can be verified rapidly. If the target is contained in the semantic set, facilitation will result relative to recognition based on the more time-consuming computations associated with the sensory set. However, if the target is not contained in the semantic set, little will be lost because verification of that set can be completed so fast that verification of the sensory set will be delayed only a small amount or not at all relative to recognition in the absence of context. Hence the antonym condition described above produces large benefit and small cost. When context supports general rather than specific expectations, the situation is different. The semantic set will be large rather than small and it will take a relatively long time to verify. If it contains the target, the serial verification process may still go through a lot of wrong candidates before reaching the right one, so that benefit may often be rather small. If it does not contain the target, the chances of cost are great because of the large number of incorrect candidates that must be rejected before exhausting the semantic set and reaching the sensory set. Hence the category condition described above produces small benefit and large cost.

In the verification model, then, variation in cost and benefit arises from variation in the size of the semantic set. From this perspective the verification approach can explain the negative correlation between cost and benefit as well as the more specific differences between the benefit-dominant pattern of context effects produced by antonyms and the cost-dominant pattern produced by category names. Both of these phenomena raise problems for the two-process theory, which combines a logogen model of word recognition with an attention mechanism in order to explain context effects.

Of course, the challenge represented by the verification approach has not gone unanswered by proponents of two-process theory. Stanovich, West, Feeman, and Cunningham (1984) have attempted to turn the tables by identifying a group of context effects that two-process theory handles but the verification model does not. These and other bones of contention in the domain of context effects are discussed by Becker and by Seidenberg in this volume.

c. *The Recognition of Isolated Words.* In order to be a viable model of word recognition, however, the verification approach would not only have to explain context effects, but it would also have to handle the results of tasks requiring recognition of isolated words that have already been reviewed. We saw in the discussion of tachistoscopic recognition that the activation-verification model offered by Paap *et al.* (1982) can do a reasonably good job in that domain. Because the verification process is disabled under the conditions of tachistoscopic recognition, however, the model requires additional assumptions to accommodate word frequency effects that fall naturally out of the logogen and PCS accounts.

With respect to pronunciation, we can only speculate, since so far none of the verification theorists has tackled any of the phenomena in that task domain. As they stand, however, the verification models make little mention of phonological coding, and they have no means for achieving any kind of integrated representation of pseudowords—they can only identify the component letters of a pseudoword and determine that those letters do not correspond to any of the words stored in the lexicon. Therefore the verification models would suffer the same difficulties as the logogen model of McClelland and Rumelhart (1981) in accounting for the results of pronunciation tasks.

Because the task of choice for verification theorists has been lexical decision (Becker, 1976, 1979, 1980, 1982; Becker & Killion, 1977), one should expect the verification model to do well in that domain. As just mentioned, the verification model does not deal explicitly with phonological codes, so we can again only speculate about its ability to handle the evidence on phonological recoding in lexical decision that was taken earlier in the article to favor PCS models over logogen models. It would appear, however, that any effects of phonological codes would be postlexical in the verification model, resulting from release of knowledge about the word's pronunciation, spelling, meaning, and other properties from word's lexical entry after verification has been completed. If so, then the verification model would face the same disadvantages as the logogen model in comparison to PCS accounts of semantic access.

There are other phenomena, though, to which the verification model has been applied directly in tests of its efficacy at isolated word recognition, and we can discuss them more concretely. Besner and Swan (1982) have drawn a detailed comparison of the ways in which the verification model and the logogen model explain the effects of stimulus repetition, word frequency, and stimulus degradation, where degradation is achieved through contrast reduction or superimposition of visual noise such as a dot pattern. The simple effect of each of these variables on lexical decision is straightforward. Decisions about repeated stimuli are made more rapidly than decisions about first occurrences, high frequency words are responded to more rapidly than low frequency words, and high-quality visual stimuli are responded to more rapidly than degraded stimuli. Besner and Swan acknowledge that both models can easily accommodate the simple effects, but argue that neither model can successfully encompass the pairwise interactions among these variables.

First, stimulus repetition and word frequency interact in an overadditive fashion: repetition helps the slower, low frequency words more than it helps the faster, high frequency words. According to additive factors-type logic (Sternberg, 1969; but see McClelland, 1979; Pieters, 1983; Taylor, 1976), such an interaction indicates that they influence the same processing mechanism. The logogen model supposes that this mechanism is the logogen system. Both frequency and repetition lower the amount of evidence a word's logogen needs to reach its threshold. The verification explanation is different, but just as effective. In the verification model, words are entered into the verification queue in order of frequency. If the model assumes that repetition, like higher frequency, also causes a word to enter the queue at an earlier position, then additive factors logic would lead one to predict such an interaction between repetition and word frequency.

Next the models must account for a similar overadditive interaction between repetition and visual degradation. Again, the most straightforward means is to suppose that repetition and degradation influence the same processing mechanism, and again the logogen model assumes that this mechanism is the logogen system—degradation reduces the rate of information accrual in the logogens, and since repetition reduces the amount of information needed to reach threshold, an overadditive interaction is predicted. Notice, though, that the logogen model has now claimed that **all three** factors influence the logogen system. Therefore it should predict that the remaining interaction, between word frequency and degradation, would also be significant and overadditive. However, these two factors do not interact (Becker & Killion, 1977; Stanners, Jastrembski, & Westbrook, 1975), which means that the logogen model has been caught in a contradiction and has some repairs to make.

What about the verification model? Because it was Becker and Killion (1977) who first reported additivity between word frequency and degradation, the verification model has been tuned to account for that effect. Whereas frequency influences the ordering of words in the verification queue, the kinds of degradation under consideration here, which are contrast reduction and superimposition of a noise mask such as a dot pattern, are held to slow the rate of feature extraction in the bottom-up process of visual encoding. The features eventually extracted, however, are equal in quality to the features extracted from undegraded stimuli, so that the candidate set and the process of verifying it are not altered. Thus frequency and degradation are assumed to influence different mechanisms and additivity between them can be explained.

This explanation sets the stage for the verification model to contradict itself in much the same way as the logogen model. If repetition works the same way as frequency, and if frequency and degradation are additive, then the verification model should predict that repetition and degradation are additive. But Besner and Swan found that they interact. Like the logogen model, then, the verification model displays a number of strengths but has some repairs to make before it can handle all the phenomena to which it ought to apply.

4. Some Conclusions about the Verification Model and Its Standing Relative to the Logogen and PCS Accounts

Having now observed the verification model in its domain of strength, we can conclude that it measures up fairly well. On the one hand, it suffers some difficulties in comparison both to the PCS model and to Glushko's activation-synthesis version of the logogen model because of its lack of provisions for phonological coding, especially of pseudowords. Furthermore, it has some work to do in order to account for the phenomena reviewed by Besner and Swan (1982). On the other hand the logogen model also has trouble in Besner and Swan's analysis, and the verification model succeeds in an impressive way with some kinds of context effects that are not easy for logogen-based models to handle. Since the kinds of difficulties raised for the logogen approach by either Besner and Swan or the research on context effects would not be easily solved by postulating a parallel encoding mechanism based on grapheme-to-phoneme translation, the PCS approach cannot simply step in and win by default. It, too, has some work to do to account for these phenomena.

The upshot of the various comparisons we have made so far, then, is that while the PCS model is to be preferred over the logogen approach, both of these models have their weaknesses and the verification model may be able to capitalize on them. Whether it or the PCS approach will turn out to be the best of the models discussed so far depends on how each responds to the weaknesses that have been identified. It seems to us, though, that the PCS model currently has fewer repairs and extensions to make than does the verification model in order to become thoroughly viable in the domains

of tachistoscopic recognition, pronunciation, lexical and semantic judgments, and context effects.

D. Multiple Morphemes, Long Words, and the Lexical Search Model

Certainly our discussion so far has exposed variety: Variety in the empirical and theoretical issues that have been investigated, variety in task
procedures that have been employed, and variety in the approaches that
have been taken to modeling the word recognition process. Nevertheless,
there is a consistent theme that can be identified. In one way or another,
all of the models have concentrated on something that is generally referred
to as "accessing the lexicon" or "lexical access." Achieving "lexical access" is a central goal of the models, though they may differ markedly in
their procedures for reaching that goal.

It is clear that in these models of word recognition, "lexical access" involves getting into the right location in memory—activating some kind of
long-term memory representation that contains experientially established
information about the particular string of letters that is currently available
or that was most recently available to the senses. What is less clear—what
is often quite vague—is the type of information that is supposed to be contained in that representation. What, exactly, does the perceiver know about
the stimulus letter string immediately upon reaching and activating the right
location in memory that was not known before its activation?

Implicit in our discussion of the relationship between models and task
situations has been the assumption that different tasks lead the subject to
rely on different codes for their performance. We have been especially concerned with two types of codes, one phonological and the other semantic,
and with how they become available to the perceiver for the purposes of
making the decisions that are required by the tasks in which word recognition has been studied. From that point of view we have portrayed models
of "word recognition" as models of how the different codes are activated
and in some cases coordinated. In our portrayals, current models use the
notion of a lexicon or a system that represents lexical instances both as a
means of getting phonological information about stimulus letter strings and
as a means of getting semantic information about them. While we have not
made a firm argument as to whether the phonological lexicon and the semantic lexicon must be completely separate from one another, we have argued that they must at least represent the two kinds of codes in a way that
allows phonological and semantic information to dissociate: perceivers
sometimes know one kind of information about a letter-string stimulus but
not the other.

As part of such an argument, it is important to be explicit about the manner in which each kind of code is represented and what processes must take place in order to activate it. We have spent a great deal of effort in discussing this matter with respect to phonological codes, but despite the fact that we began in the last section to discuss tasks that involve semantic decisions, we have not yet addressed in detail the question of how semantic information is actually represented and activated. It is to this and related issues that we now turn, and in so doing we will reach the territory of the lexical search models.

1. Morphemic Representation

When one starts to consider what it would mean to access the meaning of a word, an important question is whether a word is decomposed into its constituent morphemes and if so, how. Almost any model of reading would have to concede that words such as *headstand, bakeshop,* and *polymorphemic* are understood (in **some** sense, anyway) by understanding the component parts. The need for such a concession is most clearly illustrated by the ease with which readers can comprehend the results of a particular type of lexical generativity that involves creating novel prefixed or suffixed words. Thus while in general the degree of transparency of the internal semantic structure of polymorphemic words may vary substantially, it is hard to see how comprehension of something like *stifler* could be anything other than decomposition of the word into *stifle* plus the agentive suffix. If this is true for *stifler,* it might possibly be true for words that are more familiar but nevertheless polymorphemic. *Reading,* for example, might be comprehended by decomposing it into *read* plus the present participle. With the exception of Morton's proposals (1979; Kempley & Morton, 1982; Murrell & Morton, 1974), the logogen and PCS models make little mention of morphemic structure or any processes for dealing with it. It seems likely that if pressed, proponents of these models might suggest that decomposition, if it occurs at all, happens as a stage subsequent to accessing the semantic lexicon. For example, the lexical entry might give the meaning of the word and also its morphemic decomposition for those that are interested, in roughly the way that such information is sometimes given in Webster's dictionary. Morphemic structure has been addressed more directly in the context of the verification model, but with an outcome much like the one we have envisioned for logogen and PCS models. Rubin, Becker, and Freeman (1979) have proposed that morphemic decomposition is an optional strategy that can be adopted when task conditions make it beneficial.

An alternative possibility is that reliance on semantic decomposition is a fundamental feature of word recognition rather than a peripheral accessory. Pursuit of this possibility has been the major thrust of the work of

Taft and Forster in developing the lexical search model, as described in detail by Taft (this volume). Taft takes the position that the major problem the word recognition system tries to solve in its semantic processing is to identify the root morpheme of a word, the kernel out of which the word's meaning is constructed by adding prefixes and suffixes of various kinds. The research done in pursuit of this claim suggests that decomposition does not occur after the lexicon has been reached, but is instead an integral part of getting there, and that the semantic representations stored in memory consist of the meanings of morphemes—the products of decomposing words—rather than the meanings of the words themselves. If that conclusion were accepted, then the PCS model that we have tentatively adopted at this point, or either of the other types of models if we are wrong in favoring the PCS approach, would have to be complicated to account for some sort of morphemic analysis. Therefore we will take a look at the data that have led Taft and others to this point of view.

a. Active Subword Units in Word Recognition. We raised an argument in discussing phonological recoding that models of word recognition probably need to include either a set of rules or a set of representations that handle subword units. This need is a building block of the argument in favor of semantic decomposition.

The mature reader is, or at least can become, aware of many subword units as he or she reads. The subunits of phonology such as the syllable or the phoneme and the subunits of orthography such as the spelling pattern are clear candidates for psychological reality. In fact, a large body of work on reading development has taken the need to master phonological and orthographic units as its topic (e.g., Gleitman & Rozin, 1977; Golinkoff, 1978; Treiman, 1985; Treiman & Baron, 1981). Morphemic subunits are another candidate. It has been argued that parts of a stimulus word that happen to be words or morphemes themselves become temporarily activated, even when they are not appropriate subunits of the stimulus word. An example would be *bear* as a temporarily activated subunit of *beard* (Taft, 1979). The critical question from our standpoint is whether these morphemic units are activated prelexically as a part of the process of locating and activating information in the semantic lexicon, or only after lexical access has been achieved, either obligatorily or as a consciously controlled option on the part of the perceiver.

b. Experimental Evidence for Morphemic Subword Units. Perhaps the strongest evidence for morphemic subword units comes from experiments involving affixed words. An important finding is that words with prefixes, such as *rejuvenate* or *revive,* are classified more rapidly in a lexical decision task than "pseudoprefixed" words such as *repertoire* or *relish,* whose initial letters are the same as a commonly used prefix but do not function as one for the word. A difference in lexical decision time of about 30 msec can be found between prefixed and pseudoprefixed words that have been equated for length and frequency of occurrence (e.g., Taft, 1981).

Is there a similar effect for suffixes? That is, do people take longer to classify a word that looks as though it has a suffix but does not, such as *sister,* than a word that really has a suffix, such as *sender?* Here the answer is less clear (see Taft, this volume, for a discussion). However, a particular finding involving suffix effects is of considerable interest. Manelis and Tharp (1976) presented pairs of letter strings as stimuli and required subjects to respond positively if both were words and negatively if either or both were nonwords. Mixed pairs that contained a suffixed word and a pseudosuffixed word, such as *sister–sender*, produced slower responding than unmixed pairs, regardless of whether the unmixed pair consisted of two suffixed words or two pseudosuffixed words. The two kinds of unmixed pairs did not differ in their response times. It is as if the word recognition system could engage in two different kinds of processing, one appropriate to suffixed words and the other appropriate to pseudosuffixed words, and carrying out two instances of the same kind of processing is easier than switching from one to the other. It would be hard to accommodate such a finding without proposing at least that processes for semantic decomposition are readily available for use in the word recognition process, if not that they are always used.

The results of Manelis and Tharp (1976) are consistent with the idea that procedures for handling affixes may be primed by successfully employing the same procedure on a preceding word (or that these procedures may be inhibited by successfully employing a different one on a preceding word). A related line of inquiry has investigated specific priming effects between words that share morphemes in common. Given that words sharing morphemes will often be similar in meaning (*read, reader, reading, reread*), this might seem to be merely a reworking of the semantic priming that we discussed earlier with respect to context effects and the verification model. However, there is an aspect to the data on priming via shared morphemes that indicates that something more may be going on. It is generally the case that semantic priming due to associations between words, such as *doctor* and *nurse,* is smaller in magnitude and quicker to dissipate than repetition priming that results from previously processing exactly the same word. It appears that the priming effect due to shared morphemes bears a greater similarity in magnitude and longevity to repetition priming than to semantic priming. Stanners, Neiser, Hernon, and Hall (1979b) have even reported that over a lag of about 10 trials between presentations in the lexical decision task, an inflected form of a verb, such as *lifting,* primed the verb stem, in this case *lift,* just as much as did the stem form itself. The size of this effect was well over 100 msec, which is very large as priming effects go in this task. Furthermore, the effect of processing an inflected form on processing the stem form was not due simply to physical or orthographic similarity between the two letter strings. When pairs that were related derivationally, such as *selective-select,* were used as prime and target, only about half as much priming resulted, even though the members of derivational pairs are just as similar physically and orthographically as pairs like *lifting-lift.*

These results indicate that morphological aspects of linguistic structure, especially relationships due to inflection, are important to recognition. However, it is still possible to construct a scenario in which initial recognition depends on lexical rather than morphological representation, with decomposition occurring postlexically. It could be, for example, that the products of the postlexical decomposition feed activation back into the lexicon and it is this feedback that does the work of priming observed in the lexical decision task. As Taft (this volume) argues, however, such an account would be hard pressed to predict equal amounts of priming from inflected and identical primes. With identical primes, the entirety of the processing leading up to the lexical decision would be the same, whereas with inflected primes, which in the postlexical decomposition account would have separate entries in the lexicon, much of the processing would be different. Therefore the equivalence of priming from inflected forms and identical forms would seem to demand that semantic decomposition be an integral part of the mechanisms of word recognition that are recruited by the lexical decision task.

Another striking result was reported by Stanners, Neiser, and Painton (1979a) in a series of experiments looking at priming of prefixed words. They found that presentation of a stem and a prefix on separate trials facilitated lexical decisions about a word consisting of the prefix plus the stem on a subsequent trial (e.g., *trieve* and *remit* presented separately followed by *retrieve*). However, the magnitude of this priming was only about half that produced by identical primes. Similar priming equal to about half that of identical primes was found for changed prefixes (*progress* primed by *regress*) and for stems primed by prefixed versions of the same stem (*aware* primed by *unaware*). Complementary evidence comes from Taft (1976; Taft & Forster, 1976). Morphemic stems such as *vive* are harder to reject as nonwords than are matched "pseudostems" such as *lish* taken from *relish,* and mispaired prefixes and stems are harder to reject as nonwords than are matched prefixes and pseudostems, such as *dejuvenate* versus *depertoire.*

Despite the highly suggestive nature of these results, the fact that priming effects involving prefixes are smaller than those produced by identical primes again leaves them open to interpretation in terms of postlexical feedback processes. This problem is compounded by the fact that lexical decision is a task that has been specifically shown to tap postlexical as well as prelexical processes (Balota & Chumbley, 1984; Seidenberg, 1983; West & Stanovich, 1982). Furthermore, none of the experiments by Stanners and his colleagues included controls for semantic or associative priming of the *doctor–nurse* variety. It seems quite plausible that on seeing *trieve* subjects may have thought of *retrieve* or on seeing *aware* they may have thought of *unaware,* creating the conditions for feedback from these associative generations to produce some priming on subsequent trials.

Given these difficulties, it would be a useful contribution to replicate the effects of prefixes (and those of suffixes as well) using a task such as pronunciation that has been shown to be less susceptible to postlexical processes and to include a control for associative priming. The closest to such an experiment that we know of in visual word recognition is the study by Murrell and Morton (1974), which employed tachistoscopic whole report. In that experiment primes that were morphologically related to the target, such as *boring* as a prime for *bored,* produced significant facilitation. Primes that were equally similar visually but unrelated semantically, such as *born* as a prime for *bored,* produced no facilitation at all. Though this experiment does not control for associative priming, it does extend the possibility of morphemic priming beyond the lexical decision task. Furthermore, Kempley and Morton (1982) have reported analogous effects of morphological relatedness in an auditory word recognition task, and this time a control was included for semantic relatedness. However, we mentioned in discussing tachistoscopic recognition that data from the whole-report procedure are hard to interpret because of the large number of post-perceptual guessing strategies that subjects can successfully bring to bear in the task. Therefore the case for morphemic decomposition as a fundamental aspect of lexical access is intriguing, but it is not yet airtight.

2. Subword Units and Lexical Search: Getting to the Morphemes Represented in Memory

If semantic representations correspond to morphemes, then stimulus strings must be decomposed into morphemes and the results must be matched against the morphemic representations in the lexicon in order to achieve recognition. The lexical search model makes a number of proposals for how the processes of decomposition and matching are carried out. The essence of these proposals is that one or the other of two different types of units must be recovered from a stimulus string before going to the lexicon: its root morpheme (which, as we have stressed, is a semantic unit) or something called its basic orthographic syllable structure, or BOSS, which is a nonsemantic unit based on orthographic rules rather than meaning. The evidence in favor of the BOSS is rather shaky, so we will concentrate here on processes for recovering the root morpheme in order to use it as an access code. Detailed critiques of the notion of a subword orthographic code for accessing semantics can be found in Lima and Pollatsek (1983) and Taft (this volume).

While the relation between the word and its root morpheme may not always be completely obvious because of the extent of the transformations that link them (as in *compulsion* and *compel*), the lexical search model nevertheless sees determination of the root morpheme as perhaps the single most important component of the word recognition process. This determination requires that all prefixes and suffixes be stripped away (and any other transformations accounted for, as in the example of *compulsion,* which without its suffix *-sion* would be *compul* rather than the desired *compel*). In particular, the beginning of the stimulus string is examined for sets of letters that could form a prefix and the end is examined for letters that could form a suffix. If such letters are detected, they are separated from the remainder of the stimulus and discarded for the purposes of semantic access. This preprocessing procedure would work well for words that really do have affixes and for words whose beginnings and endings cannot be confused with affixes. However, for words with "pseudoaffixes" (e.g., the *re* in *repertoire*) there would be a considerable cost as the system tries to access the putative root *pertoire* and, finding no match, must reattach the letters that were erroneously stripped away and try again.

A check of the dictionary reveals that pseudoaffixed words are not at all uncommon. This fact would seem to argue against the theory on a priori grounds, since the proposed mechanism for recognition would hurt rather than help on a nontrivial proportion of its recognition attempts. Even if affix stripping were accepted as a fundamental process, theoretical problems would remain. Once affixes have been removed, the stimulus string is parsed left to right and the first (that is, the leftmost) morpheme is used as the access code. However, Selkirk (1982) has proposed that the morphological organization of words is considerably more complex than could be handled by a simple left-to-right parse. A clear example can be found in compound words such as *footstool*. A *footstool* is a kind of stool, not a kind of foot, so that access to meaning via the leftmost morpheme would be potentially misleading. One might argue that compound words are processed differently, but then one would need a mechanism to identify compound words. One might argue that while lexical decomposition follows the left-to-right rule as a means of achieving access, semantic recomposition follows a different set of rules once the appropriate morphological components have been activated. But this two-stage process seems contrived and hence is unattractive. Finally, one could adopt more sophisticated decomposition rules that take account of arguments such as Selkirk's, but at the risk of complicating the model relative to the competition.

On the other hand, the data show that recognition seems to suffer exactly the kinds of difficulties that affix stripping predicts. Furthermore, while it is more complex than the logogen or verification models in some respects, the lexical search model enjoys an advantage of simplicity in other respects. Information flow appears to be entirely stimulus driven on most occasions (excepting those in which the de-emphasized verification process is invoked). Forster (1979, 1981) has argued explicitly that word recognition is functionally autonomous (see also Humphreys, this volume), and Taft (this volume) has adopted that view for the lexical search model. Hence the effects of context are seen as entirely postlexical and are hardly discussed. Furthermore, Taft (this volume) argues that phonological recoding is irrelevant to semantic processing, which in his view always occurs via visual pathways. This assumption allows considerable simplification over alternative views such as the PCS approach—though we have argued that the data do not provide very strong support for the assumption.

How do these advantages and disadvantages balance out? All in all, it appears to us that the considerable edifice of the lexical search model overloads its empirical foundations. The impressive evidence for the psychological reality of morphemic decomposition clearly demands that such processes be given a place in models of word recognition. However, it is not yet very clear what that place ought to be. We consider next two chinks in the lexical search model's empirical armor that go beyond what we have discussed so far. The nature of these difficulties allows us to make a suggestion about the place of morphemic decomposition in word recognition as it is presently conceived, but ultimately, as we will argue in the final section of the article, it points toward a fundamental inadequacy in all the current models.

3. Two Problems for Lexical Search: Letter Perceptibility in Long Words and the Size of the Interference Effects

While the lexical search model discusses semantic access in far greater detail than most other models of word recognition, it is curiously silent on a matter that ought to be of great concern: Given that the first few letters and the last few letters of a word must be identified quite early in processing in order for affix stripping to do its work, just how identifiable **are** those letters? On the one hand, there is a literature on recognition of short words (say, three to five or six letters) that suggests the extremities of a word are more perceptible than letters in the interior (see Taft, this volume, for some of these findings and Carr, Lehmkuhle, Kottas, Astor-Stetson, & Arnold, 1976, for more). On the other hand, data from studies of eye movements in reading suggest that for words longer than six or seven letters this generality breaks down. The rightmost letters of such words tend to be rather poorly perceived because readers usually center their initial fixations toward the beginnings of longer words rather than at the center (for reviews, see Rayner, 1983; see also Section IV of this article). This means that for many of the words in the stimulus materials of the experiments conducted under the aegis of the lexical search model, the notion of suffix stripping, at least, makes little sense, since one of the first parts of the word to be processed is a part that is likely to be seen quite poorly during the first fixation on the word.

Just as troubling is that the magnitude of the interference with lexical decision caused by pseudoprefixing and pseudoaffixing is simply not as large as one would expect given the lexical search model's explanation of the effect. According to the model, the "affix" is stripped, then a search of the lexicon is instituted with the resulting "root," and when that search fails, the stripped letters are retrieved, reattached, and a new search is commenced, ending when the pseudoaffixed word is finally located. Yet for all this backtracking the delay in responding to pseudoprefixed words is only on the order of 30 msec relative to comparable words with real prefixes, and the delay in responding to pseudosuffixed words is even less, perhaps approaching zero.

4. An Alternative in the PCS Tradition: Multiple Pathways

To us, the two facts, (1) that the debilitative effect of pseudoaffixation is so small in general, and (2) that the effect is larger for pseudoprefixes than for pseudosuffixes, suggest parallel processing. As proposed by Stanners *et al.* (1979a), there may be two pathways by which visual-orthographic access to semantic information can occur. The first is a whole-word route that does not involve prelexical semantic decomposition. This route would require that semantic information be stored according to a lexical representation scheme rather than a morphemic one. The second pathway is the sequence of affix stripping followed by search for the resulting root morpheme postulated by Taft and Forster. This route would require the morphemic representation scheme, suggesting either that both schemes are instantiated completely, with a resulting duplication of representation for familiar polymorphemic words, or else that one scheme is followed for some word families and the other scheme is followed for the remainder. It would remain to determine which representational format is the right one, and if it is the latter, what rules determine which word families are represented with which scheme.

If the two pathways operate in parallel, such a proposal can account sensibly for a good bit of the data. The 30-msec difference between real prefixed words and pseudoprefixed words could easily arise as the magnitude of a redundancy gain defined by the difference between a situation in which either of two routes produces a correct answer (real prefixation) and a situation in which one route produces a correct answer and the other an incorrect answer (pseudoprefixation). The smaller difference between real and pseudosuffixed words would arise because of the relatively poor perceptibility of the suffixes of many of the words. Initiation of suffix stripping would have to be delayed until the end letters could be resolved (which in many cases of natural reading might not be until the second fixation on the word—see Section IV). This delay would allow the whole-word route to run much closer to completion before the effects of the semantic decomposition route would be felt, diminishing the contribution of the decomposition route to performance. Since in the whole-word route there is no distinction between real and pseudosuffixed words, the net result would be a much smaller difference between these two stimulus types than between real and pseudoprefixed words. Finally, it remains to accommodate the results of Manelis and Tharp (1976), which suggested that both a whole-word and a semantic decomposition route exist and that either route can be primed by prior usage. It is clear that the dual pathway proposal can encompass these results more easily than can the lexical search model as it stands.

III. CONCLUSION: A VERY COMPLICATED PCS MODEL WINS THE DAY

We can now conclude our look at current models of word recognition by summarizing our opinion of their relative merits. Even if a firm choice among the categories of models could be made, there are many points on which uncertainty would still exist and work would have to continue on the details. However, a firm choice is very difficult at present. Each of the major approaches has both strengths and weaknesses relative to the other approaches, so that the model deemed superior depends in large part on the particular problem one happens to be thinking about at the time of the decision. Nevertheless, we believe that some general constraints can be identified.

First, it seems that the overall organization of the PCS model should be preferred over that of the lexical instance models. This is true despite the surprising success of the lexical instance models at achieving behavior that appears to be rule governed in addition to their more expected success with behavior that is specific to a particular stimulus. We have defended the PCS organization with respect to how phonological recoding is achieved, arguing in Section II,B,2 that a lexical instance mechanism and a rule-governed, grapheme-to-phoneme translation mechanism operate in parallel. (It bears reiteration, though, that the operating characteristics of the translation mechanism remain unacceptably vague. We might agree to the need for such a mechanism, but we certainly do not know how to build one. Progress must be made on this problem in the near future if the PCS approach is to retain its viability.) We have also defended the PCS organization with respect to how semantic access is achieved. In Section II,C,1 we argued that a direct visual route to meaning operates in parallel with a route that is mediated by phonological recoding. (However, we subsequently qualified our endorsement of the PCS interpretation of semantic access in Section II,C,4, pointing out that the verification model, though in need of further development, has considerable potential in the semantic arena.) Finally, in Section II,D,4 we extended the PCS logic to the internal operation of the direct visual route to meaning, suggesting that a pathway based on whole words may work in parallel with a pathway based on morphemic decomposition. On balance, then, we have come down quite consistently in favor of the PCS approach.

As a way of summarizing our position, Fig. 6 shows an organization of the word recognition apparatus that is consistent with the arguments made so far. In essence, we have postulated that three parallel systems are involved in normal word recognition. Two of these are driven directly by the processes of visual code formation: a visual-orthographic pathway to whole-word meaning labeled (1) in the figure and a visual-orthographic pathway mediated by morphemic decomposition labeled (2). The third is a pathway based on phonological recoding, which itself has an internal structure consisting of parallel mechanisms, one working on paired associate or logogen-like principles and the other working on grapheme-to-phoneme translation rules. This pathway is labeled (3) in the figure. Besides operating to activate semantic codes, the outputs of these systems become available to conscious decision mechanisms that can do things like carry out laboratory word recognition tasks. This fact is accounted for by the pathways labeled (1A), (2A), (3A), and (S), which feed visual, morphemic, phonological, and semantic information into working memory. (The existence in the model of the oval labeled "Conscious word recognition: Working memory" and the pathways that feed it is not a profound addition—it merely takes explicit notice of people's abilities to introspect on and make relatively arbitrary use of various kinds of information about letter strings.)

In adopting such a complicated version of PCS, we clearly run a great risk. We would not want to proliferate processing mechanisms to the point that the resulting model of word recognition is either too unwieldy to use or too powerful to test. At the very least, it is necessary to seek converging evidence on the need for the various independent mechanisms we have de-

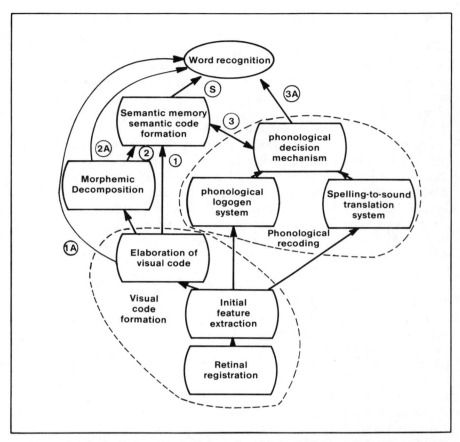

Fig. 6. Schematic diagram showing information flow through a complicated parallel coding systems model of word recognition that we believe to be the best current candidate. The portions of the system responsible for visual code formation and for phonological recoding are enclosed by dotted lines. The oval labeled "Conscious word recognition: Working memory" represents the ability of the perceiver to gain access to the outputs of the encoding mechanisms represented by the boxes for the purposes of decision and action or response production. See text for explanation of numbered pathways.

scribed. One source of such evidence is the neuropsychological literature, which we have already had recourse to in Section II,B,2. Let us examine the fruits of that literature a little more as a way of completing our argument.

In fact, there is some reason to believe that the neuropsychological literature supports the existence of only two systems. Marshall and Newcombe (1973) introduced a dichotomous classification of the syndromes of lesion-induced dyslexia that consisted of *surface dyslexia* and *deep dyslexia*. This dichotomy has gained wide popularity (see, e.g., Coltheart *et al.,* 1980). Surface dyslexics generally appear to have an intact phonological recoding system, as they can pronounce words and pseudowords with approximately equal facility and often tend to regularize the pronunciation of exception words, but they have great difficulty with semantics. Deep dyslexics, in contrast, appear to have a direct visual pathway to meaning but no phonological recoding system. Some of their characteristics were discussed in Section II,B,2. Most interesting for present purposes, however, is that deep dyslexics often have problems pronouncing function words, typically failing on them rather miserably even when the same task can be successfully performed on content words. In addition, deep dyslexics often make a disproportionately large number of derivational errors, such as producing only the stem when the stimulus is an inflected word. Some investigators, pointing to the fact that function words and bound morphemes often perform similar linguistic functions and therefore might be closely related (as in "the book of Mary" and "Mary's book"), have taken this evidence to mean that the system that handles function words and morphemic decomposition is the same system that handles phonological recoding.

However, the evidence as described above is only correlational, and cases can be found in the growing neuropsychological literature that seem to represent more extensive dissociation among functions than can be accommodated by a simple dichotomy between surface and deep dyslexia. While many deep dyslexics have problems with function words, inflections, and derivations, not all do. In fact, the occasional sparing of various aspects of morphological processing, among other details of symptomology, has lead Coltheart (1981) to propose a finer grained classification scheme that distinguishes between deep dyslexics and "phonological dyslexics." The existence of clinical patients whose injuries deprive them of phonological recoding but not of the ability to process function words or morphology suggests that phonological recoding and morphemic processes are handled by different mechanisms, as we have argued, rather than by the same mechanism. A particularly clear example of such a patient can be found in a case report by Funnell (1983).

Nevertheless, the correlation that does exist in the neuropsychological literature between phonological recoding and morphemic processes is intriguing. It could merely reflect the anatomy of the brain. The two systems may be supported by neural structures that are located close together and are therefore likely to be damaged together. Alternatively, it could be that the two systems share a common component. One possibility is that both phonological recoding and morphemic decomposition require something that the direct visual pathway does not, such as a short-term memory buffer where intermediate data can be stored while the computations leading up to semantic access are carried out. When this mechanism is damaged, both systems will be impaired, but when it is spared, then the injury could conceivably impair one but not the other, depending on its locus. This is mere speculation, but pursuit of it might help to resolve whether or not there is a need for as many independent processing mechanisms as we have proposed.

Perhaps it is in our own best interest to remind you now of the warning we gave in introducing Section II, that this article contains a complicated review of a complicated research area in which we are able to make very few succinct and unqualified summary statements. In that spirit, we will append to our conclusion a rather extended postscript, in which we raise an issue that causes difficulties for all of the models, including the PCS approach that we currently favor.

IV. POSTSCRIPT: SEQUENTIAL PROCESSING OF WORDS IN TEXT CAUSES PROBLEMS FOR ALL THE MODELS

We turn now to an issue to which we have alluded before, and which proves to cause problems for all of the models of word recognition. For this reason it constitutes an area in general need of greater consideration within the word recognition enterprise. The models we have considered have tacitly assumed that visual information from a word is ordinarily processed more or less in parallel on the basis of a single eye fixation (and hence, for example, that masked tachistoscopic presentation may be a reasonable simulation of the conditions under which words are recognized in reading). However, the data from studies of extended reading imply that many words in text are processed on more than one fixation. Before discussing the evidence for our assertion and its possible consequences for the process of word recognition, we will present a bit of background on eye movements in reading.

When reading text the eyes do not move smoothly and continuously as casual introspection might suggest. They actually move in a series of discrete, ballistic jumps known as saccades. In between saccades the eyes are relatively still, focusing on a particular point in the text, for periods of time called fixations. The saccades vary substantially in length, but average about seven to nine characters and take roughly 15–30 msec to accomplish, depending on the length of the saccade. Fixations are also highly variable, but last roughly 200–250 msec on the average. Virtually all of the information extracted from the text is acquired during the fixations (a phenomenon called saccadic suppression drastically reduces the sensitivity of the visual system and prevents useful information from being acquired during the saccades). In addition to eye movements that advance the eyes forward through the text, there are return sweeps that move the eyes from the end of one line of text to the beginning of the next line and regressions that move backwards through the text rather than forwards. Regressions account for about 10–15% of the movements during reading; most are only a few characters in length and are, for the most part, unconscious, made without the reader noticing them. Research in the last 10 years has established that much of the variability in saccade length and fixation duration can be explained by the visual and semantic characteristics of the text being fixated at the time, suggesting that eye movements are sensitive to the real-time information needs of the cognitive processes involved in reading (for reviews, see Rayner, 1983).

a. Processing Words on More than One Fixation. One datum that has resulted from the study of eye movements in reading is that longer words are often fixated twice. This datum opens the possibility that these words are not completely processed on one fixation, but instead are processed via the sequential intake (and coordination) of information from two fixations. Of course, this is not the only possibility, since the fact that the eyes fixate a word twice does not **necessarily** mean that information from that word is extracted on both fixations. This problem leads us to discuss a methodology that has been used in an attempt to diagnose what areas of text are actually being processed on a given fixation.

In the "moving window" technique, readers are presented with normal text in a certain region (the "window") around the letter that they are fixating on. Text outside this window is altered or mutilated in some way. For example, the experimenter might present the reader with a window consisting of all the letters of the word he or she is fixating and replace all other letters of the text with X's (preserving the spaces between words). Whenever the reader moves either forward or backward, the new word fixated will be normal and all the rest of the words (including the one previously fixated) will be X's. Such procedures are possible because eye position is being monitored and the display of text is being controlled by computer. To avoid having to monitor vertical as well as horizontal eye position (which increases the difficulty of the monitoring task tremendously), the technique has more often involved displaying one line of text at a time rather than extended passages, but the two situations have produced similar results.

The logic of the moving window technique is as follows. If when confronted with a situation in which only the word fixated is presented normally, readers could in fact read normally—with undiminished speed and comprehension relative to reading standard, unmutilated text—then one could conclude that the only information relevant to the reading process is the word at which the eyes are actually pointing on any given fixation. However, this turns out not to be the case. Whereas normal reading rates for skilled readers under laboratory conditions are in the neighborhood of 320 words per minute, the reading rate in the 1-word window condition is only about 200 words per minute, a reduction of some 35–40%. If the window is widened to include 4 letters and spaces to the left of the fixation point and 14 letters and spaces to the right, then readers of English will read with approximately normal speed and comprehension (Rayner & McConkie, 1977; Rayner, Well, & Pollatsek, 1980). Thus it appears that the area of text from which useful information is extracted is fairly limited but does often go beyond the boundaries of the word being fixated.

When one remembers that the average forward saccade length is about 7–9 letter spaces, which is less than the 14 spaces to the right over which information is extracted, it becomes clear that the reader's window of information extraction may overlap on successive fixations, setting up conditions under which long words could be quite regularly processed on more than one fixation. But are they? When the window of normal, unmutilated text includes only four letters to the left but all the letters to the right of fixation, fixations often occur on the last few letters of long words—which means that the first few letters would be mutilated. Nevertheless, reading proceeds normally, indicating that the mutilation of the first few letters is not disruptive. This in turn indicates either that those letters had already been processed on the previous fixation, or alternatively that the whole word had been processed and the reader, though intending to fixate the **next** word, simply fell short of his or her intended saccade length.

However, if the latter were true and the basic unit of information were the word, then windows defined in terms of words should be less disruptive to reading than windows defined in terms of numbers of letters and spaces. Rayner, Well, Pollatsek, and Bertera (1982) contrasted windows defined in these two ways, and discovered that the basic metric was the number of letters that were available to the right of fixation, regardless of whether the word being fixated was entirely visible or not. This suggests that processing of an entire word on a single fixation is not a critical parameter of the act of reading (which, if true, lends humility to theories of word recognition). In a follow-up to this experiment, Rayner *et al.* presented readers with a window defined by allowing normal viewing of the word being fixated plus three letters of the next word, with the restriction that the subject would **never** see the **entire** word to the right of the fixated one. In this condition, reading speed and comprehension were substantially better than when the window consisted only of the fixated word, and furthermore, it was only marginally worse than when the window included the whole word to the right of fixation. The implication is that information from the first three letters of the next word is often processed on the fixation in which it becomes available and then combined with the information extracted on the next fixation to complete the processing of that word. Otherwise, the condition in which those three letters are available in addition to the fixated word would not be any better than the condition in which only the currently fixated word is available.

This conclusion is buttressed by findings from a word pronunciation paradigm in which a string of letters is presented in the parafovea, 1–5° of visual angle to the right or to the left of fixation. The participant in the experiment is supposed to move his or her eyes to that string of letters and pronounce it as rapidly and accurately as possible. However, during the period of saccadic suppression while the participant is moving his or her eyes, the letters can be changed without the participant noticing it. In this paradigm pronunciation latencies are facilitated by as much as 40 or 50 msec when the "preview" string that originally appears in the parafovea is identical to the target string that must be pronounced, compared to a base line control condition in which the preview is a string of X's (Rayner, McConkie, & Erlich, 1978; Rayner, McConkie, & Zola, 1980). However, similar to the finding just cited with reading of text rather than pronunciation of single words, the size of this facilitation effect is about as large when the parafoveal preview shares only the first three letters with the target word as when the preview is identical to the target. Thus the task provides direct converging evidence that letters seen on one fixation are aiding the processing of a word seen on the next fixation that contains those letters.

The finding with individual words as previews differs from the finding with text in that facilitation occurs when the parafoveal preview is presented to the left of fixation as well as to the right. Other work involving comparisons of English with Hebrew, which is read from right to left rather than from left to right, shows that asymmetric extraction of parafoveal information is a product of attentional patterns established in response to the direction of the text (Pollatsek, Bolozky, Well, & Rayner, 1981). It is striking that in the experiments with individual words, the first three letters of the preview are the important information even when the string is presented to the left of fixation.

To summarize, the experiments we have described in this section hint rather strongly that in reading, many words are processed on more than one fixation, with the resulting information combined across fixations to constitute the total information that is obtained from that word. First, it appears to be relatively common for the first three letters or so of a word to be processed or partially processed in the parafovea before that word is actually fixated. Second, it appears that the last few letters of long words

are often not fully processed when the word is first fixated, but are completed and "added in," so to speak, on a succeeding fixation.

   b. *Implications for Word Recognition.* What are the implications of these
findings for theories of word recognition? The most straightforward implication is that the picture of word processing derived from tachistoscopic
recognition experiments may be misleading in some specific ways. Certainly
one must qualify any assumption to the effect that letter information is
available simultaneously or in parallel from all letter positions in a word
(which is explicit in McClelland & Rumelhart, 1981, and Paap *et al.,* 1982,
close to explicit in Becker, this volume, and Taft, this volume, and implicit
in the remainder of the models). Such an assumption can only be made for
relatively short words, perhaps those of six to seven letters and fewer. While
large numbers of words fall into this category, many important content
words do not, especially in expository and technical writing. Longer words
will often exceed the limits of parallel information extraction. It remains
to be seen exactly why performance is degraded when these limits are exceeded. Perhaps identification of visual features fails because of lack of
visual acuity or increased lateral inhibition in the parafovea, or perhaps
storage of information obtained on one fixation fails while waiting for information from the next fixation because of forgetting in a short-term
memory buffer of some kind. It also remains to be seen exactly how the
reading system accommodates to such performance degradations as occur.

   In order to begin to answer these questions, it is very important to discover the nature of the storage system that allows information about a word
to be held from one fixation to the next, and the two "packets" of information to be combined and integrated. Since we argued earlier in the article
that both phonological recoding and morphemic decomposition are integral
components of word recognition, it is tempting to speculate that sound-
based codes or subword morphemic units are crucial ingredients in the integration process. In fact, a plausible scenario for the involvement of these
types of codes in word processing is that a direct visual pathway to whole-
word meaning might be sufficient if words were all shorter than the six to
seven letter limit on parallel visual feature extraction, but that the need to
integrate information across fixations for words that exceed the limit is what
recruits phonological and morphemic recoding into the word recognition
activities of skilled readers.

   Unfortunately, the evidence presently available on this issue is very
sketchy. It is clear that a substantial part of the information carried from
one fixation to the next is not in the form of physical or low level visual
features. For example, Rayner *et al.* (1980) demonstrated in their experiments on pronunciation after parafoveal preview that changing from all
lower case letters in the preview to all upper case letters in the target or vice

versa did not decrease the amount of facilitation relative to that observed when preview and target were in the same case. McConkie and Zola (1981) also failed to find a decrement in the reading of extended text due to case changes. When all the words of the text were printed in mixed case (e.g., *cHeSt*) and all the letters in the text changed case every time the reader's eyes moved (e.g., *cHeSt* became *ChEsT*), reading was unaffected compared to a condition in which all the letters remained visually unaltered when the eyes moved. Furthermore, the participants in McConkie and Zola's experiment were usually unaware that the case of the letters was changing back and forth. Thus the information carried across fixations must be relatively abstract.

At what level or levels of abstraction this information is coded, however, remains unclear. First consider the extraction of the first one to three letters of a parafoveal word—the letters that have been shown to be influential in the preview and moving window experiments described above. It is possible that a candidate set of whole words or of morphemes is activated by information from these letters, and that this activation facilitates completion of the recognition process on the next fixation. There is negative evidence on this possibility. Inhoff, Lima, and Rayner (1983) presented text in which a key word had either all of its letters available before the subject fixated it, or its first three letters with the remaining letters replaced by X's, or none of its letters (the whole word was replaced by X's). The important manipulation in the experiment concerned the predictability of the word given its first three letters and its length. Inhoff *et al.* reasoned that if a major component of facilitation across fixations involved priming due to partial activation of word representations, then a greater advantage should occur for highly predictable words for which far fewer candidates would be activated than for less predictable words (this reasoning is similar to that followed in testing explanations of the word superiority effect based on sophisticated guessing, as described in Section II,A,1). However, the data showed that predictability made no difference to the amount of facilitation that accrued from having the first three letters available in advance of fixation. These data suggest that priming of word representations is not a major mechanism of cross-fixation facilitation.

On the other hand, there is positive evidence from studies monitoring eye movements that function words such as *the* are skipped more often than content words of similar length (O'Regan, 1979) and that short content words are skipped more often when they are predictable from context than when they are not (Erlich & Rayner, 1981). Thus it appears that the meaning of the entire parafoveal word may be extracted on some occasions. A reasonable conclusion would be that the meaning of a parafoveal word can sometimes be extracted, but that if on the next eye movement the reader fixates the word rather than skipping it, the extraction of meaning had not progressed very far on that occasion. It remains possible that morphemic or lexical representations play a part in cross-fixation facilitation when they are short, corresponding to the first two or three letters of a word (e.g., prefixes) or when they are relatively predictable from context. Future research will have to determine if this possibility is a reality.

As for phonological codes, there is even less relevant evidence than for morphemic and semantic codes. Rayner *et al.* (1980) found that no more facilitation was obtained from a parafoveal preview that preserved the initial phoneme of the target's pronunciation than from a preview that did not, as in *chest* as a preview for *chart* versus *clerk*. The best guess that we can make for now, then, is that the information carried across fixations appears to be something on the order of abstract letter identities or some other kind of nonphysical orthographic information.

If this guess turns out to be correct, then the role of such carryover may lead to modifications in the processes of visual code formation that are proposed by various models, but not so much in the processes of phonological recoding and semantic activation that are driven by the visual codes. In this respect Coltheart (1981), Evett and Humphreys (1981), and Besner, Coltheart, and Davelaar (1984) have all argued for the existence of a nonphonological level of representation at which *A* and *a* or *D* and *d* are the same—that is, an encoding mechanism whose outputs are abstract letter identities (see also McClelland, 1976). Boles and Eveland (1983) have raised objections to this notion, but it is certainly consistent with the work on parafoveal preview. In a PCS-type model described by Coltheart (1981), abstract letter identities constitute the information on which phonological and semantic mechanisms operate. Referring back to Fig. 6, this proposition is much like saying that the task of the process labeled "Elaboration of visual code" is to produce abstract letter identities, except that in Fig. 6 the elaborated visual code is the information base for semantic code formation but not for phonological recoding, which operates on visual features. Whether or not this difference between the conceptualization of PCS organization in Fig. 6 and Coltheart's conceptualization would turn out to be important requires further investigation (see Well & Pollatsek, 1981).

Note, though, that the foregoing discussion does not complete the work of this section. Much of the data on carryover and integration of information across fixations has been obtained from the parafoveal preview paradigm of Rayner and his colleagues. In this paradigm the preview and the target are—from the point of view of the participant—the same word, not the first and second portions of a single word, and what must be integrated are an incomplete representation obtained parafoveally from the preview and a more complete and precise representation obtained foveally from the target. Thus the preview and the target must be in some sense overlaid to be integrated in the parafoveal preview paradigm. In the problem that originally motivated this section, which was the processing of long words that are fixated two or more times, the information from the two or more foveal fixations must be concatenated rather than overlaid, though the concatenation process must take account of the possibility of overlap between the reader's successive windows of information extraction. At present there are essentially no data on the details of recognizing long words that are fixated more than once. However, plausibility arguments suggest that this situation might differ in important ways from integrating information from a parafoveal preview and a foveal fixation, if for no other reason than the fact that foveal processing is faster, more accurate, and more complete than parafoveal processing. Much research remains to be done here, and it is not clear what changes in models of word recognition will eventually be wrought as a result.

ACKNOWLEDGMENTS

We would like to thank Curtis Becker, Derek Besner, and Mary Beth Rosson for comments and criticisms during preparation of the manuscript, and Lee Brooks and James McClelland for stimulating discussions of the issues at stake. Parts of this article are based on work supported by a contract from the University of Dayton Research Institute to the first author (see Carr, 1986).

REFERENCES

Adams, M. J. (1979). Models of word recognition. *Cognitive Psychology, 11,* 133–176.

Allport, A. (1979). Word recognition in reading. In P. A. Kolers, M. E. Wrolstad, and H. Bouma (Eds.), *Processing visible language 1.* New York: Plenum.

Antos, S. J. (1979). Processing facilitation in a lexical decision task. *Journal of Experimental Psychology: Human Perception and Performance, 5,* 527–545.

Baddeley, A., Eldridge, M., & Lewis, V. (1981). The role of subvocalization in reading. *Quarterly Journal of Experimental Psychology, 33A,* 439–454.

Baddeley, A., & Hitch, G. (1974). Working memory. In G. Bower (Ed.), *The psychology of learning and motivation* (Vol. 8). New York: Academic Press.

Baddeley, A., & Lewis, V. (1981). Interactive processes in reading: The inner voice, the inner ear, and the inner eye. In A. M. Lesgold & C. A. Perfetti (Eds.), *Interactive processes in reading.* Hillsdale, NJ: Erlbaum.

Balota, D. A., & Chumbley, J. (1984). Are lexical decisions a good measure of lexical access? The role of word frequency in the neglected decision stage. *Journal of Experimental Psychology: Human Perception and Performance, 10,* 340–357.

Balota, D. A., & Rayner, K. (1983). Parafoveal visual information and semantic contextual constraints. *Journal of Experimental Psychology: Human Perception and Performance, 9,* 726–738.

Baron, J. (1973). Phonemic stage not necessary for reading. *Quarterly Journal of Experimental Psychology,* **25,** 241–246.

Baron, J. (1975). Successive stages in word recognition. In P. M. A. Rabbitt and S. Dornic (Eds.), *Attention and performance V.* New York: Academic Press.

Baron, J. (1976). The word superiority effect. In W. K. Estes (Ed.), *Handbook of learning and cognitive processes* (Vol. 4). Hillsdale, NJ: Erlbaum.

Baron, J., & Strawson, C. (1976). Use of orthographic and word-specific knowledge in reading words aloud. *Journal of Experimental Psychology: Human Perception and Performance,* **2,** 386–393.

Baron, J., & Thurston, I. (1973). An analysis of the word superiority efect. *Cognitive Psychology,* **4,** 207–228.

Barron, R. W. (1981). Reading skill and reading strategies. In C. A. Perfetti & A. M. Lesgold (Eds.), *Interactive processes in reading.* Hillsdale, NJ: Erlbaum.

Barron, R. W., & Baron, J. (1977). How children get meaning from printed words. *Child Development,* **48,** 586–594.

Bauer, D. W., & Stanovich, K. E. (1980). Lexical access and the spelling-to-sound regularity effect. *Memory and Cognition,* **8,** 424–432.

Becker, C. A. (1976). Allocation of attention during visual word recognition. *Journal of Experimental Psychology: Human Perception and Performance,* **2,** 556–566.

Becker, C. A. (1979). Semantic context and word frequency effects in visual word recognition. *Journal of Experimental Psychology: Human Perception and Performance,* **5,** 252–259.

Becker, C. A. (1980). Semantic context effects in visual word recognition: An analysis of semantic strategies. *Memory and Cognition,* **8,** 439–512.

Becker, C. A. (1982). The development of semantic context effects: Two processes or two strategies? *Reading Research Quarterly,* **17,** 482–502.

Becker, C. A. (1985). What do we know about context effects? In D. Besner, T. G. Waller, & G. E. MacKinnon (Eds.), *Reading research: Advances in theory and practice* (Vol. 5). New York: Academic Press.

Becker, C. A., & Killion, T. H. (1977). Interaction of visual and cognitive effects in word recognition. *Journal of Experimental Psychology: Human Perception and Performance,* **3,** 389–401.

Besner, D., Coltheart, M., & Davelaar, E. (1984). Basic processes in reading: Computation of abstract letter identities. *Canadian Journal of Psychology,* **38,** 126–134.

Besner, D., & Davelaar, E. (1982). Basic processes in reading: Two phonological codes. *Canadian Journal of Psychology,* **36,** 701–711.

Besner, D., Davies, J., & Daniels, S. (1981). Reading for meaning: Effects of concurrent articulation. *Quarterly Journal of Experimental Psychology,* **33A,** 415–437.

Besner, D., & Swan, M. (1982). Models of lexical access in visual word recognition. *Quarterly Journal of Experimental Psychology,* **34A,** 313–325.

Bock, J. K. (1982). Toward a cognitive psychology of syntax: Information processing contributions to sentence formulation. *Psychological Review,* **89,** 1–47.

Boder, E. (1973). Developmental dyslexia: A diagnostic approach based on three atypical reading-spelling patterns. *Developmental Medicine and Child Neurology,* **15,** 663–687.

Boles, D. B., & Eveland, D. C. (1983). Visual and phonetic codes and the process of generation in letter matching. *Journal of Experimental Psychology: Human Perception and Performance,* **9,** 657–674.

Broadbent, D. C. (1967). Word frequency effect and response bias. *Psychological Review,* **74,** 1–15.

Broadbent, D. E., & Broadbent, M. H. P. (1975). Some further data concerning the word frequency effect. *Journal of Experimental Psychology: General,* **104,** 297–308.

Brooks, L. R. (1977). Visual pattern in fluent word identification. In A. S. Reber & D. Scarborough (Eds.), *Toward a psychology of reading*. Hillsdale, NJ: Erlbaum.

Brooks, L. R. (1978). Non-analytic concept formation and memory for instances. In E. Rosch & B. Lloyd (Eds.), *Cognition and categorization*. Hillsdale, NJ: Erlbaum.

Brooks, L. R., & Miller, A. (1979). A comparison of explicit and implicit knowledge of an alphabet. In P. A. Kolers, M. E. Wrolstad, & H. Bouma (Eds.), *Processing of visible language 1*. New York: Plenum, 1979.

Brown, R. (1973). *A first language: The early stages*. Cambridge, MA: Harvard Univ. Press.

Carr, T. H. (1981). Building theories of reading ability: On the relation between individual differences in cognitive skills and reading comprehension. *Cognition, 9*, 73–114.

Carr, T. H. (1986). Perceiving visual language. In L. Kaufman, J. Thomas, & K. Boff (Eds.), *Handbook of perception and human performance*. New York: Wiley, in press.

Carr, T. H., Davidson, B. J., & Hawkins, H. L. (1978). Perceptual flexibility in word recognition. Strategies affect orthographic computation but not lexical access. *Journal of Experimental Psychology: Human Perception and Performance, 4*, 678–690.

Carr, T. H., Lehmkuhle, S. W., Kottas, B., Astor-Stetson, E. C., & Arnold, D. (1976). Target position and practice in the identification of letters in varying contexts: A word superiority effect. *Perception and Psychophysics, 19*, 412–416.

Carr, T. H., McCauley, C., Sperber, R. D., & Parmelee, C. M. (1982). Words, pictures, and priming: On semantic activation, conscious identification, and the automaticity of information processing. *Journal of Experimental Psychology: Human Perception and Performance, 8*, 757–777.

Cattell, J. M. (1886). The time taken up by cerebral operations. *Mind, 11*, 277–292, 524–538.

Chomsky, N. (1957). *Syntactic structures*. The Hague: Mouton.

Chomsky, R. (1965). *Aspects of the theory of syntax*. Cambridge, MA: MIT Press.

Coltheart, M. (1978). Lexical access in simple reading tasks. In G. Underwood (Ed.), *Strategies of information processing*. New York: Academic Press.

Coltheart, M. (1980). Reading, phonological recoding, and deep dyslexia. In M. Coltheart, K. Patterson, & J. Marshall (Eds.), *Deep dyslexia*. London: Routledge & Kegan Paul.

Coltheart, M. (1981). Disorders of reading and their implications for models of normal reading. *Visible Language, 15*, 245–286.

Coltheart, M., Besner, D., Jonasson, J. T., & Davelaar, E. (1979). Phonological recoding in the lexical decision task. *Quarterly Journal of Experimental Psychology, 31*, 489–508.

Coltheart, M., Davelaar, E., Jonasson, J., & Besner, D. (1977). Access to the internal lexicon. In S. Dornic (Ed.), *Attention and performance* (Vol. 6). New York: Academic Press.

Coltheart, M., Patterson, K., & Marshall, J. C. (1980). *Deep dyslexia*. London: Routledge & Kegan Paul.

Davidson, B. J. (1978). *Coding of individual words during reading*. Unpublished doctoral dissertation, Department of Psychology, University of Oregon.

Dennis, I., Besner, D., & Davelaar, E. (1985). Phonology in visual word recognition: Their is more two this than meats the I. In D. Besner, T. G. Waller, & G. E. MacKinnon (Eds.), *Reading research: Advances in theory and practice* (Vol. 5). New York: Academic Press.

Doctor, E., & Coltheart, M. (1980). Children's use of phonological encoding when reading for meaning. *Memory and Cognition, 8*, 195–209.

Eisenberg, P., & Becker, C. A. (1982). Semantic context effects in visual word recognition, sentence processing, and reading: Evidence for semantic strategies. *Journal of Experimental Psychology: Human Perception and Performance, 8*, 739–755.

Ellis, A. W. (Ed.) (1981). *Normality and pathology in cognitive function*. New York: Academic Press.

Erlich, S. F., & Rayner, K. (1981). Contextual effects on word perception and eye movements during reading. *Journal of Verbal Learning and Verbal Behavior, 20*, 641–655.

Evett, L., & Humphreys, G. W. (1981). The use of abstract graphemic information in lexical access. *Quarterly Journal of Experimental Psychology, 33A*, 325–350.

Fischler, I., & Bloom, P. A. (1979). Automatic and attentional processes in the effects of sentence contexts on word recognition. *Journal of Verbal Learning and Verbal Behavior, 18*, 1–20.

Forster, K. I. (1976). Accessing the mental lexicon. In R. J. Wales & E. Walker (Eds.), *New approaches to language mechanisms*. Amsterdam: North-Holland Publ.

Forster, K. I. (1979). Levels of processing and the structure of the language processor. In W. E. Cooper & E. Walker (Eds.), *Sentence processing: Psycholinguistic studies presented to Merrill Garrett*. Hillsdale, NJ: Erlbaum.

Forster, K. I. (1981). Priming and the effects of sentence and lexical contexts on naming time: Evidence for autonomous lexical processing. *Quarterly Journal of Experimental Psychology, 33A*, 465–496.

Forster, K. I., & Chambers, S. M. (1973). Lexical access and naming time. *Journal of Verbal Learning and Verbal Behavior, 12*, 627–635.

Frederiksen, J. R., & Kroll, J. F. (1976). Spelling and sound: Approaches to the internal lexicon. *Journal of Experimental Psychology: Human Perception and Performance, 2*, 361–379.

Funnell, E. (1983). Phonological processes in reading: New evidence from acquired dyslexia. *British Journal of Psychology, 74*, 159–180.

Gibson, E. J., & Levin, H. (1975). *The psychology of reading*. Cambridge, MA: MIT Press.

Gibson, E. J., Pick, A. D., Osser, H., & Hammond, M. (1962). The role of grapheme-phoneme correspondence in the perception of words. *American Journal of Psychology, 75*, 554–570.

Gleitman, L. (1981). Language. In H. Gleitman (Ed.), *Psychology*. New York: Norton.

Gleitman, L. R., & Rozin, P. (1977). The structure and acquisition of reading I: Orthographies and the structure of language. In A. S. Reber & D. L. Scarborough (Eds.), *Toward a psychology of reading*. Hillsdale, NJ: Erlbaum.

Glushko, R. J. (1979). The organization and activation of orthographic knowledge in reading aloud. *Journal of Experimental Psychology: Human Perception and Performance, 5*, 674–691.

Glushko, R. J. (1981). Principles for pronouncing print: The psychology of phonography. In A. M. Lesgold & C. A. Perfetti (Eds.), *Interactive processes in reading*. Hillsdale: NJ: Erlbaum.

Gough, P. B. (1972). One second of reading. In J. F. Kavanagh & I. G. Mattingly (Eds.), *Language by ear and by eye*. Cambridge, MA: MIT Press.

Gough, P. B., & Cosky, M. J. (1977). One second of reading again. In N. J. Castellan, D. B., Pisoni, and G. R. Potts (Eds.), *Cognitive theory* (Vol. 2). Hillsdale, NJ: Erlbaum.

Hawkins, H. L., Reicher, G. M., Rogers, M., & Peterson, L. (1976). Flexible coding in word recognition. *Journal of Experimental Psychology: Human Perception and Performance, 2*, 380–385.

Henderson, L. (1982). *Orthography and word recognition in reading*. New York: Academic Press.

Hintzman, D. L., & Ludlum, G. (1980). Differential forgetting of prototypes and old instances: Simulation by an exemplar-based classification model. *Memory and Cognition, 8*, 378–382.

Humphreys, G. W. (1985). Automaticity and functional autonomy in visual word processing. In D. Besner, T. G. Waller, & G. E. MacKinnon (Eds.), *Reading research: Advances in theory and practice* (Vol. 5). New York: Academic Press.

Inhoff, A. W., Lima, S. D., & Rayner, K. (1983). *Parafoveal information in reading: Effects of frequency and initial letter sequence.* Paper presented at the annual meeting of the Psychonomic Society, San Diego, CA, November.

Jacoby, L. L., & Brooks, L. R. (1984). Nonanalytic cognition: Memory, perception, and concept learning. In G. H. Bower (Ed.), *The psychology of learning and motivation: Advances in research and theory* (Vol. 18). New York: Academic Press.

Johnston, J. C. (1978). A test of the sophisticated guessing theory of word perception. *Cognitive Psychology, 10,* 123-153.

Johnston, J. C. (1981). Understanding word perception: Clues from studying the word superiority effect. In O. J. L. Tzeng & M. Singer (Eds.), *Perception of print: Reading research in experimental psychology.* Hillsdale, NJ: Erlbaum.

Johnston, J. C., & McClelland, J. L. (1973). Visual factors in word perception. *Perception and Psychophysics, 14,* 365-370.

Johnston, J. C., & McClelland, J. L. (1974). Perception of letters in words: Seek and ye shall not find. *Science, 184,* 1192-1193.

Johnston, J. C., & McClelland, J. L. (1980). Experimental tests of a hierarchical model of word identification. *Journal of Verbal Learning and Verbal Behavior, 19,* 503-524.

Kavanagh, J. F., & Venezky, R. L. (1980). *Orthography, reading, and dyslexia.* Baltimore: Univ. Park Press.

Kempley, S. T., & Morton, J. (1982). The effects of priming with regularly and irregularly related words in auditory word recognition. *British Journal of Psychology, 73,* 441-454.

Klapp, S. (1971). Implicit speech inferred from response latencies in same-different decisions. *Journal of Experimental Psychology, 91,* 262-267.

Kleiman, G. M. (1975). Speech recoding in reading. *Journal of Verbal Learning and Verbal Behavior, 24,* 323-339.

Lachman, R., Lachman, J. L., & Butterfield, E. C. (1979). *Cognitive psychology and information processing: An introduction.* Hillsdale, NJ: Erlbaum.

Larochelle, S., McClelland, J., & Rodriguez, E. (1980). Context and the allocation of resources of word recognition. *Journal of Experimental Psychology: Human Perception and Performance, 6,* 686-694.

Levy, B. A. (1978). Speech processing during reading. In A. Lesgold, J. W. Pellegrino, S. D. Fokkema, & R. Glaser (Eds.), *Cognitive psychology and instruction.* New York: Plenum.

Lima, S. D., & Pollatsek, A. (1983). Lexical access via an orthographic code? The Basic Orthographic Syllable Structure (BOSS) reconsidered. *Journal of Verbal Learning and Verbal Behavior, 22,* 310-332.

Manelis, L. (1974). The effect of meaningfulness in tachistoscopic word perception. *Perception and Psychophysics, 16,* 182-192.

Manelis, L., & Tharp, D. A. (1976). The processing of affixed words. *Memory and Cognition, 4,* 53-61.

Marcel, A. J., & Patterson, K. E. (1978). Word recognition and production: Reciprocity in clinical and normal research. In J. Requin (Ed.), *Attention and performance VII.* Hillsdale, NJ: Erlbaum.

Margolin, D. I. (1983). *The neuropsychology of handwriting: Linguistic, motor and perceptual processes.* Unpublished manuscript, Laboratory of Cognitive Neuropsychology, Portland, OR (Available from the author, now at Cognitive Neuroscience Laboratory, Fresno Veterans Administration Medical Center, Fresno, CA).

Marshall, J. C. (1976). Neuropsychological aspects of orthographic representation. In R. J. Wales & E. Walker (Eds.), *New approaches in language mechanisms.* Amsterdam: North Holland Publ.

Marshall, J. C., & Newcombe, F. (1973). Patterns of paralexia: A psycholinguistic approach, *Journal of Psycholinguistic Research, 2,* 175-199.

Massaro, D. W. (1973). Perception of letters, words, and non-words. *Journal of Experimental Psychology, 100, 349–353.*

Massaro, D. W. (1979). Letter information and orthographic context in word perception. *Journal of Experimental Psychology: Human Perception and Performance, 5, 595–609.*

Massaro, D. W., & Cohen, M. M. (1983). Evaluation and integration of visual and auditory information in speech perception. *Journal of Experimental Psychology: Human Perception and Performance, 9, 753–771.*

McClelland, J. L. (1976). Preliminary letter identification in the perception of words and nonwords. *Journal of Experimental Psychology: Human Perception and Performance, 2, 80–91.*

McClelland, J. L. (1979). On the time relations of mental processes: An examination of systems of proceses in cascade. *Psychological Review, 86, 287–307.*

McClelland, J. L. (1980). Perception of letters in words: A review of data and theory. Unpublished manuscript, Department of Psychology, University of California, San Diego.

McClelland, J. L., & Johnston, J. C. (1977). The role of familiar units in the perception of words and nonwords. *Perception and Psychophysics, 22, 249–261.*

McClelland, J. L., & Rumelhart, D. E. (1981). An interactive activation model of context effects in letter perception: Part 1. An account of basic findings. *Psychological Review, 88, 375–407.*

McConkie, G. W., & Zola, D. (1981). Language constraints and the functional stimulus in reading. In A. M. Lesgold & C. A. Perfetti (Eds.), *Interactive processes in reading.* Hillsdale, NJ: Erlbaum.

McCusker, L. X., Hillinger, M. L., & Bias, R. G. (1981). Phonological recoding and reading. *Psychological Bulletin, 89, 217–245.*

McGurk, H., & MacDonald, J. (1976). Hearing lips and seeing voices. *Nature (London), 264, 746–748.*

Meyer, D. E., & Gutschera, K. (1975). *Orthographic versus phonemic processing of printed words.* Paper presented at the annual meeting of the Psychonomic Society, Denver, CO, November.

Meyer, D. E., Schvaneveldt, R. W., & Ruddy, M. G. (1974). Functions of graphemic and phonemic codes in visual word recognition. *Memory and Cognition, 2, 309–321.*

Mezrich, J. J. (1973). The word superiority effect in brief visual displays: Elimination by vocalization. *Perception and Psychophysics, 13, 45–48.*

Morton, J. (1969). Interaction of information in word recognition. *Psychological Review, 76, 165–178.*

Morton, J. (1979). Some experiments on facilitation in word and picture recognition and their relevance for the evaluation of a theoretical position. In P. A. Kolers, M. E. Wrolstad, & H. Bouma (Eds.), *Processing visible language 1.* New York: Plenum.

Murrell, G. A., & Morton, J. (1974). Word recognition and morphemic structure. *Journal of Experimental Psychology, 102, 963–968.*

Neely, J. H. (1977). Semantic priming and retrieval from lexical memory: Roles of inhibitionless spreading activation and limited-capacity attention. *Journal of Experimental Psychology: General, 106, 226–254.*

Neely, J. H., Fisk, W. J., & Ross, K. L. (1983). *On obtaining facilitatory and inhibitory priming effects at short SOAs.* Paper presented at the annual meeting of the Psychonomic Society, San Diego, CA, November.

Paap, K. R., Newsome, S., McDonald, J. E., & Schvaneveldt, R. W. (1982). An activation-verification model for letter and word recognition: The word-superiority effect. *Psychological Review, 89, 573–594.*

Parkin, A. J. (1982). Phonological recoding in lexical decision: Effects of spelling-to-sound regularity depend on how regularity is defined. *Memory and Cognition, 10, 43–53.*

Parkin, A. J., & Underwood, G. (1983). Orthographic vs. phonological irregularity in lexical decision. *Memory and Cognition,* **11,** 351–355.

Patterson, K. E., & Marcel, A. J. (1977). Aphasia, dyslexia, and the phonological coding of written words. *Quarterly Journal of Experimental Psychology,* **29,** 307–318.

Perfetti, C. A., & Hogoboam, T. (1975). Relationship between single word decoding and reading comprehension skill. *Journal of Educational Psychology,* **67,** 461–469.

Perfetti, C. A., & Lesgold, A. (1978). Discourse comprehension and sources of individual differences. In M. Just & P. Carpenter (Eds.), *Cognitive processes in comprehension.* Hillsdale, NJ: Erlbaum.

Pieters, J. P. M. (1983). Sternberg's additive factor method and underlying psychological processes: Some theoretical considerations. *Psychological Bulletin,* **93,** 411–426.

Pollatsek, A., Bolozky, S., Well, A. D., & Rayner, K. (1981). Asymmetries in the perceptual span for Israeli readers. *Brain and Language,* **14,** 174–180.

Posner, M. I. (1978). *Chronometric explorations of mind.* Hillsdale, NJ: Erlbaum.

Posner, M. I., & Keele, S. W. (1968). On the genesis of abstract ideas. *Journal of Experimental Psychology,* **77,** 353–363.

Posner, M. I., & Snyder, C. R. R. (1975). Attention and cognitive control. In R. L. Solso (Ed.), *Theories in information processing.* Hillsdale, NJ: Erlbaum.

Potter, M. C., & Faulconer, B. (1975). Time to understand pictures and words. *Nature (London),* **253,** 437–438.

Purcell, D. G., & Stanovich, K. E. (1982). Some boundary conditions for the word superiority effect. *Quarterly Journal of Experimental Psychology,* **34A,** 117–134.

Purcell, D. G., Stanovich, K. E., & Spector, A. (1978). Visual angle and the word superiority effect. *Memory & Cognition,* **6,** 3–8.

Rayner, K. (Ed.) (1983). *Eye movements in reading: Perceptual and language processes.* New York: Academic Press.

Rayner, K., & McConkie, G. W. (1977). Perceptual processes in reading: The perceptual spans. In A. S. Reber & D. L. Scarborough (Eds.), *Toward a psychology of reading.* Hillsdale, NJ: Erlbaum.

Rayner, K., McConkie, G. W., & Erlich, S. (1978). Eye movements and integrating information across fixations. *Journal of Experimental Psychology: Human Perception and Performance,* **4,** 529–544.

Rayner, K., McConkie, G. W., & Zola, D. (1980). Integrating information across fixations. *Cognitive Psychology,* **12,** 206–226.

Rayner, K., & Posnansky, C. (1978). Stages of processing in word identification. *Journal of Experimental Psychology: General,* **107,** 64–80.

Rayner, K., Well, A. D., & Pollatsek, A. (1980). Asymmetry of the effective visual field in reading. *Perception and Psychophysics,* **27,** 537–544.

Rayner, K., Well, A. D., Pollatsek, A., & Bertera, H. A. (1982). The availability of useful information to the right of fixation during reading. *Perception and Psychophysics,* **31,** 537–550.

Reicher, G. M. (1969). Perceptual recognition as a function of meaningfulness of stimulus material. *Journal of Experimental Psychology,* **81,** 274–280.

Rosch, E., & Lloyd, B. (Eds.) (1978). *Cognition and categorization.* Hillsdale, NJ: Erlbaum.

Rosinski, R. R., Golinkoff, R. M., & Kukish, K. (1975). Automatic semantic processing in a picture-word interference task. *Child Development,* **46,** 247–253.

Rozin, P., & Gleitman, L. R. (1977). The structure and acquisition of reading II: The reading process and the acquisition of the alphabetic principle. In A. S. Reber & D. L. Scarborough (Eds.), *Toward a psychology of reading.* Hillsdale, NJ: Erlbaum.

Rozin, P., Poritsky, S., & Sotsky, R. (1971). American children with reading problems can easily learn to read English represented by Chinese characters. *Science,* **171,** 1264–1267.

Rubenstein, H., Lewis, S. S., & Rubenstein, M. A. (1971). Evidence for phonemic recoding in visual word recognition. *Journal of Verbal Learning and Verbal Behavior,* **10,** 645-657.

Rubin, G. S., Becker, C. A., & Freeman, R. H. (1979). Morphological structure and its effect on visual word recognition. *Journal of Verbal Learning and Verbal Behavior,* **18,** 757-767.

Rumelhart, D. E., & McClelland, J. L. (1982). An interactive activation model of context effects in letter perception: Part 2. The contextual enhancement effect and some tests and extensions of the model. *Psychological Review,* **89,** 60-94.

Saffran, E., & Marin, O. S. M. (1977). Reading without phonology: Evidence from aphasia. *Quarterly Journal of Experimental Psychology,* **29,** 515-525.

Scarborough, D. L., Cortese, C., & Scarborough, H. L. (1977). Frequency and repetition effects in lexical memory. *Journal of Experimental Psychology: Human Perception and Performance,* **3,** 1-17.

Schuberth, R. E., & Eimas, P. D. (1977). Effects of context on the classification of words and non-words. *Journal of Experimental Psychology: Human Perception and Performance,* **3,** 27-36.

Schuberth, R. E., Spoehr, K. T., & Lane, D. M. (1981). Effects of stimulus and contextual information on the lexical decision process. *Memory & Cognition,* **9,** 68-77.

Schvaneveldt, R. W., & McDonald, J. E. (1981). Semantic context and the encoding of words: Evidence for two modes of stimulus analysis. *Journal of Experimental Psychology: Human Perception and Performance,* **7,** 673-687.

Schwartz, M. F., Saffran, E. M., & Marin, O. S. M. (1980). Fractionating the reading process in dementia: Evidence for word-specific print-to-sound associations. In M. Coltheart, K. Patterson, & J. C. Marshall (Eds.), *Deep dyslexia.* London: Routledge & Kegan Paul.

Seidenberg, M. (1983). *Two kinds of lexical priming.* Paper presented at the annual meeting of the Psychonomic Society, San Diego, CA, November.

Seidenberg, M. (1985). Context and visual word recognition. In D. Besner, T. G. Waller, & G. E. MacKinnon (Eds.), *Reading research: Advances in theory and practice* (Vol. 5). New York: Academic Press.

Seidenberg, M., Waters, G. A., Barnes, M. A., & Tanenhaus, M. K. (1984). When does irregular spelling or pronunciation influence word recognition? *Journal of Verbal Learning and Verbal Behavior,* **23,** 383-404.

Selkirk, L. (1982). *The syntax of words.* Cambridge, MA: MIT Press.

Simon, D. P., & Simon, H. A. (1973). Alternative uses of phonetic information in spelling. *Harvard Educational Review,* **43,** 115-137.

Singer, M. H. (1980). The primacy of visual information in the analysis of letter strings. *Perception & Psychophysics,* **27,** 153-162.

Slowiaczek, M. L., & Clifton, C. (1980). Subvocalization and reading for meaning. *Journal of Verbal Learning and Verbal Behavior,* **19,** 573-582.

Smith, E. E., & Medin, D. (1981). *Categories and concepts.* Cambridge, MA: Harvard Univ. Press.

Smith, E. E., & Spoehr, K. T. (1974). The perception of printed English: A theoretical perspective. In B. H. Kantowitz (Ed.), *Human information processing: Tutorials in performance and cognition.* Hillsdale, NJ: Erlbaum.

Smith, M. C., & Magee, L. (1980). Tracing the time course of picture-word processing. *Journal of Experimental Psychology: General,* **109,** 373-392.

Solomon, R. L., & Postman, L. (1952). Frequency of usage as a determinant of recognition thresholds for words. *Journal of Experimental Psychology,* **43,** 195-201.

Spoehr, K. T. (1978). Phonological encoding in word recognition. *Journal of Verbal Learning and Verbal Behavior,* **17,** 127-141.

Spoehr, K. T., & Smith, E. E. (1973). The role of syllables in perceptual processing. *Cognitive Psychology,* **5,** 71–89.

Spoehr, K. T., & Smith, E. E. (1975). The role of orthographic and phonotactic rules in perceiving letter patterns. *Journal of Experimental Psychology: Human Perception and Performance,* **1,** 21–34.

Stanners, R. F., Jastrembski, J. E., & Westbrook, A. (1975). Frequency and visual quality in a word–nonword classification task. *Journal of Verbal Learning and Verbal Behavior,* **14,** 259–264.

Stanners, R. F., Neiser, J. J., & Painton, S. (1979a). Memory representations for prefixed words. *Journal of Verbal Learning and Verbal Behavior,* **18,** 733–743.

Stanners, R. F., Neiser, J. J., Hernon, W. P., & Hall, R. (1979b). Memory representation for morphologically related words. *Journal of Verbal Learning and Verbal Behavior,* **18,** 399–412.

Stanovich, K. E. (1980). Toward an interactive-compensatory model of individual differences in reading fluency. *Reading Research Quarterly,* **16,** 32–71.

Stanovich, K. E., & Bauer, K. W. (1978). Experiments on the spelling-to-sound regularity effect in word recognition. *Memory & Cognition,* **6,** 410–415.

Stanovich, K. E., & West, R. F. (1979). Mechanisms of sentence context effects in reading: Automatic activation and conscious attention. *Memory & Cognition,* **7,** 77–85.

Stanovich, K. E., & West, R. F. (1981). The effect of sentence context on ongoing word recognition: Tests of a two-process theory. *Journal of Experimental Psychology: Human Perception and Performance,* **7,** 658–672.

Stanovich, K. E., & West, R. F. (1983). On priming by a sentence context. *Journal of Experimental Psychology: General,* **112,** 1–36.

Stanovich, K. E., West, R. F., & Feeman, D. J. (1981). A longitudinal study of sentence context effects in second-grade children: Tests of an interactive-compensatory model. *Journal of Experimental Child Psychology,* **32,** 185–199.

Stanovich, K. E., West, R. F., Feeman, D. J., & Cunningham, A. E. (1984). The effect of sentence context on word recognition in second and sixth grade children. *Reading Research Quarterly,* in press.

Sternberg, S. (1969). The discovery of processing stages: Extensions of Donders' method. In W. E. Koster (Ed.), *Attention and performance II.* Amsterdam: North-Holland Publ.

Taft, M. (1976). *Morphological and syllabic analysis in word recognition.* Unpublished Ph.D. dissertation, Monash University, Australia.

Taft, M. (1979). Lexical access via an orthographic code: The Basic Orthographic Syllable Structure (BOSS). *Journal of Verbal Learning and Verbal Behavior,* **18,** 21–39.

Taft. M. (1981). Prefix stripping revisited. *Journal of Verbal Learning and Verbal Behavior,* **20,** 289–297.

Taft, M. (1985). The decoding of words in lexical access: A review of the morphological approach. In D. Besner, T. G. Waller, & G. E. MacKinnon (Eds.), *Reading research: Advances in theory and practice* (Vol. 5). New York: Academic Press.

Taft, M., & Forster, K. I. (1976). Lexical storage and retrieval of polymorphemic and polysyllabic words. *Journal of Verbal Learning and Verbal Behavior,* **15,** 607–620.

Taylor, D. A. (1976). Stage analysis of reaction time. *Psychological Bulletin,* **83,** 161–191.

Theios, J., & Muise, J. G. (1977). The word identification process in reading. In N. J. Castellan, D. B. Pisoni, & G. R. Potts (Eds.), *Cognitive theory* (Vol. 2). Hillsdale, NJ: Erlbaum.

Thompson, M. C., & Massaro, D. W. (1973). Visual information and redundancy in reading. *Journal of Experimental Psychology,* **98,** 49–54.

Tolman, E. C. (1948) Cognitive maps in rats and men. *Psychological Review,* **55,** 189–208.

Treiman, R. (1985). Phonemic analysis, spelling, and reading: The case of initial consonant clusters. In T. H. Carr (Ed.), *New directions in child development 27: The development of reading skills*. San Francisco: Jossey-Bass.

Treiman, R., & Baron, J. (1981). Segmental analysis ability: Development and relation to reading ability. In G. E. MacKinnon & T. G. Waller (Eds.), *Reading research: Advances in theory and practice* (Vol. 3). New York: Academic Press.

Treiman, R., Baron, J., & Luk, K. (1981). Speech recoding in silent reading: A comparison of Chinese and English. *Journal of Chinese Linguistics, 9,* 116–125.

Treiman, R., Freyd, J. J., & Baron, J. (1983). Phonological recoding and use of spelling-sound rules in reading of sentences. *Journal of Verbal Learning and Verbal Behavior,* **22,** 682–700.

Treisman, M. (1978). A theory of the identification of complex stimuli with an application to word recognition. *Psychological Review, 85,* 525–570.

Tulving, E., & Gold, C. (1963). Stimulus information and contextual information as determinants of tachistoscopic recognition of words. *Journal of Experimental Psychology,* **66,** 319–327.

Tulving, E., Mandler, G., & Baumal, R. (1964). Interaction of two sources of information in tachistoscopic word recognition. *Canadian Journal of Psychology, 18,* 62–71.

Tzeng, O. J. L., Hung, D. L., & Wang, S.-Y. (1977). Speech recoding in reading Chinese characters. *Journal of Experimental Psychology: Human Perception and Performance,* **3,** 621–630.

Van Santen, J. P. H. (1979). *Evidence for a recoding explanation of the word superiority effect in tachistoscopic conditions*. Unpublished doctoral dissertation, Department of Psychology, University of Michigan.

Van Wijk, O. (1966). *Rules of pronunciation for the English language*. London: Oxford Univ. Press.

Venezky, R. L. (1970). *The structure of English orthography*. The Hague: Mouton.

Venezky, R. L. (1979). Orthographic regularities in English words. In P. A. Kolers, M. E. Wrolstad, & H. Bouma (Eds.), *Processing visible language 1*. New York: Plenum.

Waters, G. A., & Seidenberg, M. (1983). Paper presented at the meeting of the Society for Research on Child Development, Detroit, Michigan.

Well, A. D., & Pollatsek, A. (1981). Word processing in reading: A commentary on the papers. *Visible Language, 15,* 287–308.

West, R. F., & Stanovich, K. E. (1982). Source of inhibition in experiments on the effect of sentence context on word recognition. *Journal of Experimental Psychology: Human Learning and Memory, 8,* 385–399.

Whittlesea, B. W. A. (1983). *The representation of concepts: An evaluation of the abstractive and episodic perspectives*. Unpublished Ph.D. dissertation, Department of Psychology, McMaster University, Canada.

READING RESEARCH: ADVANCES IN THEORY AND PRACTICE, VOL. 5

THE DECODING OF WORDS IN LEXICAL ACCESS: A REVIEW OF THE MORPHOGRAPHIC APPROACH

MARCUS TAFT

School of Psychology
University of New South Wales
Kensington, New South Wales, Australia

I. THE NOTION OF AN ACCESS CODE

A. Introduction

Despite the current popularity of top-down or context-driven approaches to reading instruction (e.g., Goodman, 1970), there is a growing body of research that supports a bottom-up or form-driven approach to word recognition in at least the majority of sentential contexts. What is meant by

Copyright © 1985 by Academic Press, Inc.
All rights of reproduction in any form reserved.

"form-driven" processing is that the meaning and syntactic function of a word become available when an abstract sensory representation of the word contacts the representation of that word stored in the reader's mental lexicon. The issue to be discussed in this article is the code in which this sensory-to-lexical contact takes place. The article draws heavily upon my previously reported research on this topic (Taft & Forster, 1975, 1976; Taft, 1976, 1979a,b, 1981).

B. Phonological Recoding

The first question to be raised when discussing the lexical access code is whether this code is orthographic or phonological; that is, whether or not the visual representation of a word is converted by rule into a phonological form in order for it to be recognized. It is not my aim here to outline the considerable body of literature devoted to this question since such reviews are available elsewhere (e.g., Bradshaw, 1975; Coltheart, 1980; McCusker, Bias, & Hillinger, 1981). However, the general conclusion arising from this literature is that words are recognized on the basis of their orthographic representation and not on the basis of any rule-generated phonological representation. Examples of evidence for this are the failure to find any difference between regular words and irregular words in a lexical decision task (Andrews, 1982; Coltheart, Besner, Jonasson, & Davelaar, 1979) and the failure to find any confusion, also in a lexical decision task, between words which are pronounced identically but which are spelled differently (Coltheart, Davelaar, Jonasson, & Besner, 1977). The finding, on the other hand, that nonsense words which are pronounced as words take longer to classify in a lexical decision task than nonsense words which are not homophonic with words (e.g., Coltheart et al., 1977; Rubenstein, Lewis, & Rubenstein, 1971) implies that phonological recoding may come into play when no lexical entry is successfully accessed on the basis of visual information. This conclusion, however, has been recently challenged by Martin (1982) and Taft (1982) who claim that the interference caused by the homophony of nonwords is a result of orthographic similarity rather than phonological identity. For example, the nonword deef leads to as much interference as does leef, even though leef and leaf are homophonic while deef and deaf are not.

So, since it appears to be the case that sensory-to-lexical contact is made in an orthographic code, the next step is to examine the nature of this orthographic access code. Is the sensory–lexical match performed on the basis of the whole word or is only a part of the word sufficient to allow the lexical information to become available? If the latter, then which part (or parts) is used? There are four types of word unit which are smaller than the word and which therefore are candidates for being the access code, along with the whole word itself. These are single letters, nonsyllabic letter groupings, syllables, and morphemes.

C. Access Codes versus Perceptual Units

The issue of the nature of the basic unit of word perception has been of interest since Cattell's early studies examining the tachistoscopic report of letter strings (Cattell, 1886). However, the idea of a perceptual unit is some-what different from that of an access code. The notion of perceptual unit refers to the grouping together of letters for processing in word recognition (e.g., Gibson, Pick, Osser, & Hammond, 1962; McClelland & Johnston, 1977; Mewhort & Campbell, 1980; Spoehr & Smith, 1973). In a hierar-chiacal model like that of Estes (1975), a word is recognized when the letters are matched with memory representations of letters, and then this letter information is combined and matched with memory representations of let-ter clusters, and then this information is combined to match with memory representations of syllables, and so on until a match is made with a memory representation of the word. Each of these levels can be termed a perceptual unit. The access code refers specifically to that "perceptual unit" which ultimately makes available all the lexical information about the word. Therefore, to say, for example, that the first letter of a word is its access code means that the first letter contains sufficient information to allow the lexical entry for the word to be accessed (an unlikely situation).

In order to clarify the above and before examining what the access code might specifically be, I will outline the framework in which I will mainly base my theoretical stance. This framework is the search model put forward by Forster (1976) and adopted in my previous discussions of the ortho-graphic access code. Later in the article, however, I will offer a description in terms of the more widely embraced logogen account (Morton, 1969, 1979).

D. The Search Framework

Figure 1 depicts Forster's search model. The lexical system is seen as being made up of a central master file or "lexicon proper" with three peripheral access files—an orthographic file for visually presented words, a phono-logical file for aurally presented words, and a semantic file for production purposes. Words in the access files are listed in order of their frequency in the language. When a word is visually presented, a search is made for it in

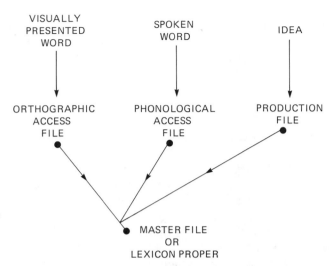

Fig. 1. A search model of lexical access based on Forster (1976).

a subset of the orthographic access file. Access to a candidate entry in the access file leads to information stored about this word in the master file. Lexical information about the orthography of the accessed word (i.e., information stored within the master file) might then be used to check back to the sensory representation of the presented word in order to confirm that the correct entry had been accessed. Therefore, the sensory-to-lexical match that is necessary for lexical access to occur actually takes place in the orthographic access file, so that the term "access code" refers to the representation of the word in the orthographic access file. What then is this representation? As stated previously, the candidates appear to be single letters, subsyllabic letter groupings, syllables, morphemes, and whole words.

E. Letters and Letter Groupings as Access Codes

It seems unlikely that single letters or small letter groupings act as access codes since there would be too many words having the same code. For example, recognition of the word *limitless* via the initial letter *l* would involve the activation of all words beginning with *l* and then a postaccess search through all those words in order to find the one that actually matched the presented word. The advantage of being able to get the access procedure underway quickly (because of the minimal initial processing involved) would be very much outweighed by the huge number of activated lexical entries that would need to be examined.

It is not so illogical, however, to suppose that it is a combination of small letter groupings that forms the access code; for example, the first few plus the last few letters of the word. In the case of *limitless* this might be *li-ss*. Such a suggestion is made by Forster and Gartlan (1975, cited in Forster, 1976) and is consistent with data presented by Stanners, Forbach, and Headley (1971), Stanners and Forbach (1973), and McCusker, Gough, and Bias (1981). The support for this suggestion will not be pursued further here, but will be brought up again later as a possible problem for the view of the access code which I will be exposing.

One criticism of the idea of the access code being some combination of letter groupings, however, is the imprecision and seeming arbitrariness of what that combination is. This is because it is based on the size of the letter grouping without taking into account the actual linguistic structure of the word. For example, does the *ss* of *limitless,* forming part of the suffix *less,* contribute as much to the recognition of the word as does the *ss* of *embarrass,* forming part of the stem? In the next section I consider an access code that is guided by linguistic characteristics of the word, namely the stem morpheme.

II. STEM MORPHEMES AS ACCESS CODES

A. Methodological Issues

In 1975 Ken Forster and I produced the first of a series of papers on the influence of morphological structure on word recognition. Much of the following constitutes a summary of that research program. Most of the experiments to be mentioned employed the lexical decision task, where subjects were required to press a response key depending upon whether the stimulus item was a word or not. Latency of response to a word was seen to reflect the time taken to access that word in the lexicon and to then decide that the accessed lexical entry was indeed the correct one. Latency of response to a nonword was seen to reflect the time taken to decide that there were no lexical representations that sufficiently matched with the stimulus item.

If a nonword is similar enough to a word for the lexical entry for that word to be accessed, then subjects will either incorrectly respond to the nonword item as a word or else they will be delayed in making a "nonword" response. Similarly, if a word item is very similar to another more common word, then access to the correct lexical entry will be delayed by the accessing of the entry for that similar word. Alternatively, subjects might respond to the word as a nonword, if they check the incorrectly accessed lexical entry, decide it is not the correct entry, and assume that the item was therefore not a word without continuing the search for another lexical entry. Another possibility, however, is that subjects might mistakenly make a "word" response to the incorrectly accessed lexical entry which would therefore be registered as a fast correct response, rather than an error or a slow correct response. Because of this possibility, it may be more difficult to observe delays and/or errors on word items caused by their similarity to other words than to observe them on nonword items.

A number of the experiments to be mentioned examined access codes by looking for such interference effects resulting from the similarity of nonwords to words and also the similarity of words to higher frequency words. The logic is that if the part of a word that constitutes the access code is presented as an item for lexical decision, then that word will be accessed and an interference effect will be observed.

B. Prefixed Words

1. Evidence for Stem Storage

The first of these interference effects reported (Taft & Forster, 1975) centers upon the stem morphemes of prefixed words. It was found that bound stems like *vive* (from *revive*) took longer to classify as nonwords and were associated with more errors than nonmorphemic nonwords which were just as similar to words as were the stems, e.g., *lish* (from the nonprefixed word *relish*). Taft (1976) additionally demonstrated that items like *lish* did not differ from nonwords that were not parts of words at all, e.g., *vith*. A similar result was found with word items, where words that could also be the stem of a prefixed word (e.g., *vent*) were found to take longer to respond to (though not associated with more errors) than words, matched for frequency, that were not stems of prefixed words, e.g., *coin*. This was only true when the stem version of the item was a more frequently occurring form than the word itself (as is the case with *vent*, where the frequency of *prevent* and *invent* is higher than that of *vent*). The conclusion drawn by Taft and Forster was that the access code for a prefixed word was its stem. Thus in order to recognize a prefixed word, the prefix must be "stripped off" for lexical access to succeed. There are several findings that support this prefix stripping notion.

2. Evidence for Prefix Stripping

a. Inappropriately Prefixed Nonwords. Taft and Forster report that when a nonword stem is inappropriately prefixed (e.g., *devive*) the interference effect is still observed relative to control items (e.g., *delish*). This implies that the prefix is stripped off, the stem accessed, but then found not to correctly combine with the presented prefix.

b. Pseudoprefixed Words. Both Rubin, Becker, and Freeman (1979) and Taft (1981) have demonstrated that words which look as though they are prefixed but are not (pseudoprefixed words like *relish*)[1] take longer to recognize than truly prefixed words (e.g., *revive*). The conclusion from this finding is that the pseudoprefixed words are mistakenly stripped of the letters that form a prefix and this leads to an abortive attempt at lexical access, using the putative stem as the access code. Rubin *et al.* claimed, however, that this prefix stripping procedure is under strategic control and only employed under particular experimental conditions, namely in the lexical decision task when prefixed nonwords are included in the experiment. This conclusion was based on their failure to find any difference between pseudoprefixed and truly prefixed words when there were no prefixed nonwords in the experiment. In reply to this, however, Taft (1981) observed difficulty with pseudoprefixed words in a naming task where there were no nonwords at all and, in fact, no truly prefixed words either. It was suggested that the result of Rubin *et al.* was an outcome of subjects being able to correctly respond in their experiment simply on the basis of whether the stimulus item began with letters that formed a prefix or not, since all of the word items and none of the nonword items began in such a way.

c. Prefixed Nonwords. A third result that suggests that prefixes are stripped off during lexical access is that prefixed nonwords like *denold* take longer to classify as nonwords than nonprefixed nonwords like *lomalk* (Taft, 1976). This would be expected if two searches are made for the former type of item, one involving prefix stripping and the other not. The problem with this experiment, though, is the possible inequality between the two conditions on their likeness to words. While the conditions were matched on digram frequency as given by Mayzner and Tresselt (1965), the digram frequencies given by this count are dependent upon word length. Thus while the frequency of *lo* might be the same as the frequency of *de* for six-letter words, it is very likely that it occurs less frequently if one were to take all words into account.

3. Evidence for Combined Storage of Prefixed Words

The conclusion from the aforementioned research is that prefixed words are recognized after the prefix is stripped off and lexical access takes place using the stem morpheme as the access code. One interesting extension of this view is that words having the same stem morpheme (e.g., *prevent* and *invent*) will use the same access code in recognition. This implies (though

---

[1]The classification of a word as "pseudoprefixed" rather than "prefixed" was made on the basis of prefixedness ratings (Taft, 1981), for want of any other more objective method. The fact that response times to prefixed words and pseudoprefixed words differed attests to the success of this rating technique. On what basis judges made their prefixedness ratings, though, is not answered by this. However, see Smith and Sterling (1982) for an examination of such a question.

not necessarily) that such words are accessed via the same representation in the access file. An experiment reported by Taft (1979b) in fact supports this implication. If representations in the access file are encountered in order of frequency then reaction times to prefixed words should be influenced by the frequency of their access codes, that is, the frequency of their stem morphemes. While the words *reproach* and *dissuade* have the same frequency of occurrence (according to Kučera & Francis, 1967), the frequency of the stem *proach* is higher than the frequency of the stem *suade*. This is because *proach* also occurs in *approach* which has a frequency of 123/ million, while *suade* occurs in *persuade* which has a frequency of only 17/million. Taft (1979b) demonstrated that words like *reproach,* with a high frequency stem were recognized faster than words like *dissuade,* with a lower frequency stem, even though the actual words that were presented were matched on frequency.

4. Evidence for Storage of Both Stem and Whole Words

While the evidence strongly suggests that prefixed words are represented by their stems in the lexicon, an argument has been made that they are represented as whole words as well (Stanners, Neiser, & Painton, 1979b). This argument was made on the basis of the finding that, while the lexical decision response to a prefixed word, like *progress,* is facilitated by the prior presentation of its stem, either on its own (i.e., *gress*) or combined with a different prefix (e.g., *regress*), this facilitation is not as great as when the actual word itself (i.e., *progress*) is previously presented. It was suggested that the lexical representation for the prefixed word is only partly activated by the presentation of its stem and hence that there is at least one lexical representation of the word that is more than just a representation of its stem. If the word *regress* were represented solely as *gress,* then presentation of *gress* should, according to Stanners *et al.,* produce as much facilitation as *regress.* The flaws of this assumption have been outlined by Taft (1981). Essentially, the argument is that the lexical classification of *gress* or of *regress* does not follow exactly the same processing pathways as does the lexical classification of *progress,* though they all include the common step of accessing the representation *gress.* Only the recognition of the word *progress* involves the recombining of *pro* with *gress* after the lexical entry has been accessed. Thus it seems that the postulation that there exists a lexical representation of both the prefixed word and its stem is an unnecessary elaboration on the basis of the experiments reported by Stanners *et al.*

Developmentally, however, it is logical that a prefixed word is initially stored as a whole word and only stored in its stem form when the person becomes aware of its morphological structure. But once access to the word takes place via prefix stripping it seems that the whole word representation would then become redundant and would never again need to be used for accessing purposes. It might be supposed though, that the whole word and the stem of the word are searched in parallel and whichever is accessed first leads to recognition.

Empirical evidence that possibly argues against parallel search, however, is, first, the delay observed with pseudoprefixed words (Rubin *et al.,* 1979; Taft, 1981), and, second, the delay observed with prefixed nonwords (Taft, 1976). The former might be explained by saying that one of the parallel searches is unsuccessful (e.g., the search for the *lish* of *relish*) and, even though the other search is successful (i.e., the search for the whole word *relish*), the failure of one search nevertheless slows down the response. Perhaps the two searches are carried out in order to act as a confirmation of each other, and response is delayed when one does not confirm the other.

The second possible experimental result that might be raised as evidence against parallel search is the finding that prefixed nonwords like *denold* take longer to classify than nonprefixed nonwords like *lomalk*. Assuming (perhaps wrongly) that it is prefixedness rather than word-likeness that leads to this difference, one might expect that the failure to access a lexical entry with both searches (one search for *nold* and one for *denold*) would not delay response times if these searches were conducted in parallel (in fact, it might be expected to speed up response times, in that the searches confirm each other). In response to this, though, one could say that parallel processing leads to a response delay in that it occupies more processing capacity than a single search. In turn, however, one can reply to this with the finding (Taft, 1976) that there appears to be no difference in reaction times between prefixed words (e.g., *revive*) and nonprefixed words (e.g., *menace*), where the former would involve two parallel searches (one for *vive* and one for *revive*) while the latter would involve only a single search (for *menace*).

Therefore, while it is conceivable that prefixed words are stored both as representations of the whole word and as representations of their stem, the evidence to date is not in its favor.

C. Suffixed Words

1. Inflected versus Derived Words

There are two broad types of suffixed words distinguished in the linguistic literature: inflected words (e.g., *cats, eating, bigger*) and derived words (e.g., *beautiful, wisdom, solidify*). There are several important differences between these two types of words.

First, the appending of an inflection to a word does not alter the syntactic category of that word, whereas the appending of a derivational suffix usually does. For example, *cat* is a noun and so is *cats,* but *beauty* is a noun while *beautiful* is an adjective—the adjective has been derived from the noun.

The second difference concerns the stem to which the suffix is attached. Finding the stem of any (regularly) inflected word can be achieved by the application of simple rules: The stem of *mats* is found to be *mat* after the *s* is removed, the stem of *matting* is found to be *mat* after the *ing* and duplicated consonant are removed, and the stem of *mating* is found to be *mate* after the *ing* is removed and an *e* is added because there was no geminated consonant. The relationship between a stem and its derived form, however, is not always so regular. For example, the stem of *retention* is *retain,* but the stem of *contention* is not *contain,* but *contend.*

Third, the relationship between an inflection and its function in a word is highly regular and predictable and thus can be reduced to a simple set of rules. For example, the addition of an *s* to a singular noun always converts that noun into a plural. The relationship between a derived suffix and its function, on the other hand, is not always regular. For example, *contention* means something like "that which is contended," whereas *attention* does not mean "that which is attended," but rather, "the act or state of attending." Thus the suffix *ion* has different functions in *contention* and *attention.*

Some derivational suffixes behave more regularly than others. For example, *ness* attaches itself to its stem in a highly regular fashion, the only rule being that *y* changes to *i* before *ness* (e.g., *happiness*). The suffix *ward* functions regularly in that it always means "in the direction of" (e.g., *homeward*) and never affects the phonology or orthography of the stem to which it is attached. When a derivational form is highly regular like this, the stem word is said to be transparent. There seem to be degrees of transparency where the suffix affects the stem more markedly in some cases compared to others (Cutler, 1981). For example, the stem word *destroy* is modified more markedly in the derived word *destruction* than is the stem word *expand* in *expansion* which, in turn, is more markedly modified than the stem word *govern* in *government.*

Finally, in production, if a word is to be inflected (e.g., pluralized, put into the past tense, made into a superlative) then there is no doubt about the suffix that must be added (e.g., *s* for plurals, *ed* for past tenses, *est* for superlatives), unless the word is marked as one of the rare exceptions (e.g., *child–children*). On the other hand, derivations are not predictable. For example, to convert a verb into its nominal form, one might need to add *ment* (as in *enjoyment*), *ion* (as in *prevention*), *al* (as in *rehearsal*), *age* (as in *shrinkage*), *ence* (as in *existence*), *ry* (as in *revelry*) or even *ing* (as in *meeting*) depending on the verb. It therefore seems likely that derivational information is represented in the lexicon in a different manner from inflectional information. Inflectional information can, in fact, be reduced to simple rules (e.g., add *s* to pluralize a noun), as long as the part of speech of the stem word is known and the stem word is not marked in the lexicon as an exception. Derivational information, though, must be either specifically listed within the lexical entry for the stem word or else represented as the derived word itself, stored separately from the stem word.

The psychological literature does appear to point strongly to a stem access code for inflected words, but the evidence for derived words is not so straightforward. Most of the experimental paradigms used to examine prefixed word recognition have also been used to study suffixed word recognition. These include examining lexical decision times to nonword stems, pseudosuffixed words, and suffixed nonwords, manipulating the frequency of the stems of suffixed words, and measuring the amount of facilitation gained by priming a suffixed word with its stem.

2. Empirical Studies

a. Nonword Stems. Examining interference in lexical decision responses to the nonword stems of inflected words is virtually impossible given the dearth of such stems in the language. Most of the items which may be thought of as nonword stems either have a dubious nonword status in that they do appear in the "Shorter Oxford Dictionary" (e.g., *doldrum, galosh, dreg*) or they are morphologically complex themselves (e.g., *painstake, oncome, unabash*).

On the other hand, nonword stems of derived words, being far more plentiful, can be examined. Taft (1976) compared stems like *daint* (from *dainty*), *groce* (from *grocer*), and *drast* (from *drastic*) to the first syllables of words that were not stems of suffixed words, like *flam* (from *flamboyant*), *trink* (from *trinket*), and *puzz* (from *puzzle*). There was absolutely no difference between these two conditions, implying that stems of derived words were no different from first syllables in their status as access codes. More will be said later about the status of first syllables as access codes.

b. Pseudosuffixed Words. If suffixes are stripped off prior to lexical search then one might expect that any final letters that appear to form a suffix should be stripped off even if this is not appropriate. Therefore pseudosuffixed words, like pseudoprefixed words, should evidence a delay in lexical decision times.

An experiment examining pseudoinflected words (Taft, 1976) provided some support for this in the case of inflections. Pseudoinflected words (e.g., *bias, kindred, whiting*) took longer and were associated with more errors than noninflected words (e.g., *boom, shuffle, outbreak*). However, there are two problems with this result. One is that truly inflected words (with bound stems, e.g., *suds, mottled, oncoming*) were intermediary in reaction times and errors between the other two conditions, differing statistically from neither. While this may have possible theoretical import, it also may be a result of the second problem with the experiment. This is that, on the whole, the words used were of very low frequency and, since it is likely that frequency counts like that of Kučera and Francis (the authority used in this experiment) are highly inaccurate at the lower end of the frequency scale, it is possible that the conditions were poorly matched on frequency. Consultation of a second word frequency count (Carroll, Davies, & Richman, 1971) in fact suggests this might be so, with the frequencies of the truly inflected words being relatively lower by this count, and the frequencies of the noninflected words being relatively higher (in relation to the frequencies of the pseudoinflected words) than given by Kučera and Francis norms. Inaccurate frequency matching is a problem confronting any research using low frequency words. My practice now is to use two frequency norms when designing experiments that use low frequency words (e.g., Taft, 1981), since it is unlikely that both norms will be inaccurate on exactly the same words in exactly the same way. The upshot of the above experiment then is that there may be a difficulty in recognizing pseudoinflected words, but it is not at all conclusive.

An experiment looking at pseudoderived words, like *bounty, petal,* and *crucible* (Taft, 1976) revealed that they were no more difficult to recognize than nonderived words, like *morsel, heron,* and *tentacle* or truly derived words (with bound stems), like *dainty, regal,* and *credible.* Frequency matching seemed to be more reasonable in this experiment on examination of the Carroll *et al.* frequency count. Thus, in agreement with the nonword stem results, it seems that derived words are treated no differently from polysyllabic words.

Manelis and Tharp (1977) also report no difference between pseudoderived and truly derived words. (Eleven of their 15 item groups had derivational suffixes; the other 4 had inflections.) On making a lexical decision response to two words at a time, subjects took no longer with two pseudoderived words (e.g., *sister-somber*) than with two truly derived words (e.g., *tester-sender*).

While this appears to be consistent with my own findings for derived words, it is in fact not convincing evidence against derivational suffix stripping. This is because mixed pairs of words (pseudoderived and truly derived, e.g., *sister-tester*) took longer to respond to than either type of unmixed pair. As pointed out elsewhere (Taft, 1979b), this finding with mixed pairs appears to support the view that truly derived words are treated differently from pseudoderived words, though it is unclear whether this leads to conflict in the case of mixed pairs or facilitation in the case of unmixed pairs, (Manelis & Tharp assume the latter; but see Taft, 1979b, for a critique of their explanation.) It is possible, however, that this inhibition or facilitation does not occur at the decomposition stage of processing, but rather at a postaccess stage (as has been suggested in the case of semantic priming, e.g., Forster, 1981; and in the case of phonological priming, e.g., Humphreys, Evett, & Taylor, 1982). That is, the structure of truly derived words and pseudoderived words (i.e., monomorphemic polysyllabic words) may be represented differently in the lexicon proper, even though their access codes may be of exactly the same form.

The results of Manelis and Tharp are problematical in another way, though. A check of the item frequencies using the Carroll *et al.* frequency norms reveals that the truly derived words (e.g., *tester*) are far less frequent than the pseudoderived words (e.g., *sister*) and this difference (using log frequency) is in fact significant [$t(14) = 2.76, p < .02$]. It is possible, therefore, that the pseudoderived words would have taken longer than the truly derived words, had frequency been properly matched. While my own results reported above suggest that they would not, the fact that Manelis and Tharp found no difference when frequency was biased against the pseudoderived words implies otherwise. So, again, the results are inconclusive.

A lack of difference between truly derived and pseudoderived words was observed in a different type of experiment by Smith and Sterling (1982). In a letter cancellation task subjects missed just as many *e*'s in the ending *er* when it functioned as a derivational suffix (e.g., *driver*) as when it did not (e.g., *river*). On the other hand, more *e*'s were missed in the ending *ed* when it functioned as an inflection (e.g., *hunted*) than when it did not (e.g., *hundred*). Drewnowski and Healy (1980) found the same thing for the inflection *ing*.

c. Suffixed Nonwords. Evidence for inflection stripping comes from a comparison of inflected nonwords (e.g., *molks, widodled*) with noninflected nonwords (e.g., *porld, vodintew*). The finding of slower reaction times to the former (Taft, 1976) suggested that inflection stripping occurred and slowed down the response. As with prefixed nonwords, however, an argument could possibly be made that inflected nonwords are more wordlike in that their final letters are so common. It is interesting to observe, though, that derived nonwords (e.g., *boithy, tivation, flasic*) were found to be no slower than nonderived nonwords (e.g., *foutha, tibariot, prasit*), even though the endings of the former were also far more common (Taft, 1976).

These data again imply that inflections are stripped off prior to access, but derivational suffixes are not. Consistent with this is the direct comparison made by Reisner (1972) of inflected nonwords (e.g., *drilked*) with derived nonwords (e.g., *dralkor*), finding longer lexical decision times for the former. Results obtained by Snodgrass and Jarvella (1972) are also consistent, in the sense that lexical decision times to derived nonsense words like *diltness* were no longer than those to their stem nonsense words (*dilt*). However, this result must be viewed with caution in that, first, they also found no difference between prefixed nonsense words (e.g., *prestul*) and their stems (*stul*), which is not consistent with the prefixed nonword results reported in Section II,B,2,c, but that second, only four items were used in each condition (and those were not matched on length).

d. Frequency Manipulations. If suffixed words and their stems are accessed through the same entry in the access file (namely, through a representation of their stem), then lexical decision times should be influenced by the frequency with which that entry is accessed. Thus response times should reflect the combined frequencies of the stem plus its suffixed forms.

Taft (1979b), Reisner (1972), and O'Connor (1975) have shown this to be true of inflected words. For example, while the words *sized* and *raked* have the same frequency of occurrence, the summed frequency of their related forms differs (*sized + size + sizes + sizing* versus *raked + rake + rakes + raking*). It was found that the relatively high base frequency of items like *sized* made them faster to respond to than items like *raked*.

In addition to this, however, matching items on base frequency and varying them on the frequency of their presented form (i.e., their surface frequency) also produced an effect (Taft, 1979b). Thus, items like *followed* were found to be faster than items like *numbered* as a result of *followed* being a more common word than *numbered,* even though the summed frequency of *followed, follow, follows,* and *following* is the same as the summed frequency of *numbered, number, numbers,* and *numbering.*

The explanation given for the fact that both base and surface frequency contribute to reaction times is that frequency has its effects at two stages of the accessing process. Base frequency has its influence in the access file where all related forms of a word are accessed through the same entry, while surface frequency has its effect in the lexicon proper where the suffix is recombined with its stem. Thus not only is the word *numbered* affected by the frequency of *number* and its related forms, but also by the frequency with which *number* is converted into its past tense, in the lexicon proper, by the addition of *ed*. This might partly (or wholly) be a reflection of the frequency with which *number* is used as a verb rather than a noun.

Frequency has also been manipulated in an examination of derived words. Using a mixture of different derivational suffixes, Reisner (1972) observed that words with a high base frequency were recognized faster than words with a low base frequency, but only when the surface frequency of the word was low. High frequency derived words (e.g., *beautiful*) appeared not to be treated as being related to their stems (*beauty*). However, there is an alternative explanation for this. Since surface frequency is a component of base frequency, high surface frequency words will also have high base frequencies. Thus, when surface frequencies are high, a comparison of low base frequency words with high base frequency words must necessarily be in fact a comparison of high base frequency words with higher base frequency words. Since lexical decison times appear to be a function of log frequency (e.g., Swift, 1977), the difference between a frequency of, say 400 and a frequency of 200 would not in fact be very great in terms of reaction time. Thus the difference in response pattern that Reisner obtained between high and low surface frequency words may well be the result of frequency insensitivity with the high frequency words.

Bradley (1979) performed a more systematic study, looking separately at four different types of derivation. For words with suffixes in *ness, ment,* and agentive *er,* Bradley observed that base frequency influenced lexical decison times whereas surface frequency did not. On the other hand, base frequency had no effect for words ending with the nonproductive, less transparent suffix *ion.* However, surface frequency had no effect here either!

One cannot, however, be completely confident in accepting Bradley's results since she used relatively low frequency words selected on the basis of only one frequency count (Kučera & Francis, 1967). This problem is particularly pertinent here because of the susceptibility to the artifact of regression to the mean resulting from the fact that the variable being manipulated (e.g., base frequency) is highly correlated with the variable on which matching is performed (surface frequency). In my own studies looking at inflected words (Taft, 1979b), the second frequency count (Carroll *et al.,* 1971) was consulted to guard against this artifact argument.

Examination of the Carroll *et al.* norms reveals that Bradley's items may, in fact, be open to this problem. In the *ness, ment,* and *er* experiments, the pairs that were matched on surface frequency using the Kučera and Francis norms (e.g., *boldness*—high base frequency versus *deftness*—low base frequency), were, according to the Carroll *et al.* norms, biased in favor of the high base frequency member of the pairs by a factor of about three to one. (For the *ion* experiment, where base frequency was not shown to have an effect, frequency seemed to be better matched, according to Carroll *et al.*). Nevertheless, when one looks at the 13 pairs of *ness, ment,* and *er* items which were actually biased against the base frequency effect (i.e., the higher base frequency member of the pair had a lower surface frequency, according to Carroll *et al.*), there still seems to be a base frequency effect, with 11 of the 13 pairs showing a difference. So, the base frequency effect does appear to be genuine.

The items matched on base frequency but varied on surface frequency are also problematical, since the Carroll *et al.* base frequencies are biased two to one against the surface frequency effect (i.e., the higher surface frequency member of the pair having a lower base frequency), thus possibly nullifying the effect. In addition to this, the Carroll *et al.* norms reveal that in half of the *ion* items, the supposedly higher surface frequency member of the pair is actually equal to or lower in surface frequency than the supposedly lower surface frequency member, and this is also true for three out of the seven *ment* items.

In conclusion, then, it does appear that derived nouns that have regular and productive suffixes like *ness, ment,* and *er* share the same access code as their stem, while derived words in *ion* do not. It is unclear, however, whether the derived words are listed separately from their stems in the lexicon proper or reconstructed from their stems. Using the logic of my experiments with inflected words (Taft, 1979b), the latter should be evidenced by a surface frequency effect in addition to the base frequency effect. Bradley's results, if they are accepted, suggest the former, indicating that derivationally related words are listed separately (while inflectionally related words are listed together).

e. Priming Experiments. Stanners, Neiser, Hernon, and Hall (1979a) conducted a series of experiments looking at the effect of priming a word with a suffixed version of that word. What they found was that responding to a regularly inflected word (e.g. *lifting*) had the same priming effect on a later response to the stem of that word (*lift*) as did prior responding to the stem of the word itself (*lift*). That is, what was observed with inflected primes was equivalent to repetition priming. This result implies that all information about the inflected form of a word is located within the lexical representation of its stem.

Notice that this result appears on the surface to be different from that described earlier with prefixed words (Stanners *et al.,* 1979b) where the prime only partially facilitated the target word. However, in that experiment the stem was the prime and the affixed word was the target, rather than the other way around. When Stanners *et al.* (1979b) looked at the situation where the prefixed word (e.g., *unhappy*) preceded the stem (*happy*), they obtained a result equivalent to the inflected word result, namely, that the prefixed word was as effective a prime as was the stem word itself. Thus the conclusion is that prefixes and inflections are treated in the same way in lexical processing, being stripped off prior to access.

Murrell and Morton (1974) also examined priming effects with inflected words, but used a tachistoscopic recognition task. They found that inflected words (e.g., *sees*) were identified more readily if they had been previously memorized than if they had not been. Facilitation was also obtained, though not as strongly, when the memorized word was a different word with the same stem (e.g., *seen*), but there was no facilitation when the memorized word was visually similar to the to-be-identified word, but not morphologically related (e.g., *seed*).

While the result was taken by Murrell and Morton to mean that inflected words are represented lexically by their stems, their experiment revealed that the stem priming effect was not as strong as the repetition effect, unlike the experiment of Stanners *et al.* (1979a). However, this was only true when responses were scored for their correctness as a whole word. When responses were scored for the correctness of their root morpheme there was no difference between stem priming and repetition priming. That is, in the stem priming condition the identification response often included the correct stem but an incorrect suffix, implying that inflectionally related words (e.g., *sees* and *seen*) were employing the same access code (namely, their stem).

Kempley and Morton (1982) have replicated Murrell and Morton's finding in a similar paradigm using spoken words. In an extension of this, however, they found that pretraining with a word had no facilitating effect on the identification of an irregularly related word. Thus pretraining with *stink* had no effect on the identification of *stank* in a background of noise. This was taken to mean that irregularly inflected words are accessed through different codes to their stems. On the other hand, the results that Stanners *et al.* (1979a) obtained with irregularly inflected words did reveal a priming effect on lexical decison times, though one that was not as great as repetition priming. They interpreted this by saying that irregularly inflected words have lexical representations that are separate from their stems, but added that the representations are related in some way, perhaps in the same way that *dog* is related to *cat*. Kempley and Morton's failure to find any priming effects for irregularly inflected words must then be put down to their auditory task not being sensitive to these lexical relationships, though why this should be so is unclear.

Stanners *et al.* drew the same conclusions about derived words as they did for irregularly inflected words in that they found that when the prime word was derivationally related to the target word (e.g., *selective–select*) there was a facilitatory effect, though one that was weaker than repetition priming. Thus a derived word was seen to have lexical representation separate from, though related to, its stem. However, Stanners *et al.* point out a further result that was not consistent with this sort of interpretation, namely, that irregularly inflected words (e.g., *hung*), took longer to recognize than noninflected stems (e.g., *hang*), even though they were matched for frequency and length, and the same appeared to be true for derived words. This then suggests that information about derived and irregularly inflected words is accessed via the lexical representation of their stem.

Consonant with this conclusion are MacKay's findings obtained when subjects were asked to produce the past tense of spoken present tense verbs and the nominal form of spoken verbs (MacKay, 1976, 1978). Not only were errors of inflection or derivation fairly common (e.g., *gived* from *give*, *collidement* from *collide*), but response times reflected the complexity of the phonological transformations that would be required to produce the inflected or derived form from the stem word. For example, it took longer to derive *suspicion* from *suspect* than to derive *connection* from *connect*, and it took longer to say that *taught* was the past tense of *teach* than to say that *sent* was the past tense of *send*.

It appeared, then, that irregularly inflected and derived words were generated by transformational rule from the stem word. If the derived forms were simply listed in complete form in conjunction with their related stems in the lexicon then the complexity of structural relationship between the word and its stem should have been irrelevant and errors like *collidement* should not have been made. Although this experiment used auditory presentation, it nevertheless has implications for visual word recognition, in that it was presumably tapping the modality-free lexicon proper.

3. Evidence from Language Dysfunction

Evidence for morphological processing has been obtained in a number of situations where language is impaired. For example, Morton (1964) lists examples of affixation errors amongst a corpus of reading errors made by normal subjects reading quickly (e.g., *Roman* read instead of *Rome*). Letters that can be recalled when in a tip-of-the-tongue state often constitute morphemes (Rubin, 1975), and typing errors that are made under pressure (Shaffer, 1975) occasionally evidence morphological decomposition (e.g., *sense ibilities*). However, most of the relevant work with language dysfunction has been in the examination of reading errors made by dyslexics and in the examination of speech production errors made by normals.

There are many examples of specifically morphological deficits in the dyslexia literature (e.g., Beyn, 1958; Jakobson, 1971; Marshall & Newcombe, 1973; Patterson, 1980) and it is not my intention to describe these in any detail. In general, however, the nature of the reading errors of dyslexics, as well as their lexical decision performance (e.g., Patterson, 1980), are consistent with the experimental studies described above, namely, that affixed words are recognized through the lexical entry for their stem.

Analyses of slips of the tongue also tend to support this view (e.g., Fromkin, 1973; Garrett, 1976; MacKay, 1979; Cutler, 1983). For example, the uttering of *dependment* rather than *dependence* is equivalent to the generating of *collidement* from *collide* in MacKay's nominalization experiment described above. While speech error data is a valuable source of information as regards the structure of the lexicon proper as well as the speech output mechanisms, it obviously cannot contribute directly to our understanding of the visual access code and input mechanisms.

4. Conclusions from Research on Suffixed Words

a. Regularly Inflected Words. All of the above research on the recognition of inflected words appears to point to a stem access code. That is, it seems that inflected words and their stems are represented by the same lexical entry, not only in the lexicon proper but also in the access file. Regularly inflected words appear to be generated from their stems by rule application within the lexicon.

The evidence also suggests that inflected words are decomposed such that the suffix is stripped off prior to lexical access. It should be noted that suffix stripping is not a necessary corollary of the conclusion that an inflected word and its stem share an access code. The stem could alternatively be isolated from its suffix by a left-to-right parsing process (see Taft, 1979a; Marcel, 1980) whereby the letters that occur at the beginning of the word are matched with a representation in the access file, namely, a representation of the stem of the word. However, the pseudoinflected word experiment (Section II,C,2,b) and inflected nonword experiments (Section II,C,2,c) point to suffix stripping in the recognition of inflected words.

Experiments which indicate that the letters which form an inflection are treated as a single unit also support the idea of suffix stripping. Gibson and Guinet (1971) found that fewer errors were made in the tachistoscopic identification of inflections attached to words and nonwords than in the identification of the final letters of noninflected items. In addition, when errors were made to inflections there was a tendency for subjects to report a suffix that was not the one that was presented (e.g., *ed* for *ing*). Unitization of the inflection *ing* was also observed by Drewnowski and Healy (1980), who found that the letter *n* was detected less often in an *ing* ending when it formed a suffix than when it formed part of the word stem (e.g., *something*). There were also fewer detections of *n* in the inflection *ing* than in the inflection *en* (i.e., used as a past participle) as well as in the derivational suffixed *ion* and *ment*. This implied that the frequency of the suffix (or perhaps productiveness) played a role, rather than whether it was an inflection or a derivation. So, when it is said that inflections are treated as single units and stripped from the word during recognition, this might be restricted to only the very common inflections (namely *ing, ed,* and *s*).

There is one experiment in the literature that appears to run counter to the notion of morphological decomposition with inflected words. This is the second experiment performed by Manelis and Tharp (1977). In this experiment, subjects were required to say whether a particular word (e.g., *lack*) was contained in a following suffixed word (e.g., *lacking*) or suffixed nonword (e.g., *lackest*). The majority of the suffixes used were inflections. If inflected items were decomposed into stem plus suffix prior to lexical access, Manelis and Tharp argue that stem words should be detected in nonwords as rapidly as they are in words. Contrary to this, however, they found longer response times to nonwords than to words.

A criticism of this experiment has been made elsewhere (Taft, 1979b). The suffixes used in the word items were not the same as the suffixes used in the nonword items. The vast majority of word items involved the common inflections *ing, ed,* and *er,* whereas not one of nonword items used these inflections. Instead, the majority of nonword items involved the far less common suffixes *est, en,* and *es* (inappropriately used, e.g., *growes*). Since the frequency of occurrence of the suffix is likely to be important in morphological decomposition (cf. Drewnowski & Healy, 1980), Manelis and Tharp's experiment cannot be seen as evidence against morphological decomposition.

b. Derived Words. The conclusions to be drawn about the recognition of derived words are less clear. Bradley's experiments suggest that words with transparent derivational suffixes like *ment, ness,* and agentive *er* have the same access code as their stem words. Words with opaque derivations (e.g., *ion*) do not. Further, her experiments may be said to show that derived words have separate entries from their stems in the lexicon proper, if her lack of a surface frequency effect is interpreted in this way. This explanation may account for the partial priming effect observed by Stanners, Neiser, Hernon, and Hall with derived words (i.e., priming in the access file, but not in the lexicon proper), and the longer reaction times to derived words compared to nonsuffixed items (i.e., going from the joint representation in the access file to the lexical entry for the stem, e.g., *bold,* prior to going to the lexical entry for the less frequently occurring derived form, e.g., *boldness*). However, it does not account for the fact that the partial priming effect was also found for words with opaque derivations (e.g., *destruction, reception*). Nor does it account for MacKay's results where derivations appeared to be generated from their stems within the lexicon proper. An alternative account is therefore required.

One possibility is that words with transparent derivations share the same representations as their stems in both the access file and the lexicon proper, while words with opaque derivations share the same representations as their stems in the lexicon proper only. By this account similar explanations are given for transparent derivations and inflected words, but the crucial difference is that inflections are not listed within the lexical entries whereas derivational suffixes are. That is, the lexical entry for *select* includes the information that it can take the suffixes *ive, or,* and *ion* and also that it is a verb. The latter is sufficient information to determine that it can take *s, ing,* or *ed* where appropriate. How then, by this account, does one explain full priming of stems from inflected words, but only partial priming for derived words regardless of their derivational transparency? And also, how does one account for a surface frequency effect for inflected words (Taft, 1979b), but not for derived words (assuming Bradley's results to be genuine)?

To answer the priming problem it may be the case that when a word is accessed, the output from its lexical representation is stored or tagged episodically (Tulving, 1972). Priming may then occur postaccess (see Section II,C,2,b), when the output from the lexical representation of the target word is compared to the episodic trace of the prime. The output of the lexical entry for *select* when the item *selective* is presented is *select + ive,* while the output of the lexical entry for *select* when the item *selects* is presented is *select* (since the *s* is not contained within the lexical entry). Hence *selects* will prime *select* as much as *select* itself does, while *selective* will not prime it as much. Similarly, the output from the lexical entry for *divide* when *division* is presented will be *divide + ion,* and thus *division* should lead to as much (partial) priming of *divide* as *selective* does of *select.*

To explain why inflected words show a surface frequency effect (Taft, 1979b), while derived words do not (Bradley, 1979), one needs to assume that the application of an inflectional rule (e.g., pluralizing a noun, forming the past tense of a verb) is affected by the time taken to determine whether the rule can be used or not. For example, to pluralize a noun one must determine if the noun can be a "countable noun," and to form a past tense one must determine if the word can be a verb. If it happens that the stem of the past-tensed form is more commonly a noun than a verb, then the decision that the past-tensed form is correct may well be delayed. The stems of many of the inflected verbs used by Taft (1979b) were indeed more common as nouns than as verbs, but only for the lower surface frequency items. For example, the word *number* is more commonly a noun than a verb, whereas the word *follow* (the stem of *followed,* which was the higher surface frequency partner of the item *numbered*) is always a verb. Thus the response to the word *numbered* may have been delayed by the low frequency of usage of the word as a verb. Also, in most of the pluralized items there might have been some doubt about whether the noun was countable or not, since the stem words of the items normally refer to something unique, e.g., *suns, fronts, worlds.* Bradley's derived words differed from this in that the derivational suffix was almost always added to the most frequent (and usually the only) part of speech of the stem. In addition, if a derivational suffix were specifically listed within the lexical entry for the stem, then there would be no doubt about whether the derivation was appropriate or not. So, by the account given, the surface frequency effect observed for inflected words results from the time taken to decide that the inflectional rule is applicable. There is no surface frequency effect for derived words since the suffix is not generated by rule, but stored within the lexical entry.[2]

It should be noted that the suggestion that derivational suffixes are listed within lexical entries does not preclude the possibility that derivations can also be generated by rule. It in fact seems necessary to make this assumption in order to account for neologisms (e.g., *de-mad-ifier;* Cutler, 1983) as well as for errors of derivation like those observed by MacKay (e.g., *collidement* for *collision*). Also, subjects do seem to be sensitive to the morphotactic conventions of the language (i.e., which morphemes can go together). For example, neologisms ending in *ity* are more acceptable than those ending in *ness* when following *ible* (e.g., *resurrectibility* versus *resurrectibleness;* Anshen & Aronoff, 1981), but less acceptable when following *ive* (e.g., *reflectivity* versus *reflectiveness;* Aronoff & Schvaneveldt, 1978), though Cutler (1981) argues that this is a result of transparency rather than productivity.

Finally, there is the issue of the preaccess parsing of derivationally suffixed words. While evidence for suffix stripping was obtained for inflectional suffixes, equivalent evidence was not forthcoming for derivational suffixes. This suggests that derivational suffixes are not removed from the stem prior to lexical access, but instead that the letters that form the stem are found to match with a representation in the access file via a reiterative left-to-right parsing procedure (Taft, 1979a; Marcel, 1980). For example, recognition of the word *dainty* would involve successive (or parallel) searches in the access file for *dai, dain,* and *daint,* the last of which is found to match with a representation (namely, the stem of the word *dainty*). Thus, the access code for derived words is seen to be the stem of the word but the means of isolating this access code is via a left-to-right parsing procedure rather than by recognizing the derivational suffix and then stripping it off. In this way, the *bull* of *bullock,* the *bath* of *bathe,* and the *crumb* of *crumble* can

[2]A similar explanation can be made for noninflected words for which Taft (1979b) also found a surface frequency effect when base frequency was controlled (e.g., *tin* versus *rib*). For these items, the higher frequency member of a pair was always the most commonly occurring form of the word (e.g., *tin* is more common than *tins, tinned,* and *tinning*), whereas the lower frequency member of the pair was never the most commonly occurring form (e.g., *rib* is less common than *ribs*). Thus recognition times to *rib* could have been slowed by the more common usage of the word as a plural.

all be isolated, despite the fact the *ock, e,* and *le* are not generally known to be suffixes.

   c. *Irregularly Inflected Words.* The data obtained by Stanners *et al.* (1979a) and MacKay (1976) suggest that irregularly inflected words behave like derived words. Thus, information about the irregularity of the inflected word is listed within the entry for the stem word in the lexicon proper. It is interesting to note that the occurrence of such neologisms as *brung, thunk,* and *shat* imply that irregular inflections can be productive to some extent. Whether or not an irregularly inflected word and its stem have the same access code has not been examined, but it could only be possible when the inflected form is quite similar to its stem. For example, the words *hang* and *hung* could have the same access code if the vowel were not included in the code (but not so for *teach* and *taught*).

D. Compound Words

   If the access code for the recognition of affixed words is the stem of the word, what is the access code when a word is composed of two stems? This is the situation with compound words like *postcard* and *seaweed.* Do both words in the compound constitute separate access codes, or is only the first or the second constituent the access code? Perhaps the whole compound word in itself is the access code. There in fact exist very few empirical studies on the recognition of compound words.

   Osgood and Hoosain (1974) used a tachistoscopic recognition task, followed by a recall task, to compare compound words like *real estate* with noncompound noun phrases like *city estate* and nonsense compounds like *post estate.* They found that noun phrases were recalled almost as well as compound words in contrast to nonsense compounds, but otherwise the noun phrases behaved more like the nonsense compounds. Compound words were easier to tachistoscopically perceive than the other two types of item, and most importantly, recognition of the constituent words of the items was facilitated by prior exposure to the noun phrases and the nonsense compounds, but not by prior exposure to the truly compound words. Therefore it seemed that compound words were being identified as whole units. This possibly implies that the access code for compound words is the whole word itself. However, it is possible that the pretraining effects observed in tachistoscopic recognition studies are a result of post access integration of some sort and have little to say about the nature of the access code, though they may reflect the structure of the representation within the lexicon proper.

   The results of several experiments by Taft and Forster (1976) support an access code that is not the whole word itself, but rather, a representation of the first constituent of the word. The first experiment involved a comparison of compound nonwords where either the first constituent was a nonword (e.g., *flurbpair*), the second constituent was a nonword (e.g., *spellcung*), both constituents were nonwords (e.g., *thrimnade*) or both constituents were words (e.g., *toastpull*). It was found that lexical decision times to items like *toastpull* and *spellcung* were equal but longer than those to items like *flurbpair* and *thrimnade,* which in turn were equal. From this it was concluded that only the lexical status of the first constituent was relevant to response times and thus the first constituent formed the access code. In other words, the lexical entry for *seaweed* is accessed via the entry *sea* in the access file.

If information in the lexicon proper is accessed on the basis of the first constituent in order to determine whether or not the second constituent can combine with the first, then one can make a further prediction. The number of possible second constituents that can combine with the first constituent should influence the time taken to recognize a compound item. For example, the entry *stone* will lead to information about the words *stonefruit, stone age, stoneware, stonemason,* and so on. Therefore, if the nonword *stonefoil* is to be rejected as a word, each of these possible compounds needs to be rejected. Hence, nonwords whose first constituent is potentially the first constituent of a word (e.g., *stonefoil*) should take longer to classify than nonwords whose first constituent is not compoundable (e.g., *smilecrop*). This comparison can be made using the nonword items of Experiment V reported by Taft and Forster (1976). Although only reported in that article as a contrast between low frequency and high frequency first constituents, the items were actually designed in a 2 × 2 factorial setup with the factors being frequency of the first constituent (high frequency, e.g., *stonefoil* and *smilecrop,* versus low frequency, e.g., *stalegrip* and *smashboss*) and compoundability (e.g., *stonefoil* and *stalegrip* versus *smilecrop* and *smashboss*). The analysis of lexical decision times revealed no significant frequency effect (as reported by Taft & Forster, 1976), but did produce a significant effect of compoundability, with the interaction being nonsignificant (Taft, 1976). The lack of a frequency effect is accounted for by exhaustive search (see Taft & Forster, 1976), while the compoundability effect suggests that recognition of compound words takes place via access to their first constituent, on the basis of which the acceptability of their second constituent is determined.

Finally, Taft and Forster report a comparison of compound words whose first constituent is of high frequency and compound words whose first constituent is of low frequency. For example, while the surface frequency of *loincloth* and *headstand* is matched, the frequency of their first constituents differs in that *loin* is less common than *head*. The finding that items like *loincloth* took longer to recognize than items like *headstand* implied that the words were being recognized through their first constituent. It should be noted, however, that the second frequency count (Carroll *et al.*) reveals a slight bias in favor of the *headstand* items. Also, the frequency of the second constituent of the word was matched between the two conditions over all the items, but was never itself manipulated. From the fact that the first experiment had revealed no difference between a word and a nonword second constituent, it was assumed that the frequency of the second constituent would also be irrelevant. However, it has not been shown directly that it is irrelevant.

An unreported experiment that I have recently carried out suggests that the situation is not in fact as clear-cut as it first seemed. In a lexical decision task, subjects were presented with compound nonwords that were actually reversed compound words (e.g., *stooltoad, berryblack, walkjay*) and these were found to be more difficult to classify as nonwords (as measured both by reaction time and errors) than ordinary compound nonwords (e.g., *brandlink, demonshort, tallmop*). The implication of this is that both constituents seem to have been accessed, not just the first one. This is puzzling given the lack of a difference between *toastpull* items and *spellcung* items reported earlier, though there was a tendency in that experiment for there to be more errors on the *toastpull* items. [Lima and Pollatsek (1983) in fact observed a difference in reaction time between *toastpull* items and *spellcung* items, but this was only significant on the analysis of the subject means and so may have been the result of a couple of oddly behaving items.] Possibly the second constituent is accessed, but normally only after the response has been given. When it is discovered early in the experiment that the two constituents form a word when reversed, the response is perhaps delayed until after the second constituent is accessed. Certainly, the reaction times in the reversed compound word experiment were very long (1146 msec for the reverse compounds and 1075 msec for the controls as opposed to 758 msec for the *toastpull* items of Taft and Forster).

Possibly, then, the conclusion one can draw about the recognition of compound words is that the primary access code is the first stem, but the second stem may also provide a secondary access route. Thus, both *sea* and *weed* may lead to lexical information about *seaweed*, though normally only the former route is used.

III. SYLLABLES AS ACCESS CODES

The evidence presented in Section II supports the idea that the (first) stem of a polymorphemic word is its access code. But is it the whole stem that forms the code? Nothing presented so far precludes the possibility that the access code is in fact the first syllable of the stem. For example, it might be demonstrated that the nonword *bezzle* accesses the lexical entry for *embezzle,* but is this because the access code is *bezzle* or might it be *bezz*? The item *spellcung* accesses the entry for *spell* but is this because *spell* forms a morpheme or because it forms a syllable? Stems of derived words (e.g., *groce* from *grocer*) were shown to be treated in the same way as first syllables of words (e.g., *trink* from *trinket*) in a lexical decision task (see Section II,C,2,a), so it is conceivable that the access code is in fact the first syllable of the stem of the word.

A. The Traditional Syllable

1. Problems of Definition

If the access code is the first syllable of the stem of the word then we must define what is meant by a syllable. The syllable is traditionally defined in pronunciational terms (e.g., Stetson, 1951; Bolinger, 1968; MacKay, 1974) though a precise and unique definition is extremely difficult (see Bell & Hooper, 1978). It is often assumed (e.g., Hansen & Rodgers, 1968) that polysyllabic words with a long or reduced initial vowel are syllabified after that vowel (e.g., *lo/cal, po/lice*), that words with a short vowel and a single following consonant are syllabified after that consonant (e.g., *hon/est*), and that words with two medial consonants are divided between those consonants (e.g., *hos/tage*), though this is by no means generally accepted. Kahn (1976), for example, puts forward an algorithm for syllabification that allows for consonants to be ambisyllabic, for example, *hon/nest* and *hos/stage*. Not only is there a difference of opinion about syllabic structure among linguists, but syllabification seems to differ depending upon whether the word is spoken slowly or quickly (e.g., Bell, 1975). Given these difficulties in specifying the syllabic structure of a word it seems unappealing to say that syllabic structure is directly represented in lexical memory, and more particularly, that the first syllable of a word can be isolated as the access code in visual word recognition. In addition, if a word is represented morphologically within the lexicon, then there will be a number of cases where it cannot also be represented syllabically at the same time. For example, the morphological structure of *actor* is *act* + *or* whereas the syllabic structure is *ac/tor* (or *ac/ctor*). It seems then that on logical grounds either the syllable is not important in visual word recognition or else the syllable must be defined differently. I will be supporting the latter alternative. What, then, is the empirical evidence for the involvement of syllables in visual word recognition?

2. Monosyllables versus Polysyllables

There have been several experiments that have directly compared mono-syllabic and polysyllabic words (e.g., Eriksen, Pollack, & Montague, 1970; Klapp, 1971; Forster & Chambers, 1973) and an account of the more recent studies is given by Henderson (1982). The conclusion drawn from this literature is that monosyllabic items have shorter verbalization latencies than polysyllabic items, but this is only obviously so when verbalization is difficult (either because the items are nonwords or because the reader is unskilled). It appears then that syllabic structure can affect the ease of pronunciation; but this says little about its importance in visual word recognition.

Forster & Chambers (1973) and Fredriksen and Kroll (1976) both failed to find syllabic effects in a lexical decision task where verbalization was not required. However, syllabic effects have been claimed in at least three other studies where pronunciation was not required.

Klapp (1971) employed a "same–different" task where subjects were to say whether two words were the same or different and response time was measured. Monosyllabic and disyllabic words of equal length and frequency were compared. Klapp combined the results for the "same" and "different" conditions and observed that disyllabic words were associated with longer latencies than monosyllabic words. However, on separating the "same" responses from the "different" responses, one finds that there is no difference at all between the "same" response times for the two conditions. If one then examines the items used in the "different" condition, it is evident that the disyllabic pairs (e.g., *cover–color*) have more letters in common in the same position (*c, o,* and *r,* in this case) than the monosyllabic pairs (e.g., *court–clear,* where only the letter *c* is in common), and this can be shown to be a significant difference across all the items that Klapp uses [$t(6) = 2.50, p < .05$]. The more letters that two words have in common, the more difficult it is to make the decision that they are different words (Chambers & Forster, 1975). Therefore, it is not surprising that the disyllabic words in Klapp's study were associated with longer latencies than the monosyllabic words.

On the other hand, Taylor, Miller, and Juola (1977) did obtain a difference between monosyllabic and disyllabic words for the "same" responses in a "same–different" task. They further claim, though, that in this task, case transitions between syllable boundaries (e.g., *MARket*) made no difference when compared to other case transitions (e.g., *MArket* or *MArkET*), implying that the syllable was not a perceptual unit in word identification. However, Taylor *et al.* present their data in such a way that this conclusion is not apparent. Three different types of six-letter disyllabic words were used, with the syllable boundary occurring after either the second letter (e.g., *de/gree*), the third letter (e.g., *mar/ket*) or the fourth letter (e.g., *prop/er*) and it is never actually revealed what happened when the case transition coincided with the syllable boundary. Instead, responses to the different types of case transitions were compared and found not to differ, regardless of whether they coincided with the syllable boundary or not.

A tachistoscopic report task was used by Spoehr and Smith (1973) where the accuracy of report was measured. What they found was that monosyllabic words were more accurately reported than disyllabic words, and they interpreted this to mean that syllables do act as perceptual units in word identification. However, subsequently, Spoehr (1978) observed that this syllable effect only occurred in a situation where phonological encoding was likely to occur for retention purposes, namely, when the stimulus was followed by a mask and there was a delay in the presentation of the response alternatives in a forced choice task.

Even if one were to conclude, however, that polysyllabic words are recognized as easily as monosyllabic words, this would not necessarily imply that syllables are not involved in word recognition. After all, the failure to find a difference between polymorphemic and monomorphemic words (e.g., *credible* versus *tentacle, revive* versus *menace*; Taft, 1976) does not preclude the existence of morphological processing in word recognition. Taft and Forster (1976), therefore, examined the role of the syllable in visual word recognition without comparing polysyllabic and monosyllabic words directly.

3. Interference Effects

If the access code of a polysyllabic word is the first syllable of that word then nonwords that form first syllables (e.g., *ath* from *athlete, scound* from *scoundrel*) should take longer to classify as nonwords than control items (either nonsyllabic first parts of words, e.g., *awf* from *awful, draugh* from *draught,* or nonwords that are not first parts of words, e.g., *arn, spoard*), but this should not be true of nonwords that form final syllables (e.g., *cule* from *molecule, lete* from *athlete*). This was in fact the result obtained by Taft and Forster (1976), along with the corresponding finding for word items; that is, words like *neigh* (the first syllable of *neighbour*) took longer to recognize than words like *shrew* (the first part of *shrewd*) and like *scoff* (not part of another word), while there was no difference between words like *band* (the last syllable of *husband*) and *seat* (not part of another word). These results therefore suggest that the access code is the first syllable of the word.

Taking this further, it follows that the first syllable of a polysyllabic word has the same access status as has an entire monosyllabic word. For example, *ath* is stored in the access file for the recognition of *athlete*, while *ash* is stored in the access file for the recognition of *ash*. This view was supported by the finding (Taft, 1976) that nonword items that began with familiar first syllables (e.g., *athpurt, scoundlan*) were responded to no differently from nonword items that began with monosyllabic words (e.g., *ashpaft, strandlan*), both taking longer to classify than nonwords that began either with the nonsyllabic first part of a word (e.g., *awfpust, draughlan*) or with a nonword that was not the first part of a word (e.g., *arnpolt, spoardlan*), which in turn did not differ. In agreement with this, Manelis and Tharp (1977) compared incorrectly suffixed words (e.g., *lendy, hairen*) with suffixed first syllables (e.g., *murdy, measen*) and suffixed nonwords (e.g., *maldy, leaben*), and found that the first two conditions took equally longer to classify than the third.

One final result that is consistent with the view that the initial syllable is important in word recognition is the finding of Mewhort and Beal (1977) that tachistoscopic identification is more accurate if the word is presented syllable by syllable in a left-to-right fashion than if it is presented nonsyllable by nonsyllable or in a right-to-left fashion. However, the words in this experiment were all eight letters long and therefore mostly polymorphemic. Thus syllable and morpheme may have been confounded.

The idea that the first syllable of a word acts as the access code for that word means that there will be a number of words that share the same access code. In many cases these words will be morphologically related in some way (e.g., *hand, handle, handy*) and the sharing of an access code may somehow facilitate lexical access (perhaps by boosting the frequency of the access code). However, there will also be cases where the words sharing an access code are not related (e.g., *kind, kindle, kindergarten*). It is possible that in these cases the access code representations are listed separately from each other, and that recognition of the lower frequency words is slowed by the mistaken access of the code for the higher frequency words. That is, the recognition of *kindergarten* may be slowed by the accessing of *kind*. Unpublished experiments by myself and Dianne Bradley lend support to this possibility, where lexical decision times to words beginning with a high frequency word (e.g., *kindergarten, bigot, dogma*) were found to be longer than those to control words.

B. The Basic Orthographic Syllabic Structure (BOSS)

In Section III,A,1 it was pointed out how there were problems involved with the idea that the lexicon includes representations of syllabic structure defined in pronunciational terms. There are additional problems if it is true that the access code is the first syllable of the word. In particular, the fact that the syllabic structure and the morphological structure of many words does not coincide (e.g., *ac/tor* and *act + or, tes/ting* and *test + ing*) means that the access code for the suffixed word (e.g., *ac, tes*) will be different from the access code for its stem (*act, test*), and this runs counter to the conclusions drawn in Section II,C,4 about suffixed word recognition.

The problem in this case might be resolved, though, if it were assumed that the access code is in fact the first syllable of the stem of the word. Thus *act*, being the stem of *actor*, is also the access code for *actor*. Similarly, while the related words *nature* and *natural* have different first syllables (*na* and *nat*, respectively) it can be claimed that the access code for *natural* is *na* since this is the first syllable of its stem (*nature*). Also one would need to claim that the access code for *gently* is *gen* since this is the first syllable of its stem (*gentle*) even though the syllabification of *gently* as *gen* and *tly* leads to the phonotactic violation /tl/ (see Taft, 1979a). It is examples like this which make this modified account of the involvement of phonologically defined syllables in visual word recognition unappealing, as well as the fact that normal visual word recognition does not appear to involve a phonological code (see Section I,B).

Instead of the access code being the syllable that is involved in pronunciation, Taft (1979a) offers an alternative. This is a syllable that is orthographically and morphologically defined, called the basic orthographic syllabic structure (or BOSS). The BOSS of a word includes all consonants following the first vowel group of the stem morpheme, unless principles of orthographic co-occurrence (e.g., *tl*) are violated (what I have termed orthotactic violations, but what Henderson, 1982, more properly has termed graphotactic violations). Thus the BOSS of both *gentle* and *gently* is *gent*, and the BOSS of both *nature* and *natural* is *nat*.

Essentially, the BOSS can be seen as a broadly defined stem. For example, the *le* of *gentle* and the *ure* of *nature* are not generally taken to be suffixes in these words (except by etymologists), yet the BOSS notion in effect treats them as such, as it does the *ain* of *certain*, the *y* of *candy*, the *on* of *button*, the *ow* of *shadow*, the *e* of *shade*, and so on. In this way, the access mechanism for polysyllabic words (or monosyllabic words with a final silent *e*) need be no different from that for derived words. For example, the access procedure for the words *closure, closet,* and *close* can be the same, namely, a left-to-right parsing procedure leading to the accessing of a representation *clos* in the access file. It is worth noting that the idea that the first syllable includes all the consonants following the first vowel has also been suggested on phonological grounds (Anderson & Jones, 1974), without consideration of morphological structure.

Evidence for the BOSS was provided by Taft (1979a). Words that were presented with their BOSS boundary emphasized by a change of case (e.g.,

LANTern) or a gap (e.g., *lant ern*) were faster to recognize in a lexical decision task than were words that were presented with their pronunciationally defined syllable so emphasized (e.g., *LANtern* or *lan tern*), though they were slower than nondisrupted words (e.g., *lantern*). It is interesting to note though that the items whose BOSS was also the BOSS of another related word, e.g., *entry* (related to *enter*), *radar* (related to *radio*), *movie* (related to *move*), *verbal* (related to *verb*), appeared, if anything, to produce a reverse effect (i.e., BOSS division being slower than syllabic division—e.g., *RADar* being slower than *RAdar*). One might have expected that such items would have actually shown the strongest effect in favor of the BOSS division. However, it is possible that the presentation of these words with their BOSS emphasized actually led to interference from the related word. For example, the presentation of *radar* as *RADar* may have facilitated access to *radio* and thus slowed down response times to *radar*.

It is possibly this observation that can account for the failure of Lima and Pollatsek (1983) to replicate the BOSS/syllable difference using the gapping procedure (e.g., *lant ern*) as well as in two experiments where a fragment of the word (e.g., *lant*) was presented prior to the presentation of the whole word. These authors looked post hoc at those cases where the BOSS was a word in its own right (e.g., the *stab* of *stable*), and this appeared to be irrelevant, but they did not look at those cases where the BOSS was also the BOSS of another word.

More likely though, it seems that the subjects in Lima and Pollatsek's experiments were doing something rather different than those in my own experiments. Though it is unclear what this was and why. In addition to their failure to find a BOSS/syllable difference, Lima and Pollatsek observed that nonwords that were disrupted (e.g., *ral parch* or *ralp arch*) took longer to respond to than nonwords that were not (*ralparch*), yet this was not so in my experiment (where disruption was achieved by a change of case). It should be noted though that, while Lima and Pollatsek failed to replicate my results, they also failed to replicate their own, in that their two experiments using the fragment-priming technique gave different patterns of results. So it seems that the BOSS effect, if it exists, is either very weak and highly transitory, or more interestingly, only manifests itself with certain subjects; for example, those with a sophisticated knowledge of language (and perhaps I happened to use more of these subjects than did Lima and Pollatsek).

A further experiment using a different paradigm was presented by Taft (1979a) to support the BOSS notion. Nonwords which were constructed by removing the final silent *e* from words (e.g., *ston, cring*) took longer to classify than control nonwords (*slon, bling*). Items like *stin* (the first part, but not the BOSS of *sting* or *stink*) were not used since it was shown by

Taft and Forster (1976; see Section III,A,3) that nonwords that were first parts of words (e.g., *draugh*) were responded to in the same way as nonwords that were not (e.g., *spoard*). The silent *e* finding was also obtained with word items, e.g., *shin* (from *shine*) and *stag* (from *stage*) taking longer than *swan* and *slum*. While it may be possible to give an explanation for this finding without resort to the BOSS account as I have defined it, it is certainly consistent with the view that the access code does not include any vowels that are separated orthographically from the first set of vowels in the word (as in the BOSS account).

In summary, support for the idea that words are accessed through their first syllable defined on orthographic and morphological grounds comes only from my own experiments (and perhaps Manelis & Tharp's suffixed nonword finding). The failure of Lima and Pollatsek to support the BOSS view does not inspire confidence in the idea, but one still needs to account for the discrepancy between our results.

Derivational relationships between words (e.g., *final, finality, finalize, finalization*) are frequently taught in schools at least to some extent, on the assumption that an understanding of the structure of words will aid reading, spelling, and vocabulary development, and the experiments described in Section II,C do indeed suggest that such relationships play a role in word recognition. What I would like to propose is that the teaching of the relationships between words could go further than just the teaching of traditional derivational relationships. For example, the words *final, finale, finish, finite, confine, refine, definite, infinitive,* and even *finicky, finance,* and *fine* all have the same origin (the Latin root *fin*—conveying the concept of "termination") and this is seen in the common component *fin* (which is the BOSS of each of these words). Teaching words in terms of their BOSSes would therefore enrich the pupil's knowledge of relationships between words and the structural composition of words, as well as allowing the words to be broken down into manageable chunks. It would be interesting to ascertain whether subjects who show a BOSS/syllable difference in word recognition experiments have a greater facility with the language than subjects who do not.

IV. AN ALTERNATIVE THEORETICAL FRAMEWORK

A. Possible Difficulties for an Inflexible Code

My description of the word recognition process to this stage has assumed that there is a single coded representation for each word in the access file, though this representation may be the same for a number of related words. Therefore this is a highly inflexible system whereby the form-driven processing of a word can only take place via this code. This strong position, however, warrants reconsideration given that there is evidence that parts of the word other than the BOSS (or even the stem morpheme) play a role in word recognition.

1. Word Extremities

It was indicated in Section I,E that the extremities of a word (i.e., initial and final letter groupings) may act as an access code. Forster and Gartlan (1975, cited in Forster, 1976) performed a lexical decision experiment where the presentation of a word (e.g., *steadily*) was immediately preceded by the display of either its first and last two letters (*st   ly*), its middle four letters (*eadi*   ), its first four letters (*stea*   ), or its last four letters (*dily*). They found that only the first of these conditions led to priming of the word, relative to a condition where there was no prior display. That is, only the presentation of the extremities of the word allowed processing to get underway. Forster interpreted this in terms of the access file being divided into "bins" whereby words with the same access code (i.e., the same first and last letter groupings) are stored together. Thus prior presentation of the first and last letters allows the correct bin to be accessed in advance of the presentation of the whole word. (The fact that presentation of the first four letters did not lead to priming is not a problem for the BOSS account or first syllable or first morpheme account, since in the majority of items the first four letters did not coincide with the BOSS, first syllable, or first morpheme).

McCusker *et al.* (1981) also observed a priming effect with the outside letters of four-letter words compared to the inside letters, in both a naming task and a semantic decision task (animal or nonanimal). Unlike Forster and Gartlan, however, McCusker *et al.* found what seemed to be a priming effect with the inside letters relative to a "no prime" condition, though no analyses of item means were presented and thus all of their results must be considered dubious (c.f. Clark, 1973).

Interpretation of results using the priming technique are complicated by the fact that responses to nonwords seem to be facilitated by the prior presentation of just about any part of the item (Forster & Gartlan, 1975; Lima & Pollatsek, 1983). Forster proposes that this is because all bins are searched when a nonword is presented, so that prior presentation of even the middle letters of the nonword would allow the search in one of the bins to get underway (namely, the bin that is appropriate for words with those middle letters). This, however, is illogical in that there can exist no bins that list words by their middle letters, or else words would be primed by their interior letters. Perhaps instead, the priming effects observed in this task are all simply letter-priming effects, and this is actually counterbalanced by an inhibitory effect when the letter grouping that preceded a word item looks like a nonword (i.e., middles like *easi,* first halves like *stea,* and second halves like *dily*).

The idea that word extremities act as access codes was also claimed by Stanners *et al.* (1971) and Stanners and Forbach (1973) on the basis of lexical decision experiments where the frequency of occurrence of the first two and last two letters of the items was varied. Words with common beginnings and endings were responded to more quickly than those with rare beginnings or endings, but as Stanners and Forbach themselves point out, this was probably a word frequency effect since letter frequency and word frequency were confounded. The important result, though, was that nonwords with common beginnings and endings were responded to more slowly than the other nonword conditions. This implies that the number of words with the same access code as the nonword item (i.e., the same first and last letters) affected reaction times. However, it could alternatively be that there was a general effect of overall word similarity, since this was confounded in the experiment. That is, the number of words which were one letter different from the nonword could have been what affected reaction time (Coltheart *et al.,* 1977), regardless of where in the nonword that one letter was.

So the evidence for the extremities of words being important in word recognition is by no means clear-cut. It is interesting to note though, that the view of the access code that I have been espousing in this paper actually predicts some sort of processing of the extremities of words independent of the processing of the rest of the word. In particular, it has been proposed that both prefixes and inflectional suffixes are strippped from the word prior to lexical access, and therefore there must be preprocessing of the beginning and the ending of a word in order to ascertain whether there is such an affix present.

2. Interference Effects

From a series of lexical decison experiments looking at interference effects, Chambers (1979) concluded that there are multiple access codes in word recognition. When words were transformed into nonwords by the substitution of one consonant (e.g., *lotor* from *motor, fibal* form *final*), Chambers found that these items took longer to classify than nonwords that were not so constructed (e.g., *tosol, gimal*), regardless of whether the substituted letter was the first, middle, or final consonant. When words were transformed into nonwords by the transposition of two letters (e.g., *ottol* from *total, pesron* from *person*) these nonwords took longer to classify than control items (e.g., *ottid, nesrol*) when the transposition occurred in both the initial and middle positions, but the middle position transformations led to greater difficulties than the initial position transformations. (Final position transformations were not examined). It appears therefore that even when the BOSS of a word is not intact within a nonword, there can still be sufficient similarity to that word for interference to occur. Chambers suggests from this that all of the letters of a word can act as an access code.

It is possible, however, to explain Chambers' results in terms of the BOSS being the primary access code if one assumes that the sensory-to-lexical match need not be exact in order for access to occur. Consider the nonwords *ottal* and *ottid* for example. If one assumes that *ott* is close enough to *tot* (the BOSS of *total*) for a match to be made, then the accessing process will go further to ascertain whether the remaining letters of the stimulus (i.e., *al*) can combine with the accessed entry (i.e., *tot*) to form a word. Since they can, there will be interference compared to *ottid*, where *id* cannot combine with *tot*. While the same argument could be stretched to explain the letter substitution results (e.g., *fib* is sufficiently similar to *fin* for *fibal* to access the lexical entry for *final*), it should be noted that many of the letter substitution items used by Chambers began with the BOSSes of other words (e.g., *fib* is the BOSS of *fibre*) while the control items did not (e.g., the *gim* of *gimal*). Thus response times could have been lengthened for this reason rather than because of letter substitution.

To say that an inexact sensory-to-lexical match is sufficient for access to occur suggests that there is a criterion of similarity that has to be met. Such a suggestion is compatible with a threshold model of word recognition, namely the logogen model of Morton (e.g., 1969, 1979).

B. The Logogen Account

According to the logogen model of lexical access, stimulus features passively raise the activation level of all logogens (or lexical entries) that correspond to words which have those features. Once a logogen reaches some preset activation threshold, the word corresponding to that logogen can be recognized. However, a modification to this account must be made in order to explain interference effects. For example, if the logogen for the word *person* were sufficiently activated by the stimulus features of *pesron*, then *pesron*, would be incorrectly recognized as *person*, rather than being responded to slowly as a nonword as Chambers found.

Coltheart *et al.* (1977) put forward a modification to the logogen model in order to account for interference effects. They supposed that a nonword response is made when no logogens reach their threshold value before a certain deadline. This deadline can be lengthened, though, if there is a lot of activity registered in the system, which would be the case when a logogen has been highly activated but not to threshold level. Such a view, however, does not account for interference effects with word items, which have been observed by Taft and Forster (1975, 1976; Taft, 1979a) as well as by Chambers (1979), who found that the letter transposition effect occurred with word items as well as nonword items (e.g., *slat* being confused with *salt*).

As an alternative, then, one can either say that the response to a word item can also be delayed by high activity in other logogens (which Morton, 1969, in fact suggests), or that when a logogen reaches threshold, the word is compared back to the sensory representation and, if it does not exactly match then the outcome of the next logogen to reach threshold is evaluated (Taft, 1979b). This latter explanation is in fact a combination of the logogen and search models, whereby the search set is restricted or "marked off" (Rubenstein, Garfield, & Millikan, 1970) on the basis of logogen activation.

Whichever of these alternatives is correct, the interference on response times to items like *ottal* could result either from there being sufficient features in *ott* to activate a logogen *tot,* or from there being sufficient features in *ottal* to activate a logogen *total.* The latter interpretation (which is suggested by Chambers, 1979) is of course the more flexible of the two, since it allows for any features of the word to potentially activate the logogen. One can account for the possibility that some features might be more important than others (e.g., the BOSS of the word) by saying that such features are given more weight when the logogens are activated.

There is a problem with this view, however. Since it assumes that each of the logogens represents a full word (though without its inflections; cf. Murrell & Morton, 1974), words coming from the same stem will be stored separately. This means that *reproach* and *approach,* for example, will be represented by different logogens; yet Taft (1979b; see Section II,B,3) has shown that response times to *reproach* are influenced by the frequency of *approach.* Similarly the word *sharpness* appears to be influenced by the frequency of its stem *sharp* (Bradley, 1979). Any view tht claims that the sensory-to-lexical matching is performed on the whole word will have difficulty accounting for these findings.

V. SUMMARY AND CONCLUSIONS

This article has attempted to provide a critical review of the evidence for and against the involvement of morphemes and syllables in the decoding of visually presented words. The position taken has been that a word is recognized when its access code, which is a representation of the first syllable (orthographically defined) of its stem morpheme, is located in the recognition device of the lexical system. The recognition device within the serial search model (Forster, 1976) is the orthographic access file, while within the logogen model (Morton, 1979) it is the set of visual input logogens.

When a word is to be read, any prefixes and common inflectional suffixes are identified and stripped off. The remaining stem of the word is then parsed, perhaps in a left-to-right fashion in order for the access code to be isolated. Once a match has been successful within the recognition device, the full details of the lexical item which has been accessed become available.

The possibility of a more flexible system than the one just described was examined in Section II,B,4 and Section IV. It was suggested that a number of access codes might be available (including a representation of the full word) and that these are all used in the recognition of a word. While this view might be embraced for its eclecticism, the evidence in favor of it is not at this stage very strong. Inter- and intrasubject flexibility has been demonstrated in the use of phonological information in visual word recognition (e.g., Hawkins, Reicher, Rogers, & Peterson, 1976; Coltheart *et al.*, 1977), but this can be seen as flexibility in the use of different recognition devices (i.e., visual and phonological) rather than flexibility within one recognition device as suggested here. It should be noted, though, that the single access code account advocated in this article need not itself be entirely inflexible, since one can incorporate into it the idea of a criterial basis for the decision that a lexical match has been made. The account is also flexible in the sense that people who are unaware of the structural relationships between words would not be expected to use a morphologically based access code.

My discussion of the decoding of words in lexical access has concentrated on experiments using single-word presentations. As such, one may wish to argue that what I have said has little if any relevance to the reading of words in text. However, as mentioned at the beginning, current experimental evidence suggests that context does not qualitatively alter the lexical access process; that is, word recognition in text is the same as word recognition out of text (except perhaps when the word is highly predictable from the context). In accord with this, the few studies on morphological processing that have looked at words in context (the letter cancellation work of Drewnowski & Healy, 1980; and Smith & Sterling, 1982) have produced results that are entirely consistent with the results of single word studies. Thus it seems fair to say that single word paradigms are a valid way of examining form-driven processing in reading.

REFERENCES

Anderson, J., & Jones, C. (1974). Three theses concerning phonological representations. *Journal of Linguistics,* **10,** 1–26.
Andrews, S. (1982). Phonological recoding: Is the regularity effect consistent? *Memory & Cognition,* **10,** 565–575.

Anshen, F., & Aronoff, M. (1981). Morphological productivity and phonological transparency. *Canadian Journal of Linguistics,* **26,** 63–72.

Aronoff, M., & Schvaneveldt, R. (1978). Testing morphological productivity. *Annals of the New York Academy of Sciences,* **318,** 106–114.

Bell, A. (1975). *If speakers can't count syllables, what can they do?* Paper presented at the Indiana University Linguistics Circle.

Bell, A., & Hooper, J. B. (Eds.) (1978). *Syllables and segments.* Amsterdam: North Holland Publ.

Beyn, E. S. (1958). Peculiarities of thought in patients with sensory aphasia. *Language and Speech,* **1,** 233–244.

Bolinger, D. (1968). *Aspects of language.* New York: Harcourt.

Bradley, D. C. (1979). Lexical representation of derivational relation. In M. Aronoff & M. L. Kean (Eds.), *Juncture.* Cambridge, Mass: MIT Press.

Bradshaw, J. L. (1975). Three interrelated problems in reading: A review. *Memory & Cognition,* **3,** 123–134.

Carroll, J. B., Davies, P., & Richman, B. (1971). *The American Heritage word frequency book.* Boston: Houghton-Mifflin.

Cattell, J. McK. (1886). The time it takes to see and name objects. *Mind,* **11,** 63–65.

Chambers, S. M. (1979). Letter and order information in lexical access. *Journal of Verbal Learning and Verbal Behavior,* **18,** 225–241.

Chambers, S. M., & Forster, K. I. (1975). Evidence for lexical access in a simultaneous matching task. *Memory & Cognition,* **3,** 549–559.

Clark, H. H. (1973). The language-as-fixed-effect fallacy: A critique of language statistics in psychological research. *Journal of Verbal Learning and Verbal Behavior,* **12,** 335–359.

Coltheart, M. (1980). Reading, phonological recoding and deep dyslexia. In M. Coltheart, K. Patterson, & J. C. Marshall (Eds.), *Deep dyslexia.* London: Routledge & Kegan Paul.

Coltheart, M., Besner, D., Jonasson, J. T., & Davelaar, E. (1979). Phonological encoding in the lexical decision task. *Quarterly Journal of Experimental Psychology,* **31,** 489–507.

Coltheart, M., Davelaar, E. Jonasson, J. T., & Besner, D. (1977). Access to the internal lexicon. In S. Dornic (Ed.), *Attention and performance VI.* New York: Academic Press.

Cutler, A. (1981). Degrees of transparency in word formation. *Canadian Journal of Linguistics,* **26,** 73–77.

Cutler, A. (1983). Lexical complexity and sentence processing. In G. B. Flores d'Arcais & R. J. Jarvella (Eds.), *The process of language understanding.* New York: Wiley.

Drewnowski, A., & Healy, A. F. (1980). Missing -ing in reading: Letter detection errors on word endings. *Journal of Verbal Learning and Verbal Behavior,* **19,** 247–262.

Eriksen, C. W., Pollack, M. D., & Montague, W. E. (1970). Implicit speech: Mechanism in perceptual encoding? *Journal of Experimental Psychology,* **84,** 502–507.

Estes, W. K. (1975). The locus of inferential and perceptual processes in letter identification. *Journal of Experimental Psychology: General,* **104,** 122–145.

Forster, K. I. (1976). Accessing the mental lexicon. In E. C. J. Walker & R. J. Wales (Eds.), *New approaches to language mechanisms.* Amsterdam: North-Holland Publ.

Forster, K. I. (1981). Priming and the effects of sentence and lexical context on naming time: Evidence for autonomous lexical processing. *Quarterly Journal of Experimental Psychology,* **33A,** 465–495.

Forster, K. I., & Chambers, S. M. (1973). Lexical access and naming time. *Journal of Verbal Learning and Verbal Behavior,* **12,** 627–635.

Forster, K. I., & Gartlan, G. (1975). *Hash coding and search processes in lexical access.* Paper presented at the Second Experimental Psychology Conference, University of Sydney.

Fredriksen, J. R., & Kroll, J. F. (1976). Spelling and sound: Approaches to the internal lexicon. *Journal of Experimental Psychology: Human Perception and Performance,* **2,** 361–379.

Fromkin, V. A. (Ed.) (1973). *Speech errors as linguistic evidence.* The Hague: Mouton.

Garrett, M. F. (1976). Syntactic processes in sentence production. In R. J. Wales & E. C. J. Walker (Eds.), *New approaches to language mechanisms.* Amsterdam: North-Holland Publ.

Gibson, E. J., & Guinet, L. (1971). Perception of inflections in brief visual presentations of words. *Journal of Verbal Learning and Verbal Behavior, 10,* 182–189.

Gibson, E. J., Pick, A., Osser, H., & Hammond, M. (1962). The role of grapheme–phoneme correspondence in the perception of words. *American Journal of Psychology, 75,* 554–570.

Goodman, K. S. (1970). Reading: A psycholinguistic guessing game. In H. Singer & R. B. Ruddell (Eds.), *Theoretical models and processes of reading.* Newark, Del.: International Reading Association.

Hansen, D., & Rodgers, T. S. (1968). An exploration of psycholinguistic units in initial reading. In K. S. Goodman (Ed.), *The psycholinguistic nature of the reading process.* Detroit: Wayne State Univ. Press.

Hawkins, H. L., Reicher, G. M., Rogers, M., & Peterson, L. (1976). Flexible coding in word recognition. *Journal of Experimental Psychology: Human Perception and Performance, 2,* 380–385.

Henderson, L. (1982). *Orthography and word recognition in reading.* New York: Academic Press.

Humphreys, G. W., Evett, L. J., & Taylor, P. E. (1982). Automatic phonological priming in visual word recognition. *Memory & Cognition, 10,* 576–590.

Jakobson, R. (1971). Toward a linguistic classification of aphasic impairments. In R. Jakobson (Ed.), *Selected writings II.* The Hague: Mouton.

Kahn, D. (1976). *Syllable-based generalizations in English phonology.* Unpublished Ph.D. thesis, Massachusetts Institute of Technology.

Kempley, S. T., & Morton, J. (1982). The effects of priming with regularly and irregularly related words in auditory word recognition. *British Journal of Psychology, 73,* 441–454.

Klapp, S. T. (1971). Implicit speech inferred from response latencies in same-different decisions. *Journal of Experimental Psychology, 91,* 262–267.

Kučera, H., & Francis, W. N. (1967). *Computational analysis of present-day American English.* Providence, R. I.: Brown Univ. Press.

Lima, S. D., & Pollatsek, A. (1983). Lexical access via an orthographic code? The Basic Orthographic Syllabic Structure (BOSS) reconsidered. *Journal of Verbal Learning and Verbal Behavior, 22,* 310–332.

McClelland, J. L., & Johnston, J. C. (1977). The role of familiar units in the perception of words and nonwords. *Perception & Psychophysics, 22,* 249–261.

McCusker, L. K., Bias, R. G., & Hillinger, M. L. (1981). Phonological recoding and reading. *Psychological Bulletin, 89,* 217–245.

McCusker, L. K., Gough, P. B., & Bias, R. G. (1981). Word recognition inside out and outside in. *Journal of Experimental Psychology: Human Perception and Performance, 7,* 538–551.

MacKay, D. G. (1974). Aspects of the syntax of behavior: Syllable structure and speech rate. *Quarterly Journal of Experimental Psychology, 26,* 642–657.

MacKay, D. G. (1976). On the retrieval and lexical structure of verbs. *Journal of Verbal Learning and Verbal Behavior, 15,* 169–182.

MacKay, D. G. (1978). Derivational rules and the internal lexicon. *Journal of Verbal Learning and Verbal Behavior, 17,* 61–71.

MacKay, D. G. (1979). Lexical insertion, inflection, and derivation: Creative processes in word production. *Journal of Psycholinguistic Research, 8,* 477–498.

Manelis, L., & Tharp, D. A. (1977). The processing of affixed words. *Memory & Cognition, 4,* 53–61.

Marcel, T. (1980). Surface dyslexia and beginning reading. In M. Coltheart, K. Patterson, & J. C. Marshall (Eds.), *Deep dyslexia*. London: Routledge & Kegan Paul.

Marshall, J. C., & Newcombe, F. (1973). Patterns of paralexia: a psycholinguistic approach. *Journal of Psycholinguistic Research, 2,* 175–199.

Martin, R. C. (1982). The pseudohomophone effect: The role of visual similarity in nonword decisions. *Quarterly Journal of Experimental Psychology, 34A,* 395–409.

Mayzner, M. S., & Tresselt, M. E. (1965). Tables of single-letter and digram frequency counts for various word-length and letter-position combinations. *Psychonomic Monograph Supplements, 1,* 13–32.

Mewhort, D. J. K., & Beal, A. L. (1977). Mechanisms of word identification. *Journal of Experimental Psychology: Human Perception and Performance, 3,* 629–640.

Mewhort, D. J. K., & Campbell, A. J. (1980). The rate of word integration and the overprinting paradigm. *Memory & Cognition, 8,* 15–25.

Morton, J. (1964). A model for continuous language behavior. *Language and Speech, 7,* 40–70.

Morton, J. (1969). Interaction of information in word recognition. *Psychological Review, 76,* 165–178.

Morton, J. (1979). Facilitation in word recognition: Experiments causing change in the logogen model. In P. A. Kolers, M. Wrolstad, & H. Bouma (Eds.), *Processing of visible language I*. New York: Plenum.

Murrell, G. A., & Morton, J. (1974). Word recognition and morphemic structure. *Journal of Experimental Psychology, 102,* 963–968.

O'Connor, R. E. (1975). *An investigation into the word frequency effect*. Unpublished honors thesis, Monash University.

Osgood, C. E., & Hoosain, R. (1974). Salience of the word as a unit in the perception of language. *Perception & Psychophysics, 15,* 168–192.

Patterson, K. (1980). Derivational errors. In M. Coltheart, K. Patterson, & J. C. Marshall (Eds.), *Deep dyslexia*. London: Routledge & Kegan Paul.

Reisner, P. (1972). *Storage and retrieval of polymorphemic words in the internal lexicon*. Unpublished Ph.D. thesis, Lehigh University.

Rubenstein, H., Garfield, L., & Millikan, J. A. (1970). Homographic entries in the internal lexicon. *Journal of Verbal Learning and Verbal Behavior, 9,* 487–494.

Rubenstein, H., Lewis, S. S., & Rubenstein, M. A. (1971). Evidence for phonemic recoding in visual word recognition. *Journal of Verbal Learning and Verbal Behavior, 10,* 645–657.

Rubin, D. C. (1975). Within word structure in the tip-of-the-tongue phenomenon. *Journal of Verbal Learning and Verbal Behavior, 14,* 392–397.

Rubin, G. S., Becker, C. A., & Freeman, R. H. (1979). Morphological structure and its effect on visual word recognition. *Journal of Verbal Learning and Verbal Behavior, 18,* 757–767.

Shaffer, L. H. (1975). Control processes in typing. *Quarterly Journal of Experimental Psychology, 27,* 419–433.

Smith, P. T., & Sterling, C. M. (1982). Factors affecting the perceived morphemic structure of written words. *Journal of Verbal Learning and Verbal Behavior, 21,* 704–721.

Snodgrass, J. G., & Jarvella, R. J. (1972). Some linguistic determinants of word classification times. *Psychonomic Science, 27,* 220–222.

Spoehr, K. T. (1978). Phonological encoding in visual word recognition. *Journal of Verbal Learning and Verbal Behavior, 17,* 127–141.

Spoehr, K. T., & Smith, E. E. (1973). The role of syllables in perceptual processing. *Cognitive Psychology, 5,* 71–89.

Stanners, R. F., & Forbach, G. B. (1973). Analysis of letter strings in word recognition. *Journal of Experimental Psychology, 98,* 31–35.

Stanners, R. F., Forbach, G. B., & Headley, D. B. (1971). Decision and search processes in word-nonword classification. *Journal of Experimental Psychology, 90,* 45–50.

Stanners, R. F., Neiser, J. J., Hernon, W. P., & Hall, R. (1979a). Memory representation for morphologically related words. *Journal of Verbal Learning and Verbal Behavior, 18,* 399–412.

Stanners, R. F., Neiser, J. J., & Painton, S. (1979b). Memory representations for prefixed words. *Journal of Verbal Learning and Verbal Behavior, 18,* 733–743.

Stetson, R. H. (1951). *Motor phonetics: A study of speech movements in action.* Amsterdam: North-Holland Publ.

Swift, D. J. (1977). *The effects of context, word frequency, and internal redundancy in reading and word perception.* Unpublished Ph.D. thesis, University of New Hampshire.

Taft, M. (1976). *Morphological and syllabic analysis in word recognition.* Unpublished Ph.D. thesis, Monash University.

Taft, M. (1979a). Lexical access via an orthographic code: The Basic Orthographic Syllabic Structure (BOSS). *Journal of Verbal Learning and Verbal Behavior, 18,* 21–39.

Taft, M. (1979b). Recognition of affixed words and the word frequency effect. *Memory & Cognition, 7,* 263–272.

Taft, M. (1981). Prefix stripping revisited. *Journal of Verbal Learning and Verbal Behavior, 20,* 289–297.

Taft, M. (1982). An alternative to grapheme—phoneme conversion rules? *Memory & Cognition, 10,* 465–474.

Taft, M., & Forster, K. I. (1975). Lexical storage and retrieval of prefixed words. *Journal of Verbal Learning and Verbal Behavior, 14,* 638–647.

Taft, M., & Forster, K. I. (1976). Lexical storage and retrieval of polymorphemic and polysyllabic words. *Journal of Verbal Learning and Verbal Behavior, 15,* 607–620.

Taylor, G. A., Miller, T. J., & Juola, J. F. (1977). Isolating visual units in the perception of words and nonwords. *Perception & Psychophysics, 21,* 377–386.

Tulving, E. (1972). Episodic and semantic memory. In E. Tulving & W. Donaldson (Eds.), *Organization of memory.* New York: Academic Press.

WHAT DO WE REALLY KNOW ABOUT SEMANTIC CONTEXT EFFECTS DURING READING?

CURTIS A. BECKER

AT&T Information Systems
Lincroft, New Jersey

I. INTRODUCTION

As Gough, Alford, and Holley-Wilcox (1981) point out, many of us take great comfort in the notion that the "context" provided by something we have just read helps us in reading what comes next. For research purposes, a context has been variously specified as a single word (Meyer & Schvaneveldt, 1971), as an incomplete sentence (Schuberth & Eimas, 1977), as the gist of a pair of sentences (Foss, 1982), and as the general theme of a passage (Bransford & Johnson, 1972). Typically, the context of interest

125

Copyright © 1985 by Academic Press, Inc.
All rights of reproduction in any form reserved.

is defined more by example than by formal description, especially for the more complex forms of context. This trade-off between complexity and definability has led many of us to work with the simpler forms of context and to assume that our findings will generalize to the more complex forms.

Gough *et al.* suggest, though, that the assumption of generality may be naive. They report a study in which a short text passage was presented one word at a time, and subjects were asked to name each word aloud as quickly as they could. Naming times for words in a normal text passage were no different from the naming times for the same words presented in a scrambled order. In other studies using single word contexts (e.g., context—*doctor,* target word—*nurse*), word naming times are faster in related contexts than in unrelated contexts (Becker & Killion, 1977; Meyer, Schvaneveldt, & Ruddy, 1975). Although many aspects of the procedures used by Gough *et al.* are comparable to those used in studies of single-word contexts, the more complex context provided by the text passage did not appear to affect word naming in the same way as the simpler contexts. It could well be, then, that the way we use contextual information differs across levels of complexity. If this conclusion stands up to additional tests, it may well signal the end of a currently active line of inquiry.

In contrast to the word-naming data, other findings have supported the notion that context has some effect for complex materials. Monitoring subjects' eye movements during the reading of short text passages, Erlich and Rayner (1981) report that words predictable in a context are fixated for a shorter time than are unexpected words. Eisenberg (1981) has shown that highly predictable content words are fixated for shorter durations than less predictable but contextually appropriate content words. Also, highly predictable function words are more likely to be skipped than are less predictable function words. Although these results suggest that there may well be context effects in complex text materials, it is an open question whether these effects are the same ones found using single-word contexts. To further complicate matters, there is considerable discussion about just what is measured by the duration of an eye fixation (Just & Carpenter, 1980; Rayner, Slowiaczek, Clifton, & Bertera, 1983) and, therefore, some uncertainty about which measure of fixation duration is most appropriate (Inhoff, 1984).

The purpose of this article is to further examine the question of whether there must be a conceptual dividing line between simple forms of context and complex forms of context. After introducing the basic procedures, I will focus on five topics that have helped to clarify our understanding of the effects of relatively simple contexts. Then, I will describe one theoretical position that has had a considerable influence on my thinking. Finally, I will present two new experiments that will directly address the generality of what we currently understand about the effects of the simpler forms of context.

II. BASIC PROCEDURES AND DATA OF INTEREST

Throughout much of this article, the discussion will focus on experiments that use a single word as a target stimulus and precede that target word with various kinds of cue stimuli. Minimally, two kinds of cues are used, cues that are semantically related to the target word and cues that are semantically unrelated to the target (e.g., Meyer & Schvaneveldt, 1971). More analytic experiments (the more recent ones) also use a third kind of cue, one that is semantically neutral, one that provides no semantic information at all (e.g., Becker, 1980; Fischler & Bloom, 1979; Neely, 1976, 1977; Schuberth & Eimas, 1977; Stanovich & West, 1979, 1981, 1983a). One of two responses is typically made to the target stimulus. Either the subject says the word aloud, or the subject classifies the target as a correctly spelled word or as a nonword (a lexical decision task). Differences in reaction time and in error rates as a function of the different kinds of cues are the data of interest. Faster reaction times and fewer errors for the related cue condition compared to the neutral cue condition is the **facilitation effect** of putting a word in an appropriate semantic context. Slower reaction times and more errors for words following an unrelated cue compared to a neutral cue is the **interference effect** from recognizing a word in an inappropriate context. The difference between related and unrelated cue conditions is the total effect of semantic context.

A second-order analysis of these data has shown promise for identifying qualitatively different context effects. The analysis focuses on the relative contributions of facilitation and interference to the total context effect. Under certain conditions, nearly all of the total effect comes from facilitation, and this pattern is labeled **facilitation dominant.** Under other conditions, most of the total context effect derives from interference in recognizing words following an unrelated context, an **interference dominant** pattern (Becker, 1980). A third pattern occasionally appears, one in which the facilitation and interference effects are about equal. These patterns appear to be a mixing of some subjects producing facilitation dominance and other subjects producing interference dominance (Eisenberg & Becker, 1982). Currently, what appears to control which of the three patterns is obtained is some combination of the general properties of the semantic relationships used in an experiment and the instructions that are given to the subjects.

III. THE EFFECTS OF SIMPLE SEMANTIC CONTEXTS

To guide this discussion of context effects for relatively simple materials, I have selected five topics that have driven much of the research. Briefly, the topics are as follows:

1. Are word recognition and the effects of context automatic, or do they demand attention?
2. Can semantic effects occur during the processing that leads to the identification of a word or are the effects produced after word identification?
3. Are there fundamental differences between single-word contexts and context provided by short sentences?
4. Are there fundamental differences between skilled and less skilled readers in their use of context?
5. What are the critical methodological issues?

As will become clear, there are merits in each of the positions that have been taken on these topics.

A. Attention, Word Recognition, and Context Effects

Considerable time, effort, and resources have been devoted to trying to decide whether the act of recognizing a stimulus occurs automatically or whether it demands some of our attentional processing capacity. A strong definition of the distinction between automatic and attentional holds that an automatic process can execute to completion and neither interfere with other ongoing processing nor be interfered with by other processing. In contrast, an attentional process is one that cannot be completed without using some central processing resource that must be shared among concurrent competing processes. Thus, an attentional process can both interfere with other processing and be interfered with by other processes. To further identify the two sides of this dichotomy, automatic processes are simple, low-level, perceptual, and unconscious processes. Attentional processes are complex, higher level, cognitive, and conscious processes. Knowing which facets of word recognition are automatic and which are attention demanding may provide us with insight into the subskills that support reading and perhaps into the ways that those subskills are best learned (LaBerge & Samuels, 1974).

Unfortunately, after many years of varying multiple messages in a dichotic listening task (Lewis, 1970; Treisman, Squire, & Green, 1974), after many years of indulging in the complex logic of dual-task experiments (Becker, 1976; Herman & Kantowitz, 1970; Keele, 1973), after several years of comparing valid and invalid cue conditions to neutral cue conditions (Becker, 1980; Fischler & Bloom, 1979; Neely, 1976, 1977; Posner & Snyder, 1975; Stanovich & West, 1979, 1981, 1983a), after decades of trying to understand the Stroop color-naming task (Kahneman & Chajczyk, 1983; Neill, 1977), after all this, the findings are equivocal (see Humphreys, this volume, for a thorough review). We still do not have a clear indication about which facets of word recognition are automatic and which are attention demanding.

Even if we could resolve this question, it could well be that the value of the resolution would not be that great. If we could decide, once and for all, that recognizing a word can be automatic (LaBerge & Samuels, 1974; but see Becker, 1976; Kahneman & Chajczyk, 1983), that context effects can occur automatically (Stanovich & West, 1981; but see Becker, 1980; Forster, 1981), that selecting an appropriate response can be automatic (Keele, 1973; but see Becker, 1976), if we could decide each of these points, we would have identified one property of the processes of interest. Knowing this property could limit our choice of methodologies for further investigations, but the label would not tell us exactly what the process is doing, how the various component tasks are accomplished, which information is relevant and which is irrelevant, which factors speed processing and which slow processing. In short, labeling a black box as automatic does not yield an understanding of what goes on within the box between input and output. Moreover, premature labeling can force certain conclusions that may not be necessary, as we shall soon see.

B. Are Semantic Effects Prerecognition or Postrecognition?

In a shift away from the direct study of questions of attention, some investigators have begun to address the question of whether semantic context effects occur solely during the processing that leads to recognizing a word. It is quite possible that some (DeGroot, 1983; West & Stanovich, 1982) or all (Forster, 1981) of the effects of context could occur during the postrecognition processing that coordinates a newly recognized word with the subject's task or integrates that word into the current stream of thought. Earlier work on this topic showed that certain manipulations of stimulus visibility interact with context effects. Less visible target words yield larger total effects of context (Becker & Killion, 1977; Meyer et al., 1975). The original interpretation of these findings used the logic of additive factors (Sternberg, 1967) and argued that the interaction forced an explanation to place at least some of the effects of context in those processes that recognize words. Over the years, the qualification "at least some" has been largely ignored in the development of word recognition models that try to explain all context effects using only prerecognition mechanisms (Becker, 1976, 1979, 1980, 1982; Becker & Killion, 1977). Renewed interest in this topic may be partly a reaction to this too restrictive view.

The work that implicates postrecognition processes in context effects has grown out of the study of attention. The basic interpretive logic here relies on conclusions about the attentional properties of word recognition, including the assumptions that word recognition is automatic and that certain processes yielding facilitation for appropriate semantic contexts are automatic (DeGroot, 1983; West & Stanovich, 1982). Given these two assumptions of automatic word recognition, virtually any interference effect for words in unrelated contexts must come from outside of the word recognition system. For instance, the lexical decision task produces an interference effect for stimulus materials that do not show interference in a word-naming task. The postrecognition process assumed to be responsible for this difference across tasks is a decision process needed for word vs nonword choices that is not involved in word naming. Ordinarily, subjects expect a new stimulus word to be congruent with the current context. When this expectation is met, there is no evidence that could conflict with the making of the choice response required in the lexical decision task. In fact, that choice might be facilitated. In contrast, when a stimulus word is presented in an unrelated context, the incongruence between word and context may well conflict with the "word" response required by the task. Thus, the interference effect for lexical decisions arises in the postrecognition decisions that coordinate the automatic output of word recognition processes with the arbitrary choice response required in the task.

A second result that has been handled by assuming certain postrecognition processing is the finding of interference for unrelated contexts in the absence of facilitation for related contexts. Forster (1981) has suggested that an integration process may be behind this pattern of results. As a subject works through a segment of text, comprehension involves building an interpretation of that text, integrating what is already known with what has just been recognized. The act of integrating may be complex enough that any automatic facilitation is offset by the time spent integrating. Further, an interference effect may be the result of the extra time and effort needed to determine that a word in an unrelated context has no connection whatever to its context. This explanation, then, focuses on what must be done to determine the congruence between a word and its context instead of the effects of contextual congruency on the subject's task.

These suggestions for postrecognition context effects are necessary consequences of accepting the assumption that word recognition is automatic.

By strict definition, an automatic process cannot, of itself, produce inter-ference. Therefore, any interference effect must be explained by the ways that subsequent processes use the output of the automatic process. As we shall see, this form of explanation is not demanded in other theoretical frameworks.

C. Single-Word Contexts vs Short-Sentence Contexts

For early work on the effects of semantic context, individual words were good enough. There was a substantial body of normative data from which to select an adequate sample of materials, especially since there was little concern about the quality of the relationships among words. In fact, it was quite some time before researchers began to examine different kinds of se-mantic relationships (Fischler, 1977). Soon, though, the work began to con-sider the effects that a short sentence context might have on recognizing a single word (Schuberth & Eimas, 1977). For sentences, the quality of the relationship between context and target can vary widely, and it seems quite different from the kinds of relations that exist between two words. Intui-tively, the context word–target word pair *dog–cat* is different from the sen-tence–word pair "The dog chased the–*cat*." Sentence contexts, at the very least, supply syntactic constraints in addition to the semantic constraints on words that can serve as appropriate completions of the sentence.

Consistent with the logical differences between word and sentence con-texts, some of the data also suggest a difference between the two forms of context. Neely (1976) used strongly associated word pairs in his related con-text condition and found that the effect of a context was facilitation dom-inant. In sentence contexts, though, Fischler and Bloom (1979) reported the opposite finding; the total context effect was largely the result of interfer-ence in recognizing words unrelated to the sentence. Schuberth and Eimas (1977) report that word frequency does not interact with context effects for sentences, whereas Becker (1979) reports an interaction between the two factors when context is provided by a single word.

More recent results, however, indicate that there may be relatively little difference between single-word contexts and short-sentence contexts. Becker (1980), using single words to provide a context, reported an interference-dominant effect of context similar to that reported by Fischler and Bloom for sentence contexts. Stanovich and West (1981) have reported facilitation-dominant sentence context effects comparable to the effect reported by Neely for single words. Stanovich and West also reported an interaction between sentence contexts and a word frequency factor. Although there has yet to be a report of a word context study showing no interaction between context and frequency, the additional data suggest that the effects of single-word contexts may not be much different from the effects of short-sentence contexts.

D. Skilled vs Less Skilled Readers

As we accrued information about how college students use a semantic context, it was inevitable that we begin to ask about how less skilled readers use context. The starting point for this work included a number of top-down theories of reading which assume that increases in reading skill are directly related to increases in the ability to use contextual information (see Stanovich, 1980, for a review). Early on, though, the data contradicted this view. Schvaneveldt, Ackerman, and Semlear (1977) correlated the magnitude of single-word context effects with standardized reading test scores for elementary school children and found a trend for context effects to **decrease** with increases in reading skill. Other results reported by West and Stanovich (1978) show convincingly that less skilled readers produce larger context effects instead of the expected smaller effects.

These and other data have been important in supporting the interactive-compensatory view of reading proposed by Stanovich (1980). Building on the assumption that skilled word recognition is automatic, Stanovich argued that context effects for skilled readers derive only from their automatic processes. These processes operate so efficiently that attentional processes do not have the time to affect the results. Less skilled readers, however, cannot rely on their automatic processes because, in less skilled readers, these processes have not developed their full efficiency (LaBerge & Samuels, 1974). Therefore, less skilled readers must turn to contextual processes that demand attention. The sum of automatic and attentional context effects for less skilled readers should be larger than just the automatic context effects found for skilled readers, and the data for less skilled readers should show some evidence of interference effects from the use of attentional processing.

In support of this view, Stanovich, West, and Feeman (1981) report that second-grade subjects show only automatic context effects (i.e., no interference) for high-frequency target words, but they show interference effects for low-frequency target words. Even for subjects this young, high-frequency words may have been recognized often enough to have achieved full automatic efficiency. For any arbitrary set of words that includes both high-and low-frequency items, though, less skilled readers should show attentional context effects. However, Becker (1982) has shown that third-grade and fifth-grade subjects do not always conform to this prediction. Using single-word contexts, one type of semantic relationship produced a large facilitation effect and no interference for both grade levels. A second type of semantic relationship produced interference dominance for both grade levels. In accord with other data, the size of the total effect of context increased for both types of relationship as grade level decreased. Thus, less skilled readers show larger context effects regardless of whether there is an indication that they are using attentional processes. In fact, these data for less skilled readers replicate the findings for skilled, adult readers (Becker, 1980). Across levels of reading skill, the pattern of facilitation and interference changes as a function of the type of semantic relationship used in the related context condition.

E. What Are the Critical Methodological Issues?

The last of the topics to be considered here encompasses several methodological points raised in existing research. In particular, three major points are covered: what defines a "good" neutral context, which task should be used, and how should subjects be instructed to use a context.

The inclusion of a neutral context condition has proved essential to our progress in understanding how simple contexts influence word recognition. A neutral condition provides a third data point against which to assess the facilitation and interference components of context effects. Clearly, though, there has been concern about just what properties a semantically neutral context must have. Certainly, a neutral context should provide as little semantic information as possible. Beyond that, a neutral cue should require about the same processing effort as other, non-neutral cues, it should retain its alerting properties, and it should not introduce any perceptual or response biases. In the existing work, no neutral cue has satisfied all of these criteria. For single-word contexts, some researchers have used a row of X's as the neutral cue (Becker, 1980, 1982; Neely, 1976, 1977). Others have suggested using nonword letter strings (Schvaneveldt & McDonald, 1981), the word "ready" (Antos, 1979), or the word "blank" (DeGroot, Thomassen, & Hudson, 1982). For sentence contexts, X's have been used (Eisenberg & Becker, 1982); spelled-out digit strings have been used (Schuberth & Eimas, 1977); repetitions of the word *the* (Stanovich & West, 1979) and random word sequences have been used (Forster, 1981); and uninformative sentences like "They said it was the. . . . " have been used (Stanovich & West, 1983a).

In each case, there are arguments that can be made against a particular neutral cue based on at least one of the criteria above. A row of repeated X's does not require the same amount of processing as a word, and it may introduce response biases (Antos, 1979; DeGroot *et al.*, 1982). Depending on the target materials, the words "ready" and "blank" may not be semantically neutral (e.g., *ready–start* as a neutral condition trial), and the repeated use of the same word may reduce its alerting property. Nonword cues may require more processing than word cues and, therefore, may introduce inappropriate delays in responding to targets. Random digit or word sequences require more processing than meaningful sentences do, and there is the possibility that unintentional associations could contaminate the neutral condition. Uninformative sentences may well come close to satisfying the criteria for a neutral cue, but again, repeating a cue may reduce its alerting properties. Using several uninformative sentences may solve this problem (Stanovich & West, 1983a), but then any analyses must begin by demonstrating the equivalence of the various sentences, and this cannot be guaranteed.

Another option for a neutral condition is that suggested by Fischler and Bloom (1979), who used two separate groups of subjects. One group saw target words in both related and unrelated contexts. The second group saw target words only in unrelated contexts. Subjects in the second group were instructed to read the context, but they had no reason to use it; so, the context for this group should be effectively neutral. Clearly, this technique equates the characteristics of the neutral cues with the related and unrelated cues, but unfortunately, it introduces the problems of comparing across independent groups of subjects. A variation of this approach would be to block trials into unrelated-only and related-plus-unrelated blocks for a single subject. Of course, this would require controlling the order of block presentation and could well introduce block-transfer effects.

Ultimately, it seems that there is no one neutral condition that is free of criticism. Therefore, we are stuck with the experiment-by-experiment evaluation of the adequacy of neutral contexts. To make that evaluation, several aspects of the data may be useful. Fischler and Bloom (1979) have suggested that the equivalence of a within-subject and a between-subject neutral condition can increase our confidence that the neutral context is a good base line. DeGroot *et al.* (1982) suggest that equal performance on word context–nonword target and neutral context–nonword target trials in a lexical decision task provides evidence that there is little, if any, bias in subjects' responses in the neutral condition. Using several neutral context cues (Stanovich & West, 1983a) and finding no differences as a function of the specific cues can also add confidence to the accuracy of the neutral condition.

The second methodological point to be considered here is which task to select. West and Stanovich (1982) have reported a set of experiments that compare a word-naming task in which subjects simply read words aloud to a lexical decision task in which subjects arbitrarily classify letter strings as words or as nonwords. Their data showed that the lexical decision task results in larger facilitation effects and in larger interference effects than does the word-naming task. West and Stanovich argued that both of these increased effects can be attributed to a postrecognition process that selects the response for lexical decisions. For words in a related context, the decision process receives two inputs that are in agreement. One input says, "Respond 'yes,' the stimulus is a word." The second input says, "Respond, 'yes,' the stimulus fits with the current context." With two positive inputs, the decision process can quickly settle on a positive word response compared to a neutral condition in which only one of the two decision inputs is available. For words in an unrelated context, the two inputs are in conflict. One says, "Respond 'yes,' the stimulus is a word," but the other says, "Respond 'no,' the word does not fit into the current context." Resolving the conflict delays response selection to the unrelated word and produces a sizable interference effect. West and Stanovich argue that the word-naming task is free of these types of response selection effects because in word naming, response selection is an integral part of the process of recognizing a word. Among the things that we ordinarily do with recognized words is to make them available to working memory, and this form of memory may well rely on a phonological code to sustain its traces. A phonological code can also provide the basis for the response of saying the name of a word.

In large part, discussions about which task is **best** are unnecessary provided that we are sensitive to the differences among tasks. Results obtained from different tasks can support the generalization of conclusions about the manipulations of interest and provide converging evidence on the properties of other independent variables. Obviously, if we limit our work to a single task, we run the risk of creating a theory of that task instead of a theory about the problem that led us to the research. The important data of West and Stanovich identify for us one of the possible differences between word naming and lexical decisions. As data become available that identify other differences across tasks (e.g., Balota & Chumbley, 1984), our analyses will need to become more sophisticated.

The final methodological point to be addressed here concerns the instructions given to subjects about how to use a context. Earlier, I described a second-order analysis of facilitation and interference effects that focused on the relative dominance of one effect over the other. The first demonstration of facilitation and interference dominance resulted from a manipulation of the kinds of related contexts that were used (Becker, 1980). A later study (Eisenberg & Becker, 1982) showed that the dominance of a given set of materials can change as a function of instructions. If the materials produce an interference effect, telling subjects to use the context to predict possible related targets can reduce or even eliminate the interference while increasing facilitation. In a way, this makes an obvious point. There are certain properties of the stimulus materials that determine how a context can be used, and there are certain abilities that the subjects can bring to bear to determine how they will treat a given set of materials.

IV. A THEORETICAL PERSPECTIVE

Now that some of the data have been described, it is time to delve into theory. Because of the high level of activity in the study of semantic context effects, clearly no single theory is going to be adequate. An in-depth consideration of just one theory, though, can prove useful to determine which implications of the theory hold up and which are in need of change. Here, the verification model (Becker, 1976, 1979, 1980; Becker & Killion, 1977) provides the focus for discussion. This model provides a consistent description of many of the findings from single-word context experiments, and there is already some indication that the basic constructs of the model extend to more complex materials.

A. The Verification Model

The model assumes two memory systems and two processes that operate between them. The first memory system is a sensory memory that is assumed to retain a veridical representation of a stimulus. The precise nature of that representation is unknown, but certain properties are assumed in the ways that the two processes operate on the contents of sensory memory. The second memory is a collection of lexical units each of which corresponds to a word. A lexical unit consists of a set of property lists. One list describes the "primitive" features of the visual representation of the word, most simply put, the line segments that make up the word. A second list contains the "relational" visual features that describe how the primitive features are interconnected. The set of relational features includes information about the angles and corners where two primitive features intersect, the relative placement of primitive features within a letter, and the relative position of letters and thereby of the space between letters in the word. A third list specifies the semantic features of the word. For immediate purposes, the details of semantic features are unimportant; it is assumed that semantic features provide for a crude description of the meaning of the word.

The two processes assumed in the verification model coordinate information across the two levels of memory and effect the mapping of sensory information onto lexical information. The first of the two processes accepts its input from the sensory memory, extracts the primitive features, and forwards those features to lexical memory. Based on the correspondence between the extracted features and the primitive-feature lists in lexical memory, a subset of the units in lexical memory is identified as at least minimally consistent with the stimulus. Because a list of primitive features is an impoverished and incomplete description of a word, little more than a set of disconnected line segments, primitive features alone cannot uniquely identify a word. The lexical units tagged by feature extraction are included in a set of stimulus-defined word candidates to be considered by the second of the two processes, the verification process. In the model, verification consists of selecting a candidate word, using the primitive **and** relational feature lists to construct what the word looks like, and comparing the constructed representation to the image in sensory memory. When the constructed representation supplies an acceptable match to the stimulus, the stimulus is identified as the candidate word currently under consideration. When the match is unacceptable, another candidate word is selected, constructed, and compared. The verification process continues, one candidate at a time, until the stimulus is recognized or until the set of candidates is exhausted.

To this skeletal structure, two major assumptions have been added. The first of these is that, within the stimulus-defined set of candidate words, the order of selection during verification is determined by word frequency. More frequently occurring words are assumed to be selected earlier in the process than less frequently occurring words. This assumption accounts for the finding of word frequency effects in word recognition tasks (Becker, 1976, 1979; Stanovich & West, 1981) and for the additivity of word frequency with certain manipulations of stimulus visibility (Becker & Killion, 1977; Stanners, Jastrzembski, & Westbrook, 1975). Since verification is a serial, one-item-at-a-time process, a difference in order of selection for verification entails a difference in the amount of time needed to recognize a word. When stimulus visibility is varied, the form of the manipulation may be such that it affects only the extraction of primitive features from the stimulus (e.g., the contrast between white stimuli and a dark background or a dot pattern superimposed over solid line stimuli). Locating frequency effects in the order of selection during verification also allows the model to account for a number of the phenomena of tachistoscopic recognition, as well (Paap, Newsome, McDonald, & Schvaneveldt, 1983). What the assumption cannot account for is the failure to find word-frequency effects in some experiments that use a word-naming task (Theios & Muise, 1977).

The second major assumption incorporated into the verification model addresses semantic context effects. It is assumed that a semantic feature system affects lexical memory in much the same way as the primitive feature extraction process. Once a word has been recognized, it becomes known to the semantic system and is used to generate semantic features appropriate to its current usage. These features are then fed back into lexical memory where they are used to identify a context-defined set of word candidates as a preparation for the next stimulus. Once identified, the words in the context-defined set can be sampled by the verification process as soon as a new stimulus is presented. Context set sampling is assumed to begin during the time that a stimulus-defined set is being created for the new stimulus. According to these assumptions, a word that is related to the current context would be included in the context-defined set and sampled early in the verification of candidates against a new stimulus. As with high-frequency words, the early sampling results in relatively fast recognition. Words that are not related to the context would not be included in the context set, and when such a word is presented as the stimulus, the context set would be exhaustively sampled without producing identification of the stimulus. Then, members of the stimulus-defined set are verified until the unrelated word is selected. Compared to related words, an unrelated word is not sampled until late in processing, resulting in relatively slow recognition. This difference in verification time provides the model with its basic mechanism for addressing semantic context effects.

1. On Pre- vs Postrecognition Context Effects

According to the verification model, all semantic context effects occur during prerecognition processing. Regardless of whether a word is in or out of context, recognition results from the successful verification of a candidate word selected from a set of words in lexical memory. Any differences in processing time as a function of context arise from the assumed differences in when a word candidate is selected. Words that are appropriate to a context are selected for verification sooner than are words that are inappropriate. Clearly, the work of preparing the inputs to define the context set for a subsequent stimulus is outside of word recognition per se. That task is assigned to an ill-defined, poorly understood semantic process. The verification model is a prerecognition model in the sense that the results of the semantic processing only affect the time required to recognize a subsequent word. There are no provisions in the model for the kinds of postrecognition processing described by West and Stanovich (1982) and DeGroot (1983).

One important implication has been drawn from the context assumptions that has allowed the verification model to account for the data that others have used to motivate assumptions about postrecognition context effects (see Section III,B). That is, the size of the context set should determine the detailed properties of observed context effects. If we assume that, on average, a word related to the context will be sampled from the context-defined set after half its members have been verified and rejected, then the smaller the context set, the faster the absolute recognition time for a word contained in the set. Conversely, the larger the context set, the slower the absolute recognition time. Within the framework of the model, this is but half of the implication. The size of the context set may determine recognition speed for unrelated words, as well. When the context set is small, all of its members may be rejected quickly enough so that the stimulus-defined set can be sampled as soon as it is created. There may even be some "slack" time (Schweikert, 1980) between the time that the context set is disposed of and the time that the stimulus set becomes available. When the context set is large, though, it may not have been exhausted by the time the stimulus set is ready. Here, sampling the remainder of the context set would delay consideration of the stimulus set, resulting in interference in the recognition of the unrelated word. Thus, for the verification model, interference effects do not necessarily point to postrecognition processes. Such effects can be subsumed under existing constructs.

To evaluate this implication requires a context manipulation that can be argued to produce context sets of different sizes. Because the predictions involve differences in absolute recognition times, a neutral context condition is also required as a base line for comparing across the different forms of context. In the initial test, different groups of subjects saw a single-word-related context that was either an antonym of the target word or the name of the category to which the target word belonged (Becker, 1980). The unrelated context condition used mismatched antonym pairs or mismatched category name–category member pairs, and the neutral context was a string of X's. For subjects in the antonym list condition, it was argued that they would be very restricted in the words that they would treat as related to the context. In a setting where the only relationship was antonymy, a subject seeing a context word like *hot* would almost certainly predict that the target would be the word *cold,* if it was related to the context. For subjects in the category list condition, it was argued that a considerable number of the members of a category would be treated as candidates for related targets. To improve the odds that subjects would view the category relationship as broadly as they could, the experiment used both typical category members (e.g., *animal–dog*) and atypical category members (e.g., *animal–mouse*) as instances of the relationship.

As described earlier, the antonym list produced a pattern of facilitation dominance. There were substantially faster response times for words in related contexts than for words in a neutral context, and there was no difference between words in the neutral context and words in an unrelated context. In contrast, the category list resulted in no difference between related and neutral contexts and substantially slower response times to words in unrelated contexts than to words in the neutral context, an interference-dominant pattern. It was also shown that response time in the neutral context condition was not affected by the different forms of relationships used, thereby validating the neutral condition as an appropriate base line for the cross-list comparisons (Becker, 1980, Experiments 3 and 4). These results, then, are a clean demonstration of two different forms of context effects that match those predicted by the verification model.

2. On Single-Word and Short-Sentence Contexts

In the earlier discussion of the context provided by a sentence, it was suggested that the intuitive differences between a sentence context and a single-word context may be reflected in the data. Typically, sentence contexts are more flexible, and continuations from an incomplete sentence are less predictable compared to the single-word context materials that have been used. For the verification model, these differences may well map onto the theoretical distinction between context sets of different sizes. To test whether the set-size notion extends to sentence contexts, Eisenberg and Becker (1982) used a task in which the context was provided by a short sentence and the target was another short sentence. The task required a true–false judgment on the target sentence. True response targets were presented following related sentences and unrelated sentences; a string of X's provided a neutral context. A list factor, comparable to the antonym vs category list distinction, was created by using strongly related cue–target filler pairs of sentences in one list and a mixture of strongly and weakly related pairs in the other list. Across this list factor, a set of critical cue–target materials was held constant, and the data were reported only for these critical materials. Subjects who saw the strongly related filler list showed facilitation dominance with target sentences in a related context 87 msec faster than sentences in neutral contexts and a 0-msec difference between the neutral and unrelated context conditions. Subjects who saw the mixed strong/weak filler list showed a 48-msec facilitation effect and a 57-msec interference effect. In a follow-up study, one group of subjects in the mixed filler list condition showed a clear interference-dominant effect with only 19-msec facilitation and 70-msec interference. These differences in sentence context effects are comparable to the differences found for single-word contexts, and they appear to be controlled by the same type of context list factor. Thus, the context set-size explanation may well extend to contexts larger than a single word.

3. On Skilled and Less Skilled Readers

When the data comparing skilled and less skilled readers are considered in the framework of the verification model, it is not necessary to assume that less skilled readers do something in addition to what skilled readers are doing. Much of the existing data can be accommodated by the mechanisms assumed to apply to skilled readers. The first point to be addressed is the fact that less skilled readers show larger overall effects of a context. Within the model, any or all of three mechanisms can contribute to this effect. First, stimulus feature extraction could be slower in the less skilled. Second, feature extraction could be less precise, leading to larger stimulus-defined candidate sets, and third, the speed of a verification cycle could be slower. The first two possibilities would affect the amount of time needed to recognize words both in neutral contexts and in unrelated contexts. The third possibility would affect recognition time for all words, regardless of context. In the verification model, then, all differences between skilled and less skilled readers are attributed to differences in the efficiency of executing the same assumed processes.

In an attempt to be more specific, about all that can be said for the moment is that it seems that less skilled readers are slower in verifying a candidate word compared to skilled readers. This is suggested by the finding of changes in the amount of interference across levels of reading skill (West & Stanovich, 1978) and by the fact that recognition time for words in related contexts increases for less skilled readers. Both of these points of support are weak, though. The changes in interference involve comparison across materials, or they involve a change from no interference to a substantial interference effect. Increases in absolute recognition time for related contexts also include the many confounding factors that contribute to speed differences between adults and children. Unfortunately, the data do not support a further choice among the three mechanisms, but the similarity of these mechanisms to those invoked to accommodate the effects of stimulus visibility (Becker & Killion, 1977) may provide the converging operations needed to make a choice.

A second point of interest under this topic is whether the set size idea applies to less skilled readers as well as to skilled readers, to children as well as to adults. To evaluate this point, Becker (1982) presented an antonym list and a category list to groups of third graders and to groups of fifth graders. For both groups, the antonym list resulted in a large facilitation effect and no interference. The third graders showed interference dominance for the category materials, and the fifth graders showed interference dominance for a more difficult set of category materials that went further into the low end of category typicality. Thus, for single-word contexts, children seem to use a context in the same way that adults use context.

B. Further Study of the Verification Model

In addressing several of the topics on the effects of context, the verification model has relied on just the implications of variations in context set size. The apparent power of the set-size mechanism makes it a worthy target for additional work to determine more of the properties of the processing that produces different sized context sets. Some of the additional work shows that particular contexts can yield either of the dominance patterns. Stimulus lists of pure category materials seem to produce interference dominance, but when category relationships are mixed in with antonym and strong associative relationships, facilitation dominance is found for all three types of related contexts (Becker, 1980, Experiment 5). This outcome suggests that subjects have some choice about how a given context is used, and that choice is at least partly controlled by the overall properties of the stimulus list.

More direct support for the conclusion that subjects have a choice in how they use a context comes from an experiment reported by Eisenberg and Becker (1982). Here, the basic category experiment was repeated with a change in the instructions given to the subjects. In the earlier experiment, subjects were simply given examples of the kinds of relationships that they would encounter. Eisenberg and Becker told subjects to use a category name context word to explicitly predict a list of category members that might appear as a related target word. Without the instructions to predict, the category materials resulted in only a 9-msec facilitation for related contexts and 61-msec interference for words in unrelated contexts. When subjects were told to predict, the facilitation effect increased to 33 msec, while the interference effect decreased to 46 msec. Without prediction instructions, only the interference effect was statistically significant. With the instructions, both effects were reliable.

There are also several other facets of the semantic set size implication that have been examined. The first of these is found in some additional data reported by Becker (1980). When the category materials used in that study resulted in an interference-dominant context effect, there were no effects of the strength of relatedness between the category name and the category member—a pair like *animal-dog* produced the same effects as a pair like *animal-mouse*. When the context effect was facilitation dominant, the more strongly related pairs produced more facilitation than the less related pairs, although both types resulted in the same small interference effect. Stated more succinctly, there appear to be graded semantic effects for "small set" processing as a function of strength of relatedness and no graded effects for "large set" processing.

So far, there has been no mention of intermediate-sized semantic sets, although that is clearly a possibility. The reason for not mentioning it is that there appear to be just the two extreme sizes. Support for this comes from an analysis of individual differences in the prediction-instructed, category experiment. Before participating in the lexical decision task with the category materials, subjects were given a reading test consisting of one practice passage, one seventh grade-level test passage and one fourteenth grade-level test passage. The instructions were to read or skim the passages as quickly as they could and to concentrate on the general content of the passage while ignoring details. Subjects whose reading rates did not change substantially across the easy and difficult test passages were assigned to one group, and subjects whose reading rate dropped by more than 20% across the two passages were assigned to a second group. The hypothesis here was that all subjects would use small-set processing for the easier of the two passages. Those who could read the more difficult passage at about the same rate were probably using the same mode of processing on the second passage as well. Those who slowed down considerably were probably forced to shift to the other mode of processing, thereby losing much of the facilitation that can come from the context. In the prediction-instructed lexical decision task with the category materials, subjects who read both passages at about the same rate showed clear facilitation dominance, and subjects who slowed down on the more difficult passage showed clear interference dominance. Thus, there appear to be individual differences in how subjects use a context. The averaged data described above for the prediction-instructed category experiment resulted from half of the subjects using one mode of context processing and the other half using the other mode of processing.

In another test of these possible individual differences, Eisenberg and Becker gave subjects the reading test followed by their sentence true–false task using the mixed strong/weak related filler materials. On average, the data showed 48-msec facilitation and 57-msec interference. When subjects were divided using their reading test results, one group showed facilitation dominance with 87-msec facilitation and −19-msec interference (the unrelated condition was slightly faster than the neutral condition). The second group of subjects showed interference dominance with 19-msec facilitation and 70-msec interference. These data both support the individual difference finding and help to extend the coverage of the verification model beyond single-word contexts.

The final point to be made here also comes from the Eisenberg and Becker study. Part of their data showed an effect of instructing subjects to use a category name context predictively. That effect was to reduce the amount of interference and increase facilitation. A second test of these instructions used the mixed list of sentence task materials that had twice before resulted in roughly equal facilitation and interference effects. Under instructions to use the context sentence to predict the content of possible related target sentences, the mixed list of materials produced facilitation dominance with 90-msec facilitation and −19-msec interference. Thus, not only are the individual differences found for both single-word and sentence contexts, but the effect of the prediction instructions are the same; interference is reduced while facilitation increases.

The data addressing the context set size assumption can be summarized by seven constraints that must be met by the structures and processes of a theory of word recognition and semantic context effects.

1. The number of potentially related words must affect the operations of recognizing words both in and out of context. The form of that effect must be that facilitation decreases and interference increases with increases in the number of words treated as related.

2. The semantic context mechanism must produce two discrete outputs, a small set or a large set. The variation in set size does not appear to be continuous.

3. The process of generating a small set must involve something like explicit prediction.

4. The process of generating a large set must not differentiate among the candidates based on their strength of relatedness to the context.

5. The semantic mechanism must not be restricted to just single words or to just multiword text elements.

6. The theory must apply in much the same way to children as it does to adults.

7. There must be a way for subjects to exercise some control over the semantic processing mechanism.

There are several ways to describe a semantic mechanism that will meet the currently known constraints. One suggestion is that the semantic processes use a distinction between a single denotation of the context and all possible connotations of the context (Becker, 1980). To emphasize the control that subjects apparently have over how a context is used, the different modes of context processing were labeled as strategies. Under a proposed **prediction strategy,** the semantic mechanism focuses on the one denotation of the context that is most appropriate and generates only the semantic features for that denotation. Within the verification model, the restricted set of semantic features should result in only a small number of lexical units in the context-defined candidate set. Under a proposed **expectancy strategy,** the semantic mechanism allows a much broader interpretation of the context and generates semantic features appropriate to all meanings of the context. The larger number of features should identify a larger number of lexical units for inclusion in the context-defined candidate set. Presumably, the features appropriate to different meanings of the context are disjoint sets. Therefore, no single meaning of the context would show a feature count advantage over any other meaning, and there would be no basis for a ranking of candidates along a strength-of-relatedness dimension. To apply this notion to multiple words, we need minimally assume that the semantic processor is capable of some form of running computation of the context. As additional words are recognized, the meaning of those words is factored into the computation, and new features are generated. Finally, this basic mechanism can be applied to children as well as to adults. The mechanism itself need not change, although a subject's knowledge and expertise clearly differ across the two populations. It could well be that the average child differs from the average adult in about the same way that an expert in a field differs from the novice. The words and concepts may be available, but the less experienced subject may not be able to use the relationships in the same way as the more experienced subject can.

This suggestion of semantic strategies is consistent with the assumptions of the verification model in using the terminology of semantic features to distinguish between two semantic strategies. It, therefore, has the advantage of compatibility with the mechanism assumed for communicating between the semantic processes and the word units in lexical memory. There is, of course, nothing sacred about semantic features. Other communication mechanisms and semantic mechanisms could easily serve the same function. For example, a semantic network (e.g., Collins & Loftus, 1975) could be used to describe the semantic mechanism, and there could be a whole-word mechanism for communicating with items in lexical memory.

C. Weaknessses of the Verification Model

Both the logical weaknesses of the model and the weaknesses in the supporting data lie in those aspects that are unique to the model. First, there is little convincing evidence supporting the firm theoretical distinction made between the primitive features of a stimulus and the relational features of a stimulus. In large part, the distinction is based on the visual masking work of Turvey (1973) showing different temporal patterns of masking effects as a function of the quality of the masking stimulus: random dots vs a line-pattern mask. For the verification model, a similar distinction should obtain for different forms of stimulus visibility manipulations. Although this distinction is central to the model, it is outside the scope of the current paper, and tests of this prediction will have to await another time.

A second weakness in the model is the distinction between what feature extraction accomplishes and what the verification process does. Feature extraction is assumed merely to limit the number of words that are to be considered during verification. Verification takes care of uniquely identifying a word. This facet of the model has received some support in the work of Paap *et al.* (1983) who assumed that tachistoscopic recognition procedures provide a look at the operations of word recognition when the verification process cannot function properly. The key assumption here is that a stimulus word is available to subjects for such a brief time that they do not have the opportunity to complete the verification of all members of the stimulus-defined set of candidates. Using a restricted stimulus population and a set of individual letter confusion matrices, Paap *et al.* estimated the stimulus set sizes for each four-letter word in their sample. After accommodating the effects of stimulus display conditions on accuracy of recognition, these investigators showed a considerable consistency between the predictions of the verification model and a wide range of tachistoscopic word recognition data. Again, though, this issue is not of primary concern here, and further work must be delayed.

The third weakness in the model is in the distinction between small and large context sets. So far, all of the supporting evidence has been obtained in experiments using the lexical decision task or a true–false sentence-judgment task. Both tasks involve an arbitrary classification of the stimulus, and therefore, both tasks may be open to the kind of criticisms made by West and Stanovich (1982). It could be that the decision involved in the task itself is affected by a semantic relationship. Another limitation in the data is that a large part of the support comes from experiments that use single-word contexts.

A logical weakness in the distinction between large and small context sets can be found in the semantic feature mechanism assumed above. There probably is no acceptable set of semantic features to provide a base for the kind of sophisticated mechanism outlined above. A "minimal" set of features would probably not work as required because it would be quite possible that the union of feature sets for all possible connotations of a word would not differ from the set of all possible features. The problem then becomes one of identifying a useful set of features, and even if that could be done to adequately describe individual words, there is other information carried by the relations among words that would not necessarily be captured. This aspect of the model, then, is weak on two counts: the semantic feature mechanism is basically flawed and the supporting data are weak. This weakness is clearly within the focus of this article, and further work in this area is forthcoming.

V. ADDITIONAL TESTS OF THE VERIFICATION MODEL

One limitation on the data supporting the distinction between large and small semantic sets is the type of task that has been used. Most of the data come from the lexical decision task, and the remainder come from a true–false judgment task using short sentences. Both tasks require an arbitrary classification response, and it has been argued that the making of such a decision is itself affected by the semantic relationships obtaining between a cue and a target stimulus. A second limitation is that most of the experiments have used single-word contexts. If the verification model is to be applied generally to how people use context during reading, both of these limitations must be tested. In the first experiment reported below, subjects were asked to read an incomplete sentence to themselves and then to name aloud a word target. This experiment addresses both of the limitations, and it also tests one of the theoretical constraints stated earlier. The experiment includes both adults and children as subjects, so it should provide evidence on whether generalizing across subject populations is warranted.

A second experiment to be presented here uses a variation of the lexical decision task that amounts to a proofreading task. Target words are embedded in short text passages, and subjects are asked to decide whether each word in the passage is spelled correctly. The results from this task may bring us even closer to the realm of normal reading.

A. Experiment 1

In this experiment, subjects read a short, three to six-word incomplete sentence to themselves and then responded to a single target word by naming it aloud. The target word either completed the sentence appropriately, was unrelated to the sentence, or finished the neutral context sentence "The next word is." The appropriate sentence completions were selected from the set of responses provided by fourth and sixth grade students in a Cloze task. The subjects in the naming task included third graders, fifth graders and adults, with the members of each grade level divided into two groups. These groups differed, first, on the type of related filler materials they saw, and second, in the type of instructions they received. At each grade level, one group saw related fillers that were highly predicted in the Cloze task data, those for which the probability of the target word was at least .85. These subjects were also instructed to use the incomplete sentence to predict the word or words that could reasonably complete the sentence. The second group saw related filler materials in which the target word was congruent with the sentence, but the target was never given as a Cloze task response. These subjects were instructed simply in the task and not told to use the context predictively.

1. Subjects

Twenty-four third-grade students, 24 fifth-grade students, and 24 adults served as subjects. The younger subjects were enrolled at a middle-class, public elementary school, and they participated during their normal morning class hours. The adults included three equally represented subgroups: the teachers of the younger subjects, the parents of the younger subjects, and friends of the experimenter. Twelve people at each level were randomly assigned to the predicted filler/prediction instruction group, and the remaining 12 were assigned to the unpredicted filler/nonprediction instruction group.

2. Procedure

The younger subjects and their teachers were tested in a section of the school library, and the remaining adult subjects were tested in the experimenter's home. The presentation of stimulus materials and the timing of events was controlled by a TRS–80 Modell III microcomputer, and the subjects' vocal responses were detected by a specially built, voice-activated switch. Each subject session began with a calibration of the switch and with a set of four demonstration trials that were experimenter paced. Next, the subjects completed a set of 12 practice trials and four sets of 18 test trials. A complete session lasted about 10–12 minutes.

Each trial in the experiment consisted of an incomplete sentence displayed for 1250, 1500, and 1750 msec for the adults, fifth graders, and third graders, respectively. The sentence was then removed from the display screen and immediately replaced by a target word located just to the right of where the sentence had ended. All subjects were told that they were to name the target word aloud, as quickly as they could without making mistakes. After each response, the experimenter could signal either a subject error or a voice switch failure. For subject errors, an error message was displayed on the screen for 1500 msec, and for voice switch failures, the experiment was interrupted to allow for recalibration. Only obvious switch failures were handled in this way, those for which the subject's response failed to trigger the switch at all. The intertrial interval was 1500 msec for all subjects.

Two sets of critical target materials were selected from Cloze task data obtained from 48 fourth- and sixth-grade students. One set included 30 incomplete sentence–target word pairs for which the Cloze task probability of the target varied between .50 and .83. The second set included another 30 pairs for which the Cloze probability of the target word ranged between .02 and .10. Both the stronger and the weaker sets were divided into three subsets of 10 pairs each. For one subject, 10 of the stronger and 10 of the weaker pairs were used in a related context condition; that is, the incomplete sentence was presented and then followed by its Cloze task completion word. Another 10 of each type were shown as unrelated pairs with one sentence followed by the completion word of a different sentence. For the final 10 stronger and weaker pairs, the incomplete sentence was replaced by the neutral sentence "The next word is." Other subjects saw a different assignment of particular sentence–target word pairs to context conditions.

Overall, each target word appeared equally often in each of the three context conditions, with no target word repeated for a single subject.

In addition to the materials just described, two sets of 12 filler pairs were selected. One set included only those sentence–target word pairs that resulted in a Cloze task probability between .85 and 1.00. The set was combined with the stronger and weaker critical sets and shown to subjects in the predicted filler/prediction instruction groups. The second set included incomplete sentences that had been used in the Cloze task paired with experimenter-generated completion words that were semantically congruent with the sentence but that had never appeared as responses in the Cloze task (e.g., "Everyone likes to eat–*peas*"). This set was combined with the two critical sets and shown to subjects in the unpredicted filler/nonprediction instruction groups. The filler pairs served two purposes. First, they biased the overall list of relationships that subjects saw, and second, a filler pair was always used as the first trial in a block of test trials as a "buffer" to allow subjects to get started again without affecting the data from the critical materials.

The two factors of filler list and instructions were purposely confounded here because of a small subject population. The experiment was intended to provide the theoretical best case for obtaining facilitation dominance and the theoretical best case for obtaining interference dominance. The relative importance of the list factor and of the instructions factor can be determined elsewhere, if necessary.

3. Results

All of the data reported here are taken from the critical materials, materials that were exactly the same across groups of subjects. Trials on which the equipment malfunctioned were eliminated, and the remainder of the data were trimmed at ± 2 standard deviations from the mean for each subject for each condition. This procedure was used to remove those extreme trials on which the subject's response failed to trigger the voice switch until late in the utterance and those trials on which background noise may have triggered the switch early. The eliminated trials accounted for about 2% of the total with the younger subjects having more trials eliminated for both reasons. The data are shown in Table I.

In an overall analysis of variance, there was a main effect of grade level, $F(2,66) = 29.60$, $p < .001$, and of context condition, $F(2,66) = 14.49$, $p < .001$. Obviously, adults were faster than fifth graders, who were faster than third graders. The related context condition was faster than the neutral condition, which was faster than the unrelated condition. The error rates showed the same main effects, with the faster conditions also producing

TABLE I

Mean Reaction Times and Percentage Errors for the Naming Task, Experiment 1

	Context condition		
	Related	Neutral	Unrelated
Predicted filler/prediction instructed			
Third grade			
RT[a]	652	708	783
% error	6.0	10.4	9.7
Fifth grade			
RT	514	550	589
% error	2.2	6.5	6.3
Adults			
RT	440	471	482
% error	1.7	2.5	1.7
Unpredicted filler/nonprediction instructed			
Third grade			
RT	733	738	847
% error	3.0	4.7	8.1
Fifth grade			
RT	559	550	629
% error	1.3	1.7	6.7
Adults			
RT	504	503	550
% error	0.0	0.4	0.4

[a]RT, reaction time.

fewer errors. In the reaction time data, there was a marginal effect of filler list/instruction condition, $F(1,66) = 2.99$, $p < .10$, with the predicted filler/prediction instructed condition slightly faster. This condition also resulted in more errors, however, $F(1,66) = 6.67$, $p < .05$, suggesting a speed–accuracy trade-off across conditions.

There are also two significant interactions in these data. First, grade level interacted with context condition, $F(4,132) = 4.89$, $p < .01$, with third graders showing the largest effect of context condition and adults showing the smallest effect. The increase in context effects for younger subjects is consistent with numerous other studies (Becker, 1982; Schvaneveldt, Ackerman, & Semlear, 1977; West & Stanovich, 1978; see Stanovich, 1980, for one treatment of this effect).

The second interaction is of particular interest because it provides the test of the effect of filler list/instructions. In the reaction time data, the interaction between filler list/instructions and context condition was significant, $F(2,132) = 4.55$, $p < .05$. For the predicted filler/prediction instruction condition, facilitation was 41 msec and interference was 42 msec. For the unpredicted filler/nonprediction instruction condition, facilitation was -2 msec averaged across grade levels, and interference was 79 msec. In the error data, this interaction was marginally significant, $F(2,132) = 2.95$, $p < .10$. The shift in error rates paralleled the change in reaction time. Subjects in the predicted filler/prediction instruction condition showed more facilitation and less interference than subjects in the unpredicted filler/nonprediction instruction condition.

If the verification model is to apply to the word-naming task and to incomplete sentence contexts, this is the kind of effect that the filler list/instruction factor must have. In the data, there is clearly an interference-dominant effect of context for one condition, but there is no clear facilitation dominance. The finding of interference dominance, though, is an important one for the model. Far and away the most common result from this type of study is facilitation dominance. In fact, in only two experiments has there been interference dominance. Forster (1981) reports an interference-dominant effect of context, but that was the result of a change in the type of neutral context in an experiment using the rapid sequential visual presentation (RSVP) technique to present the context. The second report of interference dominance is that of Stanovich and West (1983b) in their Experiment 1. All other experiments in that study and in the other work of these investigators have resulted in facilitation dominance, and therefore, the importance of Experiment 1 was downplayed. There was one critical difference between the materials of Experiment 1 and the materials used in the other experiments, however. That difference was in the strength of the semantic relationships used in the two sets of materials. Those that resulted in facilitation dominance "were 'loaded' with semantic relationships" (Stanovich & West, 1983b, p. 54) perhaps to a point that allowed subjects to read predictively. The materials that produced interference dominance were not "loaded."

In the current experiment, the data from just the adult subjects strengthen the results of Stanovich and West in clearly showing each form of dominance. This outcome here does two things. First, it confirms the existence of interference dominance in word naming when just adult subjects are considered. Second, it allows a further test of the generality of the verification model by examining the effects of the strength-of-relatedness factor across the patterns of context effect. In the earlier lexical decision studies, stronger and weaker contexts were equivalent when the data were interference dominant, but stronger contexts produced more facilitation than weaker contexts when the overall effect was facilitation dominant. Table II shows the strength-of-relatedness data for the adult subjects.

The analysis of these data used planned comparisons to assess facilitation

TABLE II

Mean Reaction Times for the Stronger
and Weaker Critical Materials, Experiment 1[a]

	Context condition		
List/materials	Related	Neutral	Unrelated
Prediction			
Stronger	418	474	485
Weaker	461	471	481
Nonprediction			
Stronger	492	493	555
Weaker	518	513	546

[a]Data are for the adult subjects only.

and interference effects across levels of strength of relatedness. For the facilitation-dominant, predicted filler/prediction instruction group, the more strongly related materials produced 46 msec more facilitation than did the weakly related materials, 56 msec vs 10 msec, $t(11) = 2.76$, $p <$ .05. The interference effects for this group did not differ as a function of strength of relatedness, 11 msec vs 10 msec for the stronger and weaker items, respectively, $t(11) = .011$. For the unpredicted filler/nonprediction instruction group, the stronger and weaker items differed by only 6 msec in facilitation, 1 msec vs -5 msec, respectively, $t(11) = 0.59$. Each of these results conforms well to the earlier results in the lexical decision task. The final comparison, that for interference effects in the interference-dominant data, differs from the earlier results. Here, the target items from the stronger set produced 29 msec more interference than did the target items from the weaker set, 62 msec vs 33 msec, $t(11) = 2.63$, $p <$ .05.

For the most part, the test of the strength-of-relatedness effects is consistent with the earlier findings. The one exception is a difference in interference where none was expected. There are two ways that this result might be handled. First, the exception occurred under interference dominance, and there are two other groups that produced clear interference-dominant context effects, the third and fifth graders. An examination of the data for the younger subjects shows no difference in interference effects as a function of strength of relatedness. The third graders had interference effects of 110 and 109 msec for the stronger and weaker materials, respectively, and the fifth graders had interference effects of 76 and 81 msec for the stronger and weaker materials. Thus, the difference in interference effects may not be particularly robust. At the least, the difference in interference effects across levels of strength of relatedness does not extend to the younger subjects.

A second possible explanation comes from the fact that there was an unintended confound in the assignment of contexts to targets in the unrelated context condition. When target words from the weaker set were used in the unrelated condition, the context was always provided by an incomplete sentence from the more strongly related set of materials. When the target words from the stronger set were used in the unrelated condition, context was always provided by a sentence from the weaker set of materials. A re-examination of these materials suggests that there could have been an effect of this confound. In the Cloze task, subjects generated an average of 7.4 different words as possible completions for the sentences used in the stronger set. For sentences in the weaker set, subjects generated an average of 13.4 words. This observed difference could reflect an underlying difference in the size of the semantic sets that can be generated for items in the two sets of materials. It could be that only the adult subjects were sensitive to this subtle difference.

With some support for applying the verification model to word naming and sentence contexts, it is now time to address the data for the younger subjects. In the predicted filler/prediction instruction condition, these subjects showed roughly equal facilitation and interference effects, and the only way that the model can address the data is to rely on individual differences in context use. With no independent means to divide subjects, any analysis must be post hoc. Another problem is that there are only 12 subjects in each grade-level group. Nevertheless, let us proceed speculatively. For the purpose of looking at individual differences, an extra six subjects were added to the fifth-grade group, bringing the total there to 18. Unfortunately, there were no extra third graders.

The post hoc method used to divide subjects began with the computation of a "dominance score." For each subject, facilitation was subtracted from interference to yield a single composite score. A negative dominance score results when facilitation is larger than interference for a given subject. A positive score obtains when interference is larger than facilitation. Next, subjects within each of the materials-defined subgroups (i.e., those subjects who saw the same assignment of target words to the three context conditions) were ranked on dominance scores. Subjects above the median for each group were assigned to a positive dominance group within their grade level, and subjects below the median were assigned to a negative dominance group. This method of assignment resulted in dividing each of the two grade-level groups in half while preserving the balancing of particular materials within each half. The results of this post hoc division are shown in Table III.

For the 18 fifth graders, the division produced two distinct groups, one that shows a facilitation-dominant context effect and one that shows an interference-dominant context effect. For the third graders, there is one

TABLE III

Mean Reaction Times for the Third Grade and Fifth Grade Individual Differences Analysis, Experiment 1

Grade level	Dominance	Context condition		
		Related	Neutral	Unrelated
Third	Negative	635	724	782
	Positive	669	692	783
Fifth[a]	Negative	496	554	573
	Positive	539	544	612

[a]The fifth grade group includes six additional subjects.

group that shows interference dominance, but the other group continues to show both facilitation and interference. Although this result is not as expected, it may simply be that the limits of effectiveness of the prediction inducements have been reached for this set of materials and this group of subjects.

Overall, the results of Experiment 1 are fairly consistent with the verification model. There are, of course, some points of inconsistency, but the suggestions made for accommodating the data may lead to additional sophistication of the model. In particular, if subjects are sensitive to highly constrained contexts even though using the large-set mode of processing, this may serve as a signal to switch processing modes. If this sensitivity is limited to adults, it could indicate that adults are more facile at switching modes than are children. The failure to find clear patterns of individual differences for the third-grade subjects presents a more awkward problem. The suggestion for dealing with this result was basically that the materials were not properly calibrated for this subject group. While that may well be true, it is not especially satisfying. To blame the materials is an escape, not an explanation. To more completely generalize the verification model, an "appropriate" set of materials must be found.

B. Experiment 2

The purpose of this experiment was to test a novel procedure that is closer to normal reading than most of the other tasks that have been used to study context effects. The procedure amounts to a proofreading task in which subjects decide whether each word in a short text passage is correctly spelled or not. The materials were selected from among the short articles appearing in a local newspaper and modified to eliminate proper names and other peculiarities. In the experiment, a passage was started with its first word at the top left corner of a computer display. When the subject responded, the next word was presented one space to the right of the preceding word. As the subject responded to each word, a new word was added to the display. Eventually, the passage more or less filled the display screen. Randomly distributed throughout a passage were 15 misspelled words and 15 "unrelated" words that did not fit into the context provided by the passage. Each subject saw three passages, two of them presented as normal text and one in which the order of the words in the pasasge was randomized. It was thought that the randomized passage would provide a neutral context condition against which to assess the facilitation for words that fit with the normal passages and the interference for those words that did not fit into the normal passages.

1. Subjects

Six friends and 18 co-workers of the experimenter served as subjects in this experiment. The friends were tested in the experimenter's home, and the co-workers were tested at a facility of AT&T Information Systems. The two types of subjects were assigned equally to the two groups described below.

2. Procedure

Subjects were tested individually using a TRS–80 Model III computer to present the stimulus materials and to collect and time the subject's responses. As part of the instructions, subjects were shown two three-sentence passages as practice on the proofreading task. The first practice passage was presented normally and the second passage was randomized. Subjects were told that a text passage would be presented on the screen, one word at a time. They were to read each word as it came on, decide whether it was correctly spelled, and pull the right-hand switch of the response box for correct words or the left-hand switch for misspelled words. After the two practice passages, subjects were informed that there were three passages yet to come, two normal passages and one randomized passage.

Each passage was initiated by a subject response. After that, the presentation of the passage was determined by the subject's response rate, with each successive word added to the display as soon as the subject had responded to the preceding word. There were two exceptions to this rapid mode of presentation. First, when the subject made an error, an error message was flashed at the bottom of the display for 4 seconds. Second, subjects were allowed 50 msec in which to release the switch from their response to the preceding word. When they failed to do so, a message instructing them to release the switches quickly was flashed at the bottom of the screen for 4 seconds. Following either type of message, there was a 1-second interval before the next word in the passage was presented.

Presentation of the passages began in the upper left corner of the computer's 64 character by 16 line display. Successive words were displayed one character space to the right of the preceding word if the new word would fit entirely on the same line. When a new word would not fit on the remainder of a line, it was displayed at the left margin of the following line. Only 15 of the 16 display lines were used for the passages. The sixteenth line was reserved for messages. When the passage required more than 15 lines, the entire screen was scrolled up and the passage was continued on the now empty fifteenth line.

The materials used here were modifications of six articles selected from a local newspaper. The modifications eliminated proper names and other oddities, reformatted the text into a single paragraph, and removed occasional duplicates of certain critical words. The six passages ranged in length from 124 words to 161 words. In each passage, 15 critical words were selected with the constraints that the set of words be evenly distributed across the passage and that each word occur once across all passages. Critical words also were not allowed within the first 10 words or the last 5 words of a passage. All the critical words were content words. Next, three pairs of passages were formed by combining passages with dissimilar content (e.g., a passage on clam digging was paired with a passage on Arab–Israeli tensions). A given subject would see only one member of each pair of passages, and the critical words from the other passage in a pair were used as unrelated words. The content dissimilarity within a pair was used to guard against unwanted relationships between the passage and the unrelated words embedded within the passage. Finally, 15 misspelled words were created for each of the three pairs of passages. The misspellings preserved the pronunciation of the words from which they were derived (e.g., *chain* was misspelled as *chane*).

Each subject saw one member of each of the three pairs of passages, and each subject saw two normal passages and one randomized passage. Across subjects, the passage pairs were balanced so that half the subjects saw one member of each pair, and half the subjects saw the other member. Also, the order of the normal and randomized passages was balanced so that one-third of the subjects saw the randomized passage first, one-third saw it second, and one-third saw it as their third passage. Finally, the passage that was randomized varied across subjects so that each particular passage was randomized once for each subgroup of six subjects.

During the presentation of a passage, unrelated and misspelled words were inserted randomly after the first 10 words of the passage. At any given point in a passage, the probability that an unrelated word or a misspelled word would be presented was determined by the number of that type yet to be shown, divided by the total number of words yet to be shown. For example, if there were 10 unrelated words left, 8 misspelled words, and 82 words from the passage, the probability of getting an unrelated word next was .10.

In all passages, the misspelled words remained on the screen only until the subject had responded. The misspellings were removed and replaced by whatever came next in the passage. For the normal passages, the unrelated words were handled in the same way; as soon as the subject responded, the unrelated word was erased and replaced by the next stimulus. By removing both the misspellings and the unrelated words from normal passages, subjects always had coherent text in front of them.

The 24 subjects tested here were randomly assigned to one of two groups that differed in instructions. One group was given the instructions described above telling them about the task and how they were to respond. Subjects in the second group were further instructed to use the context of the passages predictively. Specifically, they were told: "As you read along in a passage, try to think ahead about what words or topics might come up next in the passage. Try to outguess the author." The counterbalancing of materials and of the order of the randomized passage was identical across the two groups.

3. Results

About 1% of the data was lost because the subject failed to release the switch from the preceding response. The reaction times for correct responses and the error rates for this experiment are shown in Table IV. In the randomized passages, the data were collected separately for the critical words from the passage and for the unrelated words embedded in the passage. There was no difference between these two types of critical words in the randomized passage, thus suggesting that a randomized passage is, in fact, contextually neutral. In the data reported below, the "related" and "unrelated" words in the randomized passages are averaged together to provide a single neutral context value.

For the subjects in the standard instruction group, the facilitation effect was $-3 + 19.28$ msec, $t(11) = -0.15$, and the interference effect was $77 + 20.46$ msec, $t(11) = 3.74$, $p < .01$. The pattern here was clearly interference dominant. In part, this condition replicates the data reported by Gough *et al.* (1981). These investigators compared words in normal text to words in randomized text using a naming task. They found no difference between words in normal text and words in randomized text, and that finding is supported here. What is added here is the data point for the unrelated words in normal text. Unrelated words were clearly interfered with.

TABLE IV

**Mean Reaction Times and Percentage Errors for the Proofreading
Task, Experiment 2**

Instruction condition	Context condition		
	Related	Neutral	Unrelated
	Critical items		
Prediction			
RT[a]	508	550	588
% error	0.6	0.0	4.2
Nonprediction			
RT	541	538	615
% error	0.8	1.2	4.6

	Filler material			
	Passage type			
	Normal		Random	
	Words	Nonwords	Words	Nonwords
Prediction				
RT	461	751	477	713
% error	0.4	16.5	0.6	16.9
Nonprediction				
RT	488	740	465	748
% error	0.2	14.9	0.3	16.5

[a]RT, reaction time.

For the subjects in the prediction-instructed group, facilitation was 42 + 17.90 msec, $t(11) = 2.38$, $p < .05$, and interference was 38 + 18.41 msec, $t(11) = 2.06$, $p < .10$. The data here show a substantial facilitation effect and a marginally significant interference effect. Comparisons across the two groups show that the increase in facilitation for the prediction-instructed group was marginally reliable, $t(22) = 1.75$, $p < .10$, and the change in interference was not significant, $t(22) = 1.42$. The fact remains, however, that under prediction instructions, subjects show a facilitation effect, whereas without the instructions, there is no facilitation. There are also other more stable data that may be used to test for differences in facilitation between the two groups. The noncritical words in the various passages provide a second look at facilitation effects. The stimulus materials are properly balanced for this comparison as well as for the comparisons of critical words. Here, the facilitation effect for the prediction-instructed group was significantly larger than the facilitation effect for the standard instruction group, $t(22) = 2.60$, $p < .05$.

Within the prediction-instructed group, the pattern of facilitation and interference effects is of the sort that the verification model ascribes to individual differences. To evaluate this possibility, dominance scores were computed as in Experiment 1. The subjects within a materials group were divided based on dominance scores derived from the critical word data, and then the means for the filler words were calculated for each group. The availability of the filler words in this experiment allows for a bit of independence between the data used to identify the groups and the data to be examined. The subject group that showed facilitation dominance for the critical materials had a 30-msec facilitation effect of the filler words. The group that showed interference dominance for the critical materials had only a 3-msec facilitation effect for the filler words. Thus, there is some suggestion that the pattern of results for this group as a whole are the result of averaging across individual differences.

There remain two comments to be made about the proofreading task itself. First, it seems to show a good deal of promise for future work. After their sessions, subjects were asked their opinion of the task, and most mentioned that the task did not seem unnatural, but there was one objection that many voiced. They complained that they fell into the trap of using the "correct" switch as a means of simply advancing through the passage, only to get caught on the next misspelled word, either with an error or an extremely long response time. Although this may be a procedural hazard, it would seem to lend greater credibility to any context effects obtained with this task. Using the "correct" switch to advance the text should have the effect of equalizing response times across words and thereby of minimizing context effects.

The second comment addresses why the proofreading task was selected here. As mentioned above, others have used the word-naming task in related experiments. That task was not used here because of the delay that must be built into the experiment to accommodate the often long vocal responses. To have used a naming task would have required at least a 500-msec delay between words to allow the subject to finish saying one word before having to say the next word. In the proofreading task, there was only a 50-msec switch-reset delay used, and that delay was started after the new word had been presented. This rapid mode of presentation accomplished one of the main goals of this work, to come as close as possible to normal reading while retaining the same measures used in earlier studies. A quick look at Table IV shows that subjects were responding to words in about 500 msec. This translates to a reading rate of around 120 words per minute. This rate is considerably slower than the rate of normal reading, but it is also considerably faster than the rates that have typically been studied when examining context effects.

VI. SEMANTIC CONTEXT EFFECTS—A RETROSPECTIVE

Three of the issues introduced earlier have been explicitly addressed here. Both experiments extend our knowledge about how different forms of context affect word recognition, and both experiments address the methodological issues of selecting a task, selecting an appropriate neutral condition, and instructing subjects. Experiment 1 also addresses the topic of how skilled and less skilled readers might differ in their use of context.

On the possible differences between simple contexts and that provided by normal text, both of the experiments described here suggest that the two forms of context yield similar effects instead of disparate effects. Experiment 1 showed that the factors that influence the pattern of context effects produced by single words yield the same effects on the pattern of results for incomplete sentence contexts, and Experiment 2 extended this finding to short text passages. The opposing view, that single-word and multiple-word contexts differ, has been stated most strongly by Gough *et al.* (1981). These investigators suggested that the consistent context effects found for single words do not extend to multiword contexts. In fact, they argued that context may have no effect at all in text passages. Given their data showing no difference in naming times for words in normal text compared to words in randomized text, this conclusion was clearly warranted. The proofreading task of Experiment 2 here replicated this finding, but the experiment also showed that there are context effects that Gough *et al.* did not detect. In one condition, there was no difference between words in normal and randomized passages, but the data did show a context effect in the substantial difference between unrelated words in a normal passage and words in a randomized passage. In the other condition, when subjects were told to use the context predictively, the context provided by a normal passage did significantly decrease the response time for words related to the passage. The passage context effects found here were detected in conditions that Gough *et al.* did not include. They did not have an unrelated condition so they could not detect interference effects for unrelated words. They did not examine the effect of prediction instructions so they did not detect the facilitation effect. Now that more of the data are in, the view tht context has no effect in normal text passages becomes untenable. In fact, the various patterns of context effects found in text passages seem effectively the same as those found for single-word contexts.

The methodological issues of task selection, neutral-context selection, and instructions were also addressed in both of the experiments. On the point of task selection, the thrust here was to examine the effects of "old" variables in "new" tasks as a test of generality of the variables. The data here suggest that the list factor may influence how subjects use an incomplete sentence context and that instructions to predict may determine how subjects use both incomplete sentences and normal text passages regardless of the task set the subject. If the kinds of context effects of interest here are task independent, as they seem to be, the possibilities for further extension expand considerably.

The identification of an appropriate neutral condition was approached in two different ways. In the first experiment, an arbitrary incomplete sentence was created as the neutral context. This form of neutral context can be viewed as comparable to the neutral conditions investigated by Stanovich and West (1983a). They examined several uninformative sentences and found no differences among them. Here, only one neutral sentence was used, but the finding of facilitation dominance and interference dominance using that sentence suggests that it is at least close to an accurate neutral context. From the data here and those provided by Stanovich and West, it would seem that any well-formed but uninformative incomplete sentence may well serve as an acceptable neutral context in this type of research. In Experiment 2, there was an explicit test of the neutrality of a randomized passage. Critical words that came from the original passage were not responded to any differently than the unrelated words taken from another passage.

On the final methodological point, each experiment shows the effect that a change in the subjects' instructions can have. Along with the semantic relationships in the materials, telling subjects to use the relationships predictively can substantially change the characteristics of the context effects.

The issue of potential differences between skilled and less skilled readers is addressed only in Experiment 1. Although the data from that study were not definitive, the general properties of the results were consistent with the view that there are no fundamental differences in the way that skilled readers use a context and the way that less skilled readers use a context. Clearly, there are differences in the data across groups in the speed of processing and in the precise context pattern for a given set of materials. But, the main point here is that the difference is not a qualitative difference in the type of processing, in the way that contextual information is used during word recognition. Instead, it was suggested that the differences can be found in different levels of knowledge across the groups. Those subjects with a richer knowledge base are perhaps in a better position to predict from the context.

VII. SEMANTIC CONTEXT EFFECTS—A PROSPECTIVE

The data presented here add considerable generality to the characterization of semantic processing developed in the verification model. There seem to be two ways that subjects use semantic information regardless of level of reading skill, amount or form of context, or specific task requirements. With the basic distinction more firmly established, there now may be an opportunity to use that distinction to explore the semantic structures that lie behind context effects. Currently, the verification model does not provide a way to determine, a priori, how a particular set of materials will be used. What is available, though, is a set of tools that may provide the experimental leverage for a finer grained analysis of semantic knowledge that will lead to the necessary predictive power.

The first step in this line of inquiry is to explicitly incorporate a semantic structure and content analysis into the selection of materials. Candidates for this type of analysis are the propositional descriptions suggested by Anderson (1976) and by Kintsch (1974). Regardless of the specific mode of representation, what is needed is a description of materials that reflects complexity (e.g., the number of propositions, the level of nesting of propositions) and connectivity (e.g., redundancy across propositions, anaphoric reference). It may also be necessary to consider higher levels of structure, such as the expository organization of a long text passage, the inferential cohesiveness of a passage, or how well or poorly it maps onto a story grammar (see Mandl, Stein, & Trabasso, 1984). It will then be a matter of testing the materials to see whether the structural descriptions capture the kind of differences that affect how subjects can use a context.

If the first step is successful, it may show that the content of a set of materials can define the boundary conditions for context use. Extremely difficult materials may not be used predictively by any subjects, and extremely easy materials may be used predictively by all subjects. Once away from the boundaries, though, other factors become important. Among those factors are the subjects' pre-existing familiarity with the content and the subjects' ability to predict. These two may be particularly difficult to separate. The effect of degree of familiarity or expertise may make it difficult to detect differences in general ability to predict.

In addition to the investigation of the factors that determine how a context can be used, it is important to find out whether the two modes of context use result in differential learning of the material that has been read. There are several intriguing possibilities here. It could be that predictive reading merely reinforces that which is already known. Or, it could be that predictive reading serves to highlight the failures of prediction and mark these parts of the input for incorporation into existing memory structures. Nonpredictive reading may be used to build new memory structures that are integrations of several pre-existing structures. It would also be that nonpredictive reading supports the addition of a substantial amount of new information to an old memory structure. In any case, we need to know whether the different uses of context affect what is remembered.

Early on in this article, I mentioned that the data reported by Gough *et al.* (1981) suggested that we may have reached the end of the line in research on semantic context effects in word recognition. Those data were originally interpreted as showing that context does not affect processing time in normal text passages. The extensions described here have demonstrated that this conclusion was based on a special case of context effects, and instead of being at the end of the line, we now may face a challenging future of trying to understand a much broader range of context effects.

ACKNOWLEDGMENTS

This research was supported entirely by the author. I would like to thank the Board of Education, the Superintendent, Mr. G. Wuesthoff, the Assistant Principal, Ms. M. Merritt, the teaching staff, and the students of the Atlantic Highlands Elementary School for their cooperation and their participation in Experiment 1. I would also like to thank my co-workers (many of whom are also friends even though the description of subjects in Experiment 2 implies that they are not) for donating their free time to serve as subjects in Experiment 2.

REFERENCES

Anderson, J. R. (1976). *Language, memory, and thought.* Hillsdale, NJ: Erlbaum.

Antos, S. J. (1979). Processing facilitation in a lexical decision task. *Journal of Experimental Psychology: Human Perception and Performance, 5,* 527–545.

Balota, D. A., & Chumbley, J. I. (1984). Are lexical decisions a good measure of lexical access? The role of word frequency in the neglected decision stage. *Journal of Experimental Psychology: Human Perception and Performance, 10,* 340–357.

Becker, C. A. (1976). Allocation of attention during visual word recognition. *Journal of Experimental Psychology: Human Perception and Performance, 2,* 556–566.

Becker, C. A. (1979). Semantic context and word frequency effects in visual word recognition. *Journal of Experimental Psychology: Human Perception and Performance, 5,* 252–259.

Becker, C. A. (1980). Semantic context effects in visual word recognition: An analysis of semantic strategies. *Memory & Cognition, 8* 493–512.

Becker, C. A. (1982). The development of semantic context effects: Two processes or two strategies? *Reading Research Quarterly, 17,* 482–502.

Becker, C. A., & Killion, T. H. (1977). Interaction of visual and cognitive effects in word recognition. *Journal of Experimental Psychology: Human Perception and Performance,* **3**, 389–401.

Bransford, J. D., & Johnson, M. K. (1972). Contextual prerequisites for understanding: Some investigations of comprehension and recall. *Journal of Verbal Learning and Verbal Behavior,* **11**, 717–726.

Collins, A. M., & Loftus, E. F. (1975). A spreading-activation theory of semantic processing. *Psychological Review,* **82**, 407–428.

DeGroot, A. M. B. (1983). *Lexical-context effects in visual word recognition.* Unpublished doctoral dissertation, Katholieke Universiteit te Nijmegen.

DeGroot, A. M. B., Thomassen, A. J. W. M., & Hudson, P. T. W. (1982). Associative facilitation of word recognition as measured from a neutral prime. *Memory & Cognition,* **10**, 358–370.

Ehrlich, S. F., & Rayner, K. (1981). Contextual effects on word preception and eye movements during reading. *Journal of Verbal Learning and Verbal Behavior,* **20**, 641–655.

Eisenberg, P. (1981). Word expectancies in reading: The effect of text constraints on error detection and eye movements during real-time reading. Unpublished doctoral dissertation, University of Minnesota, 1981. *Dissertation Abstracts International,* **42/10-B,** 4228.

Eisenberg, P., & Becker, C. A. (1982). Semantic context effects in visual word recognition, sentence processing, and reading: Evidence for semantic strategies. *Journal of Experimental Psychology: Human Perception and Performance,* **8**, 739–756.

Fischler, I. (1977). Semantic facilitation without association in a lexical decision task. *Memory & Cognition,* **5**, 335–339.

Fischler, I., & Bloom, P. A. (1979). Automatic and attentional processes in the effects of sentence contexts on word recognition. *Journal of Verbal Learning and Verbal Behavior,* **18**, 1–20.

Forster, K. I. (1981). Priming and the effects of sentence and lexical contexts on naming time: Evidence for autonomous lexical processing. *Quarterly Journal of Experimental Psychology,* **33A**, 465–495.

Foss, D. J. (1982). A discourse on semantic priming. *Cognitive Psychology,* **12**, 1–31.

Gough, P. A., Alford, J. A., & Holley-Wilcox, P. (1981). Words and context. In O. J. L. Tzeng, & H. Singer (Eds.), *Perception of print,* Hillsdale, NJ: Erlbaum.

Herman, L. M., & Kantowitz, B. H. (1970). The psychological refractory period effect: Only half of the double-stimulation story? *Psychological Bulletin,* **73**, 74–88.

Inhoff, A. W. (1984). Two stages of word processing during eye fixations in the reading of prose. *Journal of Verbal Learning and Verbal Behavior,* **23**, 612–624.

Just, M. A., & Carpenter, P. A. (1980). A theory of reading: From eye fixations to comprehension. *Psychological Review,* **87**, 329–354.

Kahneman, D. & Chajczyk, D. (1983). Tests of the automaticity of reading: Dilution of Stroop effects by color-irrelevant stimuli. *Journal of Experimental Psychology: Human Perception and Performance,* **9**, 497–509.

Keele, S. W. (1973). *Attention and human performance.* Pacific Palisades, CA: Goodyear.

Kintsch, W. (1974). *The representation of meaning in memory.* Hillsdale, NJ: Erlbaum.

LaBerge, D., & Samuels, S. J. (1974). Toward a theory of automatic information processing in reading. *Cognitive Psychology,* **6**, 292–323.

Lewis, J. L. (1970). Semantic processing of unattended messages using dichotic listening. *Journal of Experimental Psychology,* **85**, 51–58.

Mandl, H., Stein, N. L., & Trabasso, T. (1984). *Learning and comprehension of text.* Hillsdale, NJ: Erlbaum.

Meyer, D. E., & Schvaneveldt, R. W. (1971). Facilitation in recognizing pairs of words: Evidence of a dependence between retrieval operations. *Journal of Experimental Psychology,* **90**, 227–234.

Meyer, D. E., Schvaneveldt, R. W., & Ruddy, M. (1975). Loci of contextual effects in visual word recognition. In. P. M. A. Rabbitt & S. Dornic (Eds.), *Attention and performance, V.* New York: Academic Press.

Neely, J. H. (1976). Semantic priming and retrieval from lexical memory: Evidence for facilitatory and inhibitory processes. *Memory & Cognition,* **4,** 648–654.

Neely, J. H. (1977). Semantic priming and retrieval from lexical memory: Roles of inhibitionless spreading activation and limited-capacity attention. *Journal of Experimental Psychology: General,* **106,** 226–254.

Neill, W. T. (1977). Inhibitory and facilitatory processes in selective attention. *Journal of Experimental Psychology: Human Perception and Performance,* **3,** 444–450.

Paap, K. R., Newsome, S. L., McDonald, J. E., & Schvaneveldt, R. W. (1983). An activation-verification model for letter and word recognition: The word-superiority effect. *Psychological Review,* **89,** 573–594.

Posner, M. I., & Boies, S. J. (1971). Components of attention. *Psychological Review,* **78,** 391–408.

Posner, M. I., & Snyder, C. R. R. (1975). Facilitation and inhibition in the processing of signals. In P. M. A. Rabbitt & S. Dornic (Eds.), *Attention and performance, V.* New York: Academic Press.

Rayner, K., Slowiaczek, M. L., Cilfton, C., & Bertera, J. H. (1983). Latency of sequential eye movements: Implications for reading. *Journal of Experimental Psychology: Human Perception and Performance,* **6,** 912–922.

Schuberth, R. E., & Eimas, P. D. (1977). Effects of context of the classification of words and nonwords. *Journal of Experimental Psychology: Human Perception and Performance,* **3,** 27–36.

Schuberth, R. E., Spoehr, K. T., & Lane, D. M. (1981). Effects of stimulus and contextual information on the lexical decision process. *Memory & Cognition,* **9,** 68–77.

Schvaneveldt, R. W., Ackerman, B. P., & Semlear, T. (1977). The effect of semantic context on children's word recognition. *Child Development,* **48,** 612–616.

Schvaneveldt, R. W., & McDonald, J. E. (1981). Semantic context and the encoding of words: Evidence for two modes of stimulus analysis. *Journal of Experimental Psychology: Human Perception and Performance,* **7,** 673–687.

Schweikert, R. (1980). Critical path scheduling of mental processes in a dual task. *Science,* **18,** 704–706.

Stanners, R. F., Jastrzembski, J. E., & Westbrook, A. (1975). Frequency and visual quality in a word–nonword classification task. *Journal of Verbal Learning and Verbal Behavior,* **14,** 259–264.

Stanovich, K. E. (1980). Toward an interactive-compensatory model of individual differences in the development of reading fluency. *Reading Research Quarterly,* **16,** 32–71.

Stanovich, K. E., & West, R. F. (1979). Mechanisms of sentence context effects in reading: Automatic activation and conscious attention. *Memory and Cognition,* **7,** 77–85.

Stanovich, K. E., & West, R. F. (1981). The effect of sentence context on ongoing word recognition: Tests of a two-process theory. *Journal of Experimental Psychology: Human Perception and Performance,* **7,** 658–672.

Stanovich, K. E., & West, R. F. (1983a). On priming by a sentence context. *Journal of Experimental Psychology: General,* **112,** 1–36.

Stanovich, K. E., & West, R. F. (1983b). The generalizability of context effects on word recognition: A reconsideration of the roles of parafoveal priming and sentence context. *Memory & Cognition,* **11,** 49–58.

Stanovich, K. E., West, R. F., & Feeman, D. J. (1981). A longitudinal study of sentence context effects in second-grade children: Tests of an interactive-compensatory model. *Journal of Experimental Child Psychology,* **32,** 185–199.

Sternberg, S. (1967). The discovery of processing stages: Extensions of Donders' method. In W. G. Koster (Ed.), *Attention and performance, II.* Amsterdam: North-Holland Publ.

Theios, J., & Muise, J. G. (1977). The word identification process in reading. In N. J. Castellan, D. B. Pisoni, & G. R. Potts (Eds.), *Cognitive theory* (Vol. 2). Hillsdale, NJ: Erlbaum.

Treisman, A. M., Squire, R., & Green, J. (1974). Semantic processing in dichotic listening? A replication. *Memory & Cognition, 2,* 641–646.

Turvey, M. T. (1973). On peripheral and central processes in vision: Inferences from an information processing analysis of masking with patterned stimuli. *Psychological Review, 80,* 1–52.

West, R. F., & Stanovich, K. E. (1978). Automatic contextual facilitation in readers of three ages. *Child Development, 49,* 717–727.

West, R. F., & Stanovich, K. E. (1982). Source of inhibition in experiments on the effect of sentence context on word recognition. *Journal of Experimental Psychology: Learning, Memory and Cognition, 8,* 385–399.

PHONOLOGY IN VISUAL WORD RECOGNITION: THEIR IS MORE TWO THIS THAN MEATS THE I

IAN DENNIS,* DEREK BESNER,† AND EILEEN DAVELAAR‡

*Department of Psychology
Plymouth Polytechnic
Plymouth, England

†Department of Psychology
University of Waterloo
Waterloo, Ontario, Canada

and

‡Department of Psychology
Wilfrid Laurier University
Waterloo, Ontario, Canada

Copyright © 1985 by Academic Press, Inc.
All rights of reproduction in any form reserved.

Studies of the role of phonological recoding in visual word recognition
have an extensive history and have been the subject of a number of reviews
(e.g., Coltheart, 1978, 1980; McCusker, Hillinger, & Bias, 1981; see also
Carr & Pollatsek, this volume). It is no part of our present purpose to re-
capitulate or extend these reviews; rather, we wish to focus on one particular effect in the area. In recent years a prominent role has been played by
the lexical decision task in which subjects are required to distinguish between words and nonwords. One of the first apparently phonological effects to emerge in this task was the pseudohomophone effect, first reported
by Rubenstein, Lewis, and Rubenstein (1971), whereby nonwords which
sound like words (e.g., *brane*) receive a slower response than other pronounceable nonwords (e.g., *slint*). As Coltheart, Davelaar, Jonasson, and
Besner (1977) pointed out, as an effect involving responses to nonwords,
this phenomenon need not carry any necessary implications for the role of
phonological recoding in recognizing words. Despite this possibility, the
pseudohomophone effect is not without interest. It appears to provide one
of the few clear examples of an effect arising from the phonological properties of a visually presented letter string, and to demonstrate the generation
of a phonological code despite the fact that the production of this code
leads to a slower response to pseudohomophones. There have also been
attempts to exploit the effect in the study of other issues. It has been applied, for example, to investigating differences in the derivation of a phonological code between patients suffering from an acquired reading disorder
(deep dyslexia) and normals (Patterson & Marcel, 1977) or between good
and poor readers (Barron, 1978), and for subtyping poor readers (Mitterer,
1982). It has also been used as a tool for investigating functional capacities
of the left and right hemispheres (Cohen & Freeman, 1978; Barry, 1981)
and in attempts to explore the mechanism of spelling–sound conversion
(Pring, 1981).

    In this light it is worthwhile to give further consideration to the contro-
versy which has recently arisen about whether the effect is truly phonological in character; that is one of the aims of this article. A second aim
arises from the nature of a possible resolution of that controversy. It has
become increasingly clear in recent years that performance on a particular
set of stimuli in a task such as lexical decision is not an absolute property

of those stimulus items but depends also on the other items in the list which form the context in which they are presented. Examples of such context effects are the frequency blocking effect (Glanzer & Ehrenreich, 1979; Gordon, 1983), the variation in the homophone and pseudohomophone effects depending on the proportion of psuedohomophones in the list (Davelaar, Coltheart, Besner, & Jonasson, 1978; McQuade, 1981) and the effect reported by Andrews (1982) whereby words received faster and more accurate responses when half the nonwords were pseudohomophones. In the light of effects such as these it seemed worthwhile to consider the possibility that the pseudohomophone effect is also context sensitive and that some of the apparent inconsistencies in recent work on the effect arise out of another example of the same class of phenomena.

The view that the pseudohomophone effect is phonologically based has recently been challenged by Martin (1982). Martin argues that earlier studies had failed to control adequately the visual similarity between nonwords and real words. Thus, the longer reaction times obtained for pseudohomophones in these studies might reflect the fact that the pseudohomophones looked more like words than the controls. Martin reports an experiment in which pairs of pseudohomophones and controls were created by carrying out analogous orthographic transformations on two real words (thus, for example, *werd* was derived from *word* and *cest* similarly derived from *cost*). The pseudohomophones and controls were also equivalent in the number of words which could be derived from them by changing a single letter (*n*). In this experiment responses to pseudohomophones were no slower than to their controls.

Besner and Davelaar (1983) have shown that matching controls to pseudohomophones on *n* does not necessarily abolish the pseudohomophone effect. In their study the pseudohomophones used by Coltheart *et al.* (1977) were paired with controls created by changing a single letter in the pseudohomophone and matched to the pseudohomophones on *n*. These stimul showed a clear pseudohomophone effect. This suggests that the pseudohomophone effect is genuinely phonological but leaves Martin's (1982) failure to obtain a pseudohomophone effect unexplained. One difference which Besner and Davelaar point out between their experiment and that of Martin is that in the former the pseudohomophones sounded like two English words whereas in the latter they sounded like only one. However it seems worthwhile considering whether there might be other factors contributing to the discrepant outcomes of the two studies.

In general, little consideration has been given to the **words** used in studies of the pseudohomophone effect. However it is well known that the frequency of the words used in a lexical decision task can have a substantial effect on the latency of the response to nonwords (Glanzer & Ehrenreich, 1979; Richardson, 1976; see also Gordon, 1983). There is also reason to believe that phonological effects are more likely to be manifest when responding is relatively slow (Coltheart *et al.*, 1977; Stanovich & Bauer, 1978; Dennis & Newstead, 1981). On this view it would be expected that the pseudohomophone effect would be stronger when the words used are of low frequency and the rejection of nonwords is therefore slower than when the words are of high frequency. The first two experiments which are reported here set out to test this suggestion by comparing the pseudohomophone effects obtained in separate groups of subjects given either only low frequency words or only high frequency words. In Experiment 1 this comparison was carried out using the pseudohomophones and controls used by Besner and Davelaar (1983). Experiment 2 used the same pseudohomophones and controls as Martin (1982).

I. EXPERIMENT 1

A. Method

Two groups of 30 subjects each were paid for their participation in the experiment. All subjects were presented with 156 letter strings; half were words and half were nonwords. For both groups of subjects the **nonwords** were the 39 pairs of pseudohomophones and matched controls used by Besner and Davelaar (1983). For one group of subjects the **words** had Thorndike–Lorge frequencies in excess of 30 occurrences per million. With the exception of the three-letter words, the words were taken from those used by Fredriksen and Kroll (1976). For the other group of subjects the words had frequencies in the range of 2–5 occurrences per million. The stimulus set can be seen in Appendices A and B.

The letter strings were presented one at a time on a CRT screen slaved to an Apple II+ microcomputer. The letter string remained on the screen until the subject responded; subjects made positive responses with the first finger of their dominant hand and negative responses with the first finger of their nondominant hand. Each trial was initiated by the subject pressing a button with the thumb of the dominant hand. Subjects were instructed to respond positively if the word displayed on the screen was a real English word and negatively if it was not. Thirty practice trials preceded the 156 test trials. Feedback about speed and accuracy was displayed during practice, following each trial; no feedback was given during the experimental trials.

B. Results

Mean reaction times and error rates across subjects for nonwords are shown in Table I. Analysis of variance on mean nonword reaction times for subjects showed a main effect of the frequency of the accompanying words [$F(1,58) = 14.6, p < .01$] but no reliable main effect of pseudohomophones versus controls [$F(1,58) = 2.8$]. There was no significant interaction between these two factors [$F(1,58) = 0.38$].

Because of computing problems the analysis of stimulus means was restricted to the data from 28 subjects in each group. Mean reaction times for each nonword in the two conditions are listed in Appendix B. Analysis of variance on these data showed an effect of word frequency [$F(1,38) = 177.4, p < .01$] but no pseudohomophone effect [$F(1,38) = 1.8$] and no interaction [$F(1,38) = .02$].

Analysis of variance on the number of errors made by each subject in each condition showed that more errors were made on pseudohomophones than on controls [$F(1,58) = 14.7, p < .01$] but produced no other significant outcomes. However on the analysis of errors over stimuli only the effect of frequency of the background words was significant [$F(1,38) = 7.68, p < .01$].

C. Discussion

The anticipated effect of frequency of the accompanying words on latency of responding to nonwords emerged clearly in this experiment. However, a pseudohomophone effect on reaction times was obtained neither against a background of high frequency words nor against one of low frequency words. This failure to obtain the pseudohomophone effect is surprising in view of the results of Besner and Davelaar (1983) and the relatively large number of subjects used here. It will be discussed more fully after the

TABLE I

Mean Reaction Times (msec) and Error Rates to Nonwords in Experiment 1

	Pseudohomophones		Controls	
	Reaction time	% Error	Reaction time	% Error
High frequency words as background items	598	7.7	591	5.4
Low frequency words as background items	727	11.4	712	7.9

results of Experiment 2 have been presented. Experiment 2 was analogous to Experiment 1 but the nonwords used were taken from Martin (1982).

II. EXPERIMENT 2

A. Method

Two groups of 30 subjects each were used. Each subject saw a total of 100 letter-strings consisting of the 25 pairs of pseudohomophones and controls used by Martin (1982) and 50 words. The words presented to the two groups of subjects were a subset of those presented to the corresponding group in Experiment 1. The stimulus set is given in Appendices A and C. In all other respects, Experiment 2 was identical to Experiment 1.

B. Results

The mean reaction times and error rates across subjects are shown in Table II. An analysis of variance on subject mean reaction times shows a significant main effect of frequency of the accompanying word [$F(1,58) = 10.9$, $p < .01$] and a significant interaction of this factor with pseudohomophone versus control [$F(1,58) = 9.1$, $p < .01$]. The same effects were also significant in an analysis across stimuli [for the main effect $F(1,24) = 228.9$, $p < .01$, for the interaction $F(1,24) = 8.1$, $p < .01$].

The interaction was explored further by carrying out tests of the simple main effect of pseudohomophones versus controls for each level of frequency of the background words. With a high frequency background the comparison between pseudohomophones and controls was not significant either across subjects [$F(1,58) = 2.9$] or across stimuli [$F(1,48) = 0.84$]. With a low frequency background pseudohomophones were significantly **faster** than controls across subjects [$F(1,58) = 7.7$, $p < .01$] though this

TABLE II
Mean Reaction Times (msec) and Error Rates to Nonwords in Experiment 2

	Pseudohomophones		Controls	
	Reaction time	% Error	Reaction time	% Error
High frequency words as background items	680	6.8	666	7.3
Low frequency words as background items	756	7.7	782	9.2

effect did not reach significance across stimuli [$F(1,48) = 3.2$]. Mean reaction times for each nonword are listed in Appendix C. There were no significant error effects in this experiment.

C. Discussion

The results of Experiments 1 and 2 clearly provide no support for the specific suggestion that the pseudohomophone effect will be greater when the words used in the lexical decision task are of low rather than high frequency. In Experiment 1 no interaction between the type of nonword and word frequency was obtained and the interaction which was obtained in Experiment 2 involved a reversal of the pseudohomophone effect with low frequency words.

In more general terms, however, the notion that the nature of the words moderates the pseudohomophone effect merits further consideration in the light of these experiments. One pointer to a role for the words used was the interaction obtained in Experiment 2 and a second one was the failure to obtain a pseudohomophone effect for either the low or high frequency group in Experiment 1. This suggests that some feature of the **words** used by Besner and Davelaar (1983) is critical to the pseudohomophone effect which they obtained. The only transparent difference between the words used by Besner and Davelaar (1983) (which were, in fact, the same as the words used by Coltheart *et al.*, 1977) and those used in Experiments 1 and 2 was that half of the Besner and Davelaar words were the lower frequency member of a pair of homophones. This suggests that the presence of homophones among the words used may enhance the pseudohomophone effect and hence that the absence of homophones among the words used may have contributed to Martin's (1982) failure to obtain the effect. In order to test this suggestion Experiment 3 used Martin's nonword stimuli together with homophones and their matched controls taken from Coltheart *et al.* (1977).

III. EXPERIMENT 3

A. Method

Thirty subjects were paid for their participation in this experiment. Each subject made lexical decisions to a total of 100 letter strings. This total was made up of the 25 pseudohomophones and their controls used by Martin (1982) and 25 pairs of homophones and controls taken from Coltheart *et al.* (1977). The remaining details of the experiment were the same as those for Experiments 1 and 2. A list of the pseudohomophones and their controls can be seen in Appendix C.

B. Results

Mean reaction times and error rates for the pseudohomophones and their controls and for the homophones and their controls are shown in Table III. The pseudohomophone effect was significant across subjects [$t(29) = 2.55$, $p < .02$] but not across stimuli [$t(29) = 1.08$]. The difference in error rates between the two conditions was not significant across subjects [$t(29) = .70$] or across stimuli [$t(24) = .12$].

Homophones were significantly slower than their controls across subjects [$t(29) = 2.08$, $p < .05$] but not across stimuli [$t(24) = 1.32$]. There were also significantly more errors on homophones than on their controls both across subjects [$t(29) = 3.94$, $p < .001$] and across stimuli [$t(24) = 2.41$, $p < .05$].

C. Discussion

Stimuli which had failed to yield a pseudohomophone effect when used by Martin and in Experiment 2 did give a pseudohomophone effect which was significant across subjects when presented against a background which included homophones in Experiment 3. The results of Experiment 3 were therefore supportive of the view that the pseudohomophone effect is more readily obtained when there are homophones among the words. The evidence supporting this suggestion and the difficulties raised by the failure of the effect tor each significance across stimuli will be discussed more fully after the presentation of Experiment 4.

The homophones used in Experiment 3 all had lower frequencies than

TABLE III

**Mean Reaction Times (msec) and Error Rates
in Experiment 3**

	Reaction time	% Error
"No" responses		
Pseudohomphones	652	11.9
Controls	624	13.1
"Yes" responses		
Homophones	579	13.9
Controls	556	7.7

their homophonic mates. The same is true of most previous experiments which have obtained the pseudohomophone effect in the presence of homophones (e.g., Coltheart *et al.*, 1977; Besner & Davelaar, 1983). It may therefore be the case that it is not simply the presence of homophones in general but more specifically the presence of the lower frequency member of a homophone pair which is of importance in determining whether or not a pseudohomophone effect is obtained. Experiment 4 examined this question by comparing two groups of subjects. For both groups of subjects half the words with which they were presented were homophones. However for one group of subjects these were the higher frequency members of a homophone pair while for the other group of subjects they were the lower frequency member. In the hope of confirming the results of Besner and Davelaar (1983) and strengthening the contention that the failure to obtain a pseudohomophone effect in Experiment 1 was due to the absence of homophones, the nonword stimuli were the same as those of Experiment 1.

IV. EXPERIMENT 4

A. Method

Two groups of 25 subjects were paid for their participation in this experiment. For both groups of subjects the nonwords were the same as those used in Experiment 1 and in Besner and Davelaar (1983). For one group of subjects the words were 39 homophones and their matched controls taken from Coltheart *et al.* (1977). For the other group of subjects the 39 homophones were replaced by their higher frequency homophonic mate. The remaining details of the experiment were the same as for previous experiments.

B. Results

For "no" responses mean reaction times across subjects and error rates are shown in Table IV. Analysis of variance on the reaction times showed a pseudohomophone effect which was significant both across subjects $[F(1,48) = 17.72, p < .01]$ and across stimuli $[F(1,38) = 10.15, p < .01]$.

The main effect of group was significant across stimuli $[F(1,38) = 10.21, p < .01]$ but not across subjects $[F(1,48) = 0.23]$. Group showed no significant interaction with the size of the pseudohomophone effect on either analysis. Stimulus mean reaction times are listed in Appendix B. There were significantly more errors on pseudohomophones than controls both for subjects $[F(1,48) = 9.81, p < .01]$ and for stimuli $[F(1,38) = 5.03, p < .05]$ but no other effects in the error analysis approached significance.

TABLE IV

Mean Reaction Times (msec) and Error Rates to Nonwords in Experiment 4

	Pseudohomophones		Controls	
	Response time	% Error	Response time	% Error
High frequency member of homophone pair as background item	651	8.7	629	5.8
Low frequency member of homophone pair as background item	669	8.2	644	5.4

For "yes" responses only the data from the group with the lower frequency member of a homophone pair are of interest since in the other group the comparison between homophones and controls is confounded with word frequency. For the former group the mean reaction time to homophones was 604 msec while to controls it was 599 msec. This difference was not significant across either subjects [$t(24) = 0.93$] or stimuli [$t(38) = 0.88$]. There were 11.5% errors on homophones and 9.5% errors on controls. This error effect was significant across subjects [$t(24) = 2.13, p < .05$] but not across stimuli [$t(38) = .66$].

C. Discussion

The results of Experiment 4 suggest that as long as there are homophones present among the words it matters little whether these are the high or low frequency members of homophone pairs. The results of this experiment can be compared with those of Experiment 1 in which the same nonword stimuli were used but failed to give a significant pseudohomophone effect. Although the comparison between Experiment 4 and Experiment 1 is less striking than that between Experiment 3 and Experiment 2, it provides further support for the suggestion that the pseudohomophone effect is more readily obtained in the presence of homophones.

V. GENERAL DISCUSSION

A. Empirical Claims

The set of pseudohomophones and matched controls produced by Martin (1982) seem able to produce a conventional pseudohomophone effect as in Experiment 3, no effect as in the high frequency group of Experiment 2 and in Martin's Experiment 1, and a reversed pseudohomophone effect as in the low frequency group of Experiment 2. This clearly indicates the importance of the **words** used in experiments on the pseudohomophone effect. Neither the conventional pseudohomophone effect nor the reversed pseudohomophone effect was significant over stimuli. Hence we cannot be sure that this pattern of outcomes would generalize to other letter strings generated in the same way as those of Martin. However, even if the outcome is specific to the particular set of letter strings used here it cannot be dismissed as trivial; an explanation of why the difference between a particular set of pseudohomophones and their controls should be sensitive to the word context is still required.

One feature of the words which appears important is whether or not they include homophones. With three different sets of words not including homophones, namely those used by Martin (1982) and the high and low frequency words used in Experiment 2, Martin's stimuli failed to yield a pseudohomophone effect. When homophones were included in the words in Experiment 3 a pseudohomophone effect was obtained. Similarly, the stimuli used by Besner and Davelaar (1983) yielded a pseudohomophone effect both in their experiment and in Experiment 4 with homophones present but failed to do so with the two different sets of words in Experiment 1 which did not include homophones. The fact that the presence of homophones has proved to be important with two different sets of stimuli provides reassurance that this effect at least has reasonable generality.

Despite the apparent consistency of the effect of homophones, a direct demonstration of the interaction between the size of the pseudohomophone effect and the presence or absence of homophones is clearly desirable. In order to provide such a demonstration the difference scores between pseudohomophones and controls from the four experiments were entered into an analysis of variance with stimulus set (i.e., that of Martin versus that of Besner and Davelaar) and the presence or absence of homophones as two between-subject factors. When this analysis was carried out on the latency data the difference scores proved to be significantly larger in the presence of homophones than in their absence [$F(1,196) = 8.31, p < .01$]. However, neither the main effect of stimulus set nor its interaction with the presence or absence of homophones reached significance [$F(1,196) = 1.79$ and $F(1,196) = 2.27$, respectively].

An analysis with the same two factors was also carried out on the difference between each pseudohomophone and its control nonword. This analysis across stimuli yielded essentially the same result as the analysis across subjects; the main effect of the presence or absence of homophones reached significance [$F(1,62) = 5.27, p < .05$] but the main effect of stimulus set [$F(1,62) = 0.95$] and the interaction [$F(1,62) = 1.47$] failed to do so.

Analagous analyses were also carried out on the error data. Across subjects there was a main effect of stimulus set [$F(1,196) = 14.68, p < .01$] whereby the error effect was larger with the Besner and Davelaar stimulus set than with Martin's stimulus set. The effect of stimulus set in the error data did not, however, reach significance in the analysis across stimuli [$F(1,62) = 2.51, p < .10$]. The main effect of the presence versus absence of homophones and the interaction fell well short of significance in both the analysis across subjects and the analysis across stimuli ($F < 1$ in all four cases).

It seems reasonable to conclude that in the present series of experiments the pseudohomophone effect on latencies was larger in the presence of homophones than in their absence. There was no indication of any increased error effect when homophones were absent which might vitiate the increased latency efect. There was a suggestion that the error effect is larger with the set of stimuli used by Besner and Davelaar than with that used by Martin. However, since this effect was not reliable in the analysis over stimuli it may be that it is specific to these two samples and does not reflect any general aspect of the way in which the two stimulus sets were constructed. Despite this it may be worth noting that very often one of the two words which sounds like Besner and Davelaar's double pseudohomophones is of very low frequency and some of the subjects' errors on these stimuli may be a manifestation of uncertainty about the spelling of these low frequency words.

A review of the remaining literature on the pseudohomophone effect is broadly consistent with the view that larger pseudohomophone effects are obtained when homophones are included in the word stimuli. Previous studies of the effect are listed in Table V classified according to the proportion of homophones among the words used. In this table the designation "Studies in which words did not include homophones" is used for studies in which there was no explicit attempt to include homophones among the words and for which the list of words used was either not published or did not show an incidence of homophones which seemed strikingly different from that in the language as a whole. The experiment which is briefly mentioned by Gough and Cosky (1977) has been omitted from this table since no indication of the number of subjects, number of trials, or the type of words used is given. The various groups and conditions of five studies in which homophones have been included in the words used (Rubenstein *et al.,* 1971; Coltheart *et al.,* 1977; Barron, 1978; Barry, 1981; Besner & Davelaar, 1983) have yielded pseudohomophone effects ranging from 30 to 68 msec. In contrast, the largest effect obtained in seven studies which have not included homophones among the words (Fredriksen & Kroll, 1976; two studies reported by Cohen & Freeman, 1978; McQuade, 1981; Martin, 1982;

TABLE V
Summary of Previous Studies of the Pseudohomophone Effect

Study	Number of subjects	Number of pseu- dohomo- phones	Size of pseudohomophone effect	
			Msec	Errors (%)
Studies in which words did not include homophones				
Fredriksen & Koll (1976)	10	20	25	—
Cohen & Freeman (1978)				
(a) Case alternation present, RVF	10	64	30	+7
(b) Case alternation present, LVF	10	64	−32	0
(c) Case alternation absent, RVF	6	32	23	—
(d) Case alternation absent, LVF	6	32	11	—
McQuade (1981)				
(a) Low proportion pseudohom- ophone	40	20	36	—
(b) High proportion pseudohom- ophone	40	20	2	—
Andrews (1982)	20	40	−7	—
Martin (1982)	18	25	−10	−1.6
Parkin & Ellingham (1983)	8	40	32	—
Studies in which 50% of words were homophones				
Rubinstein *et al.* (1971)				
(a) Pseudohomophones of low frequency words	44	20	47	+12
(b) Pseudohomophones of high frequency words	44	19	63	+2
Coltheart *et al.* (1977)	20	39	62	+3.2
Barron (1978)				
(a) Good readers	32	40	68	+10.3
(b) Poor readers	32	40	30	+10.4
Barry (1981)				
(a) RVF	20	16	48	+15.6
(b) LVF	20	16	55	+7.2
Besner & Davelaar (1983)	22	39	34	+2.2
Studies with intermediate proportion of homophones				
Pring (1981)				
(a) FSU[a] intact	20	38	44	+1.3
(b) FSU degraded	20	38	4	+0.6
Taft (1982)	30	20	−2	+0.6

[a]FSU, functional spelling unit.

Andrews, 1982; Parkin & Ellingham, 1983) was 36 msec, and four of these seven studies failed to yield significant pseudohomophone effects. An experiment by Pring (1981) in which stimuli with case alternations which did not disrupt spelling units produced a pseudohomophone effect of 44 msec is a marginal case. Although there was no deliberate attempt to include homophones in her study, inspection of the stimulus list shows that roughly 20% of the words were homophones. The study by Parkin and Ellingham (1983) has been assigned to the category where the words did not include homophones. There is, however, a degree of arbitrariness here. As with Pring's experiment there was no deliberate attempt to include homophones among the words, and while there was only one homophone among the 40 regular words, there were 10 among the 40 irregular words. (Parkin & Ellingham classified a word as irregular if its pronounciation was specified in the "Oxford Paperback Dictionary," and one suspects that the compilers of this dictionary may well have been influenced by considerations of homophony; it is difficult to see why else they should provide a pronounciation for *yolk* but not *folk*). Although the Parkin and Ellingham experiment appears to provide one of the large effects in this category, it should be noted that the comparison is based on only eight subjects and that no statistical test of the pseudohomophone effect is reported. The one study which is hard to reconcile with the claim that the pseudohomophone effect is more readily obtained in the presence of homophones is that of Taft (1982), who failed to obtain a pseudohomophone effect when 25% of the words were homophones; this study is discussed later.

Where they are available from the original accounts of the studies in question, Table V also gives the size of the error effect. Unfortunately, error data are not available for many of the studies which did not include homophones among the words. Nevertheless, such data as have been reported suggest that there is a robust error effect when homophones are present and provide no support for the view that the larger latency effect with homophones present is offset by a smaller error effect.

One point which needs to be considered in relation to the data in Table V is that the presence of **homophones** among the words used in an experiment has largely been confounded with the use of double rather than single **pseudohomophones**. Thus the studies by Coltheart *et al.* (1977), Barron (1978), Barry (1981), and Besner and Davelaar (1983) all used double pseudohomophones, whereas none of the studies in which the words did not include homophones used double pseudohomophones. This confound is resolved in the original Rubenstein *et al.* (1971) study which produced a large pseudohomophone effect with single pseudohomophones, in the present Experiment 1 which failed to produce a pseudohomophone effect with double pseudohomophones, and in the present Experiment 3 which produced a 28-msec pseudohomophone effect with single pseudohomophones. It seems reasonable to claim that the data in Table V provide further support for the contention that the pseudohomophone effect is more readily obtained when there are homophones among the words used.

In summary, our main empirical claim is that the pseudohomophone effect is more easily found in the presence of homophones than in their absence. A subsidiary and more tentative claim based on the results of Experiment 2 is that the pseudohomophone effect can reverse in the presence of low frequency words. The next section of the discussion aims to provide a theoretical account of these phenomena.

B. A Hypothesis

In attempting to explain why the presence of homophones should influence the pseudohomophone effect, we will discount Martin's (1982) contention that the effect is solely attributable to the greater visual similarity of pseudohomophones to words and will instead assume that the effect is phonologically mediated. The primary reason for this is that the effect has been obtained with two sets of stimuli in which the visual similarity of the pseudohomophones to words has been carefully matched to that of the controls, including the stimulus set produced by Martin herself. Additionally, if the effect arose from visual similarity to words it is difficult to see why incidental differences in the visual similarity of pseudohomophones and their controls to words should have produced a 62-msec effect in experiment 1 of Coltheart et al. (1977) whereas a deliberate attempt to manipulate visual similarity in their experiment 2 produced only a 37-msec effect.[1]

Our attempt to explain why the presence of homophones should influence the size of the pseudohomophone effect is based on the nature of the task which confronts subjects when they are asked to distinguish between words and nonwords. When there are pseudohomophones present in the stimuli, but no homophones, then sounding like some word but not being spelled like that word is a property which is only found among nonwords and might therefore logically be used to provide evidence for a nonword response. However, homophones also have the property of sounding like some word that does not match their spelling. Thus, once there are homophones present among the words this property can no longer be used as a reliable clue to identify a stimulus as a nonword. There is thus a source of evidence which can be used in making negative responses to pseudohomophones which is eliminated by the presence of homophones. Hence the latency of pseudohomophones relative to other nonwords might be expected to be longer in the presence of homophones.

---

[1]See also Besner and Davelaar (1983) for further problems with the claim that n exerts an effect on response time.

This approach might also help to explain an otherwise very puzzling phenomenon reported by Andrews (1982). Andrews examined the latencies of responses to the same set of words in two versions of a lexical decision experiment. The two versions differed by virtue of the fact that in one version half of the nonwords were pseudohomophones while in the other no pseudohomophones were included among the nonwords. Responses to words were both faster and more accurate when there were pseudohomophones among the nonwords. Andrews attempted to explain this effect in terms of reduced reliance on phonological recoding in the presence of pseudohomophones but had difficulty in generating a version of this account which predicted improvements on both latency and accuracy. A second difficulty facing an account of this type is that Andrews' study showed no interaction between the presence or absence of pseudohomophones and the effect of consistency (as defined by Glushko, 1979). If the presence of pseudohomophones was reducing reliance on phonology then this might be expected to reduce the effect of consistency. The view proposed above would explain Andrews' finding by supposing that the additional evidence that pseudohomophones are not words makes the task of word–nonword discrimination easier and hence leads to faster and more accurate responses on words.

It is reasonable that when homophones are absent the fact that a letter string sounds like some word but is not spelled like that word provides evidence for a nonword response. However, the question arises as to whether it is possible to develop an account of how that potential source of evidence might be exploited within the framework provided by contemporary views on lexical access. It is probably feasible to elaborate the notion sketched out above within a variety of accounts of lexical access; however, there is one model which seems particularly well suited to this purpose. This is the extension of the logogen model produced by Coltheart *et al.* (1977). This was originally conceived partly in order to account for the pseudohomophone effect, and many of the reasons which made it attractive for this purpose still seem valid. In particular, the fact that visual and phonological evidence can be pooled in a straightforward manner is an advantage over search models where the search must be based on either visual comparisons or phonological comparisons or at best on some Boolean combination of the two. A further attraction of this model in the present context is that the most satisfactory account of the frequency blocking effect available at present, namely, that of Gordon (1983), is essentially an elaboration of the same model. For these reasons the Coltheart *et al.* model is appealing as a starting point for the present account.

The Coltheart *et al.* model assumes that there is a single set of logogens collecting both visual and phonological evidence but that phonological evidence alone is insufficient to take a logogen past threshold.[2] "No" responses are produced when a deadline expires without a logogen having passed threshold. However, the deadline is flexible, so that if a logogen is approaching threshold the deadline is delayed to see whether the logogen fires. It is this last assumption that is used to explain why responses for pseudohomophones are slower than those for controls. Although phonological evidence cannot take a logogen past threshold it can bring it sufficiently close to postpone the deadline and hence delay the response. In order to use this model to explain why the presence of homophones might moderate the pseudohomophone effect it is necessary to suppose that there is an alternative procedure by which "no" responses can be made to pseudohomophones. This alternative procedure involves registering the fact that a pseudohomophone sounds like a word but does not have the correct spelling for that word. This can be achieved if phonological evidence takes a logogen past threshold and there is some postaccess spelling check. In the absence of homophones the failure of this spelling check can be taken to indicate that the presented letter string is a nonword. This will be referred to as the spelling check procedure for rejecting pseudohomophones.

There is clearly a conflict between the requirement of the spelling check procedure which assumes that phonological evidence from a pseudohomophone can take the corresponding logogen past threshold and the assumption in the Coltheart *et al.* model that this cannot occur. It is therefore necessary to assume that the system operates somewhat differently when the spelling check procedure is being used and when it is not. When the spelling check procedure is not being used logogen thresholds are raised or the weight given to phonological evidence is modified so that the phonological evidence from pseudohomophones cannot take a logogen past threshold. Under these conditions all nonwords are dealt with in the same way, that is, by failure of a logogen to fire before the deadline expires (the deadline procedure). In contrast, when the spelling check procedure is in use, logogen thresholds are reduced (or the system is otherwise adjusted) so that pseudohomophones can fire a logogen. Under these circumstances pseudohomophones are rejected by the spelling check procedure while other

[2]It should be noted that the model need only suppose that visual evidence and phonological evidence derived from **visually presented** words are pooled. The validity of Morton's (1979) espousal of separate auditory and visual input logogens is orthogonal to this question providing it is assumed that the visual logogens can be activated through phonological recoding as well as by direct visual evidence. If the alternative assumption that phonological evidence derived from visually presented letter strings activates only auditory logogens is made then some modifications of the account are required. However, much of the logic of the explanation and in particular the notion that pseudohomophones might be rejected by the spelling check procedure could still be maintained.

nonwords continue to be rejected by the deadline procedure. The spelling check procedure cannot be used when homophones are present because if the lexical entry for the homophonic mate is accessed the postaccess spelling check will fail and this will lead to an erroneous nonword response.

In the absence of homophones the likelihood of subjects using the deadline and spelling check procedures may be determined by their relative speed. It is impossible to specify *a priori* whether the deadline procedure or the spelling check procedure will lead to faster rejection of pseudohomophones. However, if the deadline procedure were always faster than the spelling check procedure then it is difficult to see why subjects should not continue to use the deadline procedure when homophones are absent. In order to explain the lack of a pseudohomophone effect when homophones are absent it is necessary to assume that the spelling check procedure can sometimes lead to a faster "no" response for pseudohomophones than the deadline procedure does. Whether the absence of homophones leads simply to the reduction of the pseudohomophone effect or to its elimination or reversal depends on the speed of the spelling check procedure for pseudohomophones relative to that of the deadline procedure for controls. Although it is again impossible to specify these relative speeds *a priori* it is possible to identify a variable which is likely to alter the speed of the deadline procedure but not that of the spelling check procedure and hence to indicate the circumstances under which a reversal of the pseudohomophone effect is most likely to be found. In order to account for the effects of the frequency of the background words in lexical decision on the latency of nonword responses it is necessary to assume that the deadline procedure is slower in the presence of low frequency words than in the presence of high frequency words. Under a logogen-type model this is explained by assuming that it is possible to operate with a shorter deadline when all the words are of high frequency (cf. Gordon, 1983). On the other hand, there seems to be no obvious reason why the speed of the spelling check procedure should be altered by the frequency of the accompanying words. Thus the spelling check procedure for pseudohomophones is most likely to be faster than the deadline procedure for controls, and hence a reversed pseudohomophone effect is most likely to be found when background word frequency is low. This is precisely what was found in Experiment 2. It is notable that pseudohomophones as well as controls receive a slower response in the presence of low frequency words than in the presence of high frequency words. Since the spelling check procedure is assumed to be insensitive to the frequency of the words this must be explained by assuming that at least for high frequency words some use is still made of the deadline procedure, even in the absence of homophones.

Since the account of the pseudohomophone effect which is being proposed here is one that is capable of explaining either the conventional pseudohomophone effect or its absence, or even its reversal, it is important, if it is to remain testable, that it should be successful in predicting the circumstances under which each of these outcomes is obtained. Insofar as it correctly suggests that a conventional pseudohomophone effect is most likely to be obtained in the presence of homophones, while a reversed effect is most likely to be obtained when the words do not include homophones and are of low frequency, the account is successful. One outstanding difficulty is that it is unclear why word frequency should have interacted with the pseudohomophone effect in Experiment 2 but not in Experiment 1. It is notable that in Experiment 1 the variance between subjects in the difference between pseudohomophones and controls was greater for the low frequency group than for the high frequency group $[F(29,29) = 3.45, p < .01]$. It may therefore have been the case that while some subjects in the low frequency group adopted the spelling check procedure and showed the anticipated reversal of the pseudohomophone effect, others adhered to the deadline procedure.

The use of the spelling check procedure is supposed to lead to errors on homophones whenever phonological access leads a homophone to access the entry of its homophonic mate and a subsequent spelling check fails. This will only happen when access to the wrong lexical entry precedes access to the correct lexical entry. Thus, if access to the entry for the higher frequency member of a homophonic pair always occurred first, no errors should occur when the higher frequency member of the pair is presented. Hence under this assumption it might have been expected that the use of the higher frequency members of homophone pairs would have led to the pseudohomophone effect being reduced or absent in the relevant group of Experiment 4; this did not occur. The simplest way of explaining this would seem to be to assume that although, on the average, access is faster for the higher frequency member of the pair, there are some occasions when the entry for the lower frequency member is accessed first. These occasions would result in an error whenever the presented word was the higher frequency member of the pair. In order to explain the results of Experiment 4 it is necessary to assume that these occasions are sufficiently frequent to discourage the use of the spelling check procedure even when the higher frequency members of homophone pairs are present.

Martin (1982) argued that the pseudohomophone effect is an artifact which occurs when the pseudohomophones have greater visual similarity to words in general than do their controls. Taft (1982) has also argued that the pseudohomophone effect is not a phonological effect but rather that it arises because the pseudohomophones can be transformed into words by rules for interchanging sets of graphemes which can give rise to the same pronunciation (e.g., *ea* may be exchanged for *ee* and *g* for *j*). Taft has called these rules grapheme–grapheme conversion rules, and has shown that pseudohomophones give lexical decision latencies which are no longer than those given by controls which can also be converted to words by grapheme–grapheme rules. Taft's failure to obtain a pseudohomophone effect with these controls cannot be attributed to an absence of homophones since 25% of the words in his experiment were homophones.[3] Can Taft's account of the pseudohomophone effect be extended to explain why the presence of homophones is important in obtaining the effect? Since one member of a pair of homophones can generally be converted to the other by means of a grapheme–grapheme rule the presence of homophones will, if anything, discourage the application of these rules. Hence the effect cannot be explained in terms of the likelihood of such rules being used. An alternative account in terms of grapheme–grapheme rules might propose an analog of the spelling check procedure for the rejection of pseudohomophones whereby if there is a grapheme–grapheme rule which can convert the stimulus to a word then the subject makes a negative response. There are, however, difficulties with this account, some of which serve to illustrate aspects of the grapheme–grapheme notion which are underspecified. One problem is that there are many words which are not homophones but which can be converted to other words by grapheme–grapheme rules (e.g., *sweat* may be converted to *sweet* and *gust* to *just*). Any attempt to apply the proposed analog of the spelling check procedure could lead to incorrect "no" responses to these words. The severity of this problem depends on how frequently two graphemes must map onto the same phoneme before a grapheme–grapheme rule is established.

The second problem is that the procedure can only work if the system can distinguish between lexical access achieved by the original letter string and lexical access consequent on the application of grapheme–grapheme rules. It is impossible to evaluate the importance of this problem without some specification of how grapheme–grapheme rules are incorporated into the system as a whole. This highlights the point that it is unclear what useful role grapheme–grapheme rules can play.

Further difficulties for Taft's theory arise from experiments on priming of word responses in lexical decision by a matching pseudohomophone on the preceding trial. Besner, Dennis, and Davelaar (1985) showed that if *wreath* is preceded by *wreeth* the "yes" response is faster than if it is preceded by an unrelated nonword. Taft would presumably explain this by

[3]It should be noted, however, that the nonwords which Taft considers to be proper controls contain a large number of embedded words (e.g., *dreed, froast, putch*). As discussed by Besner and Davelaar (1983), this will lead to inflated reaction times relative to nonwords without embedded words.

claiming *wreeth* can be converted to *wreath* by a grapheme–grapheme rule. On this basis the effect should still occur with a prime that can be converted into the following word by a grapheme–grapheme rule but is not a pseudohomophone of that word. Thus, for example, *breeth* should prime *breath*. This latter effect did not occur.

An experiment carried out by Sheena Leach with the first author also poses problems for Taft's view of the pseudohomophone effect (as well as for Martin's). Pseudohomophones were used in a lexical decision experiment in one of three conditions. The three conditions were differentiated by the word which occurred on the trial preceding the pseudohomophone in the sequence. In one condition the pseudohomophone was preceded by a regularly pronounced word ending with the same set of letters as the pseudohomophone (e.g., *kave* preceded by *wave*). In a second condition the pseudohomophone was preceded by a word with the same set of letters pronounced irregularly (e.g., *kave* preceded by *have*), the third condition was a control in which the pseudohomophone was preceded by an unrelated word (e.g., *kave* preceded by *last*). The mean reaction time for pseudohomophones with a regular prime was 963 msec; for pseudohomophones with an irregular prime it was 877 msec, and for the control it was 921 msec. The respective error rates were 17, 13, and 14%. Graphemic effects, whether mediated by grapheme–grapheme rules or not, should be equivalent for both regular and irregular primes; the slowing of responses by regular primes must have a phonological basis. Thus these results provide a further indication that the pseudohomophone effect is, at least in part, a phonological effect, contrary to Taft's suggestions. It might also be noted in passing that this effect creates the same sort of difficulties for an account of phonological recoding based on grapheme–phoneme rules as do the results of Kay and Marcel (1981).

For these reasons we prefer to retain the view that the pseudohomophone effect is phonological and that the role of homophones is the one previously indicated. However, Taft's data clearly require explanation; this remains an unsolved problem.

C. Wider Implications

Coltheart *et al.* (1977) point out that since the pseudohomophone effect is an effect on **nonword** decisions its occurrence has no strong implications for the role of phonological recoding in lexical access for words. The conclusion that phonological access does not occur for **words** in a lexical decision task has since been reiterated by Coltheart, Besner, Jonasson, and Davelaar (1979) and by Coltheart (1980). Although the mere occurrence of the pseudohomophone effect cannot tell us anything about lexical access for words, it may be that the way the effect is moderated by the presence of homophones is more informative. The assumption that homophones (and hence presumably other words) (cf. Stanovich & Bauer, 1978; Bauer & Stanovich, 1980; Barron, 1981; Parkin, 1982) can achieve phonological access is crucial to the foregoing account of the influence of their presence on the pseudohomophone effect. Without this assumption there would be no explanation of why the spelling check procedure is not used in the presence of homophones. A more general argument for the involvement of phonology in lexical decisions about words can also be made. This argument rests on the fact that it is only when a phonological representation is involved that the properties of homophones differ from those of other words. Thus, any account of the influence of homophones on the pseudohomophone effect will need to invoke a phonological representation for words at some stage. It is, of course, possible that this stage is postlexical or is not involved in the production of "yes" responses. However, while we recognize this as a logical possibility we are unable to devise any specific account of this kind. There are also other lines of evidence which suggest that phonological access can occur for words in lexical decision. Although homophone effects have sometimes proved elusive with pseudohomophones present (e.g., Coltheart *et al.*, 1977; Barron, 1978) they can be obtained when pseudohomophones are absent (Davelaar *et al.*, 1978). Even with pseudohomophones present a greater error rate was obtained on homophones than on controls both in the present Experiments 3 and 4 and in the work by Barry (1981).

Whether the specific account of the comings and goings of the pseudohomophone effect proposed here is correct or not remains to be seen. More important, perhaps, is its heuristic value in alerting us to the possibility that the absence of a pseudohomophone effect may not be evidence that a phonological code is inoperative.

This point may be illustrated by considering an argument advanced by Parkin and Ellingham (1983). They state that their data, "which show a gradual weakening of the pseudohomophone effect over successive blocks of trials, would seem to support Taft's contention that increased rejection latencies to pseudohomophones arise from their visual as opposed to phonemic properties." It should be noted parenthetically that it is far from clear that their data do show a gradual weakening of the pseudohomophone effect over successive blocks of trials. They do not report a direct test of the interaction between blocks and trials and the size of the pseudohomophone effect in the four successive blocks was 10, 52, 44, and 14 msec, respectively. Suppose, however, that the evidence that the pseudohomophone effect was getting weaker had been clear, and that the contention that subjects are not abandoning phonological recoding, which is based on a sustained regularity effect in the word data, is also accepted. This would still be consistent with a phonologically-based pseudohomophone effect. In the terms of the previous discussion it would be explicable by a switch from the deadline procedure to the spelling check procedure. It may also be unwise to make the common assumption that differences in the size of the pseudohomophone effect reflect differences in the degree of reliance on a phonological code, or in the ease of grapheme–phoneme translation. Instead, it may be necessary to seek evidence for the use of a phonological code more indirectly. For example, when we pitted a phonological account against a grapheme–grapheme account, evidence for the use of phonologically based priming emerged in the context of an experiment where there were no homophones in the background (and hence presumably a pseudohomophone effect would not have emerged) (Besner et al., 1985).

The general claim that the failure of a factor identified with phonological processing to affect performance cannot necessarily be taken as evidence that phonological processes are inoperative has been documented elsewhere. For example, it is well known that articulatory suppression has large detrimental effects upon memory span, and eliminates both word length and phonemic similarity effects when material is visually presented. The received interpretation of these effects is that suppression prevents the translation of visual information into a phonological code (e.g., Baddeley, Thomson, & Buchanan, 1975). Yet it is possible to demonstrate the availability and use of a phonological code despite suppression since subjects can do phonological lexical decision (does this letter string **sound** like a real word?) without any inteference from suppression (e.g., Besner, Davies, & Daniels, 1981, experiment 6). A related finding is that pseudohomophones are better recalled than nonword controls in a memory span task under conditions of visual presentation accompanied by suppression, despite the fact that phonemic similarity and word length effects are completely eliminated (Besner & Davelaar, 1982). It seems difficult to explain these effects without assuming the operation of a phonological code.

Finally, we ruefully note that the general question(s) concerning the relationship between phonology and visual word recognition in reading has, like many other issues, turned into an investigation of the microstructure of the task (in this case, lexical decision) rather than giving a clear-cut answer to the original question. Perhaps that is as it should be; behavior, after all, is multiply determined! Nevertheless, it may be time to readjust our sights and to attempt to move closer to understanding what part phonology may have to play in the reading of connected text. The fact that many of the phonological effects which have been obtained with single-letter strings are small in magnitude and do not always emerge consistently may not make this task any easier. More difficult than the methodological problems, though, may be the problem of establishing what part phonology is playing when phonological effects do emerge. Thus, for example, Baron (1973) demonstrated that subjects who were required to decide whether phrases make sense made more errors on pseudophrases which sounded sensible (e.g., "It's knot so") than no nonphrases which did not (e.g., "I am kill"). Superficially this effect appears to be an extension of the pseudohomophone effect into the domain of phrases. However the problems which arise with pseudophrases in this paradigm may be due to the part played by addressed (i.e., whole word) phonology in the assessing the meaningfulness of the phrase as a whole. More recent work by Treiman, Freyd, and Baron (1983) has produced more convincing evidence that assembled phonology has some part to play when dealing with phrases. These authors have produced evidence for two effects with phrases that it does not seem possible to attribute to addressed phonology. First subjects showed a greater delay in selecting an appropriate completion to sentences in which the same string of letters is pronounced in conflicting ways (e.g., "He made a nasty hasty. . . . ") than in selecting an appropriate completion to sentences in which the same string of letters was repeated and pronounced in the same way (e.g., "I will never sever our. . . . "). Addressed phonology cannot be sensitive to the fact that two words share a common string of letters and hence these effects must arise in assembled phonology. Second, there were indications that acceptability judgments were less accurate for sentences containing irregular words than for matched sentences containing regular words. This also seems to imply a role for assembled phonology, though the effect was rather marginal. Of course, the role played by assembled phonology may be in contributing to a representation which is used in comprehending the meaning of the phrase as a whole arther than in extracting the meaning of individual words. If so, assembled phonology could prove to have a more important role in the reading of phrases than in the reading of single words. At the moment such suggestions are highly speculative, but the results of Treiman *et al.* make it clear that it would be premature to be too dismissive about the role of assembled phonology. Insofar as the pseudohomophone effect has contributed to our understanding of assembled phonology it may have had a useful contribution to make.

D. Closing Remarks

The results of the very first published study of homophone and pseudohomophone effects in lexical decision by Rubenstein *et al.* (1971), when reanalysed by Clark (1973), showed a pseudohomophone effect but no homophone effect when both factors were studied within a single experiment. Davelaar *et al.* (1978) showed that the homophone effect **can** be obtained when pseudohomophones are absent while the present results suggest that the pseudohomophone effect is difficult to obtain when homophones are absent. Thus, quixotically, if Rubenstein *et al.* had studied these phenomena in separate experiments they might have obtained a homophone effect but no pseudohomophone effect, and the development of this area could have been very different. We conclude that, indeed, there is more to phonology than meets the eye.

VI. APPENDIX A

Words Used in Experiments 1 and 2

High frequency words

cat	coat	greet	unto	about	car*[a]	doubt*	pity*
rate	boat	twelve	mild	money	hat*	press*	oxen*
hung	milk	course	army	party	ill*	flash*	pony*
tell	bean	square	into	cover	told*	steam*	argue*
trap	clear	tap	deny	level	dish*	air*	fully*
aunt	goose	papa	iron	image	jump*	pot*	maybe*
pick	swept	only	ugly	active	fade*	bat*	smile*
arch	plane	easy	echo	person	bent*	mama*	major*
lawn	shame	acid	even	author	cook*	evil*	
dumb	ghost	hire	spoil	wall	weigh*	over*	

Low frequency words

irk	jade	batch	aver	untie	aid*	whack*	user*
cove	toot	larch	gala	adder	aze*	greed*	dewy*
vane	pith	morgue	halo	affix	ink*	noose*	polo*
prod	hash	arched	hazy	cower	balk*	drave*	dowry*
watt	mace	mosque	anti	parry	safe*	lee*	hoary*
bulk	quaff	tad	arid	miser	muck*	ode*	cooky*
main	crock	undo	oval	inert	womb*	sod*	colon*
gilt	chafe	avow	doer	fusion	coop*	atop*	zebra*
romp	champ	lacy	emit	centre	lank*	bony*	
sulk	trump	aver	puny	disuse	bulge*	epic*	

[a]Words with an asterisk were used only in Experiment 1.

VII. APPENDIX B

Mean Reaction Times (msec) to Each of the Nonwords in Experiments 1 and 4 as a Function of Type of Background Item[a]

	Experiment 1		Experiment 4	
	HF[a] words	LF[a] words	HF homophone	LF homophone
Pseudohomo-phone				
ile	666	850	729	731
bloo	645	673	635	607
boaled	745	767	732	794
brude	672	726	728	678
brooze	871	854	871	842
bild	697	755	681	776
chuze	614	737	569	616
kord	519	698	573	629
fraze	557	759	609	699
grone	666	816	638	782
horl	591	681	596	623
hele	579	650	565	613
hoal	677	699	647	698
laks	651	666	617	622
leke	593	588	578	567
mone	814	776	851	679
wun	559	685	613	616
porze	575	649	606	614
peese	694	672	625	606
rie	576	748	596	703
taks	603	710	658	605
throo	565	699	678	636
throan	657	741	674	815
tode	640	696	587	588
waid	616	721	704	762
wate	663	844	719	830
stawk	760	676	664	665
wurld	611	772	686	605
woar	596	655	623	659
flore	616	727	636	648
ahms	592	744	687	638
borl	574	595	602	565
bair	551	673	662	672
bor	575	616	539	605
braik	553	627	570	696
grait	690	746	688	669
soal	736	784	686	761
cort	610	733	605	750
floo	598	716	663	670

VII. APPENDIX B *(Continued)*

	Experiment 1		Experiment 4	
	HF[a] words	LF[a] words	HF homophone	LF homophone
Control				
ite	604	753	601	644
ploo	541	632	585	578
loaled	699	829	742	771
trude	663	823	672	697
drooze	609	800	734	702
sild	791	837	694	681
thuze	527	610	557	606
korm	553	610	565	610
frize	577	662	641	658
brone	625	731	706	766
dorl	631	611	620	597
hege	698	692	608	626
joal	564	669	645	666
gaks	546	785	606	617
leme	663	657	597	560
mobe	610	724	650	654
jun	586	664	598	587
corze	613	722	608	590
jeeze	618	721	592	619
fie	739	679	700	744
caks	601	643	634	611
phroo	591	648	622	604
phroan	617	821	700	656
dode	560	672	609	673
baid	675	720	675	718
jate	733	678	687	690
stoak	543	711	560	615
murld	631	745	600	615
woal	741	724	593	739
flere	550	637	622	590
ahns	588	636	593	596
birl	680	697	567	618
gair	590	665	602	594
bon	632	782	660	712
graik	594	650	552	606
brait	536	690	604	724
soat	649	723	678	715
bort	619	694	565	598
sloo	560	654	646	600

[a]HF, high frequency; LF, low frequency.

VIII. APPENDIX C

Mean Reaction Times (msec) to Each of the Nonwords Used in Experiments 2 and 3 as a Function of Type of Background Item[a]

	HF[a] words, Experiment 2	LF[a] words, Experiment 2	50% homophones, Experiment 3
Pseudohomophone			
werd	680	754	695
sune	651	736	652
groe	599	702	558
gerl	614	660	527
werk	637	682	594
meen	642	728	672
turm	733	742	698
dert	617	691	650
wite	705	763	653
whife	704	825	647
rufe	603	743	640
whall	681	756	636
ded	645	674	629
gard	704	755	625
consept	863	965	725
shure	606	726	642
reech	672	757	611
sertain	735	866	735
breth	659	760	621
hert	659	805	635
sircle	661	751	639
merder	678	761	690
munny	817	871	837
lern	677	706	560
Controls			
snoe	787	854	742
cest	681	809	642
buke	687	920	639
dree	730	809	751
feve	632	712	581
leng	621	711	602
plen	579	729	563
nuck	598	721	613
vece	598	675	575
tink	734	894	708
sheen	672	753	565
fute	641	831	701
thalk	641	753	638
ner	579	623	575
gand	629	899	627
resords	833	888	735

VIII. APPENDIX C *(Continued)*

	HF[a] words, Experiment 2	LF[a] words, Experiment 2	50% homophones, Experiment 3
thell	669	698	655
plent	670	854	673
sountry	685	797	653
tught	652	794	633
pesh	597	726	581
sloser	716	801	606
jenior	794	856	680
tuddy	672	813	625
trin	678	836	612
gree	704	790	659

[a]HF, high frequency; LF, low frequency.

ACKNOWLEDGMENTS

This work was carried out while the first author was visiting the University of Waterloo and was supported by Grant U0051 from the Natural Sciences and Engineering Research Council of Canada to Derek Besner. We are grateful to Sheryl Dickens for running subjects and Keith McGowan for programming assistance.

REFERENCES

Andrews, S. (1982). Phonological recoding: Is the regularity effect consistent? *Memory & Cognition, 10,* 565–575.

Baddeley, A. D., Thomson, N., & Buchanan, M. (1975). Word length and the structure of short term memory. *Journal of Verbal Learning and Verbal Behavior, 14,* 575–589.

Baron, J. (1973). Phonemic stage not necessary for reading. *Quarterly Journal of Experimental Psychology, 25,* 241–246.

Barron, R. W. (1978). Reading skill and phonological coding in lexical access. In M. M. Gruneberg, R. N. Sykes, & P. E. Morris (Eds.), *Practical aspects of memory.* New York: Academic Press.

Barron, R. W. (1981). Reading skill and reading strategies. In A. M. Lesgold & C. A. Perfetti (Eds.), *Interactive processes in reading.* Hillsdale, NJ: Erlbaum.

Barry, C. (1981). Hemispheric asymmetry in lexical access and phonological encoding. *Neuropsychologia, 19,* 473–478.

Bauer, D. W., & Stanovich, K. E. (1980). Lexical access and the spelling to sound regularity effect. *Memory & Cognition, 8,* 424–432.

Besner, D., & Davelaar, E. (1982). Basic processes in reading: Two phonological codes. *Canadian Journal of Psychology, 36,* 701–711.

Besner, D., & Davelaar, E. (1983). Suedohomofoan effects in visual word recognition: Evidence for phonological processing. *Canadian Journal of Psychology, 37*, 300–305.

Besner, D., Davies, J., & Daniels, S. (1981). Reading for meaning: The effects of concurrent articulation. *Quarterly Journal of Experimental Psychology, 33A*, 415–437.

Besner, D., Dennis, I., & Davelarr, E. (1985). Reading without phonology? *Quarterly Journal of Psychology,* in press.

Clark, H. (1973). The language-as-fixed-effect fallacy: A critique of language statistics in psychological research. *Journal of Verbal Learning and Verbal Behavior, 12*, 355–359.

Cohen, G., & Freeman, R. (1978). Individual differences in reading strategies in relation to handedness and cerebral asymmetry. In J. Requin (Ed.), *Attention and performance VII.* Hillsdale, NJ: Erlbaum.

Coltheart, M. (1978). Lexical access in simple reading tasks. In G. Underwood (Ed.), *Strategies of information processing.* New York: Academic Press.

Coltheart, M. (1980). Reading, phonological recoding and deep dyslexia. In M. Coltheart, K. Patterson, & J. C. Marshall (Eds.), *Deep dyslexia.* London: Routledge & Kegan Paul.

Coltheart, M. (1981). Disorders of reading and their implications for models of normal reading. *Visible Language, 15*, 245–266.

Coltheart, M., Besner, D., Jonasson, J. T., & Davelaar, E. (1979). Phonological encoding in the lexical decision task. *Quarterly Journal of Experimental Psychology, 31*, 489–507.

Coltheart, M., Davelaar, E., Jonasson, J. T., & Besner, D. (1977). Access to the internal lexicon. In S. Dornic (Ed.), *Attention and performance VI.* Hillsdale, NJ: Erlbaum.

Davelaar, E., Coltheart, M., Besner, D., & Jonasson, J. T. (1978). Phonological recoding and lexical access. *Memory & Cognition, 6*, 391–402.

Dennis, I., & Newstead, S. E. (1981). Is phonological recoding under strategic control? *Memory & Cognition, 9*, 472–477.

Fredriksen, J. R., & Kroll, J. F. (1976). Spelling and sound: Approaches to the internal lexicon. *Journal of Experimental Psychology: Human Perception and Performance, 2*, 361–379.

Glanzer, M., & Ehrenreich, S. L. (1979). Structure and search of the internal lexicon. *Journal of Verbal Learning and Verbal Behavior, 18*, 381–398.

Glushko, R. J. (1979). The organization and activation of orthographic knowledge in reading aloud. *Journal of Experimental Psychology: Human Perception and Performance, 5*, 674–691.

Gordon, B. (1983). Lexical access and lexical decision: mechanisms of frequency sensitivity. *Journal of Verbal Learning and Verbal Behavior, 22*, 24–44.

Gough, P. B., & Cosky, M. J. (1977). One second of reading again. In N. J. Castellan, D. B., Pisoni, & G. R. Potts (Eds.), *Cognitive theory* (Vol. 2). Hillsdale, NJ: Erlbaum.

Kay, J., & Marcel, A. J. (1981). One process not two in reading aloud: Lexical analogies do the work of non-lexical rules. *Quarterly Journal of Experimental Psychology, 33A*, 397–413.

McCusker, L. X., Hillinger, M. L., & Bias, R. G. (1981). Phonological recoding and reading. *Psychological Bulletin, 89*, 217–245.

McQuade, D. V. (1981). Variable reliance on phonological information in visual word recognition. *Language and Speech, 24*, 99–109.

Martin, R. (1982). The pseudohomophone effect: The role of visual similarity in nonword decisions. *Quarterly Journal of Experimental Psychology, 34A*, 395–409.

Mitterer, J. O. (1982). There are at least two kinds of poor readers: Whole-word poor readers and recoding poor readers. *Canadian Journal of Psychology, 36*, 445–461.

Morton, J. (1979). Facilitation in word recognition: Experiments causing change in the logogen model. In P. A. Kolers, M. Woolstad, & H. Bouma (Eds.), *Processing of visible language I.* New York: Plenum.

Parkin, A. J. (1982). Phonological recoding in lexical decision: Effects of spelling to sound regularity depend on how regularity is defined. *Memory & Cognition,* **10,** 43-53.

Parkin, A. J., & Ellingham, R. (1983). Phonological Recoding in lexical decision: The influence of pseudohomophones. *Language and Speech,* **26,** 81-89.

Patterson, K. E., & Marcel, A. J. (1977). Aphasia, dyslexia and the phonological coding of written words. *Quarterly Journal of Experimental Psychology,* **29,** 307-318.

Pring, L. (1981). Phonological codes and functional spelling units: Reality and implications. *Perception & Psychophysics,* **30,** 573-578.

Richardson, J. T. E. (1976). The effects of stimulus attributes upon latency of word recognition. *British Journal of Psychology,* **67,** 315-325.

Rubenstein, H., Lewis, S. S., & Rubenstein, M. A. (1971). Evidence for phonemic recoding in visual word recognition. *Journal of Verbal Learning and Verbal Behavior,* **10,** 645-657.

Shallice, T., Warrington, E. K., & McCarthy, R. (1983). Reading without semantics. *Quarterly Journal of Experimental Psychology,* **35A,** 111-138.

Stanovich, K. E., & Bauer, D. W. (1978). Experiments on the spelling-to-sound regularity effect in word recognition. *Memory & Cognition,* **6,** 410-415.

Taft, M. (1982). An alternative to grapheme-phoneme rules? *Memory & Cognition,* **10,** 465-472.

Treiman, R., Freyd, J. J., & Baron, J. (1983). Phonological recoding and use of spelling-sound rules in reading of sentences. *Journal of Verbal Learning and Verbal Behavior,* **22,** 682-700.

READING RESEARCH: ADVANCES IN THEORY AND PRACTICE, VOL. 5

THE TIME COURSE OF INFORMATION ACTIVATION AND UTILIZATION IN VISUAL WORD RECOGNITION

MARK S. SEIDENBERG

Department of Psychology
McGill University
Montreal, Quebec, Canada

Copyright © 1985 by Academic Press, Inc.
All rights of reproduction in any form reserved.

I. INTRODUCTION

Word recognition continues to engage the interest of psychologists who study reading. Although more attention has been directed in recent years toward issues concerning knowledge structures, inference processes, and other higher level aspects of comprehension, the amount of research on word recognition has also been increasing rapidly. In part this is because many of these higher level structures and processes are not specific to reading. More importantly, knowledge of the recognition process is critical to understanding skilled reading, the acquisition of reading ability, reading impairments, and the neurological basis of language. This article is concerned with two traditional, continuing issues in the study of reading. The first concerns the manner in which the linguistic context in which a word occurs influences the recognition process. The second concerns the manner in which knowledge of the lexicon itself influences recognition. I will argue that a unified account of these issues can be obtained within an approach to the study of word recognition that emphasizes the time course of processing events. This approach involves tracking the information that becomes available in the course of recognition, and the interactions among different types of information over time. I will present evidence suggesting that information provided by the context of occurrence contributes to the recognition process only in limited and specifiable ways, at least among skilled readers under the conditions that normally prevail in reading. Research on this issue provides support for the view that language comprehension results from the operation of modular subsystems, of which the lexicon is one (Fodor, 1983; Seidenberg & Tanenhaus, 1984; Tanenhaus, Carlson, & Seidenberg, 1984). What is important to the recognition process is not the information provided by the **literal** context in which a word appears, but rather the reader's knowledge of lexical structure and the relations that hold among words. This knowledge, which I will term the **virtual** context of occurrence, provides the basis for rapid and efficient recognition of words without contextual support.

II. CONTEXTUAL EFFECTS ON WORD RECOGNITION

I begin by developing the hypothesis that word recognition results from the operation of a modular subsystem, and then consider how this hypothesis fares in light of the enormous literature on contextual effects.

A. Modularity and Lexical Access

The notion that complex processes such as language comprehension result from the operation of subsystems or modules derives from several sources. In linguistics, Chomsky has always conceived of grammar as consisting of separate components (a conception that has often been criticized). In psychology, related ideas are Posner's (1969) concept of "isolable subsystems" and Pylyshyn's (1981) "cognitively impenetrable" processes. Perhaps the clearest statement of this point of view comes from Marr (1982), whose principle of modular design is "the idea that a large computation can be split up and implemented as a collection of parts that are as nearly independent of one another as the overall task allows" (Marr, 1982, p. 102). Fodor (1983) has developed this idea within a general theory of the structure of intelligence.

As applied to language comprehension, the modularity thesis suggests that different types of linguistic knowledge and processes by which this knowledge is utilized may be conceptualized as separate, though cooperative, subsystems. Psychologists often say that complex cognitive processes such as language comprehension result from interactions among different types of knowledge, which is surely true. The modularity hypothesis represents a claim about the **scope** of interactive processes. It suggests that there are constraints on interactive processes, such that some are bounded within specifiable domains. These domains are differentiated with respect to such things as the types of knowledge representations involved, the types of procedures that operate upon them, and possibly their neurological bases (Fodor, 1983). Identifying such constraints is probably a necessary step in developing an explanatory theory of the comprehension process, if only because of the complexity of the interactions involved (Seidenberg, 1985a).

Our recent work has evaluated the hypothesis that the lexicon can be construed as a module in the comprehension system (Seidenberg & Tanenhaus, 1985; Seidenberg, Tanenhaus, Leiman, & Bienkowski, 1982; Seidenberg, Waters, Sanders, & Langer, 1984b; Tanenhaus *et al.*, 1985). The idea derives from Forster's (1979) observation that, among skilled users of a language, lexical processing is autonomous, and from a similar suggestion by Gough (1972). The autonomy hypothesis is simply that word recognition is not influenced by nonlexical ("message-level") information provided by the context. Although nonlexical information contributes to the comprehension of text or discourse, it does not affect the recognition of words per se. Processes within the lexicon are not penetrated by these other types of information; rather, the lexicon automatically makes available information which is then available to be acted upon by other comprehension processes involved in interpreting sentences. These processes operate upon the **output** of the lexical module, but do not affect its internal operations.

Within this framework, lexical priming due to semantic or associative relations among words (Meyer & Schvaneveldt, 1971; Warren, 1977) has a special status. To the extent that such priming occurs in comprehending spoken or written language, it refutes a strict version of the autonomy hypothesis in which context has no effect whatsoever on lexical processing. However, the mechanism by which lexical priming occurs is spreading activation among entries in the mental lexicon. In this case, it is wholly internal to the lexicon ("intralexical" in Forster's terminology), a consequence of the manner in which the lexicon is organized. There are also other types of interactive processes within the lexicon mediated by spreading activation mechanism, some of which are discussed in later sections of this chapter. The lexicon is said to be modular, then, in the sense that its operations are not affected by nonlexical information.

Two predictions follow from the view that lexical processing occurs within an autonomous module. The first is that the information made available as a consequence of lexical processing should be invariant across contexts. The second is that the speed with which that information is made available should be unaffected by context. These predictions can be contrasted with those made by unconstrained interactive models such as those of Rumelhart (1977) and Marslen-Wilson and Tyler (1980). In these models, contextual information is combined with sensory information during lexical processing. In the cohort model developed by Marslen-Wilson and his colleagues, contextual information combines with sensory information to facilitate discriminating among a candidate set of words which have been activated by the sensory input. This model predicts that the speed with which a word can be recognized depends on the information made available by the context of occurrence (Tyler & Wessels, 1983). Words in informative contexts are processed more rapidly than words in noninformative contexts. The historical precedent for this model is analysis by synthesis (Neisser, 1967). A stronger claim might be that context can influence which candidates are activated by priming words that are congruent with the processing context. In this view, different information becomes available in different contexts.

My goal in this section is to evaluate the hypothesis that the lexicon forms an autonomous processing module in light of empirical studies of the visual recognition of words in context.[1] In later sections of the chapter, I develop some ideas about the structure and operations of the lexical module itself.

---

[1] Note that I am less concerned with the fate of the modularity thesis as it applies to other aspects of human performance. It could well be that the properties of the lexicon that make it modular are not preserved in other parts of the comprehension system.

It might appear that this first section could be very short because the modular hypothesis is easy to refute. After all, why would there be so many studies of contextual effects on word recognition if none exist? However, the empirical literature must be interpreted with regard to three issues. The first concerns the loci of contextual effects. The lexical modularity hypothesis is a claim about processes leading to the recognition of words, not what happens to lexical information once it is accessed. It does not deny the obvious relevance of contextual information to the process of interpreting sentences; it merely denies that this information either facilitates or inhibits the recognition of individual words. It then becomes important to consider not merely whether a contextual variable had an effect in a particular experiment, but whether it affected word recognition or some other aspect of the comprehension process. The second issue concerns the experimental tasks used to evaluate the role of context. Simple tasks such as lexical decision and naming are affected by contextual information in very different ways. By developing a theory of how the tasks are performed, we gain more precise information concerning the relationship between context and word recognition. Finally, it is necessary to consider the results of these laboratory studies in light of the somewhat different conditions that prevail in normal reading.

B. Loci of Contextual Effects

Although word recognition occurs very rapidly it is not instantaneous. The lexical modularity hypothesis can be formulated more clearly by differentiating among several component processes (Seidenberg *et al.*, 1982; see also Tabossi & Johnson-Laird, 1980). **Prelexical processes** involve analyses of the written or spoken input which result in its identification as a particular word. Identification (or recognition) is achieved when a unique entry in the mental lexicon (e.g., a logogen) is activated. **Lexical access** involves the activation of information associated with the lexical item, including its semantic, phonological, and orthographic codes. Other information is probably also made available at this stage; theories of the lexicon developed within linguistics (e.g., Jackendoff, 1975; Bresnan, 1978; Wasow, 1977) include many other types of information concerning, for example, the kinds of syntactic structures words can enter into. There is good evidence that at least some of this information is accessed in word recognition (Frazier, Clifton, & Connine, 1984). On the view I am proposing, then, word recognition entails prelexical processing and lexical access. **Postlexical processes** involve the selection, elaboration, and integration of lexical information for the purpose of comprehending a text or utterance (Cairns, Cowart, & Jablon, 1981; Seidenberg *et al.*, 1982). Clearly, postlexical processes defined in this way are influenced by contextual information. In fact, I will argue below that many of the contextual effects reported in the literature actually have a postlexical locus. The lexical modularity hypothesis only concerns the processes that result in recognition. The interest of the claim lies in the fact that these constitute an important part of the comprehension process.

The strongest evidence for this hypothesis derives from studies of lexical access. Much of this evidence comes from research on the processing of ambiguous words (such as *tire* or *bug*), which have multiple meanings. Except in degenerate cases (such as puns), only a single meaning of an ambiguous word is appropriate to a particular context. Clearly, there is an obvious sense in which deciding which meaning of *tire* is appropriate in the sentence "John began to tire" depends on contextual information; to a first approximation it is correct to say that resolving ambiguities involves interactions between lexical and contextual sources of information. However, the modularity hypothesis is more specific: it asserts that the lexical module yields information that is invariant across contexts. By hypothesis, the module does not have access to other, nonlexical information that has been recognized, such as the meaning of the context or its syntactic form. It follows that the lexicon itself does not possess any mechanism for determining which meaning of an ambiguous word is appropriate to a particular context. This predicts that inappropriate meanings will sometimes be accessed, and that is what recent studies show.

These studies (Onifer & Swinney, 1981; Seidenberg & Tanenhaus, 1980; Seidenberg *et al.,* 1982; Simpson, 1981; Swinney, 1979; Tanenhaus, Leiman, & Seidenberg, 1979) used a cross-modal priming methodology developed by Conrad (1974) to probe the availability of alternate meanings over time. An auditorally presented sentence such as "John began to tire" might be followed by visually presented target words related to the alternate senses of *tire* ("sleep" and "wheel"). For control conditions, the ambiguous word would be replaced by an unambiguous item such as "laugh." The logic of the methodology is that if a particular meaning of an ambiguous word is available, it should facilitate the recognition of a target related to that meaning. If the meaning is not available, the target related to it should be recognized about as rapidly as when preceded by a totally unrelated word. By presenting targets at variable delays following the ambiguous word or its control, we can trace the time course of the availability of alternate meanings. If processing within the lexicon is influenced by information provided by the context, only the contextually appropriate reading should be considered. If the lexicon has no basis on which to select the correct reading, however, multiple alternatives should be considered when the meanings are equally common. In general, these studies have shown that both of the common meanings of ambiguous words are transiently (and unconsciously) activated, a pattern termed "multiple access." Within about 200 msec, however, the contextually appropriate reading is selected and the alternate meaning is suppressed.

This result is striking because it shows that, acting as an autonomous processing module, the lexicon yields more information than is required in a given context. This outcome would only obtain if the lexicon lacked access to the results of other comprehension processes, as the modularity hypothesis suggests. The processing of lexical ambiguities provides a clear illustraton of the distinction between lexical and postlexical processes. The access of meaning, a lexical process, is autonomous. The selection of a particular meaning, a postlexical process, is determined by reference to information provided by particular contexts of occurrence. Thus, by looking at the timecourse of processing events, we can determine exactly how contextual information is (and is not) used. The evidence suggests that it only comes into play after lexical information has been activated. A more detailed model of ambiguity resolution is presented in Seidenberg et al. (1982), and there have been several computational implementations of similar models (Cottrell, 1984; Hirst, 1983; Milne, 1983).

As is typical of psychological research, the ambiguity studies have methodological complexities which threaten this simple account. A basic question is whether access of a contextually inapproprite meaning might be an artifact of cuing from the related target, a kind of "backwards priming." That is, subjects could access the contextually inappropriate reading of *tire* in the sentence "John began to tire" because it is cued by the target *wheel*. Below (Section II,D) I discuss the backward priming phenomenon, which is indeed real, and provide evidence that while it may occur when subjects perform a lexical decison to the target word, it does not occur when the target must be named. The Seidenberg et al. (1982) and Tanenhaus et al. (1979) studies used the naming response, suggesting that backward priming did not affect their results. Frazier and Rayner (1984) and Carpenter and Daneman (1981) also found evidence for multiple access in studies using eye fixation data, in which the backward priming issue is moot.[2]

---

[2]The ambiguity research illustrates some of the methodological complexities in studying the on-line processing of language. Conrad (1974) first used the cross-modal priming methodology to study lexical ambiguity. Subjects performed the Stroop task, naming the color of the ink the targets were printed in. Color-naming interference occurred for targets related to both appropriate and inappropriate meanings, indicating multiple access. Tanenhaus et al. (1979) had subjects name the targets aloud; naming latencies for targets related to both appropriate and inappropriate meanings were facilitated when they were presented immediately after the ambiguous word; only targets related to appropriate meanings were facilitated when they were presented after a 200-msec delay. Swinney (1979) used a third paradigm, in which subjects

The autonomy of lexical access is also illustrated by studies that do not involve ambiguous words. Merrill, Sperber, and McCauley (1981) examined the processing of words such as *cat* either in isolation or in sentences such as (1–2). The property of cats relevant to understanding (1) is that they are

1. John petted the cat.
2. John was scratched by the cat.

soft and furry; the property relevant to (2) is that they have claws. Using a priming paradigm, Merrill *et al.* presented each word or sentence followed by a target related to either the contextually appropriate or the contextually inappropriate property of cats. In control conditions, the same targets were preceded by unrelated word or sentence contexts. The subjects were fifth grade students who differed in their reading abilities. Presented in isolation, words such as *cat* primed targets related to both properties, compared to unrelated controls, for both good and poor readers. When the words were presented in biasing sentence contexts, priming was only observed for targets related to contextually appropriate properties for good readers, while priming occurred for both appropriate and inappropriate targets for poor readers. The suggestion from this study is that, for both good and poor readers, recognizing the word *cat* involved the activation of associated properties such as "having claws" and "having fur." Good readers rapidly select the information that is relevant to a particular context, and suppress

---

performed lexical decisions to targets, and obtained results consistent with the Conrad (1974) and Tanenhaus *et al.* (1979) studies. However, lexical decision will produce multiple access because of backwards cuing from the targets (Koriat, 1981; Seidenberg *et al.*, 1984b). The finding which is at risk because of backwards priming artifacts concerns the fate of subordinate (less frequent) meanings that are contextually inappropriate. Although there is some evidence that subordiante meanings are activated (e.g., Onifer & Swinney, 1981), they have only been studied using the lexical decision task, for which backwards priming is a definite possibility.

The fate of subordiante meanings is important because it bears on whether meaning access is exhaustive or not. In Onifer and Swinney's (1981) model, all of the meanings of ambiguous words are initially accessed, regardless of relative dominance. However, Seidenberg *et al.* (1982) assumed that meanings that differ greatly in frequency are accessed at different latencies. It could well be that a high frequency, dominant reading is accessed and integrated with the context prior to the activation of a lower frequency, subordinate reading. According to our model, then, while the access of meaning is autonomous, it is not necessarily exhaustive. Thus, subordinate meanings raise questions concerning the timing of the activation of meanings relative to the postlexical processes involved in selection, but they do not bear on the autonomy issue per se. It remains to be determined how different in frequency the readings must be for there to be differences in availability over time. It is also unclear exactly how many readings are accessed; existing studies have only looked at the activation of the two most common meanings, and do not provide direct evidence concerning the number of other readings that become available.

irrelevant information. Poor readers continue to retain both appropriate and inappropriate information, indicating a deficit in postlexical processing. The results for good readers are analogous to those in the ambiguity studies, suggesting that the model of lexical access we have proposed easily generalizes to the processing of nonambiguous words.

Additional evidence is provided by studies of the comprehension of idioms such as *kick the bucket* (Swinney & Cutler, 1979), metaphors such as *some jobs are jails* (Glucksberg, Gildea, & Bookin, 1982) and contextual expressions such as *Henry really Nixoned that one* (Clark & Gerrig, 1983) in which words are used nonliterally. In each case, the lexical module yields as output information concerning the literal meaning of the relevant words; further processing yields the nonliteral interpretation. Swinney and Cutler (1979) suggest that familiar idioms are processed in exactly the same way as ambiguous words, with both literal and idiomatic senses accessed from the lexicon, and postaccess selection of one based on the context. The correct interpretation of metaphors and contextual expressions involves inferences based on many other types of knowledge external to the lexicon (concerning, for example, episodic memory, knowledge of the world, and the intentions of the speaker or author). In the processing of these nonliteral expressions, the modularity hypothesis would be violated only if, as a result of information provided by the context of occurrence, the perceiver failed to derive the literal meanings of the words. In the case of metaphors and contextual expressions this appears to be a logical impossibility; it is hard to see how they could be comprehended unless the literal meaning were first determined. Understanding what it means to "do a Nixon" depends on knowing that the person in question is Nixon, not Kissinger.

In sum, studies of lexical access suggest that the information that becomes available in word recognition is not affected by the context of occurrence, in line with the lexical modularity hypothesis, and they validate the distinction between lexical and postlexical processes. Of course, it could be that while lexical access is autonomous, prelexical processing is not. I turn now to studies addressing this question.

C. Sentence–Context Studies

If contextual information influences prelexical processing, a word should be recognized more quickly when it occurs in a valid, informative context than in an invalid, uninformative context. Two related research paradigms have been used to sudy this question. In one paradigm (created by Schuberth & Eimas, 1977), a target word appears in a sentence context. The subject reads the context and then either names the target aloud or performs a lexical decision. Response latencies are then measured as a function of the type of information provided by the context. For example, the target could be a meaningful and highly predictable completion of the sentence ("The captain stayed with his *ship*"); meaningful but not predictable ("The whale was injured by the *ship*"); or anomalous ("The Bedouin lived in the *ship*"). Neutral contexts are created by preceding the target with a row of XXX's or a vague phrase such as "They said it was the *ship*." Essential studies of this type include Fischler and Bloom (1979, 1980); Schuberth and Eimas (1977); Schuberth, Spoehr, and Lane (1981); Stanovich and West (1979, 1981, 1983); and West and Stanovich (1982). The second paradigm is lexical priming. Here a target word is preceded by a single context word; primes and targets are related along different dimensions (e.g., they are associated: *doctor–nurse;* semantically related but unassociated: *mother–nurse;* or form a syntactic constituent: *the–nurse*). Representative studies include Fischler (1977a,b), Meyer and Schvaneveldt (1971), Neely (1977), and Warren (1972, 1977).

Henderson (1982) provides an insightful review of the literature on sentence–context effects. The discussion here will focus on the fact that contextual effects vary depending on the type of recognition task employed; the lexical decision and naming tasks yield different results. One clear finding is that naming latencies are facilitated when the target is highly predictable from the context (Fischler & Bloom, 1979). Discussion of word recognition in predictable contexts will be deferred until Section II,E. For words that are not predictable from the context, the naming task yields a pattern termed facilitation dominant: the facilitation in naming targets in congruent contexts is larger than the inhibition when the targets are named in incongruous contexts. When the task is lexical decision, the pattern is inhibition dominant: the inhibitory effects of incongruent contexts are larger than the facilitative effects of congruent contexts. The facilitative effects in naming also tend to be smaller in absolute magnitude than the inhibitory effects in lexical decision.

Stanovich and West's interpretation of these results is as follows: contextual facilitation in the naming task mainly derives from a spreading activation process within the lexicon. Words in the context can prime a semantically or associatively related target before it is encountered, yielding faster naming latencies. This process also contributes to facilitation in the lexical decision task. These effects do not violate the autonomy hypothesis for reasons discussed above. The inhibitory effects, which largely occur with the lexical decision task, are quite different: they are due to postlexical processes involved in making the decision. Essentially, making a lexical decision to a word in context creates a task very much like the Stroop task. In principle, the subject could make the decision based only on the processing of the target. A relevant context might then make the target easier to decode, facilitating the word/nonword response. However, subjects appear unable to resist judging the relatedness of word and context, i.e., whether the target forms a meaningful completion or whether it confirms a prior expectation concerning the type of target. This relatedness judgment, which occurs after the target has been recognized, also affects the decision. Hence, lexical decison latencies reflect both the difficulty of identifying the target and the judgment of the congruence of the target with the context. The analogy to the Stroop task is clear. Subjects performing the Stroop task are only required to name the color a word is printed in, but the meaning of the word affects their response. Subjects performing a lexical decision in context are only required to judge the target as a word or nonword, but the relationship between target and context affects their response.

The naming task does not appear to be as sensitive to these postlexical processes. A theory of the tasks explaining the different effects of context is presented by Seidenberg et al. (1984b), drawing upon earlier suggestions by Forster (1979), Theios and Muise (1977), and West and Stanovich (1982). Lexical decison is a signal detection task for which performance depends on the discriminability of words and nonwords, and the subject's response criteria, both of which may vary across studies and individuals. The naming task differs in that (1) the subject does not have to discriminate between words and nonwords, and (2) performance on the task is constrained by the requirement that the targets be named correctly. When lexical decision is the response measure, the question of primary interest is whether contextual information influences sensitivity to the target, or bias toward a word or nonword response. When the task is naming, context can only influence sensitivity, because there is no decision to bias. Hence, the observed differences between naming and lexical decision performance are due to postlexical bias specific to the latter task. On this view, only priming due to spreading activation among semantically or associatively related entries in lexical memory influences sensitivity; thus it occurs with both tasks. Other types of contextual effects are due to postlexical processes, which only influence the decision stage in the lexical decision task.

There are several reasons why judgments of the congruence of context and target might bias lexical decisions. One is simply that the word and nonword stimuli in these experiments are very difficult to discriminate. Subjects might use expectations concerning the relatedness of context and target to facilitate performing this difficult task. For example, knowing that the target forms a meaningful completion of the sentence provides an additional basis for deciding that it is a word. The semantic matching strategy described by Neely (1977) in a lexical priming study operated in this way. Given that the target is a nonword, the context and target must be incongruent; hence subjects might be biased to respond "nonword" whenever the context and target are judged to the incongruent. These response strategies will work as long as a target is not both a word and incongruent with the context. In this case, the subject's judgment of context–target congruence biases her or him toward a nonword response, but the target is actually a word. This yields the inhibition-dominant pattern observed in sentence-context studies using lexical decision.

According to this view, contextual effects in lexical decision result—at least in part—from the subject's strategy for performing the task. This implies that it should be possible to manipulate the relative magnitudes of facilitation and inhibition by varying the proportions of stimuli from different conditions. For example, the proportion of trials in which the target is a nonword should affect the magnitude of the inhibition effect when the target is a word but incongruent with the context. If the proportion of nonword trials were high, incongruence would provide a very strong cue that the target is a nonword, yielding increased inhibition on the trials when the target is a word but incongruent with the context. If there were a high proportion of trials in which the target is a word but incongruent with the context, there might be inhibition for congruent word targets. In general, if the relatedness of context and target influence the subject's bias toward a word or nonword response, it should be possible to manipulate these biases to produce widely varying patterns of results.

It is also possible, however, that contextual effects in the lexical decision task are due at least in part to processes that are not under strategic control. If these contextual effects are genuinely Stroop-like, they should occur regardless of subject strategies based on the proportions of stimuli from various conditions. The relatedness of context and target may be determined as a result of postlexical processes that are an automatic part of comprehension. Thus, as the task is currently used, it is not possible to determine which of these context effects occur as part of a task-specific strategy for performing lexical decisions, and which are due to processes that are a normal part of the comprehension process. In either case, however, the effects are postlexical.

The naming task typically does not show postlexical effects because it does not involve discriminating word and nonword stimuli. The subject's task is to say each word correctly; no expectations concerning the relatedness of stimuli along a particular dimension can assist in identifying particular targets (Forster, 1979).

In sum, it is difficult to determine the effects on contextual information on word recognition when the task is lexical decision because the decision process is influenced by postlexical judgments of context–target relations. Naming appears to be less influenced by such postlexical processes, although there is no guarantee that it is entirely immune to them. Although the sentence–context studies are not definitive, they suggest that contextual information can exert two kinds of effects: first, there is priming due to semantic or associative relations between a word in the context and the target. This effect is internal to the lexicon and occurs with both response measures. Second, contextual information can influence processes that occur after a word is recognized. In normal reading, these postlexical processes are involved in integrating a word with the preceding context after it has been recognized. In the lexical decison task, postlexical processes influence the decision stage, and are responsible for the inhibition-dominant pattern.

D. Lexical Priming

Studies of lexical priming provide further support for this analysis of the loci of contextual effects. The basic lexical priming phenomenon is that a word is recognized more quickly when preceded by a semantically or associatively related word (e.g., Fischler, 1977a,b; Meyer & Schvaneveldt, 1971; Warren, 1972, 1977). This outcome holds whether the task is naming or lexical decision. The standard interpretation of this effect is that it is due to a spreading activation process within the lexicon (Collins & Loftus, 1975). Activation spreads from the node of the prime to the node of the related target, decreasing its recognition threshold. The existence of such effects refutes a very strong version of the autonomy hypothesis in which context exerts no influence whatsoever over lexical processing. However, they are compatible with the view I am proposing, in which the operations within the lexical module are not influenced by other types of (nonlexical) information. These priming effects are due to the manner in which the mental lexicon is organized; this organization is probably a consequence of the role of the lexicon in speech production. Nonetheless, the semantic and associative priming effects are important because they represent contextual effects that are not postlexical.

Within the basic priming paradigm, however, other relationships between prime and target have been found to facilitate lexical decisions. Goodman, McClelland, and Gibbs (1981) obtained faster lexical decision latencies when a prime and target formed a simple syntactic constituent (e.g., *he–said*) than when the prime and target did not form a constituent (e.g., *the–said*). This outcome was obtained even though the stimuli were neither semantically nor associatively related. Koriat (1981) obtained a backwards priming effect. The prime–target pairs were stimuli such as *apple–fruit* that are associated in a backwards direction, but not forwards. Lexical decisons to the targets were facilitated when presented both forward (*fruit–apple*) and backward (*apple–fruit*). Finally, Tweedy, Lapinski, and Schvaneveldt (1977) found that the magnitude of the associative priming effect depended on the proportion of related trials. The effect was larger with a greater number of associative trials.

The importance of these findings is that they raise questions concerning the spreading activation interpretation of semantic and associative priming effects. The syntactic priming effect cannot be due to spreading activation, because activation would have to spread throughout the lexicon to all the entries for words of a particular syntactic class. The set of these words is enormous. Koriat assumed that the backward priming effect was due to spreading activation, but reintepreted the forward priming effect as due to subject expectations, an attentional process. Changes in the magnitude of associative priming as a function of the number of trials are inconsistent with the idea that associative priming derives only from a passive and automatic spread of activation through lexical memory. Hence, these results called into question the basic mechanism for lexical priming, and with it the autonomy hypothesis.

As Seidenberg *et al.* (1984b) observed, however, all of these effects were obtained with the lexical decision task, raising the possibility that they were due to postlexical processes. If the theory of the lexical decision and naming tasks presented above is correct, and these effects are postlexical, they should not occur when the target must be named. Seidenberg *et al.* tested this prediction; their findings were as follows. First, they replicated the finding that semantic and associative priming occur with both tasks; the effects were consistently larger in lexical decision than in naming. Increasing the proportion of associated trials increased the magnitude of the priming effect only in lexical decision. Syntactic priming and backward priming also occurred only with lexical decision, not with naming. Thus, the results suggest that the original interpretation of semantic and associative priming is correct: it is a result of automatic spreading activation within the lexicon. The other types of priming effects are due to postlexical judgments of prime–target relatedness along other dimensions (syntactic congruence, backwards association), which is why they are specific to the lexical decision task. Semantic and associative priming effects are larger in lexical decision than in naming because in the former case they result from both spreading activation and postlexical processing, while in the latter they only result from spreading activation.

In sum, the sentence–context and lexical priming studies suggest that the primary way in which contextual information can facilitate word recognition is through semantic or associative priming. These effects are mediated wholly within the lexicon itself. The extent to which semantic or associative priming contribute to the processing of normal text is unclear. On the one hand, the conditions under which semantic and associative priming are obtained in lexical priming studies are rarely preserved in normal texts (Henderson, 1982). For example, highly related words seldom occur contiguously in texts. On the other hand, Foss (1982) has suggested that priming effects may extend beyond these laboratory conditions because a word can be primed by an element in the reader or listener's mental representation of the text or discourse. In effect, the mental representation of a word can cause priming within the lexicon in the same way as an actual word in the text. Thus, while the reality of lexical priming is clear, its importance to actual reading is not. Nonlexical contextual information influences postlexical processes involved in integrating a word with the preceding context. However, this information has little bearing on the decoding of individual words. The reason these types of contexts function differently is because only semantic and associative priming are a consequence of the structure of the lexicon itself. The lexicon is probably organized in terms of semantic and associative relatedness because of the demands of speech production. This implies that priming is an artifact of the production system, rather than essential to comprehension.[3]

E. Generalizations to Normal Reading

The influence of contextual information on word recognition is further constrained by the conditions presented by normal texts. Recall the finding of Fischler and Bloom (1979) that naming latencies were facilitated only when the target was highly predictable from the context—on the order of 90% on a Cloze procedure. This finding indicates that when the target is highly predictable, subjects can make use of this information to perform the experimental task. Leaving aside questions concerning the locus of this predictability effect, we can inquire as to whether this kind of predictive mechanism would ever come into play in reading normal texts. Granting that subjects have the capacity to make use of contextual information in this fashion, would they ever do so under more natural conditions? Several facts about the composition of actual texts suggest that they would not. Using a Cloze procedure, Gough, Alford, and Holley-Wilcox (1981) obtained data concerning the predictability of words in several kinds of texts.

[3]Several other cautions should also be noted. First, contextual effects may differ as a function of modality; there may be greater contextual influences in comprehending speech, for which the sensory signal is necessarily distributed over time. There is also a question concerning the scope of semantic and associative priming. In the absence of independent evidence concerning this issue, there is a danger that the autonomy hypothesis is unfalsifiable, because any contextual effect can be attributed to priming.

The idea that the lexicon is organized along semantic lines because of its role in production was suggested to me by Michael Tanenhaus.

The subjects accurately predicted from 20 to 39% of the words. The one exception to this pattern was a subject who was asked to predict the words in a text he had co-authored; his accuracy was 74%. These data indicate that the words in actual texts rarely reach the 90% predictability level of the targets in the Fischler and Bloom (1979) study.

It could nonetheless be the case that readers use this predictive mechanism for those words that **are** this predictable. However, the use of expectations based on contextual information would be efficient only if there were no penalty associated with incorrect guesses. Studies such as that of Neely (1977) strongly suggest that recognition is inhibited when an expectation is disconfirmed. Thus, the benefits associated with accurate anticipations of a word would be limited to the small proportion of highly predictable cases; inhibition would obtain in the large number of cases where a prediction was disconfirmed. Unless the reader could know in advance whether a particular expectation would be confirmed or not, this would seem to be an inefficient strategy. It is hard to imagine the processing system evolving in a manner so unsuited to the characteristics of normal text. Some researchers (e.g., Goodman, 1970; Taylor & Taylor, 1984) suggest that readers are highly flexible in their use of contextual information, relying upon it only where it is useful. However, it is not clear what aspects of the text could confer this kind of prescience upon a person reading it for the first time. Gough and Hillinger (1980) also observed that the words that can be successfully predicted from context tend to be higher frequency items. These are exactly the items for which bottom-up decoding processes are likely to yield rapid recognition, obviating reliance upon context entirely.

These considerations suggest that the kind of contextual facilitation observed by Fischler and Bloom (1979) has little role in normal reading. It appears that the effect simply results from a task-specific guessing strategy induced by the presence of highly predictable target words on a large proportion of trials. A complementary effect is obtained when a degraded stimulus is presented in an informative context. A typical finding is that tachistoscopic recognition thresholds are lower when the context is relevant to the target (e.g., Tulving & Gold, 1963). When the stimulus is degraded, the subject has no choice but to guess based on information provided by the context. Some researchers have suggested that a similar process occurs in reading words in normal nondegraded texts, with less information extracted from the target when the context is informative (e.g., Goodman, 1970). However, it probably is invalid to generalize from performance under conditions which *prevent* readers from extracting full information from the target, forcing them to rely on context, to performance when the stimulus is in plain view. There is no evidence that readers are able to modify the sensory analysis of a nondegraded stimulus in the suggested way. This degree of flexibility seems unlikely if, as is widely assumed, these early sensory processes are automatic (LaBerge & Samuels, 1974). Thus, the Fischler and Bloom (1980) result shows that subjects can use a guessing strategy when the experimental conditions permit it, though these conditions are not representative of most texts; the stimulus degradation studies show that they can use the strategy when the experimental conditions **demand** it.[4]

F. Summary

The discussion to this point can be summarized as follows:

1. The naming and lexical decision tasks are both affected by lexical priming, but lexical decisions are more influenced by postlexical processes, because of the signal detection character of the task. In a limited way, the tasks provide a means for identifying the loci of contextual effects.

2. The primary facilitating effect of context on word recognition occurs through semantic or associative priming, which is a consequence of the organization of the lexicon. The extent to which this kind of priming actually occurs in reading normal texts is unclear.

3. Other types of information provided by the linguistic and extralinguistic contexts of occurrence influence postlexical processes, not recognition. Some postlexical processes are an essential part of the comprehension process involved in integrating a word with prior context once it has been recognized. It will be important to understand these postlexical processes as part of a general theory of comprehension. Other postlexical processes are specific to tasks such as lexical decision.

4. Facts about the structure of actual texts do not favor the evolution or use of a highly predictive, context-based decoding process.

In conclusion, the modularity hypothesis with regard to the lexicon is consistent with a wide range of empirical data. This conclusion must be tentative, however, because of the absence of information concerning the recognition of complex words. Most of the studies discussed above were

---

[4]Tyler and Wessells (1983) and Grosjean (1980) have used a third methodology in studying contextual effects on auditory word recognition, the gating paradigm. In a gating study, the stimuli are truncated versions of auditorally presented words. The primary finding is that less of the signal is required for a word to be recognized if it is presented in an informative context; more of the signal is required if the context is uninformative. The question raised by these and other studies of contextual effects on degraded stimuli (e.g., Tulving & Gold, 1963) is whether context influences sensitivity to the word target, or bias toward a particular response. If the effects are of the latter sort, they are postlexical and do not bear on the autonomy claim.

concerned with the processing of words that are relatively short, high in frequency and morphologically simple. It is possible that contextual information has greater influence on the processing of more complex words, especially those that are fixated more than once. This possibility raises questions concerning the domain over which lexical processing is autonomous. It could be that the relevant perceptual unit is a sublexical structure such as the syllable, in which case the above studies only considered the special case in which this unit also happens to coincide with a word. With this cautionary note in mind, I turn to the operation of the lexical module itself.

III. WHAT IS THE CONTEXT RELEVANT TO WORD RECOGNITION?

The previous sections presented evidence concerning the extent to which nonlexical information provided by the context in which a word occurs affects recognition. This evidence suggested that for persons who are skilled in using a language, the effects of the literal context are quite limited, at least under the conditions that typically prevail in reading. This review makes clear the kinds of information that are **not** relevant to word recognition, raising questions as to which kinds of information **are** relevant. In this section, I survey recent research suggesting that what is important is the reader's knowledge of the structural relationships that hold among words. This information—which is in the reader's head, rather than the actual text—represents the **virtual** context of occurrence, and it is the focus of current theories of the recognition process.

A. Multiple Pathway Models of Word Recognition

It is useful to begin by considering several related models of the recognition process that have been proposed over the past 15 years. These constitute the first information-processing models of recognition, in that they attempt to represent the flow of information through a sequence of stages, beginning with sensory input and ending with the correct identification of meaning. The first proposal of this type was Morton's (1969) logogen model. This model has undergone successive elaborations by Morton and others (e.g., Coltheart, 1978, 1980; Morton & Patterson, 1980; Newcombe & Marshall, 1981). Forster (1976) has developed a very similar proposal. Central to these models is the idea that a word could be recognized through different processes (also termed "routes" or "pathways"). Rubenstein, Lewis, and Rubenstein (1971) and Gough (1972) had proposed that visually presented words are recognized on the basis of their phonological codes. The reader was thought to process the visual input and derive its phonological form based on knowledge of how the orthography represents sound. This code was then used to search lexical memory. In this way, word recognition was said to be "phonologically mediated."

It soon became clear that, while this process might sometimes occur in recognition, it is not obligatory. This conclusion was based in part on evidence that subjects were able to recognize words under conditions where access of phonology was apparently inhibited through experimental manipulation. For example, they were able to determine the meanings of words in sentences while simultaneously shadowing digits (e.g., Kleiman, 1975). The secondary task was thought to interfere with access to phonology, implying that identifying the meaning of a word did not require phonological mediation. The logic of these experiments is open to serious question, however, because it is not clear that the secondary task had its effect by interfering with phonology per se. Subsequent studies (e.g., Waters, Komoda, & Arbuckle, 1985b) produced similar effects with nonarticulatory secondary tasks. Furthermore, it is not clear whether these manipulations affected the use of phonology in decoding a word, or a postlexical phonological code used in remembering words (Besner & Davelaar, 1982). A vast number of other experimental studies involving judgments of homophone sentences, lexical decisions to homophones and pseudohomophones, and other artificial stimuli also addressed the question (cf. Carr & Pollatsek; Dennis, Besner, & Davelaar, this volume). Several reviews of this research concluded that it had failed to demonstrate that phonological mediation is obligatory (Banks, Oka, & Shugarman, 1981; McCusker, Hillinger, & Bias, 1981; Perfetti & McCutchen, 1983). This conclusion is perhaps unsurprising given the simple observation that there are many nonspeaking deaf persons who are able to read.

This research was widely interpreted as indicating that a word could be recognized either on the basis of phonology or directly from an analysis of the visual input, leading to the development of dual route models. In most versions, the visual and phonological routes were thought to operate in parallel, with a race between them determining whether phonological mediation occurred (Forster & Chambers, 1973). The alternate recognition pathways represented two different ways of deriving the pronunciation of a word. First, in alphabetic orthographies, it could be generated on the basis of rules governing the correspondence between spelling and sound (sometimes known as grapheme–phoneme correspondence rules or GPCs; Coltheart, 1978). This is often termed **nonlexical** phonology, because the rules describe mappings between orthography and phonology that are not specific to particular words. Nonlexical phonology was also thought to be used **prelexically,** i.e., as part of the process by which a word is identified; this was Rubenstein *et al.'s* (1971) hypothesis. Phonology could also be accessed **postlexically** in the dual route model, without reliance on spelling–sound rules. In cases where the visual pathway wins the race, identification of the word provides access to a stored representation of its pronunciation, which can simply be read out of memory storage. This is in keeping with Morton's original logogen model, in which a logogen provided access to the meaning, spelling, and sound codes of a word, and it is consistent with Forster's (1976) model in which recognition involves access to an entry in a master file cross-indexed with a phonological file. The code accessed in this manner was termed **lexical** phonology, because it involved associations between particular words and their pronunciations. In sum, a word could be pronounced either on the basis of nonlexical phonology (i.e., spelling–sound rules) or through lexical phonology (read-out of memory following recognition). In the former case, recognition is phonologically mediated, while in the latter it is not.

The dual route model succeeded in capturing the intuition that access of phonology is not a necessary stage in recognition; it also provided a context for understanding some forms of dyslexia consequent to stroke or other brain injury (see Patterson, 1981; Newcombe & Marshall, 1981, for reviews). At the same time, the assumption that there are alternate recognition pathways introduced other problems. These have led, over a period of years, both to elaborations of the basic dual process theory and to completely new models that dispense entirely with the notion of alternate recognition pathways.

B. What Are the Spelling–Sound Rules of English?

A basic problem for the dual route model is that it has been difficult to provide a coherent formulation of the putative rules governing spelling–sound correspondences in English. There has been a problem in determining the type of orthographic structure over which the rules operate. For example, it might be assumed that the rules map between graphemes and phonemes. However, a unit this small is difficult to reconcile with lexical influences on pronunciation (Glushko, 1979; Kay & Marcel, 1981; Rosson, 1983). In Venezky's (1970) formulation of the rules, several different orthographic structures are involved (individual graphemes, grapheme clusters, syllables). It is difficult to preserve the notion of spelling–sound rules when they involve several heterogeneous structures. This is a serious problem for English, although not for a writing system such as Japanese Kana, in which the orthographic units are well-defined and their pronunciations entirely regular.

A related problem is presented by the morphophonemic character of English orthography. The pronunciations of many words depend on the fact that they are derived from related words (*sign, signature; bomb, bombard,* etc.). Spelling–sound rules that state simple correlations between orthographic forms and their pronunciations ignore this type of information. At best, then, spelling–sound rules could contribute to recognition without themselves being sufficient. An alternate possibility is that all words are pronounced by reference to other words (i.e., by "analogy"), permitting the elimination of the spelling–sound component entirely. This approach is considered again below.

C. Why Are There Redundant Pathways?

Although the dual route model accounted for the fact that phonological mediation was not obligatory, it did so by introducing an enormous degree of redundancy into the processing system. This can be seen by examining how the model accounts for the task of naming words aloud. In principle, every word could be recognized on a visual basis, providing postlexical access to phonology, which could then be used in naming. In effect, words could be named in the same way as numerals and other nonalphabetic symbols such as $ or +. In this way, naming a visually present word would draw on processes that are also involved in speech production in the absence of visual cues. However, only some words can be correctly named on the basis of nonlexical phonology. While English orthography systematically encodes phonological information, the mapping between the two codes is not entirely consistent. For several reasons [e.g., because the orthography is a "deep," morphophonemic one (Lukatela, Popadić, Ognjenović, & Turvey, 1980), because of diachronic changes in pronunciation, and because of lexical borrowing], many English words have idiosyncratic pronunciations. Thus, while the correspondences between spelling and sound in English can be described, to a first approximation, by a set of mapping rules (e.g., Venezky, 1970)), even the most felicitous statement of these rules will generate incorrect pronunciations for irregular words such as *have, deaf, said,* and *dose* (which are also termed **exceptions**). These words can *only* be correctly pronounced by reference to lexical phonology.

In the dual route model, then, pronouncing an exception word requires the reconciliation of an incorrect pronunciation derived on the basis of spelling–sound rules with a correct pronunciation accessed postlexically. Given that it cannot be determined in advance whether a particular word is regular or irregular, the naming of regular words will also require this postaccess check. The mismatch between the phonological code generated on the basis of prelexical phonology and the postlexical code was presumed to account for the common finding that regular words are named faster than exception words. In the dual route model, then, **naming always requires the use of both pathways.** This presents a paradox: If word recognition utlimately requires acccess to postlexical phonology, why does the reader even attempt to generate a pronunciation on the basis of spelling–sound knowledge? The plausibility of this model would increase if there were an independent explanation for the existence of the nonlexical route, or for the apparent inability of skilled readers to use the visual pathway exclusively.[5]

One possibility is that the benefits associated with using nonlexical phonology outweigh the costs. Perhaps nonlexical phonology facilitates the recognition of the majority of words, which are regular, and only interferes with the recognition of a much smaller pool of exceptions. Since it cannot be determined in advance of recognition whether a given word is regular or irregular, the processor minimizes costs and maximizes benefits by trying the spelling–sound route. According to this view, then, although postlexical phonology is necessary for naming, prelexical phonology speeds access to this code, thereby facilitating recognition. However, it is not obvious how the use of spelling–sound information could facilitate recognition compared to direct visual access, given the character of English orthography. Rubenstein *et al.* (1971), for example, proposed that recognition involves a phonologically based search through lexical memory. Given the degree of homophony in English (i.e., the fact that most sounds do not have unique spellings), it is not clear that a phonologically based search will involve a smaller space of possibilities than an orthographically based search. Furthermore, it is clear that the search cannot be exclusively phonological; orthographic information must be retained to permit homophone disambiguation (as Rubenstein *et al.* noted). It is possible that a search process

---

[5]The dual route theory holds that regular words in English can be named on the basis of nonlexical phonology. I have suggested that readers could not name words in this way unless they knew in advance whether a word was regular or irregular. A weaker assumption might be that readers use this pathway under conditions that permit it—perhaps in a reading experiment in which all the stimuli are regular. However, I know of no direct evidence that readers are able to process words (or nonwords) strictly on the basis of nonlexical phonology under **any** conditions. In my own lab, we have been unsuccessful in attempts to create conditions under which words could be named nonlexically. For example, we embedded a small number of high and low frequency words within a much larger list of regular nonwords. The subjects were not informed as to the presence of words, and their task was simply to name each stimulus. By including a high percentage of nonwords, we had hoped to induce subjects to name all stimuli nonlexically, thereby eliminating the frequency effect. However, it remained. It is possible that words could be named nonlexically in phonologically transparent scripts such as Kana or Serbo-Croatian. However, I know of no decisive evidence on this point. The fact that there are differences in the latencies to name words and nonwords in each script (Feldman, 1981; Besner, Hildebrandt, & McCann, 1984) argues against the operation of a strictly nonlexical mechanism.

utilizing both types of information would be most efficient, but this cannot be determined without a more specific account of the computation (which the dual route model does not provide). A recognition process that involved both types of information could as well be **more** complicated than a simple orthographic search. Assuming that it were determined how prelexical phonology facilitates recognition, there would be a further problem in explaining why it does not **always** enter into the recognition process. Evidence indicates that skilled readers recognize common words directly on a visual basis, with phonology only entering into the processing of lower frequency items (Seidenberg, Waters, Barnes, & Tanenhaus, 1984a; Section IV,B). It would need to be explained, then, why the visual pathway is faster in some cases, and the phonological pathway in others. In sum, the dual route model asserts that recognition proceeds along two pathways in parallel, but there is no principled explanation for either how spelling–sound information could facilitate recognition, or why it would facilitate in some cases (mediated access) but not in others (direct access).

A second possibility is that use of nonlexical phonology is a reflex of the manner in which reading skills were acquired. In the early stages of learning to read, many children sound out words, using their knowledge of spelling–sound correspondences (Backman, Bruck, Hébert, & Seidenberg, 1984; Waters, Bruck, & Seidenberg, 1985a; Waters, Seidenberg, & Bruck, 1984); many are explicitly taught to read in this manner. Residual use of the nonlexical route in skilled reading could then be seen as a consequence of early reliance on sounding out. However, this view implausibly suggests that readers continue to mechanistically apply spelling–sound rules in reading exception words such as *have* even though such words have been read many thousands of times, simply because of the manner in which decoding skills were acquired. This explanation is also inconsistent with the view that use of prelexical phonology is under the strategic control of the reader (see next section).

A third possibility is that the nonlexical route exists because of its role in reading unfamiliar words (or, in reading experiments, nonwords). The advantage of alphabetic orthographies over writing systems organized along other principles (e.g., logographies) is that knowledge of how the orthography represents sound provides a simple means for pronouncing unfamiliar words. However, as Glushko (1979) observed, naming unfamiliar stimuli does not necessarily require the use of nonlexical phonology. Novel stimuli could be pronounced by analogy to known words. Glushko proposed that the analogy process underlay the naming of both familiar words and novel words or nonwords. Assuming that a workable model could be developed along these lines, the phonological route could not be justified on the basis of its role in reading novel stimuli.

Finally, it could be assumed that the redundancy is peculiar to the naming task. Reading rarely involves overt pronunciation; subjects might attempt to use prelexical phonology to generate the pronunciation of a word simply to meet the demands of the speeded naming task. This is an interesting possiblility, but it can be rejected on two grounds. First, I present evidence below that **faster** naming latencies are associated with **smaller** effects of irregular pronunciation; hence it cannot be the case that forcing subjects to name words quickly yields greater reliance on prelexical phonology. Second, the differences in performance on the naming task compared to silent reading tasks can be explained without assuming that the naming task entails special processing strategies (see Section IV,F). To the contrary, it is silent reading tasks such as lexical decision that involve task-specific strategies.

D. Is There Strategic Control over Alternate Pathways?

In the dual route model, it is assumed that the visual and phonological pathways are attempted in parallel, with the fastest finishing process determining whether direct or mediated access occurs. However, it has also been proposed that use of nonlexical phonology is under the strategic control of the reader. This assumption was necessary because phonological effects on word recognition depend on the type of reading task. Various studies have shown that there are greater phonological effects in the naming task than in silent reading tasks such as lexical decision. Coltheart, Besner, Jonasson, and Davelaar (1979) and Seidenberg *et al.* (1984a) established that the exception effect is larger in naming than in lexical decision; often the lexical decison task yields no effect of irregular pronunciation at all. Shulman, Hornak, and Sanders (1978) found that phonological effects on lexical decison latencies depend on the type of nonword stimuli. When the nonwords were pronounceable, there was evidence of phonological access; when the nonwords were nonpronounceable letter strings, there were no phonological effects. Results of the large number of pseudohomophone studies (reviewed by Dennis *et al.,* this volume) also show that phonological effects depend on the composition of the stimuli in an experiment. The fact that access of phonology appears to depend on the type of reading task and stimulus material led Coltheart and others to conclude that its use is under the tacit control of the individual. The subject performing the naming task is thought to use prelexical phonology because it facilitates performance of the task; the subject performing the lexical decision task eschews phonology because it does not facilitate performance. Interpreted within the dual route model, this suggests that subjects can control the use of the nonlexical pathway. This leads to the view that skilled readers use flexible decoding strategies, relying on phonology only where necessary (Doctor & Coltheart, 1980), and to a view of reading education in which the goal is to develop intelligent and efficient use of these alternative strategies (Jorm & Share, 1983). These beliefs are consistent with those of many educators who assume that skilled readers have learned to avoid the use of phonological information almost entirely. Accessing phonology is thought to involve extra processing; thus, word recognition would be more efficient if this extra step were eliminated.

The problem with this point of view is that it explains task-related differences in the use of phonology by assuming that readers can control aspects of the initial decoding process. This conflicts with another favorite assumption of reading researchers, namely that initial decoding processes are automatized among skilled readers (e.g., LaBerge & Samuels, 1974). There is little evidence directly supporting the assumption that readers can strategically control processes involved in word recognition. In fact, readers show little ability to control initial decoding; for example, as we have seen, they cannot control access to the meanings of ambiguous words, even when contextual information clearly indicates which meaning is appropriate. Most compelling, perhaps, is evidence that subjects access phonological information even under conditions where it has a negative effect on performance. Tanenhaus, Flanigan, and Seidenberg (1980) had subjects perform a Stroop task, naming the color of the ink a target word was written in. Each target was preceded by a single priming word. Primes and targets were either phonologically similar (*stone-blown*), orthographically similar (*clown-blown*), both orthographically and phonologically similar (*flown-blown*) or unrelated (*chair-blown*). Color-naming latencies were longer when primes and targets rhymed than when they were unrelated. Subjects accessed phonology even though it had a detrimental effect on performance. If access of phonology were under strategic control, subjects should have avoided using it, but they did not (see also Dennis & Newstead, 1981). Further evidence is provided by complementary findings concerning the access of orthographic information in auditory word recognition. Seidenberg and Tanenhaus (1979) discovered that latencies to judge two auditorily presented words as rhymes are longer if they are spelled differently (*sky-tie*) than if they are spelled similarly (*pie-tie*). Here access of the orthographic code has a negative effect on performance, and subjects are again unable to inhibit its use.

In sum, skilled word recognition appears to be cognitively impenetrable (Pylyshyn, 1981): given the presence of certain triggering conditions, and the attention of the perceiver, recognition occurs. It seems clear that at least some higher level processes can be modified by the individual (consider the difference between skimming and "reading for meaning"). However, the idea that subjects can control initial decoding processes—that they can use different decoding "strategies" or suppress the use of phonology—is simply unsupported by empirical evidence. Nonetheless, this is how the dual route model accounts for the differing phonological effects on naming and lexical decision.

E. Explanatory Adequacy

The above discussion has identified some of the problems associated with current versions of the dual route model. It could be argued that these considerations merely point to areas in which the model must be modified or elaborated. However, there may be more basic deficiencies in the approach to theory development embodied in the dual route model. There is reason to doubt whether an explanatory theory (in the sense of Chomsky, 1965) could ever develop within this approach.

The dual route model and recent variants exemplify an information-processing approach to model building which flourished for a time in cognitive psychology (other examples are Smith, Shoben, & Rips, 1975; Carpenter & Just, 1975). These models make use of a flow-chart formalism borrowed from computer programming. The flow of information could be charted using a small number of formal elements (e.g., data paths, decision boxes, and the like). It has become clear that this approach has serious limitations. The questions raised above in connection with the dual route model derive from more basic limitations in this general approach to model building (see also Tanenhaus, Carroll, & Bever, 1976).

There are two basic problems with the flow-chart formalism: (1) the boxes and arrows that are the primary structural components of these models are arbitrary graphical conventions lacking a consistent formal or theoretical interpretation, and (2) there are no constraints on their use. In regard to (1) the problem is that boxes are used to represent many different kinds of structures and operations. Several negative consequences follow from this practice. First, the models cannot be evaluated in terms of parsimony (e.g., is a model with four large boxes more restrictive than one with six small ones?). Second, the ambiguity in the formalism breeds ambiguity in interpreting the resulting models. For example, arrows are sometimes intended to represent the temporal sequence of processing events; other times they merely indicate possible pathways without regard to sequence (as in the widespread use of double-ended arrows). As a result, it is unclear whether such models represent a claim about the time course of processing events or not. Third, the grain of these models is very coarse; it is common to see boxes labeled "word recognition," "word comprehension," and "phonological recoding." Because the internal operations of the boxes are rarely specified, the models are not genuinely computational, even though they make use of computational jargon.

In regard to (2), although these models make use of a finite number of primitive structures and operations, there are few constraints on how these elements can be employed (and these are for the most part informal). As a consequence, model building within this framework has an ad hoc character. This judgment is borne out by the history of the dual route model (summarized by Morton and Patterson, 1980). The model underwent successive elaborations and modifications over the years, with the introduction of a third recognition pathway, and various input and output buffers. These developments were largely in response to neurolinguistic data indicting specific patterns of impairment in cases of acquired reading disability; they were motivated on the basis of the case studies they were intended to explain. The explanatory value of these models is limited because new pathways and other mechanisms can be stipulated as necessary. This lack of constraint on the introduction of new structures and processes presents a serious problem. It also means that the models have little predictive value—little capacity to rule out the occurrence of particular forms of reading impairment, for example.

The particular problems with dual route models identified above may simply point to ways in which they must be revised or elaborated. Given the flexibility of the box-and-arrow formalism, I do not want to suggest that models of this type cannot in principle account for any given phenomenon, an issue to which I return in Section IV,H. However, it may be that while these models have led to increased understanding of the recognition process, they are rapidly reaching the limits of their usefulness. There is another approach to model building which has recently led to the development of models of word recognition dispensing with the notion of alternate recognition pathways entirely.

IV. WORD RECOGNITION AS A PARALLEL DISTRIBUTED PROCESS

Recent models of word recognition make use of a formal apparatus termed parallel distributed processing. This general computational framework is being used in developing theories of many aspects of neural processing, motoric activity, perception, and cognition (Fahlman, Hinton, & Sejnowski, 1983; Feldman & Ballard, 1982; Hinton & Anderson, 1981; Hummel & Zucker, 1980). The core concept is that complex phenomena may result from interactions among a large network of simple processing elements. Elements become activated, and the pattern of activation through the network changes by means of excitatory or inhibitory spread of activation. In essence, this framework represents a computationally sophisticated elaboration of the Hebbian notion of cell assemblies; one can think of these models as what Hebb might have developed had he access to a LISP machine, or a parallel computational architecture.

This computational framework has been applied to the problem of word recognition by McClelland and Rumelhart (1981). Strictly speaking, theirs is not a model of word recognition per se; it was developed in order to account for word superiority effects (the fact that a letter is perceived more rapidly in a word or orthographically legal nonword than in isolation). However, the model provides the basis for developing an explanatory theory of word recognition. The following sections describe a model of word recognition, using the parallel interactive framework, which accounts for a wide range of phenomena. In particular, it provides an account of phonological effects on word recognition among skilled readers, subsuming both direct and mediated access; it explains task-related variation in the use of phonology and differences as a function of reading skill; and it provides a framework for understanding commonalities in the processing of orthographies organized along different principles.[6]

A. A Time Course Model

In several papers, my colleagues and I have developed a time course model of word recognition (Seidenberg *et al.,* 1984a; Seidenberg, 1985a; Waters *et al.,* 1984; Waters & Seidenberg, 1985), building on proposals by McClelland and Rumelhart (1981), Glushko (1979), and others. The core idea is that various facts about phonology and word recognition can be explained by considering the time course of orthographic and phonological code activation. We assume that recognition is initiated with the extraction of visual information from the input, resulting in interactive processes of the type detailed by McClelland and Rumelhart (1981). In their model, information accrues over time at nodes representing several different types of information (words, letters, letter features). The nodes are arrayed in a hierarchical network structure; nodes sharing common information (e.g., *a* and *and*) are linked by excitatory pathways; nodes that do not share information are linked by inhibitory pathways (e.g., *a* and *but*). Recognizing a particular type of information increments the activation level of its node

---

[6]Rumelhart and McClelland (1982) discussed some ways in which their model might be extended to handle phonological phenomena. My proposals represent an attempt to make these extensions more explicit. I am very indebted to Jay McClelland for suggestions that contributed greatly to this formulation.

and activation spreads by means of the excitatory and inhibitory links through the network. Detecting a feature such as |, for example, would increase the activation of the nodes for all letters containing this feature (*E, T, L,* etc.), and decrement the activation of letters that do not contain it (*S, C, A,* etc.). Similarly activation of the letter *A* would increment the activation associated with words containing this letter, and decrement the activation associated with words that do not contain it. Information at various levels accrues over time, resulting in continuous changes in activation throughout the network. A word or letter is recognized when its activation level passes a threshold amount. The explanation for the word superiority effect is straightforward: a letter is perceived better in a word than in isolation because it receives additional activation from word-level detectors only when it appears in a word context.

The McClelland and Rumelhart model can be construed as representing interactive processes within the mental lexicon. It is clear that the model must be elaborated, however, because several types of information relevant to word recognition are not represented. In particular, the model does not make reference to phonology. Assume, then, that as orthographic units are identified, they activate phonological representations that are also interconnected by excitatory or inhibitory links (depending upon phonological similarity or dissimilarity). Under such an arrangement, access of phonological information necessarily lags behind access of orthographic information. Differences in the availability of these two types of information over time provide the basis for explaining the various word recognition phenomena mentioned above.

B. Direct vs Mediated Access

The time course model provides a framework for resolving the debate over whether lexical access is direct or phonologically mediated. The important contrast between this model and the dual route model is that, rather than postulating separate orthographic and phonological processes operating in parallel, the time course model emphasizes a single interactive process with differences in the availability of orthographic and phonological information over time. Whether direct or mediated access occurs simply falls out from facts about the time course of code activation. "Direct access" results when sufficient orthographic information is extracted from the input to permit recognition prior to the access of phonology. In the absence of pathology, recognition on a visual basis results in automatic access to a stored representation of the phonological code (postlexical phonology), which may be used in overt naming, or because it facilitates retention of information in working memory (Baddeley, 1979). "Mediated access" occurs if a word cannot be recognized prior to the activation of phonological information. Recognition then depends upon interactions among both orthographic and phonological units.

This model makes the clear prediction that phonological mediation should be associated with words that are recognized relatively slowly. This prediction is confirmed by recent research. Word recognition latencies are inversely related to frequency of use. Among skilled readers, higher frequency words tend to be recognized on a visual basis; lower frequency words show effects of phonological mediation. The evidence is provided by studies of words that have either regular or irregular pronunciations. If phonology enters into the process by which a letter string is identified, words whose pronunciations are regular (such as *just* or *make*) should be recognized more quickly than words whose pronunciations are irregular (e.g., *have, deaf*). If phonology does not enter into the recognition process, regular and exception words that are similar in other respects (e.g., frequency, length, syllabic structure, orthographic regularity) should be read with comparable facility. The time course model predicts that only lower frequency, more slowly recognized words should be influenced by phonology (as originally suggested by McCusker *et al.,* 1981).

In a series of studies, we have examined this prediction. Regular and exception words were defined in the following way. Both types of words have common spelling patterns that occur in many words. For each regular word (such as *just*), all words with similar spellings rhyme (*must, lust,* etc.). Such words contain spelling patterns with pronunciations that are predicted by the spelling–sound rules of English proposed by Venezky (1970) and Wijk (1966). Exception words contain spelling patterns that are typically pronounced otherwise; for example, the *-ave* in *have* is usually pronounced as in *gave, rave,* etc. Nor are the pronunciations of exception words correctly specified by spelling–sound rules. Our studies use a simple design: We compared recognition latencies for regular and exception words that were either relatively high in frequency, or relatively low, as indexed by standard frequency norms (Kuçera & Francis, 1967; Carroll, Davies, & Richman, 1971). The results consistently indicate that while lower frequency words are read more slowly than higher frequency words, exception words are read more slowly than regular words only when they are low in frequency. A typical result (from Seidenberg, 1985a) is presented in Table I. The stimuli were monosyllabic words, which subjects read aloud (naming task). The data summarize the results of two versions of the stimuli, yielding a total of 50 words in each condition. Higher frequency words had frequencies greater than 200 on the Carroll *et al.* norms; lower frequency words had frequencies less than 100. There was a main effect of frequency, because higher frequency words were named faster than lower fre-

TABLE I

Mean Naming Latencies in msec and Percentage Errors,
Seidenberg (1985a), Experiment 2[a]

Word type	Set A	Set B	Both sets
High frequency regular	549	531	540 (0.4)
High frequency exception	540	542	541 (0.9)
Low frequency regular	555	557	556 (2.3)
Low frequency exception	589	578	583 (5.1)

[a]The experiment was run twice with different sets of stimuli.

quency words, and a main effect of type of word. However, the critical finding was an interaction between type of word and frequency, with only lower frequency exception words yielding longer naming latencies than regular words. The exception effect for higher frequency words could be expected to be smaller in absolute magnitude than that for lower frequency words simply because higher frequency words are named more rapidly; however, the higher frequency effect is not merely smaller—it is nonexistent. Replications are reported in Seidenberg *et al.* (1984a), Waters *et al.* (1984), and Waters and Seidenberg (1985).

The results indicated that, among skilled readers of English, a large pool of words is recognized on a visual basis, with the phonological code accessed postlexically. Lower frequency words are decoded more slowly, allowing time for phonological information to be activated; this yields longer latencies for exception words whose pronunciations are irregular. For higher frequency words, then, the phonological code is automatically activated following recognition; for lower frequency words, the phonological code is computed prelexically as part of the process by which the words are recognized. This is in keeping with the predictions of the time course model.[7]

---

[7]Balota and Chumbley (1984) have obtained evidence that the frequency effect in naming may be due at least in part to differences in the difficulty in pronouncing words. This suggests that frequency may affect production, rather than recognition. In their studies, frequency effects were obtained even when subjects named words after a delay of 1–2 sec. Since recognition is completed within a few hundred milliseconds, the residual frequency effect was apparently due to differences in ease of articulation. This result suggests the possibility that our frequency-related effects of irregular pronunciation are also due to production, rather than lexical access. Several points should be noted, however. First, Balota and Chumbley's results suggest that only part of the frequency effect is due to production. The frequency effects in the delay conditions were much smaller than those that were obtained with no delay. Thus, their results indicate that the frequency effect is not limited to lexical access, but they do not indicate that frequency has no effect on access. Second, their high and low frequency words were not equated in terms of difficulty of pronunciation. Their results may reflect the fact that lower frequency words tend to contain sounds that are more difficult to pronounce.

C. How to Make Words Hard to Read

Our studies revealed an effect of irregular pronunciation much smaller than that reported in other work (e.g., Baron & Strawson, 1976; Treiman, Freyd, & Baron, 1983; Bauer & Stanovich, 1980; Glushko, 1979; Parkin, 1982). However, three important factors account for the differing pattern of results. First, these studies did not examine the critical frequency variable. The only other study to examine frequency (Andrews, 1982) also yielded an exception effect limited to lower frequency items. Other studies (such as Parkin, 1982) only included lower frequency items; therefore the results are consistent with ours. In studies that included a wider range of frequencies (such as Treiman *et al.* 1983), it is possible that the exception effect was carried by lower frequency items, although this cannot be determined from the data provided.

A second factor is that the effects of irregular pronunciation can be inflated by repeating spelling patterns with different pronunciations. Both Glushko (1979) and Treiman *et al.* (1984) found longer latencies for exception words compared to regular words using higher frequency stimuli. In the Glushko study, however, the stimuli were matched pairs such as *have* and *gave*. *Have* is a high frequency exception word. *Gave* is a regular but inconsistent word (Glushko, 1979); although the pronunciation of -*ave* in *gave* is correctly specified by spelling–sound rules, its pronunciation is not entirely consistent because it also appears in a matched exception word. In the Treiman *et al.* study, each regular word was matched with an exception word chosen so that if the exception was pronounced using the major spelling–sound rule for its spelling pattern, it would rhyme with the matched regular word. This yielded orthographically similar but phonologically dissimilar pairs such as *size–seize* and *greet–great*. Because the stimuli in both experiments were presented in a within-subjects design, exposure to one member of a pair could have biased subsequent processing of the matched item. Seidenberg *et al.* (1984a) showed that if the subject reads an exception word such as *have* without prior exposure to an orthographically similar but nonrhyming word such as *gave,* its naming latency is comparable to

---

This would not be surprising in light of other structural differences associated with frequency (Landauer & Streeter, 1973). This yields the possibility that the phonological characteristics of the lower frequency exception words we used are responsible for the longer naming latencies obtained. Gloria Waters and I have recently obtained two findings bearing on this issue. The first is that we do not obtain a difference between high and low frequency words under Balota and Chumbley's delay condition when the phonological characteristics of the stimuli are equated by using homophones. Second, when lower frequency regular and exception words are presented after a delay, no regularity effect obtains. These results suggest that the lower frequency exception effect in our studies is not due to differences in the pronounceability of the words.

that for a regular word (e.g., *must*). After prior exposure to *gave,* however, *have* takes longer to name than a regular word. Thus, prior exposure to the spelling pattern influences the processing of a subsequent word with a similar spelling; this produces an interference effect similar to one Meyer, Schvaneveldt, and Ruddy (1974) and Tanenhaus *et al.* (1980) obtained for stimuli such as *couch–touch* in lexical priming studies. By repeating spelling patterns in this way, it is possible to obtain longer latencies for exception words compared to regular words. When subjects are not biased by prior exposure, the exception effect is limited to lower frequency words.

The repetition of spelling patterns with different pronunciations also contributed to the regular inconsistent effect in the study by Glushko (1979). He found that, like exception words, regular inconsistent words yielded longer naming latencies that regular words. This effect is important for two reasons. The dual route model provides no basis for expecting that a word such as *gave* will be harder to read than a regular word such as *must.* In both cases, the pronunciations are correctly specified by spelling–sound rules, yet Glushko found that both regular inconsistent and exception words yielded longer naming latencies than regular words. The regular inconsistent effect also implied that the effects of irregular pronunciation were much more widespread than previously thought; they occurred not only for genuine exceptions such as *have,* but also for seemingly regular words such as *gave.* When the spelling patterns are not repeated with different pronunciations, however, the regular inconsistent effect is limited to lower frequency items (Seidenberg *et al.,* 1984a). This result does militate against the spelling–sound rule account, but it also confirms that phonology only enters into the recognition of lower frequency items.

Finally, in many studies, the orthographic properties of the regular and exception words were not well controlled; as Henderson (in press) has noted, widely varying criteria have been used in classifying words as exceptions. In particular, the exception–word stimuli have often included items containing uncommon spelling patterns (e.g., *ache, yacht*). This has the effect of confounding orthographic regularity of spelling–sound correspondences; a difference between regular words and this type of exception word could be due to either factor. Seidenberg *et al.* (1984a) and Waters *et al.* (1984) examined this question empirically. Recall the definitions of regular and exception words given above: Both types have common spelling patterns that occur in many words; however, the exception words have irregular pronunciations. Seidenberg *et al.* and Waters *et al.* also examined a class of words with unusual spelling patterns, which they termed "strange." A difference between regular and exception words could only be attributed to regularity of pronunciation, because the words are similar in terms of orthographic structure. Strange words could be expected to be processed more slowly than regular and exception words due to both their atypical spelling patterns and associated difficulties in deriving their pronunciations. The following results obtained: for lower frequency items, strange words were harder to read than both regular and exception words (in terms of latencies and errors); exception words were harder to read than regulars. For higher frequency words, there were no statistically reliable differences in performance for the three classes of words. Thus, there were effects of both irregular spelling and irregular pronunciation, limited to lower frequency items.

These results demonstrate that there is an effect of irregular spelling independent of the effect of irregular pronunciation. This conclusion follows from the fact that results from the exception and strange words differed in several respects. Lower frequency strange words produced longer latencies than regular words on both the naming and lexical decision tasks, and the effects were not dependent upon the composition of the stimuli. Lower frequency exception words produced longer latencies on the naming task, but their occurrence in lexical decision depended on the composition of the stimuli. Furthermore, the strange words were more difficult than exception words. The strange words are difficult both because of their irregular spellings and because of the difficulties involved in deriving their pronunciations. Exception words are difficult only because of their irregular pronunciations.

The fact that higher frequency, irregularly spelled strange words did not yield longer naming latencies than regular words of comparable frequency is also important. In essence, it means that if a word is very familiar, its similarity to other words is irrelevant to the recognition process. In Glushko's (1979) terms, the neighborhood effects for common words are very small. A word is exceptional or strange only in virtue of its relationship to other words, its neighbors. The McClelland and Rumelhart (1981) model is largely concerned with ways in which structural relationships among words could influence recognition (the "gang" effect, the "rich-get-richer" effect, etc.). While these interconnections may be relevant to the processing of lower frequency items, they have little bearing on the recognition of common words. This means that the recognition process is simplified for higher frequency words.[8]

Our results also provide an explanation for the larger exception effect in studies such as Baron and Strawson (1976), Bauer and Stanovich (1980),

---

[8]In our studies, we have consistently obtained slightly faster latencies for high frequency strange words compared to regular words. These effects are rarely significant, but they have recurred across experiments and materials. It is probably the case that, for a small number of very common words, orthographic irregularity facilitates recognition. These words are very easily discriminated from other possibilities.

and Parkin (1982). Their effects were probably due to the inclusion of words with irregular spellings, not to irregular pronunciation per se.

D. Differences in Phonological Mediation as a Function of Decoding Skill

The frequency-by-regularity interaction in the above studies indicated that phonology only enters into the decoding of lower frequency words. On the view I am proposing, then, phonological effects simply depend on the amount of time a word is processed. Lower frequency words tend to be recognized more slowly, yielding greater phonological effects. However, while frequency is negatively correlated with naming latency, there may be differences among skilled readers in the magnitude of the frequency effect. It is important to realize that the lower frequency stimuli in the above studies were common, monosyllabic words well within the vocabularies of our college student subjects. There may be some readers who are able to recognize even these lower frequency words on a visual basis. As a further test of the time course model, I sought to determine whether the phonological effects in reading lower frequency words were associated with subjects whose decoding latencies tended to be slow. Consider again the data in Table I (from Seidenberg, 1985a). The subjects in this experiment were McGill University undergraduates who are native speakers of English. The subjects were randomly solicited without regard to reading speed. After the data were collected, the subjects were partitioned into fast, medium, and slow reader groups based on their overall mean naming latencies. The results of this analysis are presented in Table II. They clearly indicate that the exception effect for lower frequency words was carried by the subjects who were slower decoders. Note that the fastest subjects read **lower** fre-

TABLE II

Data from the Seidenberg (1985a) Study Analyzed by Speed of Subject[a]

Word type	Subject group		
	Fastest	Medium	Slowest
High frequency regular	475	523	621
High frequency exception	475	517	631
Difference	0	−6	+10
Low frequency regular	500	530	641
Low frequency exception	502	562	685
Difference	+2	+32	+44

[a]There were 16 subjects in each group.

quency words over 100 msec more quickly than the slower subjects read **higher** frequency words. It was during this interval that phonological information was apparently activated for slower subjects. These results (and similar findings reported by Waters and Seidenberg, 1985) indicate differences among skilled, college student readers in the size of their "sight" vocabularies. Thus, lower frequency words tend to show greater effects of phonological mediation because they are recognized more slowly; however, even among skilled adult readers, there are differences in decoding speed which determine whether phonological effects occur or not.[9]

E. Developmental Trends in the Use of Prelexical Phonology

The time course model also provides a context for understanding how the use of phonology in recognizing words changes over the course of learning to read. It has long been argued that beginning readers rely more upon phonology in decoding words than do skilled readers, and that the ability to use phonology facilitates the acquisition of reading skills. Most children have good speaking and listening skills when they learn to read, allowing rapid access to the meaning of a word from its spoken form. By learning the correspondences between spelling and sound, the child gains a powerful tool for reading unfamiliar words. Words can be recoded into a phonological representation, permitting access to meaning in the same manner as in listening. Many children are explicitly taught to read in this manner; with practice, they learn to recognize words on a visual basis. Thus, there is a developmental shift away from the use of phonology in decoding words (Edfeldt, 1959). Among educators it has been widely assumed that the goal of reading instruction should be the development of direct, visual access because it is more efficient. Our studies of adult readers provide some support for this view; faster readers recognize a larger pool of words without phonological mediation.

There has been a surprising amount of controversy over the validity of this developmental scenario, however. Several studies have been interpreted as failing to support it (e.g., Barron & Baron, 1977; Condry, McMahon-Rideout, & Levy 1979; Rader, 1975), because they suggested that even beginning readers recognize words on a visual basis. Some of the apparent inconsistency in the literature may be due to a failure to distinguish between the use of prelexical phonology in decoding words, and postlexical phonology in remembering the words in a sentence (Baddeley & Lewis, 1981;

[9]Frederiksen (1978) reports a number of findings consistent with ours. For example, word length and number of syllables influenced naming latencies only for slower, less skilled readers.

Besner & Davelaar, 1982). Even if a word is recognized on a visual basis, postlexical access of phonology may facilitate processes involved in comprehending text. While younger readers may rely more upon phonology in decoding, older readers who recognize words on a visual basis may make better use of the postlexical code.

In several studies, we have examined developmental changes in the use of phonology in word recognition (Backman, Bruck, Hébert, & Seidenberg, 1984; Seidenberg, Bruck, Fornarolo, & Backman, 1985; Waters *et al.*, 1984, 1985a). Backman *et al.* evaluated children's abilities to read words and nonwords that varied in terms of the regularity of their pronunciations. The stimuli included regular, exception, and regular inconsistent words, as defined above; they also included a class of words containing spelling patterns termed "ambiguous." These are spelling patterns such as *-ove* or *-own* that have multiple pronunciations, each of which occurs in many words (e.g., *love, glove, above, cove, stove, grove,* etc.; *town, crown, frown, clown, blown, flown, known,* etc.). The exception, regular inconsistent, and ambiguous words contain spelling patterns that are **homographic** (associated with more than one pronunciation). The words were all higher frequency items that are learned in the early grades. Nonwords were derived from the word stimuli. The subjects were good readers in grades 2, 3, and 4 and high school, and poor readers in grades 3 and 4. Good readers scored above the seventy-fifth percentile for their grade on the reading comprehension subtest of the Stanford Diagnostic Reading Test; poor readers scored below the fortieth percentile. The children's task was simply to name the words and nonwords aloud, with naming latencies and errors the primary dependent measures.

Predictably, older children named words more quickly than younger children, and good readers named words faster than poor readers. Within each subject group, latencies across word classes did not differ. The effects of word class were manifested in the error data, which are summarized in Fig. 1. The results for the younger good readers and for the poor readers were similar: they made more errors in reading words containing homographic spelling patterns than in reading regular words. By grade 4 however, there were no differences among word classes for the good readers; their performance was similar to that of high school students. These data provide clear evidence for a developmental transition from phonological mediation to direct access. Both these quantitative data and analyses of the types of errors indicated that the grade 3-4 poor readers' decoding processes were very similar to those of the good readers in grade 2, indicating a developmental delay among the poor readers. The nonword data yielded comparable results. Waters *et al.* (1984) report similar results. Waters *et al.* (1985a) provide complementary data concerning spelling, and Seidenberg *et al.*

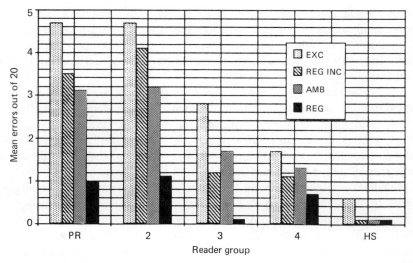

Fig. 1. Results from the Backman *et al.* (1984) study. PR, poor readers from grades 3 and 4; HS, high school students; EXC, exception words (e.g. *have*); REG INC, regular inconsistent words (e.g., *gave*); AMB, ambiguous words (e.g., *town*); REG, regular words (e.g., *must*).

(1985) provide a comparison between poor readers and those diagnosed as developmental dyslexics.

The Backman *et al.* study revealed two complementary processes in the child's acquisition of reading skill. First, good readers learn to recognize common words on a visual basis. The data indicate that learning to cope with the irregularities and ambiguities in the correspondence between spelling and sound in English presents a problem for the beginning reader. A hallmark of learning to read skillfully is acquisition of the ability to read common words on a visual basis. Poor readers have difficulty achieving this skill. They appear to be able to learn the correspondences between spelling and sound; their performance in reading regular words was similar to that of good readers, and most of their errors were due to using the wrong pronunciation associated with a spelling pattern (e.g., *have* pronounced to rhyme with *gave, town* rhymed with *flown*), rather than a wholly inappropriate pronunciation. Apparently, only the skilled readers obviate the problem of remembering which pronunciation is associated with a spelling pattern in a particular word by reading on a nonmediated basis.

At the same time that good readers are learning to recognize words without relying upon phonology, they are consolidating their knowledge of spelling–sound correspondences. This second developmental trend was revealed by the increasing systematicity of naming errors among good readers, and gains in the ability to read nonwords. Although its use in reading common words is limited, knowledge of the spelling–sound correspondences of English is presumably employed in learning new words.

In sum, younger and less skillful readers rely more upon prelexical phonology than do older, more skillful readers. In the terms of the time course model, skilled readers are able to recognize common words prior to the activation of phonological information. For younger readers, many fewer words are recognized in this manner. Although good readers have learned to recognize common words on a visual basis by about grade 4 or 5, they continue to refine their recognition skills for several years. Recognition speed continues to decrease, expanding the pool of words recognized on a visual basis.

F. Task-Related Differences in the Access of Phonology

The time course model also accounts for the fact that effects of phonological mediation depend on the type of reading task. As noted above, there are greater phonological effects on naming than on tasks such as lexical decision. Our studies employing both the naming and lexical decision tasks confirm this finding. The exception effect was limited to lower frequency words; however, while it occurred consistently with the naming task, it rarely occurred when the identical stimuli were used in the lexical decision task (Seidenberg et al., 1984a; Seidenberg, 1985a; Waters et al., 1984). Results similar to these led Coltheart et al. (1979) and others to the view that readers can strategically control the use of prelexical phonology. The subject performing the lexical decison task is thought to by-pass this pathway, as a strategy for performing the task. The problem with this proposal is that it accounts for task-dependent effects of phonology on word recognition by assuming that subjects can control the mechanics of the recognition process. This is at variance with a broad range of evidence indicating that initial decoding processes are automatic, hence immune to conscious (or tacit) control.

The time course model accounts for these differences without assuming that subjects strategically control phonological access. An explanation for the different effects of phonological information on naming and lexical decision follows from our assumptions about the time course of code activation and an understanding of the demands of each task. Access of phonological information necessarily lags behind the visual analysis of the written input because it depends on the identification of orthographic units. The naming task requires the subject to process each word to the point at which its pronunciation is known; however, the lexical decison task does not require processing to this depth. Lexical decision is a signal detection task; subjects must establish criteria for deciding whether to respond word or nonword (Seidenberg *et al.,* 1984b). These criteria may vary depending on factors such as the discriminibility of word and nonword stimuli and the instructions to the subject. Smaller phonological effects on lexical decisions would be expected if subjects were able to make lexical decisions based on information available prior to the access of phonology. Because of the requirement that subjects pronounce stimuli correctly, however, subjects performing the naming task cannot respond until they have identified the correct pronunciation. Hence there are greater phonological effects on naming than on lexical decision.

Task-specific differences in the use of phonology derive, then, not from strategic control over the access of phonology, but rather from the different demands of the naming and lexical decision tasks. Further evidence supporting this conclusion is provided by Waters and Seidenberg (1985). We attempted to determine why the lower frequency exception effect occurred inconsistently in various lexical decision studies. For example, Parkin (1982) and Parkin and Underwood (1983) obtained the effect with this task; Coltheart *et al.* (1979) did not, and we obtained the effect in some experiments (Seidenberg *et al.,* 1984a, Experiment 1; Waters *et al.,* 1984), but not in others (Seidenberg *et al.,* 1984a, Experiment 3). In contrast, the lower frequency exception effect in naming has appeared in all of our studies. Given our conception of the lexical decision task, variable effects would occur if subjects established different criteria for making their responses. If subjects were able to make reliable lexical decision prior to the activation of phonological information, no exception effect would occur. If they established more conservative criteria for making their decisions—because the word and nonword stimuli were difficult to discriminate, for example—an exception effect would emerge.

In comparing the studies in which an exception effect was obtained for lower frequency words with lexical decision with those in which no such effect appeared, we noticed one important difference in design. In the studies in which the effect did not appear, the stimuli only included words with regular spelling patterns (regular and exception words). In the studies in which the effect did appear, the stimuli consisted of a more heterogeneous pool of words. For example, the stimuli in Experiment 1 of the Seidenberg *et al.* (1984a) study included both words with ambiguous spelling patterns and homographs, while the stimuli in the Waters *et al.* (1984) and Parkin studies included orthographically atypical "strange" words. Hence the presence of a mixed pool of words seemed to control the use of phonological information. We hypothesized that including a mixed pool of words made the word–nonword discrimination especially difficult, slowing decision latencies, producing phonological effects. When the stimuli were more homogeneous and only included words with common spelling patterns, subjects were able to make the word–nonword decision prior to the access of phonology.

In order to test this hypothesis, Waters and Seidenberg (1985) looked at subjects' performance on the naming and lexical decision tasks when the composition of the stimuli varied. In one experiment, the stimuli included high and low frequency regular, exception, and strange words. In a second experiment, the strange words were deleted; in all other respects the experiments were identical. When the stimuli contained all three types of words, there were low frequency exception and strange effects (i.e., longer latencies for these words compared to regular controls). Furthermore, the effects were carried by subjects whose decision latencies were slowest. When the stimuli only consisted of regular and exception words, the exception effect in latency was eliminated, although it remained in the error data. As a further test of this hypothesis, we replicated the Parkin and Underwood (1983) experiment using their stimuli but deleting the orthographically irregular words. When the stimuli only consisted of regular and exception words, the exception effect was eliminated.

In another experiment, Waters and Seidenberg (1985) evaluated the performance of subjects on the lexical decison task with all three types of stimuli, using a response deadline technique (Stanovich & Bauer, 1978). For each subject, a deadline was imposed which yielded response latencies 150–200 msec faster than in the above experiments. Under this condition, the exception effect for lower frequency words was also eliminated. This finding provides further evidence for the hypothesis that the presence of phonologicl effects depends on the timing of subjects' responses. When lexical decision latencies are slowed by the inclusion of orthographically irregular words, an exception effect results. When subjects are required to respond more quickly than usual, the effect is eliminated.

These experiments were also run with the naming task. In contrast to lexical decision, results for the naming task do not depend on the composition of the stimuli. The exception effect occurred whether or not the stimuli included strange words. Performance is less variable with naming because subjects cannot shift their response criteria because of the requirement that each word be named correctly.

In sum, the occurrence of the exception effect in the lexial decision task depends on the composition of the stimuli. This factor accounts for the discrepant results of previous experiments. In naming, however, the effect occurs regardless of the composition of the stimuli. The different results follow from the different demands of the two tasks. Phonological effects on lexical decisions vary because subjects can establish different criteria for making their responses depending on the discriminability of word and nonword stimuli. The effects in naming are very consistent because subjects cannot respond until they have correctly identified the phonological code.

In general, effects of phonology on word recognition depend upon the timing of phonological code activation relative to when subjects are able to respond. Responses on the naming task are constrained by the requirement that words be pronounced correctly. Subjects control the criteria by which they respond in lexical decision (and thus the amount of time phonological information has to accrue), not the access of phonology.

Given that the effects of phonology on word recognition differ in the lexical decision and naming tasks, a question arises as to which result reflects what is likely to occur in reading under more natural conditions. Although very general conclusions about the reading process are often suggested on the basis of results from these tasks, both differ from normal reading in important respects. Skilled reading seldom involves overt pronunciation; thus it could be argued that the naming task overestimates the extent to which phonology enters into word recognition in silent reading. Lexical decision is a silent reading task, but it introduces the additional requirement that subjects discriminate between words and nonwords. As we have noted, the discriminability of the word and nonword stimuli determines whether phonological effects occur with this task. Performance on these tasks does not provide a clear basis for determining what occurs in reading under more natural conditions.

In order to investigate this question, Waters *et al.* (1984) compared subjects' performance on three tasks: naming, lexical decision, and a sentence-meaningfulness judgment task. The stimuli were high and low frequency regular and exception words. The naming and lexical decison tasks were run as in previous experiments. For the judgment task, each word was presented in a sentence context. The subject read the context; when it was understood, the subject pressed a button, erasing the context and presenting a target word. The task was to decide whether the target completed the sentence in a meaningful way. For example, the sentence context "Marion says that John is. . . . " might be followed by the target *deaf*. On filler trials, the targets did not form meaningful completions, e.g., context: "We ate hot dogs at the. . . . "; target: *tape*. Latencies to make the meaningfulness judgment were timed from the onset of the target. The main finding was that lower frequency exception words produced longer latencies than regular words on this task, as on the pronunciation task. Hence, the access of phonology is not an artifact of naming words aloud or performing lexical decisions. This result should be interpreted with caution, however. The judgment task was a difficult one, yielding relatively long latencies. It is possible that phonological information was activated during the interval when the decision was being made. Nonetheless, this result suggests that phonological information enters into the recognition of lower frequency words even when they are read in context by skilled readers.

G. Access of Phonology in Different Writing Systems

If the time course model is correct, it has important implications concerning the processing of different writing systems. Orthographies differ in the manner in which they represent spoken languages and in other respects. I assume that there are basic commonalities in the processing of different writing systems because human information-processing capacities constrain the structure of human languages and the manner in which they are comprehended. Nonetheless, there are differences among orthographies that could be relevant to processing or to the acquisition of reading skill.

Reading researchers have tended to stress differences in the processing of writing systems organized along different principles. One of the primary ways in which orthographies differ is in the extent to which they encode phonology. At one extreme are writing systems such as Japanese Kana, for which the correspondence between written symbols and pronunciation is regular and direct; there are no exception words in Kana. At the other extreme are writing systems such as Chinese, in which phonology is represented indirectly or not at all, depending on the character. Many Chinese characters are entirely arbitrary with respect to pronunciations; others provide partial phonological information. The English writing system lies somewhere between these extremes; English makes use of a morphophonemic representation in which the relationship between spelling and sound is systematic but nontransparent (Rozin & Gleitman, 1977).

It has often been assumed that these differences among orthographies influence the manner in which they are processed. In the terms of the dual route model, orthographies differ with respect to the viability of the nonlexical route to phonology. Writing systems with more regular correspondences to pronunciation (such as the Kana syllabary, the shallow alphabetic orthography of Serbo-Croatian, and, to a lesser extent, the deep alphabetic orthography of English) in principle provide a basis for using nonlexical phonology that is absent in writing systems for which the correspondence is arbitrary or indirect. These considerations yield two implications. First, the extent to which phonology enters into word recognition may depend on the manner in which it is represented, with greater reliance on phonology in reading orthographies with very regular spelling–sound correspondences (Katz & Feldman, 1983). Second, if nonlexical phonology facilitates word recognition, words should be easier to read in writing systems with regular spelling–sound correspondences (Makita, 1968).

However, the time course model makes a very different prediction. We have shown that in English, a large number of common words are recognized on a visual basis, without phonological mediation. For higher frequency words, the extent to which the written forms indicate their

pronunciations is irrelevant. If a similar outcome held in reading other orthographies—in particular, if the common words in all languages are recognized on a visual basis—differences among orthographies in the manner
in which they represent phonology will be irrelevant to these words. This
observation is important because of the type–token facts about various languages. It appears to be a universal property of languages that the distri-
bution of words by frequency is highly skewed. In English, for example,
the 133 highest frequency words account for about 50% of the tokens in
the Carroll *et al.* (1971) corpus; similar facts hold for other languages as
well (McCusker *et al.*, 1981). The type–token facts suggest that if the common words in various writing systems are recognized on a visual basis, the
effects of differences among orthographies in the encoding of phonology
are quite limited. This would suggest that there are deeper similarities in
the processing of different writing systems than the superficial differences
among them seem to indicate.

Seidenberg (1985a) provided evidence supporting this conclusion in a
study that compared word recognition in English and Chinese. The English results were discussed above; they are presented in Tables I and II. Only
lower frequency words showed evidence of phonological mediation. Analogous results were obtained in a study of Chinese. Seidenberg examined the
role of phonology in reading Chinese by having subjects name characters
that differ in the extent to which phonology is represented. Some Chinese
characters are arbitrary with respect to pronunciation. Other characters,
termed phonograms, contain elements that provide clues to pronunciation.
Many characters contain phonetics that provide all information relevant to
pronunciation except tone. A particular phonetic may appear in a cohort
of phonograms that are pronounced very similarly. To create conditions
analogous to those in the English study, Seidenberg examined both high
and low frequency phonograms and nonphonograms. If Chinese readers
do not use phonology in recognition, only differences in frequency would
be expected. If the phonological information encoded in some characters
is used in recognition, phonograms would be easier to recognize than nonphonograms. Finally, if, as in English, common lexical items in Chinese
are recognized on a visual basis, phonograms would be read faster than
nonphonograms only when they are low in frequency.

The results confirmed the last hypothesis: While higher frequency characters were named more rapidly than lower frequency characters, phonograms were read faster than nonphonograms only when they were low in
frequency. Contrary to common folklore, the phonological information encoded in some Chinese characters is used in recognition; as in English, however, its use is limited to lower frequency items. In both languages, the time
course of phonological code activation is such that this information does
not enter into the recognition of common items. It follows that high fre-

quency words in writing systems such as Kana or Serbo-Croatian should also be read on a visual basis, even though the phonology is transparent. These results point to the conclusion that there are greater similarities in the processing of orthographies structured according to different principles than previously assumed. If there are differences among orthographies related to the manner in which phonology is represented, they are limited to the lower frequency words.

Theories of reading often distinguish between "logographic" and "analytic" decoding strategies (Baron & Strawson, 1976; Smith, 1971). The former, often thought to be involved in reading scripts such as Chinese, involves the recognition of familiar, wholistic, Gestalt-like patterns. The latter, thought to be involved in reading alphabetic scripts such as English, involves analyses based on knowledge of orthographic subunits and rules governing orthographic–phonological correspondences. It has also been suggested by Baron and Strawson (1976) that there are differences among English readers in their reliance on each type of decoding process (the "Chinese" vs "Phoenician" distinction). The Seidenberg (1985a) studies suggest that while such a distinction is useful, use of each process is correlated not with type of orthography, but with word frequency and familiarity. Higher frequency words in both English and Chinese are read "logographically"; lower frequency words are read "analytically." Differences among readers may simply reflect, as in the data presented in Table II, differences in the number of items recognized on a visual basis, which is a function of decoding speed.

The time course model captures the basic similarities in the processing of different writing systems. Of course, there are other differences among orthographies that are relevant to skilled processing and acquisition; for example, it may be easier to learn to read alphabetic orthographies; it may be easier to derive the phonological codes for lower frequency items in alphabetic orthographies; words may be easier to discriminate from one another in some orthographies than in others; etc. Presumably the parameters of the parallel activation process differ across orthographies. Nonetheless, despite radical differences in the structure of different writing systems, it appears that readers are able to recognize common items without relying upon phonology. This fact receives a natural and direct representation in the time course model, which emphasizes the availability of orthographic and phonological information over time.

H. Summary

I have outlined a model of word recognition that accommodates a wide range of empirical and developmental phenomena. The primary achievement of this model is that it explains the role of phonology in word recognition. Its primary limitation is a lack of specificity owing to the fact that the model has not been implemented computationally as yet. Further progress in this area will require observing the behavior of working models.

In closing, it should be noted that the facts about the recognition process I have been concerned with probably could be subsumed by a suitably modified version of a dual route model. I am *not* claiming that data of the sort presented in this chapter cannot in principle be accommodated within a dual route type of model. In the absence of any constraints on the introduction of new pathways or recognition processes, models in the dual route framework can always be adapted to fit the empirical data. Although specific proposals might be refuted on the basis of empirical data, the general approach cannot. The same is true of the parallel activation type of model. The computational power of the formalism suggests that it probably can be adapted to fit any pattern of results. These observations imply that the choice between these alternative frameworks does not rest solely on their capacity to account for empirical data.

I have opted for the parallel activation framework for several reasons. One is simply that the parallel activation model seems better suited to describing changes in the availability of information over time, which I view to be the central problem for a theory of word recognition. A more important reason, however, has to do with beliefs about how an explanatory theory of word recognition is likely to evolve. Both the dual route and the parallel activation models are too powerful, but for different reasons. The power of the dual route models derives from the freedom to introduce new structures and operations and their lack of computational explicitness. Consider, for example, the spelling–sound rules, which are central to the dual route models. There is no explicit theory as to the formal properties of these rules, and because of the noncomputational character of these models, the rules are never explicitly stated. Under these conditions, it is very difficult to argue that a model employing spelling–sound rules is inconsistent with particular facts about word recognition. So, for example, while Rosson (1983) has argued that lexical influences on naming are inconsistent with the notion of spelling–sound rules, there is no reason why the rules could not be stated so as to take into account the frequencies of the lexical types in which they occur. Studies such as Rosson's provide important empirical data relevant to any model of word recognition; however, they do not provide a basis for deciding between the dual route and parallel activation frameworks.

Unlike the dual route models, the computational and representational properties of the parallel activation models are explicit. Although these models are also too powerful, they hold out the possibility of discovering principled constraints on their operation. This represents their primary advantage over dual route models. This claim may seem absurd on the face of it. After all, in order to account for relatively modest word superiority phenomena, the McClelland and Rumelhart (1981) model included some 18 parameters governing the parallel activation process. The large number of parameters in such models, and the freedom to adjust them as necessary to account for particular empirical phenomena, raise questions as to whether such models could ever be falsified and as to how important generalizations about perceptual phenomena could be discovered or represented.

I suggest that the answer is provided by recognizing that this problem is analogous to that of constraining the power of transformational grammars (Seidenberg, 1985b). Such grammars make use of an explicit formalism (base rules, transformations, and the like) known to be sufficient for the purpose of representing facts about linguistic structure. As with the parallel activation framework, however, the formalism is too powerful; while it is known to be able to account for the facts about the structure of human languages, it is also necessary to explain why certain structures do *not* occur. In transformational linguistics, this has led to a search for principled constraints on various components of the grammar (e.g., on the form of phrase structure rules or the operation of transformations). Similarly, developing an explanatory theory within the parallel activation framework will require the discovery of principled constraints on its basic computational mechanisms. These constraints will then become an important part of the theory. In other words, the parameters of the parallel activation process have to be theoretically motivated. The modularity hypothesis represents a first step in this direction. It postulates a basic constraint on the scope of interactive processes. Other such constraints may be discovered if they are sought.

Principled constraints on the parallel activation model may also be discovered in the attempt to cope with a wider range of lexical phenomena. The McClelland and Rumelhart model was developed in order to deal with word superiority effects. Their model provides several different ways to accommodate these effects. However, the word recognition phenomena I have considered in this article are of a very different sort. Dealing with both sets of phenomena simultaneously may constrain the range of possible solutions.

The choice between dual route and parallel activation models, then, is not simply a matter of evaluating which provides a better fit to the empirical data. It may be that, as the dual route and parallel activation models develop, they will converge on a common model. The parallel activation model may provide a computationally explicit basis for the general processing mechanisms in the dual route model. Conversely, parallel activation is a process, not a theory; abstracting generalizations about word recognition from the complexities of the parallel activation process may require recourse to a theory stated at the level of the dual route model. A hint of things to come is provided in a paper by Shallice, Warrington, and Mc-Carthy (1983), in which some convergences between the two types of models become apparent. Finally, it should also be noted that dual route models have been enormously helpful in understanding acquired forms of dyslexia (e.g., Patterson, 1981; Coltheart, 1980). There have been no attempts as yet to account for clinical data on language disorders within the parallel activation framework. This is an important area for future research.[10]

V. CONCLUSIONS

In this article, I have considered a number of basic issues concerning word recognition in reading, casting them as questions concerning the time course of processing. The research I have reviewed suggests the following conclusions. The modularity hypothesis with regard to the lexicon is consistent with a wide range of data. What is important to recognition is the reader's knowledge of lexical structure, not the information provided by the context of occurrence. The parallel activation model provides a promising framework for describing the operations of the lexical module. The long history of psychological research on the issues I have discussed suggests that we should be wary of prematurely considering any of them to be settled. Whatever the eventual fate of these ideas, it seems likely that experimental research will continue to challenge traditional assumptions about the reading process.

ACKNOWLEDGMENTS

This research was supported by grants from the Natural Science and Engineering Research Council of Canada (A7924) and the Quebec Ministry of Education (EQ-2074). I would like to thank my colleagues Michael K. Tanenhaus and Gloria S. Waters, who collaborated with me on much of the work described herein and influenced my thinking in important ways.

REFERENCES

Andrews, S. (1982). Phonological recoding: Is the regularity effect consistent? *Memory & Cognition, 10*, 565–575.

Baddeley, A. D. (1979). Working memory and reading. In P. A. Kolers, M. E. Wrolstad, & H. Bouma (Eds.), *Processing of visible language.* New York: Plenum.

Baddeley, A. D., & Lewis, V. (1981). Inner active processes in reading: The inner voice, the inner ear, and the inner eye. In A. M. Lesgold & C. A. Perfetti (Eds.), *Interactive processes in reading.* Hillsdale, NJ: Erlbaum.

Backman, J., Bruck, M., Hébert, M., & Seidenberg, M. (1984). Acquisition and use of spell-

---

[10]Issues concerning the choice between alternate models of word recognition are considered in greater detail in Seidenberg (1985c).

ing–sound correspondences in reading. *Journal of Experimental Child Psychology,* **38,** 114–133.

Balota, D. A., & Chumbley, J. K. (1984). The locus of word frequency effects in the pronunciation task: Lexical access and/or production? *Journal of Memory and Language,* in press.

Banks, W. P., Oka, E., & Shugarman, S. (1981). Recoding of printed words to internal speech: Does recoding come before lexical access? In O. J. L. Tzeng & H. Singer (Eds.), *Perception of print.* Hillsdale, NJ: Erlbaum.

Baron, J., & Strawson, C. (1976). Use of orthographic and word-specific knowledge in reading words aloud. *Journal of Experimental Psychology: Human Perception and Performance,* **2,** 386–393.

Barron, R. W., & Baron, J. (1977). How children get meaning from printed words. *Child Development,* **48,** 587–594.

Bauer, D., & Stanovich, D. E. (1980). Lexical access and the spelling-to-sound regularity effect. *Memory & Cognition,* **8,** 424–432.

Besner, D., & Davelaar, E. (1982). Basic processes in reading: Two phonological codes. *Canadian Journal of Psychology,* **36,** 701–711.

Besner, D., Hildebrandt, N., & McCann, R. (1984). *Visual and phonological codes in the oral reading of Japanese Kana.* Paper presented at the Psychonomic Society Meeting. San Antonio, TX.

Bresnan, J. (1978). A realistic transformational grammar. In M. Halle, J. Bresnan, & G. Miller (Eds.), *Linguistic theory and psychological reality.* Cambridge, MA: MIT Press.

Cairns, H. S., Cowart, W., & Jablon, A. D. (1981). Effects of prior context upon the integration of lexical information during sentence processing. *Journal of Verbal Learning and Verbal Behavior,* **20,** 445–453.

Carpenter, P. A., & Daneman, M. (1981). Lexical retrieval and error recovery in reading: A model based on eye fixations. *Journal of Verbal Learning and Verbal Behavior,* **20,** 137–160.

Carpenter, P. A., & Just, M. A. (1975). Sentence comprehension: A psycholinguistic model of verification. *Psychological Review,* **82,** 45–73.

Carroll, J. B., Davies, P., & Richman, B. (1971). *The American Heritage word frequency book.* Boston: Houghton-Mifflin.

Chomsky, N. (1965). *Aspects of the theory of syntax.* Cambridge, MA: MIT Press.

Clark, H. H., & Gerrig, R. J. (1983). Understanding old words with new meanings. *Journal of Verbal Learning and Verbal Behavior,* **22,** 591–608.

Clifton, C., Frazier, L., & Connine, C. (1984). Lexical expectations in sentence comprehension. *Journal of Verbal Learning and Verbal Behavior,* **23,** 696–708.

Collins, A. M., & Loftus, E. F. (1975). A spreading- activation theory of semantic processing. *Psychological Review,* **82,** 407–428.

Coltheart, M. (1978). Lexical access in simple reading tasks. In G. Underwood (Ed.) *Strategies of information processing.* New York: Academic Press.

Coltheart, M. (1980). Reading, phonological recoding, and deep dyslexia. In M. Coltheart, K. Patterson, & J. Marshall (Eds.), *Deep dyslexia.* London: Routledge & Kegan Paul.

Coltheart, M., Besner, D., Jonasson, J. T., & Davelaar, E. (1979). Phonological recoding in the lexical decision task. *Quarterly Journal of Experimental Psychology,* **31** 489–507.

Condry, S. M., McMahon-Rideout, M., & Levy, A. A. (1979). A developmental investigation of selective attention to graphic, phonetic, and semantic information in words. *Perception & Psychophysics,* **25,** 88–94.

Conrad, C. (1974). Context effects in sentence comprehension: A study of the subjective lexicon. *Memory & Cognition,* **2,** 130–138.

Cottrell, G. W. (1984). *A model of lexical access of ambiguous words.* Manuscript, University of Rochester Department of Computer Science.

Dennis, I., & Newstead, S. E. (1981). Is phonological recoding under strategic control? *Memory & Cognition, 9*, 472-3477.

Doctor, E. A., & Coltheart, M. (1980). Children's use of phonological encoding when reading for meaning. *Memory & Cognition, 8*, 195-209.

Edfeldt, A. W. (1959). *Silent speech and silent reading.* Stockholm: Almqvist & Wiksell.

Fahlman, S. A., Hinton, G. E., & Sejnowski, T. J. (1983). Massively parallel architectures for AI: NETL, Thistle, and Boltzmann machines. *Proceedings of the national conference on artificial intelligence.*

Feldman, L. B. (1981). Visual word recognition in Serbo-Croation is necessarily phonological. *Status report on speech research SR-66.* New Haven, CT: Haskins Laboratories.

Feldman, J. A., & Ballard, D. (1982). Connectionist models and their properties. *Cognitive Science, 6*, 205-254.

Fischler, I. (1977a). Semantic facilitation without association in a lexical decision task. *Memory & Cognition, 5*, 335-339.

Fischler, I. (1977b). Associative facilitation without expectancy in a lexical decision task. *Journal of Experimental Psychology: Human Perception and Performance.* 3, 18-26.

Fischler, I., & Bloom, P. (1979). Automatic and attentional processes in the effects of sentence contexts on word recognition. *Journal of Verbal Learning and Verbal Behavior, 18*, 1-20.

Fischler, I., & Bloom, P. (1980). Rapid processing of the meaning of sentences. *Memory & Cognition, 8*, 216-225.

Fodor, J. A. (1983). *Modularity of mind.* Cambridge, MA: MIT Press.

Forster, K. I. (1976). Accessing the internal lexicon. In R. J. Wales & E. C. T. Walker (Eds.), *New approaches to language mechanisms.* Amsterdam: North Holland Publ.

Forster, K. I. (1979). Levels of processing and the structure of the language processor. In W. E. Cooper & E. C. T. Walker (Eds.), *Sentence processing: Psycholinguistic studies presented to Merrill Garrett.* Hillsdale, NJ: Erlbaum.

Forster, K. I., & Chambers, S. (1973). Lexical access and naming time. *Journal of Verbal Learning and Verbal Behavior, 12*, 627-635.

Foss, D. J. (1982). A discourse on semantic priming. *Cognitive Psychology, 14*, 590-607.

Frazier, L., & Rayner, K. (1984). *Resolution of syntactic category ambiguities: Eye movements in parsing lexically ambiguous sentences.* Manuscript, University of Massachusetts Linguistics Department.

Frederiksen, J. (1978). Assessment of perceptual, decoding, and lexical skills and their relation to reading proficiency. In A. M. Lesgold, J. W. Pellegrino, S. D. Fokkema, & R. Glaser (Eds.), *Cognitive psychology and instruction.* New York: Plenum.

Glucksberg, S., Gildea, P., & Bookin, H. A. (1982). On understanding nonliteral speech: Can people ignore metaphors? *Journal of Verbal Learning and Verbal Behavior, 21*, 85-98.

Glushko, R. J. (1979). The organization and activation of orthographic knowledge in reading aloud. *Journal of Experimental Psychology: Human Perception and Performance.* 5, 674-691.

Goodman, K. S. (1970). Reading: A psycholinguistic guessing game. In H. Singer & R. B. Ruddell (Eds.), *Theoretical models and processes of reading.* Newark, Delaware: International Reading Association.

Goodman, G. O., McClelland, J. L., & Gibbs, R. W., Jr. (1981). The role of syntactic context in word recognition. *Memory & Cognition, 9*, 580-586.

Gough, P. B. (1972). One second of reading. In J. F. Kavanagh & I. G. Mattingly (Eds.), *Language by ear and by eye.* Cambridge, MA: MIT Press.

Gough, P. B., Alford, J. A., & Holley-Wilcox, P. (1981). Words and contexts. In O. J. L. Tzeng & H. Singer (Eds.), *Perception of print.* Hillsdale, NJ: Erlbaum.

Gough, P. B., & Hillinger, M. L. (1980). Learning to read: An unnatural act. *Bulletin of the Orton Society, 30*, 1-17.

Grosjean, F. (1980). Spoken word recognition processes and the gating paradigm. *Perception & Psychophysics, 28*, 267–283.

Henderson, L. (1982). *Orthography and word recognition in reading*. New York: Academic Press.

Henderson, L. (1984). Issues in the modelling of pronunciation assembly in normal reading. In J. C. Marshall, M. Coltheart, & K. Patterson (Eds.), *Surface dyslexia and surface dysgraphia*. Hillsdale, NJ: Erlbaum.

Hinton, G. E., & Anderson, J. A. (1981). *Parallel models of associative memory*. Hillsdale, NJ: Erlbaum.

Hirst, G. (1983). *Semantic interpretation against ambiguity*. Unpublished Ph.D. dissertation, Brown University Department of Computer Science.

Hummel, R. A., & Zucker, S. W. (1980). *On the foundations of relaxation labelling processes*. TR 80-7, McGill University Computer Vision and Robotics Laboratory.

Jackendoff, R. S. (1975). Morphological and semantic regularities in the lexicon. *Language, 51*, 639–671.

Jorm, A. F., & Share, D. L. (1983). Phonological recoding and reading acquisition. *Applied Psycholinguistics, 4*, 103–147.

Katz, L., & Feldman, L. B. (1983). Relation between pronunciation and recognition of printed words in deep and shallow orthographies. *Journal of Experimental Psychology: Human Perception and Performance, 9*, 157–166.

Kay, J., & Marcel, A. J. (1981). One process, not two, in reading aloud: Lexical analogies do the work of nonlexical rules. *Quarterly Journal of Experimental Psychology, 33A*, 397–414.

Kleiman, G. (1975). Speech recoding in reading. *Journal of Verbal Learning and Verbal Behavior, 14*, 323–339.

Koriat, A. (1981). Semantic facilitation in lexical decisions as a function of prime–target association. *Memory & Cognition, 9*, 587–598.

Kuçera, H., & Francis, W. N. (1967). *Computational analysis of present-day American English*. Providence, RI: Brown Univ. Press.

LaBerge, D., & Samuels, S. J. (1974). Toward a theory of automatic information processing in reading. *Cognitive Psychology, 6*, 293–323.

Landauer, T. K., & Streeter, L. A. (1973). Structural differences between common and rare words: Failure of equivalence assumptions for theories of word recognition. *Journal of Verbal Learning and Verbal Behavior, 12*, 119–131.

Lukatala, G., Popadić, D., Ogjenović, P., & Turvey, J. (1980). Lexical decision in a phonologically shallow orthography. *Memory & Cognition, 8*, 124–132.

Makita, S. (1968). The rarity of reading disability in Japanese children. *American Journal of Orthopsychiatry, 38*, 599–614.

Marr, D. (1982). *Vision*. San Francisco: Freeman.

Marslen-Wilson, W. D., & Tyler, L. K. (1980). The temporal structure of spoken language comprehension. *Cognition, 8*, 1–71.

McClelland, J., & Rumelhart, D. M. (1981). An interactive-activation model of context effects in letter perception, Part I: An account of basic findings. *Psychological Review, 88*, 375–407.

McCusker, L. X., Hillinger, M. L., & Bias, R. G. (1981). Phonological recoding and reading. *Psychological Bulletin, 89*, 217–245.

Merrill, E., Sperber, R. D., & McCauley, C. (1981). Differences in semantic coding as a function of reading comprehension skill. *Memory & Cognition, 9*, 618–624.

Meyer, D. M., & Schvaneveldt, R. W. (1971). Facilitation in recognizing pairs of words: Evidence for a dependence between retrieval operations. *Journal of Experimental Psychology, 90*, 227–234.

Meyer, D., Schvaneveldt, R., & Ruddy, M. (1974). Functions of graphemic and phonemic codes in visual word recognition. *Memory & Cognition, 2,* 309-321.

Milne, R. (1983). *Parsing against lexical ambiguity.* Technical Report, Department of Artificial Intelligence, University of Edinburgh.

Morton, J. (1969). The interaction of information in word recognition. *Psychological Review, 76,* 165-178.

Morton, J., & Patterson, K. E. (1980). A new interpretation, or, an attempt at a new interpretation. In M. Coltheart, K. Patterson, & J. Marshall (Eds.), *Deep dyslexia.* London: Routledge and Kegan Paul.

Neely, J. H. (1977). Semantic priming and retrieval from lexical memory: Roles of inhibitionless spreading activation and limited-capacity attention. *Journal of Experimental Psychology: General, 106,* 226-254.

Neisser, U. (1967). *Cognitive psychology.* New York: Appleton.

Newcombe, F., & Marshall, J. (1981). On psycholinguistic classifications of the acquired dyslexias. *Bulletin of the Orton Society, 31,* 29-46.

Onifer, W., & Swinney, D. (1981). Accessing lexical ambiguities during sentence comprehension: Effects of frequency, meaning, and contextual bias. *Memory & Cognition, 9,* 225-236.

Parkin, A. J. (1982). Phonological effects in lexical decision: Effects of spelling-to-sound regularity depend on how regularity is defined. *Memory & Cognition, 10,* 43-53.

Parkin, A. J., & Underwood, G. (1983). Orthographic versus phonological irregularity in lexical decision. *Memory & Cognition, 11,* 351-355.

Patterson, K. E. (1981). Neuropsychological approaches to the study of reading. *British Journal of Psychology, 72,* 151-174.

Perfetti, C. A., & McCutchen, D. (1983). Speech processes in reading. In N. Lass (Ed.), *Advances in speech and language* (Vol. 7). New York: Academic Press.

Posner, M. I. (1969). Abstraction and the process of recognition. In G. H. Bower & J. T. Spence (Eds.), *The psychology of learning and motivation* (Vol. 3). New York: Academic Press.

Posner, M. I., & Snyder, C. R. R. (1975). Attention and cognitive control. In R. L. Solso (Ed.), *Information processing and cognition: The Loyola symposium.* Hillsdale, NJ: Erlbaum.

Pylyshyn, Z. (1981). The imagery debate: Analogue media versus tacit knowledge. *Psychological Review, 88,* 16-45.

Radar, N. (1975). *From written words to meaning: A developmental study.* Unpublished doctoral dissertation, Cornell University.

Rosson, M. B. (1983). From sofa to louch: Lexical contributions to pseudoword pronunciation, *Memory & Cognition, 11,* 152-160.

Rozin, P., & Gleitman, L. R. (1977). The structure and acquisition of reading II: The reading process and the acquisition of the alphabetic principle. In A. S. Reber & D. L. Scarborough (Eds.), *Toward a psychology of reading.* Hillsdale, NJ: Erlbaum.

Rubenstein, H. H., Lewis, S. S., & Rubenstein, M. A. (1971). Evidence for phonemic recoding in visual word recognition. *Journal of Verbal Learning and Verbal Behavior, 10,* 645-657.

Rumelhart, D. E. (1977). Toward an interactive model of reading. In S. Dornic (Ed.), *Attention and performance VI.* Hillsdale, NJ: Erlbaum.

Rumelhart, D. E., & McClelland, J. L. (1982). An interactive-activation model of context effects in letter perception, part 2: The contextual enhancement effect and some tests and extensions of the model. *Psychological Review, 89,* 60-94.

Schuberth, R. E., & Eimas, P. D. (1977). Effects of context on the classification of words and nonwords. *Journal of Experimental Psychology: Human Perception and Performance, 3,* 27-36.

Schuberth, R. E., Spoehr, K. T., & Lane, D. M. (1981). Effects of stimulus and contextual information on the lexical decision process. *Memory & Cognition, 9,* 68–77.

Seidenberg, M. S. (1985a). The time-course of phonological code activation in two writing systems. *Cognition, 19,* 1–30.

Seidenberg, M. S. (1985b). Lexicon as module (commentary). *Behavioral and Brain Sciences,* in press.

Seidenberg, M. S. (1985c). Constraining models of word recognition. *Cognition,* in press.

Seidenberg, M. S., Bruck, M., Fornarolo, G., & Backman, J. (1985). Word recognition skills of poor and disabled readers: Do they necessarily differ? *Applied Psycholinguistics,* in press.

Seidenberg, M. S., & Tanenhaus, M. K. (1979). Orthographic effects on rhyme monitoring. *Journal of Experimental Psychology: Human Learning and Memory, 5,* 546–554.

Seidenberg, M. S., & Tanenhaus, M. K. (1980). Chronometric studies of lexical ambiguity resolution. *Proceedings of the 18th annual meeting of the Association for Computational Linguistics.*

Seidenberg, M. S., & Tanenhaus, M. K. (1985). Modularity and lexical access. In I. Gopnik & M. Gopnik (Eds.), *From models in modules: The McGill cognitive science workshops.* Norwood, NJ: Ablex, in press.

Seidenberg, M. S., Tanenhaus, M. K., Leiman, J. L., & Bienkowski, M. (1982). Automatic access of the meanings of ambiguous words in context: Some limitations of knowledge-based processing. *Cognitive Psychology, 14,* 489–537.

Seidenberg, M. S., Waters, G. S., Barnes, M. A., & Tanenhaus, M. K. (1984a). When does irregular spelling or pronunciation influence word recognition? *Journal of Verbal Learning and Verbal Behavior, 23,* 383–404.

Seidenberg, M. S., Waters, G. S., Sanders, M., & Langer, P. (1984b). Pre- and post-lexical loci of contextual effects on word recognition. *Memory & Cognition, 12,* 315–328.

Shallice, T., Warrington, E. K., & McCarthy, R. (1983). Reading without semantics. *Quarterly Journal of Experimental Psychology, 35A,* 111–138.

Shulman, H., Hornak, R., & Sanders, E. (1978). The effects of graphemic, phonemic, and semantic relationships on access to lexical structures. *Memory & Cognition, 6,* 115–123.

Simpson, G. B. (1981). Meaning, dominance, and semantic context in the processing of lexical ambiguity. *Journal of Verbal Learning and Verbal Behavior, 20,* 120–136.

Smith, E. E., Shoben, E. J., & Rips, L. J. (1975). Structure and process in semantic memory: A featural model for semantic decisions. *Psychological Review, 81,* 214–241

Smith, F. (1971). *Understanding reading.* New York: Holt.

Stanovich, K. E., & Bauer, D. (1978). Experiments on the spelling-to-sound regularity effect in visual word recognition. *Memory & Cognition, 6,* 410–415.

Stanovich, K. E., & West, R. (1979). Mechanisms of sentence context effects in reading: Automatic activation and conscious attention. *Memory & Cognition, 7,* 77–85.

Stanovich, K. E., & West, R. F. (1981). The effect of sentence context on ongoing word recognition: Tests of a two-process theory. *Journal of Experimental Psychology: Human Perception and Performance, 7,* 658–672.

Stanovich, K. E., & West, R. F. (1983). On priming by a sentence context. *Journal of Experimental Psychology: General, 112,* 1–36.

Swinney, D. A. (1979). Lexical access during sentence comprehension: (Re)consideration of context effects. *Journal of Verbal Learning and Verbal Behavior, 18,* 645–660.

Swinney, D. A., & Cutler, A. (1979). The access and processing of idiomatic expressions. *Journal of Verbal Learning and Verbal Behavior, 18,* 523–534.

Tabossi, P., & Johnson-Laird, P. N. (1980). Linguistic context and the priming of semantic information. *Quarterly Journal of Experimental Psychology, 32,* 595–603.

Tanenhaus, M. K., Carlson, G. N., & Seidenberg, M. S. (1985). Do listeners compute linguistic representations? In A. Zwicky, L. Kartunnen, & D. Dowty (Eds.), *Natural language parsing: Psycholinguistic, theoretical, and computational perspectives.* London and New York: Cambridge Univ. Press.

Tanenhaus, M. K., Carroll, J. M., & Bever, T. G. (1976). Sentence-picture verification models as theories of sentence comprehension: A critique of Carpenter and Just. *Psychological Review,* **83,** 310–317.

Tanenhaus, M. K., Flanigan, H., & Seidenberg, M. S. (1980). Orthographic and phonological code activation in auditory and visual word recogniton. *Memory & Cognition,* **8,** 513–520.

Tanenhaus, M. K., Leiman, J. L., & Seidenberg, M. S. (1979). Evidence for multiple stages in the processing of ambiguous words in syntactic contexts. *Journal of Verbal Learning and Verbal Behavior,* **18,** 427–441.

Taylor, I., & Taylor, M. M. (1984). *The psychology of reading.* New York: Academic Press.

Theios, J., & Muise, J. G. (1977). The word identification process in reading, In N. J. Castellan, D. B. Pisoni, & G. R. Potts (Eds.), *Cognitive theory* (Vol. 2). Hillsdale, NJ: Erlbaum.

Treiman, R., Freyd, J. J., & Baron, J. (1983). Phonological recoding and use of spelling-sound rules in reading sentences. *Journal of Verbal Learning and Verbal Behavior,* **22,** 682–700.

Tulving, E., & Gold, C. (1963). Stimulus information and contextual information as determinants of tachistoscopic recognition of words. *Journal of Experimental Psychology,* **66,** 319–327.

Tweedy, J. R., Lapinski, R. H., & Schvaneveldt, R. W. (1977). Semantic-context effects on word recognition: Influence of varying the proportion of items presented in an appropriate context. *Memory & Cognition,* **5,** 84–89.

Tyler, L. K., & Wessels, J. (1983). Quantifying contextual contributions to word recognition processes. *Perception & Psychophysics.*

Venezky, R. L. (1970). *The structure of English orthography.* The Hague: Mouton.

Warren, R. E. (1972). Stimulus encoding and memory. *Journal of Experimental Psychology,* **94,** 90–100.

Warren, R. E. (1977). Time and the spread of activation in memory. *Journal of Experimental Psychology: Human Learning and Memory,* **3,** 458–466.

Wasow, T. (1977). Transformations and the lexicon. In P. Culicover, T. Wasow, & A. Akmajian (Eds.), *Formal syntax.* New York: Academic Press.

Waters, G. S., Bruck, M., & Seidenberg, M. S. (1985a). Do children use similar processes to read and spell words? *Journal of Experimental Child Psychology,* **39,** 511–530.

Waters, G. S., Komoda, M. K., & Arbuckle, T. Y. (1985b). The effects of concurrent tasks on reading: Implications for phonological recoding. *Journal of Memory and Language,* **24,** 27–45.

Waters, G. S., & Seidenberg, M. S. (1985). *Spelling–sound effects in reading: Time course and decision criteria. Memory & Cognition,* in press.

Waters, G. S., Seidenberg, M. S., & Bruck, M. (1984). Children's and adults' use of spelling-sound information in three reading tasks. *Memory & Cognition,* **12,** 293–305.

West, R. F., & Stanovich, K. E. (1982). Source of inhibition in experiments on the effect of sentence context on word recognition. *Journal of Experimental Psychology: Learning, Memory and Cognition,* **8,** 385–399.

Wijk, A. (1966). *Rules of pronunciation for the English language.* London and New York: Oxford University Press.

ATTENTION, AUTOMATICITY, AND AUTONOMY IN VISUAL WORD PROCESSING

GLYN W. HUMPHREYS

Department of Psychology
Birkbeck College
London, England

I. INTRODUCTION

One of the most striking changes which occurs as children become more skilled at reading is that their processing of words becomes faster and apparently less effortful. Such a change, characteristic of developing skills in information processing tasks, is often conceptualized in terms of the transformation of a mental operation from being "controlled" or nonautomatic to being automatic (e.g., Hasher & Zacks, 1979; Laberge, 1973; Laberge &

253

Copyright © 1985 by Academic Press, Inc.
All rights of reproduction in any form reserved.

Samuels, 1974; Schneider & Shiffrin, 1977; Shiffrin & Schneider, 1977). This binary classification between automatic and control processes is useful if it enables disjoint operations to be distinguished. For instance, it can be argued that automatic and control processes can be distinguished operationally using a number of criteria:

1. Control processes draw on the limited resource capacity of the subject and so are vulnerable to interference, and interfere with other concurrent operations which demand the same capacity (Posner & Boies, 1971); automatic processes do not demand resource capacity and are neither subject to interference nor do they interfere with other concurrent operations (Posner, 1978)[1];

2. Control processes operate serially; automatic processes operate in parallel (Schneider & Shiffrin, 1977; Shiffrin, & Schneider, 1977; Treisman & Gelade, 1980);

3. Control processes are effected intentionally and are not obligatory; automatic processes do not require intention and may be obligatory (Posner & Snyder, 1975a)[2];

4. Automatic processes only develop following extensive practice, and, once learned, they are difficult to suppress; control processes are flexible and can be applied to new situations (e.g., Laberge & Samuels, 1974; Logan, 1979; Shiffrin & Schneider, 1977).

Taken alone, each of these criteria merely describes the properties of a particular information-processing function (see also Ryan, 1983). Taken together, the criteria provide a converging set of operations for differentiating two classes of functions, and they therefore provide a powerful tool for analyzing behavior. For instance, according to the conjoint constraints of the criteria, to state that a process is automatic does not merely mean that it has been extensively practiced, it also means that it does not demand resource capacity, it can operate in parallel with other concurrent processes and that its operation cannot be altered intentionally by subjects.

---

[1] I am careful here **not** to distinguish between general demands made to some central set of processing resources (Norman & Bobrow, 1975) and selective demands made to independent sets of resources which support the activity of specialized processes (Allport, 1980; Navon & Gopher, 1979; Wickens, 1983). I am therefore outlining the strong position that automatic processes ought not to demand resources either from a central source or from specialized subprocesses.

[2] The implication here is that a process may occur unintentionally but still not be obligatory. This possibility is elaborated when I consider the effects of spatial attention upon word processing (Section III,A,1); suffice it to note here that the operation of a given process may depend on whether a stimulus falls within a region of (voluntarily) attended space, though its operation may occur unintentionally when it falls within that space.

In this article, I evaluate whether the processes involved in word recognition and identification in skilled readers should be classified as automatic. The article comprises three main sections. First, I discuss evidence for the proposal that processes up to and including word recognition and identification operate automatically. Some of the implications of this proposal for understanding the differences between skilled and less skilled readers are outlined. In the second section I discuss contrary evidence suggesting that there are dissociations between the criteria for automaticity, as applied to word recognition and identification and to other information processing tasks. These dissociations indicate that some alternative conceptualization of word processing in skilled readers is necessary. One alternative, that word processing is functionally autonomous rather than automatic, is outlined in the third section. In this section I also present a model which distinguishes between two levels of word processing: an autonomous first level, concerned with the perceptual analysis of words, perhaps with its own set of limited resources; and a nonautonomous second level concerned with the episodic representation of words and their integration with textual and real-world knowledge. This model provides a framework for understanding a wide set of results on the processing of words by skilled readers.

II. AUTOMATIC PROCESSES IN WORD
RECOGNITION AND IDENTIFICATION

Clearly, not all the processes carried out by skilled readers when reading text can be considered automatic. For instance, college students find it difficult to read a story silently while copying words to dictation, and read considerably more slowly than under normal circumstances (Hirst, Spelke, Reaves, Caharack, & Neisser, 1980). Indeed, even with two such dissimilar tasks as silent reading and copying to dictation subtle trade-offs between performance can still occur after extensive practice (see Broadbent, 1982). These trade-offs between performance on two concurrent tasks are characteristic of demands on control processes.

It is necessary, then, to define exactly which processes in skilled reading, if any, operate automatically. The processes involved in word recognition and identification seem appropriate candidates for this classification since their development as automatic processes should in theory allow control processes to be devoted to the analysis of meaning and text comprehension (see Laberge & Samuels, 1974). This would be an economic way to develop a system with limited processing resources for fluent reading and comprehension.

The primary evidence that the processes involved in word recognition and identification are automatic is drawn from two experimental procedures: Stroop tasks and priming studies.

A. Stroop Effects

In the standard Stroop task (Stroop, 1935), subjects have to name the ink color of a printed color word (e.g., they respond "red" to the word *blue* printed in red ink). Performance is affected by the identity of the word. Relative to a neutral condition (e.g., a color patch presented alone or a colored row of X's), performance is facilitated by the presence of a congruent color word and interfered with by the presence of an incongruent color word (e.g., Dyer, 1973). Since the identity of the color word can disrupt the primary task, it seems that the word's identity is processed involuntarily.

Interestingly, the Stroop effect is not confined to use of a color word as the interfering stimulus. Klein (1964) showed that reliable Stroop interference can also be found when an object name with a strong color association is used (e.g., when subjects have to respond "red" to the word *grass* printed in red ink). This suggests that words associated with the irrelevant word (in this case, the color word *green*) are activated in addition to the word's own identity. Seymour (1977) has also argued that at least part of the Stroop effect is due to conflict between color attributes during semantic, or at any rate preresponse, stages of processing. He reported experiments based on color associations of month and season names. Season or month names were printed in either green, yellow, brown, or white ink (colors associated with spring, summer, autumn, and winter, respectively). Subjects either had to name the season associated with the ink color (direct naming) or the season opposite to the one associated with the color (opposite naming). Seymour found that direct naming responses were facilitated when the printed season or month name was associated with the ink color. Further, this result was also obtained in the opposite naming condition. That is, the response "winter" to yellow ink was facilitated by the word *summer* or the name of a summer month; the response was not facilitated by the word winter or the name of a winter month. These results provide little support for the argument that the printed word directly activates a verbal response, and that competition between the word response and the color response is the source of Stroop interference; they are, however, consistent with Stroop interference arising from competition between alternative color attributes at earlier stages of processing. Whatever the case, evidence from Stroop tasks indicates that words can activate identity and associative information unintentionally and, in this sense, the processes involved in word recognition and identification can be considered automatic (e.g., Keele, 1972; Posner & Snyder, 1975a).

B. Priming with Unmasked Primes

The studies of priming present rather more complex evidence, though the details of the effects and the procedures used to elicit different forms of priming are important for evaluating the case for automaticity. I therefore outline these effects in some detail.

In studies of priming, experimenters examine the effects of a single contextual stimulus (or prime) on the processing of an independent target stimulus. For our present purposes, the most important proposal is that, under some circumstances, primes may automatically affect the processing of a target (in particular, priming appears both to be involuntary and to make no demands on processing resources). By varying the relations between primes and targets to see which ones generate priming effects under such circumstances we may evaluate which processes operate automatically in word recognition and identification.

The circumstances under which "automatic" priming effects occur were first discussed in detail by Posner and Snyder (1975b). They used a task in which subjects responded according to whether two simultaneously presented letters were identical or not (*aa* but not *ab*). The target pair of letters was preceded either by a prime which might be one of the target letters or by a neutral prime (a cross). The neutral prime served as an uninformative warning signal for the target's occurrence, and, since it carries no information about the target's identity, the neutral prime condition can serve as a base line for estimating whether other primes aid (facilitate) or impede (inhibit) target processing. It turns out that estimates of facilitatory or inhibitory priming effects are crucial to the argument that priming occurs automatically.

Posner and Snyder manipulated the predictive utility of primes (i.e., the probability that the prime was related to the target). In three difference conditions, the letter prime matched the target letters either on 80% of the "same" response trials (the 80–20 condition), on 50% of the "same" response trials (the 50–50 condition), or on 20% of the "same " response trials (the 20–80 condition). For "same" response trials (i.e., *aa*-type trials) Posner and Snyder found that, relative to the neutral prime condition, performance was facilitated when primes and targets matched and inhibited when primes and targets mismatched in the 80–20 condition. That is, there were both benefits and costs from priming. In contrast, in the 20–80 condition, there was only facilitation from matching primes and no difference between the mismatching primes condition and the neutral control. That is, there were benefits without costs from priming. In the 50–50 condition, performance fell between the other two probability treatments.

Posner and Snyder also varied the interval between the prime and target event; here they found that facilitation occurred with fairly short prime–target intervals (50 msec and above), while inhibition only occurred with relatively longer prime–target intervals (300 msec and above).

From these data, Posner and Snyder (1975b) propose a two-factor account of priming. One form of priming, termed automatic priming, takes place when the prime activates a representation mediating target processing (this may occur when the prime and target are identical or when they share a learned relationship, when activation may "spread" from the prime's representation to that of the target). When a target's representation is preactivated, less stimulus-driven activation is thought to be required for a decision threshold to be reached; accordingly, responses to the target are facilitated relative to the neutral prime condition, where no preactivation occurs. This form of priming occurs simply because the prime is processed to an appropriate level; therefore it can occur quickly following the processing of the prime to that level, and it does not depend on the predictive utility of the prime. Further, prime-driven activation does not alter the level of activation in other unrelated representations, and so there are no effects on the processing of unrelated targets when this form of priming occurs. That is, **there are benefits without costs.**

The second form of priming, termed expectation-dependent priming, occurs because subjects use prime information to predict the target. Posner and Snyder propose that such predictions raise the level of activation in the representation(s) of the expected target. However, such predictions are also thought to draw upon the limited resource capacity of the subject, lowering the level of activation in other, unrelated representations. When a prediction is correct, performance is facilitated because subjects can again respond on the basis of less target-driven information. When a prediction is incorrect, performance is inhibited because of the reduced activation in unrelated representations. That is, **expectation-dependent priming produces both costs and benefits.** Expectation-dependent priming should only occur when the prime has high predictive validity (e.g., in the 80–20 condition used by Posner & Snyder, 1975b), and, since predictions of targets from primes take some time to be generated, expectation-dependent priming occurs only with relatively long prime–target intervals.

Posner and Snyder (1975b) thus distinguish expectation-dependent priming effects, which demand resource capacity, and automatic priming effects, which do not. Inhibitory priming effects are diagnostic of the involvement of resource capacity, and, therefore, of expectation-dependent priming. Expectation-dependent and automatic priming can be separated by varying the predictive utility of primes and by varying the prime–target interval.

This two-factor account of priming has been most successfully applied to word processing by Neely (1977). He used a superordinate category name as a prime and presented word or nonword targets, to which subjects made a lexical decision. Neely manipulated the predictive utility of primes by creating a task-specific relationship between certain categories. For instance, on a high proportion of trials subjects were led to expect that the target would be a member of a second category (such as "building part"), given the presentation of a different category superordinate prime (such as "part of the human body"). In this "shift" condition, lexical decisions to expected targets (e.g., *door*) were facilitated relative to a neutral prime condition (a row of X's) when correctly primed (e.g., by *body*), but only when there were fairly long intervals between primes and targets (e.g., 700 msec). With shorter intervals (below 400 msec), target processing was the same in this condition as in the neutral control condition. Interestingly, response to unexpected target words from the primed category (e.g., *arm*) were facilitated with short intervals between the stimuli, but they were inhibited when there were long intervals.

These findings demonstrate that, with short intervals between prime and target words, priming depends on the learned relationship between the stimuli. There are benefits in lexical decision latencies for targets related to primes without costs for unrelated targets. With longer prime–target intervals the effects of learned relationships between the stimuli decrease, presumably because the activation of the target representation by the prime decays over time. Priming then depends on the predicted relationship between primes and targets. Benefits for predicted targets are produced at the expense of costs for unpredicted targets.

Neely (1977) argues that his data are consistent with Posner and Snyder's (1975a,b) distinction between automatic and expectation-dependent priming. Similarly to Posner and Snyder (1975b), he distinguishes these effects operationally on the presence of inhibitory priming. However, Neely demonstrates two further operational distinctions. One is that, unlike expectation-dependent priming, automatic priming is determined by primes and targets sharing a learned, rather than a task-specific, relationship. The second is that automatic priming can occur even when subjects should predict stimuli other than targets from primes (e.g., in the *body–arm* condition).

One interpretation of Neely's (1977) automatic priming results is that words are automatically processed to a level at which their semantic relations with other words are represented. The spread of activation between the representations of semantically related words then reduces the amount of target-driven activation required for a correct lexical decision to a related target to be made.

In a similar fashion, we could argue that data reported by Hillinger (1980, Experiment 3) demonstrate that words are automatically processed to a level at which their phonological representations are specified. In Hillinger's study, subjects made lexical decisions to both prime and target letter strings. In a test for phonological priming effects, performance when targets were primed by phonologically similar but graphemically different words (*eight-mate*) was compared with performance when primes were neutral (******_mate*). Hillinger found that lexical decisions were facilitated by phonological priming relative to the neutral condition, while, importantly, there were no inhibition effects when primes and targets were phonologically unrelated (*veil–mate*). This result of benefits without costs is indicative of automatic phonological priming, with spreading activation between the representations of phonologically related primes and targets facilitating target recognition.

However, these interpretations are not demanded by the data. Automatic priming of the form demonstrated by Hillinger and by Neely may occur when subjects do not intentionally use the information activated by primes to predict targets, but it may still be that the primes themselves are intentionally processed to the appropriate level of representation. For instance, when subjects have to distinguish between words and orthographically regular, pronounceable nonwords in a lexical decision task they may strategically process stimuli to a phonological or semantic level to facilitate performance. Indeed, changing the nature of the nonwords can reduce both phonological and associative priming effects (Shulman & Davison, 1977; Shulman, Hornak, & Sanders, 1978). Nevertheless, if the information accessed by the prime takes some measurable amount of time to decay, target processing may be affected, even though subjects do not use prime information to predict targets.

C. Priming with Masked Primes

A more stringent test of the levels of representation which words can be automatically processed to is provided by studies investigating word priming under conditions which minimize prime report. Usually, prime report is minimized by presenting an irrelevant masking stimulus (often a random pattern of lines) shortly after the prime. The strongest claim here is that associative priming can occur under masking conditions which prevent subjects from detecting the presence of primes (Balota, 1983; Fowler, Wolford, Slade, & Tassinary, 1981; Marcel, 1983a). If this claim is correct, it would seem clear that words can be processed automatically to levels at which their associative relations are specified, since, by definition, intentional processes cannot operate on undetected stimuli.

Unfortunately, the evidence for the above claim is equivocal. In the studies investigating priming under conditions where primes cannot be detected, prime detection thresholds are typically estimated in a separate session from the experimental priming trials. In the threshold session, prime detection is assessed under conditions of short stimulus durations and backward pattern masking. The detection threshold is set by gradually decreasing the interval between the prime and the mask until subjects cannot judge whether a prime is present at an above-chance level, a procedure which may underestimate the amount of information subjects have available (Merikle, 1982). In the experimental sesson reaction times (RT's) to targets are measured; in this case primes presented at threshold durations are followed by long target exposures (since experimenters seek to ensure that subjects make few errors to targets). However, by using long target exposures experimenters may unwittingly light-adapt subjects, so raising primes above the detection threshold level (since backward masking is less effective with increasing light adaptation; Purcell & Stewart, 1974). It is therefore quite possible that subjects have more explicit information about primes in the experimental session than seems apparent from their threshold session performance (see Purcell, Stewart, & Stanovich, 1983).

One way to assess more accurately the information subjects have available to them when priming occurs is to require them to respond to primes as well as targets within the experimental session. Using this procedure, Evett and Humphreys (1981) and Fischler and Goodman (1978) have both shown that associative priming can occur between words on trials where subjects fail to identify primes. In the experiments reported by Evett and Humphreys, subjects were presented with two briefly exposed words, which were preceded and followed by pattern masks. Subjects were asked to report any words they could, in any order. Despite these instructions, subjects were only able to identify the second, target word at an above-chance level. Indeed, in other studies we have conducted subjects have been unable to identify either prime words or their constituent letters above chance even when the second, target word is replaced with a row of X's which does not have to be reported (Evett, Humphreys, & Quinlan, 1985). Yet, under similar conditions Evett and Humphreys (1981) also demonstrated priming dependent on the number of letters in common between primes and targets irrespective of their physical similarity, and Humphreys, Evett, and Taylor (1982) have shown phonological priming betweeen homophonic prime and target words, over and above any orthographic priming effects. These studies did not evaluate prime detection and so they do not address the issue of whether priming can occur without awareness. Nevertheless, the inability of subjects to report primes in these studies does strongly suggest that associative, orthographic, and phonological priming effects can occur when primes have not been processed intentionally to those levels of representation.

One further piece of evidence favoring the above argument has been reported by Marcel (1980). The importance of this evidence is that it shows **qualitative** differences between priming with masked and unmasked primes. In an earlier study, Schvaneveldt, Meyer, and Becker (1976) had shown that if a polysemous word (e.g., *bank*) is interpolated between two words which both relate to one of its meanings (e.g., *save, bank, money;* the congruent condition), lexical decision time to the third word is facilitated relative to when the polysemous word is primed by an unrelated word (*day, bank, money;* the terminal condition), and the terminal condition is in turn facilitated relative to when the three words are unassociated (*river, date, money*). However, relative to the unassociated condition, lexical decision time is inhibited when the first and third words relate to different meanings of the second, polysemous word (*river, bank, money;* the incongruent condition). According to Posner and Snyder's (1975a,b) two-factor account of priming, such an inhibition effect indicates that subjects generated an incorrect expectation of the third word from the primed meaning of the second, polysemous word. Marcel (1980) pattern-masked the polysemous word.[3] Similarly to Schvaneveldt *et al.,* he found a strong facilitation effect on lexical decisions to targets in the congruent condition; however, he also found small facilitation effects in **both** the terminal and the incongruent conditions, relative to the unassociated control. The magnitude of the facilitation effects in the terminal and incongruent conditions did not differ. Marcel interprets his findings in terms of Posner and Snyder's two-factor theory. Inhibitory priming in the incongruent condition is thought to occur when subjects intentionally use information from the polysemous word to select one particular meaning (that primed by the first word). When the intentional use of such information is prevented by pattern masking, both meanings of the polysemous word are shown to be available, and performance is facilitated.

Overall, it seems reasonable to argue from the studies of priming that there is convergence between the criteria separating automatic and control processes and those separating different forms of priming effect. One form

---

[3]The prime–mask durations were established for each subject so that prime could not be detected above chance level. These threshold durations were established in a separate session to the experimental trials, making the study open to the criticism that primes were above threshold during the experimental trials (Purcell *et al.,* 1983). However, since qualitative differences between priming with masked and unmasked words emerged, this criticism is not fatal.

of priming apparently shows interference effects when targets do not match expectations; it is dependent on the intentional use of prime information, and it is determined by the task-specific predictive utility of primes. Such priming seems dependent on control processes. Another form of priming does not show interference effects when priming is incorrect; it is dependent on learned relationships between the stimuli, and it occurs even when subjects **cannot** use prime information intentionally (e.g., because of masking). These three attributes conform to three of the criteria defining automatic processes. Since such priming effects can be based on associative, orthographic, and phonological relationships between words, it appears that words can be processed automatically to these levels of representation.

D. Automatic Processing and Reading Skill

The above account of priming in terms of automatic and control processes can also provide a framework for understanding differences in the use of context by subjects differing in reading skill.

Typically, the magnitude of sentential context effects varies as a function of reading skill, with less skilled readers showing larger effects than more skilled readers (e.g., Perfetti, Goldman, & Hogaboam, 1979; Perfetti & Roth, 1981; Stanovich, 1980). West and Stanovich (1978) compared the time taken by subjects from three age groups (fourth graders, sixth graders, and adults) to name target words preceded by an incomplete sentence congruent with the target, by an incomplete sentence incongruent with the target, or by the word *the*. The latter condition was used as a neutral control condition for assessing the relative effects of the congruent and incongruent contexts (cf. Posner & Snyder, 1975b). West and Stanovich found that, while all three age groups showed facilitated target naming in the congruent condition relative to the neutral control, only fourth and sixth graders showed inhibition in the incongruent condition. The sizes of the facilitation effects did not differ.

The contrasting effects of the sentence contexts on adults, producing only benefits, and on fourth and sixth graders, producing both costs and benefits, calls to mind Posner and Snyder's (1975a,b) distinction between automatic and expectation-dependent priming effects. According to Posner and Snyder's two-factor account, adult readers show only automatic contextual priming while the younger readers show expectation-dependent priming. West and Stanovich argue that the difference between the adult and the fourth- and sixth-grade readers is primarily a function of reading speed. Word identification in skilled adult readers operates sufficiently fast to minimize sentential context effects dependent on control processes. On the other hand, word identification in less skilled younger readers is sufficiently slow to enable context effects dependent on control processes to occur. Presumably, the younger readers intentionally use the sentence contexts to generate expectations of possible targets; performance is facilitated when an expectation is correct and inhibited when it is incorrect. The level of representation mediating the automatic sentential context effects in adults is not clear from the results of West and Stanovich; however, if we are correct in supposing that automatic priming must be based on learned relationships between words, we may suppose that skilled adult readers manifest sentential context effects when the target word has a learned relationship with other words in the sentence (see Section IV,A for a more detailed discussion on this point).

Thus, the distinction between automatic and control processes appears to differentiate how skilled and less skilled readers use contexts, and it is therefore useful for understanding some of the components of reading skill.

III. A CASE AGAINST WORD RECOGNITION AND IDENTIFICATION AS AUTOMATIC PROCESSES

I now consider four aspects of word recogniton and identification in skilled readers where there are dissociations between the various criteria defining automatic processes. This evidence suggests that word recognition and identification are not accurately characterized in these terms.

A. The Obligatory Processing of Words

The strongest evidence for the obligatory processing of words comes from the Stroop effect and from studies showing automatic priming effects based on learned relationships between primes and targets even when primes cannot be identified. However, a body of evidence has now begun to emerge which demonstrates that both the Stroop effect and apparently automatic priming effects can be diluted by instructing subjects to attend to or process displays in particular ways, and, further, that primes masked to prevent identification can interfere with target processing. This evidence is consistent with the view that the processes involved in word recognition and identification can be affected by control processes and that they demand at least some resources.

1. The Dilution of Stroop Effects

In the standard Stroop task, subjects are presented with a color word printed in colored ink and they have to name the ink color. It is possible that at least part of the interference effect when the color word's identity and the ink color are incompatible arises because the lexical and print color information are grouped to form a single perceptual object and the task demands that subjects respond only to one dimension of that object (cf. Treisman, 1969). Recently, investigators have examined whether Stroop interference still obtains when the incongruent lexical and color information are spatially separated. If the effect is modifiable by this form of manipulation, it would suggest that some aspects of word processing in the Stroop procedure are related to attentional processes, since, so long as separation does not produce greater data limitation to the word than the color, automatic processes should not be differentially affected.

Kahneman and Henik (1981) report the most dramatic effects of this manipulation. In one experiment (Experiment 3), they presented two words, one printed in a colored ink, one printed in black, randomly on either side of fixation. Subjects were asked to name the colored ink as quickly as possible. Displays were presented for 200 msec to prevent eye movements. In different conditions, either word could be a color name or they could be neutral (i.e., unrelated to color). Kahneman and Henik found that, relative to when both words were neutral, there was a strong (159-msec) interference effect when subjects named the ink color of an incompatible color word and the other word was neutral. However, there was no interference effect when subjects named the color of the neutral word and the incompatible color word was printed in black. That is, when the conditions allowed subjects to attend to a target color at a separate location from incongruent lexical information, Stroop interference was eliminated. Other investigators have reported less dramatic effects. In similar experiments by Kahneman and Henik themselves (1981, Experiment 2) and by Lowe and Mitterer (1982), small Stroop interference remained with spatially separated displays. Gatti and Egeth (1978) presented a color patch at fixation and varied the distance of the word from the patch (so producing greater data limitation to the word). They found that Stroop interference decreased as the spatial separation of the word and the color increased, but it was still reliable even when the word was as far as 5° of visual angle away. In general, the results indicate that the magnitude of Stroop interference is affected by separating the word and the color, though some residual effect may remain. This suggests that at least some aspects of word processing are affected by attentional processes: the full extent of Stroop interference is not generated simply by the presentation of an incongruent word; it is contingent on subjects attending to that word.

Further recent work by Kahneman and Chajczyk (1983) using the Stroop task also supports this argument. They presented a color patch at fixation accompanied by either one word, randomly above or below fixation, or two words, one on either side of fixation. The words could be color words or they could be neutral, and subjects made naming RT's to the color patch. When a single word was presented, there was a 49-msec facilitation effect when it was a congruent color word and a 72-msec interference effect when it was an incongruent color word, relative to when the word was neutral. When the color word was accompanied by a neutral word, these effects were diluted. There was then only a 29-msec facilitation effect and a 36-msec interference effect in the congruent and incongruent conditions, relative to when both words were neutral. This result was not due to a sensory interaction between the two words since the dilution effect was relatively constant when the words were varied betweeen 2 and 4° away from the color patch. A small dilution effect (about three-quarters the size of that produced by a neutral word) also occurred when a row of X's replaced the neutral word, illustrating that dilution is not due solely to the color word and the neutral word competing for a verbal response. The findings suggest that the color word and the neutral stimulus compete for common resources, either because resources must be shared between the stimuli or because resources are allocated to either one in an all-or-none fashion (in which case the color word might not be allocated any resources on some trials, so diluting its interfering effects). In order to obtain the maximum Stroop effect, the color word must be attended.

However, despite the above results it remains unclear which aspects of the Stroop effect are dependent on control processes. For instance, it would be interesting to examine whether the residual Stroop effect, found even when the color and lexical information are separated, is attributable to conflict between color attributes at prereponse levels of processing (Seymour, 1977); conversely, it may be that facilitating attention to the ink color eliminates that portion of the effect due to response competition. In the data reported by Kahneman and Chajczyk, the dilution produced by the presentation of a neutral stimulus elsewhere in the field was somewhat less on the facilitatory effect of a congruent color word than on the inhibitory effect of an incongruent color word, suggesting that at least part of the dilution effect is due to reduced response competition. Unfortunately, Kahneman and Chajczyk do not analyze whether the dilution effect was contingent on the direction of the Stroop effect, so this suggestion is unconfirmed. Further, we need to specify the level at which competition occurs. The finding of Kahneman and Chajczyk that presenting a row of X's along with an irrelevant color word produced some dilution to the Stroop effect suggests the competiton for verbal response processes may not be the only form of competition present. What form of competition may take place between the row of X's and the color word? One possibility is that these stimuli compete for covert perceptual identification.[4] When the row of X's

[4]A more detailed outline of what is meant here by an identified percept is given in Section IV,C. However, in passing we may note that an identified percept is one that subjects can make a unique discriminatory response to, if required. This response may of course by verbal, but it need not be.

achieves perceptual identification first, the effect of the color word at later stages of processing (e.g., verbal response preparation) is mitigated. Interestingly, in some of the experiments reported by Kahneman and Chajczyk the presentation of a neutral word along with a color word produces about 50% dilution of the Stroop effect, a finding which accords with the simple notion that the neutral word gains perceptual identification first on half the trials. Also, when the neutral stimulus (word or row of X's) achieves rapid perceptual identification, it may initially preclude the perceptual identification of the color patch, generating a small interference effect in its own right relative to when the patch alone is presented. This is indeed what Kahneman and Chajczyk found.

According to the above arguments, some aspects of word processing in the Stroop procedure are contingent on control process (e.g., those involved in achieving perceptual identification and in generating a verbal response to the ink color). However, experimenters have not yet specified which aspects of word processing are unaffected by the manipulations of attention in the Stroop procedure. If, as seems likely, those aspects involve the processing of word meaning, then it remains possible that words are automatically processed to levels at which their associative relations are represented.

2. The Dilution of Priming Effects

Dilution effects are not only obtained with the Stroop task; priming effects can also be lessened by instructing subjects to process primes in particular ways. The first study showing this was reported by Parkin (1979). In this study, subjects were presented with two successive stimuli on each trial. The first stimulus was a word to which subjects either made a semantic judgment (does it have pleasant or unpleasant connotations?) or a nonsemantic judgment (does it have one syllable or two?). The second stimulus was a word printed in colored ink, and subjects had to name the ink color (the Stroop task). In one condition the first word was associatively related to the second word, while in another condition the two words were unassociated. When subjects made semantic judgments of the first word, color naming times were slower when the second word was associatively related than when it was unassociated (see also Warren, 1974). Presumably, this increased Stroop effect occurred because the lexical representation of the second word was activated by its prior associate, making it more difficult to ignore. More interestingly, there was no difference in the size of the Stroop effect in the associated and unassociated conditions when subjects made a nonsemantic judgment of the first word. This result indicates that associative priming may be dependent on the way in which primes are processed. Unfortunately, we cannot be sure what type of processing was invoked by the semantic and nonsemantic judgment tasks used by Parkin. The syllable (nonsemantic) judgment task could be carried out using a phonological representation of a word; however, unless care is taken to match words with differing numbers of syllables for word length it may also be made on the basis of word length. One- and two-syllable words were not matched for word length in Parkin's study, and it is therefore possible that subjects only used length information in their nonsemantic judgments.

An experiment similar to that of Parkin (1979) has been reported by Smith, Theodor, and Franklin (1983). Smith *et al.* had subjects carry out one of five tasks on a prime word and followed the prime by a target letter string on which they made a lexical decision. In one condition primes and targets were associates; in another condition they were unassociated. The five tasks carried out upon primes were to (1) judge whether primes were preceded by a star (visual analysis); (2) judge whether a particular letter was present (letter search); (3) judge whether there was more than one syllable (phonological analysis); (4) read the word silently; or (5) decide if it represented a living thing (semantic analysis). They found reliable associative priming effects (i.e., differences between lexical decisions to targets in the associated and unassociated conditions) after subjects had judged the syllable lengths of primes, read primes silently, or judged whether primes represented living things. However, there were no associative priming effects both when subjects judged whether primes were preceded by a star and when they searched primes for a particular letter. Again, the findings suggest that the mode of processing the prime can determine whether associative priming occurs. Unlike Parkin's results, though, the findings of Smith *et al.* show that associative priming can occur once subjects have generated a phonological representation of the prime, and that it is only diluted when subjects make judgments on visual or orthographic representations of primes.

Does the mode of prime processing only influence associative priming? The answer here appears to be no. Smith (1979) had subjects carry out a letter search on both a prime and a target word, and primes amd targets could be either identical, associated, or unrelated. She found no priming effects on target responses under these circumstances. Nevertheless, strong priming effects were present when subjects only made a letter search to the **target** and made no response to the **prime**. Thus, in this case, making subjects perform a letter search on primes eliminated a repetiton effect as well as an associative priming effect.

The results of Smith (1979; Smith *et al.,* 1983) with the letter search task are somewhat puzzling since skilled readers typically conduct letter searches more rapidly with words than with pronounceable, orthographically regular nonwords (Krueger & Weiss, 1976), suggesting that lexical information may be accessed in this task. It may be that, although subjects access lexical information when searching for a letter in a word, they do not use this information when they search for letters in both primes and targets (as in Experiments 2 and 3, Smith, 1979). This may be because the search is performed upon a prelexical level of representation (e.g., a visual representation of the stimulus). However, if this were true subjects ought to show priming when they must discriminate the target from a pronounceable nonword in a lexical decision task, since this should require judgments at at least a lexical level of representation (cf. James, 1975). Since Smith *et al.* failed to obtain this result, it appears that subjects can preclude lexical information from being activated in letter search tasks [though the reason(s) why this occurred in Smith's experiments but not in experiments contrasting letter searches with words and nonwords remains obscure]. This conclusion clearly contradicts the argument that the processes involved in lexical activation operate automatically.

However, an alternative possiblility is that lexical activation did occur but the priming procedures were not appropriate to demonstrate this. For instance, we have already noted that automatic associative and semantic priming decreases rapidly as the interval between primes and targets increases (Neely, 1977; see also Gough, Alford, & Holley-Wilcox, 1981; Meyer, Schvaneveldt, & Ruddy, 1975). In both Parkin's and Smith's experiments the intervals between the onsets of primes and targets were relatively long (the time taken to judge primes plus at least a 1-second interval in Parkin, 1979; at least 1700 msec in Smith, 1979; 1500 msec in Smith *et al.,* 1983). This in itself could have minimized any automatic associative priming.

The above explanation is less easy to apply to Smith's (1979) repetition experiment, since other workers have claimed that long-lasting automatic repetition effects can occur (e.g., Scarborough, Gerard, & Cortese, 1979). Certainly, long-lasting word repetition effects can be found when subjects have not been told that words will be repeated (Scarborough *et al.,* 1979), and when recall and recognition memory for the stimuli are poor (Jacoby & Dallas, 1981; Scarborough, Cortese, & Scarborough, 1977), indicating that such effects can be achieved without the subject generating expectations of targets from primes. It is important to realize, though, that the above repetition effects are only crucial to the present argument if they reflect long-lasting activation in the input lexical representations of the words, since they would then suggest that activation in the input lexical system lasts sufficiently long to be effective in the Smith's (1979) repetition study. However, recent data collected by Philip Quinlan, Derik Besner, and myself (Humphreys, Quinlan, & Besner, 1983) have given us grounds for doubting this. I present these data in some detail because they are relevant to a number of further issues that will be raised later in the article.

We were interested in comparing the duration of word repetition effects when primes were masked to prevent their identification and when primes were not masked and could be identified. When primes were masked, both the prime and the target were briefly presented and they were immediately preceded and followed by pattern masks (see Evett & Humphreys, 1981). When primes were not masked, the first mask was omitted and primes were presented for a relatively long duration (300 msec); targets were again briefly presented and followed by a pattern mask. In both cases, subjects were asked to make written responses to both words on a trial if they could, and to write responses in the case the words were seen in. Repetition priming was examined at two intervals; prime and target either occurred on the same trial or they were separated by six intervening trials. To prevent contour summation effects when primes were repeated as targets on the same trial, primes were in lower case and targets were in upper case. When the prime was repeated as a target six trials later, the prime on the repetition trial was a neutral row of X's. The base line for this repetition condition was a condition in which a row of X's prime preceded a nonrepeated target. However, the use of a neutral prime also meant that subjects had two words to report in the immediate repeat condition but only one in the delayed repeat and its neutral control condition. In order to provide a control for report load, a further condition was included in which an unrelated word prime preceded a nonrepeated target (the unrelated control condition). This meant that on half the trials targets were preceded by another word (either the same or an unrelated word in lower case), while on the other half targets were preceded by a row of X's. This enabled us to assess whether subjects could make discriminations based on the visual format of masked primes. When primes were masked, subjects were first asked to report whether they thought two words were present in the displays or whether there was one word and a row of X's, before they reported the identities of the words.

The percentage correct target identifications when primes were masked and the percentage trials on which subjects reported two words as present are given in Table Ia. Table Ib contains the percentage correct target identifications when primes were not masked. When primes were masked, there were no correct prime identifications in the word prime conditions (out of 480 trials per condition); when primes were not masked they were identified on every trial.

When primes were masked there were no differences between the percentage trials on which subjects reported the presence of two words in the word–prime and the neutral–prime conditions. That is, subjects were unable to discriminate whether the prime was a word or a row of X's. This indicates that subjects could not use prime information intentionally in the masked prime condition. Nevertheless, target identification was more accurate in the immediate repeat condition than in any of the other condi-

TABLE Ia

**The Percentage Correct Target Identifications and the Percentage Trials
on Which Subjects Reported Two Words as Present with Masked Primes,
in Humphreys *et al.* (1983)**

Condition	Percentage correct	Percentage two-word reports
1. Immediate repeat e.g., *bent–BENT*	61.45	48.33
2. Delayed repeat e.g., *bent–WALK*	49.48	47.30
. . . .		
xxxx–BENT		
3. Neutral prime e.g., *xxxx–BENT*	49.48	47.72
4. Unrelated word prime e.g., *dark–BENT*	30.97	49.99

tions; performance in the delayed repeat and its neutral control did not differ, though it was better in both of these conditions than when primes were unrelated words.

The results were quite different when primes were not masked. Target identification was then reliably better in the delayed repeat condition than in the neutral control condition, though both were again better than the unrelated word control. Surprisingly, performance was worst in the immediate repeat condition.

The finding that is most relevant to the current argument is the contrast in the delayed repetition effect when primes were not masked relative to when they were. When primes were not masked there was a strong delayed repetition effect. When primes were masked there was a strong immediate repetition effect but no delayed repetition effect. Indeed, in other experiments we have conducted we have been able to establish a repetition effect under masking conditions **only** when primes are repeated as targets on the same trial (Humphreys *et al.,* 1983). The lack of delayed repetition effects

TABLE Ib

**The Percentage Correct Target Identification with Unmasked
Primes in Humphreys *et al.* (1983)**

Condition	Percentage correct
1. Immediate repeat e.g., *bent–BENT*	25.00
2. Delayed repeat e.g., *bent–WALK*	68.13
. . . .	
xxxx–BENT	
3. Neutral prime e.g., *xxxx–BENT*	55.42
4. Unrelated word prime	42.93

under masking conditions suggests that, in order to generate delayed repetition effects, it is critical that subjects form an episodic representation of the prime word. This episodic representation is independent of the lexical activation process involved in word recognition, since preventing the formation of an episodic representation (e.g., by masking) does not prevent lexical activation, as evidenced by associative and phonological priming effects (Evett & Humphreys, 1981; Humphreys *et al.*, 1982). If this argument is valid, then the long-lasting repetition effects found even when subjects do not predict targets from primes do **not** reflect activation in the input lexicon. Consequently, it remains possible that Smith's (1979) failure to find repetition effects when subjects searched for letters in primes and targets was due to her use of prime target intervals too long to obtain any effects of automatic activation in the input lexical system.

In summary, experiments have shown that associative and repetition priming effects can be diluted by instructing subjects to attend to or process primes in particular ways. Dilution effects are most apparent when subjects make judgments based on visual or orthographic representations of primes. It is almost as if subjects, given the task of searching for a particular letter (Smith, 1979; Smith *et al.*, 1983) or of judging whether a prime is preceded by a star (Smith *et al.*, 1983), can restrict their attention to discrete parts of the visual representation and only process in detail those parts which are attended. This suggestion is stronger than that made from studies showing dilution of the Stroop effect, since it maintains that lexical activation itself is dependent upon the strategy of the subject. However, the suggestion cannot yet be validated because experimenters have used relatively long prime–target intervals when investigating dilution effects, which may have precluded automatic priming irrespective of the strategy of the subject.

3. Interference Effects from Masked Stimuli

The dilution of effects due apparently to the obligatory processing of words indicates that at least some aspects of word processing are dependent on the attentional or process set (Duncan, 1980a) adopted by the subject, contradicting the claim that all processes in word recognition and identification are automatic in skilled readers. Further evidence against automaticity comes from studies showing that a pattern-masked stimulus can interfere with responses to a target word. In some cases, information from a masked word may be activated without intention (Evett & Humphreys, 1981; Humphreys *et al.*, 1982). The criteria defining an automatic process hold that it can be unintentional **and** that it does not interfere with other operations. Evidence of interference from a stimulus processed without intention would indicate a dissociation between the criteria defining automaticity.

Findings relevant to this proposal have been reported by Kahneman and Treisman (1983). They required subjects to name an upper case word from a display that could contain a single upper case word, an upper case word and a lower case word, an upper case word and an upper case nonword, or an upper case word and a row of X's. Displays were pattern masked to limit report accuracy. Kahneman and Treisman found that report accuracy was lowered by the presence of either the lower case word, the nonword, or the row of X's. Performance was worst when either a lower case word or a nonword was present. A similar result was obtained when subjects were simply asked to report whether or not the masked display contained an animal word. These findings indicate that subjects are limited in their ability to identify or detect a particular type of word in a display. Performance may be more impaired when the distractor is a lower case word or a nonword than when it is a row of X's either because the row of X's provides less competition for a common resource or because subjects can discriminate a row of X's from an upper case target word more easily.

The results of Kahneman and Treisman's (1983) demonstrate limitations in word processing, but they do not specify the level of processing at which such limitations occur. It is possible that impairments to performance were produced in their experiments because the target word and the distractor competed for an overt response. This possibility is less likely in studies showing interference from words pattern masked to minimize their identification. For instance, Allport (1977) presented a target word at fixation, which could be accompanied by a prime word simultaneously exposed 1° above it. The whole display was backward pattern masked and subjects attempted to identify targets. Under this circumstance, subjects reported that they were aware only of the target word. Allport found that, relative to when the target was presented alone, target identification was worse when an unrelated prime word was presented. This interference was overridden when the prime and target were associates. Given the distance separating the two words, it is unlikely that interference was due to lateral masking (Eriksen & Hoffman, 1972; Flom, Weymouth, & Kahneman, 1963); the purported lack of awareness of primes also suggests that there was little competition between them and targets for overt responses.

In a series of experiments similar to those of Allport, Taylor (1982) has further shown that the interfering effect of the prime on target identification is equivalent irrespective of whether the prime is a word unrelated to the target, an orthographically regular nonword, or a nonword with zero order of approximation to English. However, Taylor found **no** interference when the prime was constructed from "pseudoletters" (these were characters containing line segments present in letters but not resembling any particular letter). This illustrates that primes must activate letter or possibly lexical information to interfere with target word report. In the studies reported by Allport (1977) and by Taylor (1982), no direct measures of prime identification were taken, and post hoc reports of awareness by subjects are weak tests of the explicit information available (cf. Merikle, 1982). Nevertheless, interference effects have been shown when direct measures reveal minimal prime identification. For instance, Humphreys (1981a) found that single letter or digit primes interfered with categorization responses to letter or digit targets from the opposite category, even when the prime was pattern masked so that subjects could not categorize it at a better than chance level. Interference occurred both when target categorization was measured relative to a no-prime base line and when the prime was a random line pattern (Humphreys, 1978). This suggests that interference is dependent on both stimuli activating similar stored representations (i.e., letters or digits). Interestingly, interference was more likely when the stimuli were within 1° of each other than when they were further apart (Humphreys, 1979). This was not because of effects on the resolution of primes, since the result occurred when the prime was always at fixation and the target was presented randomly at various distances from fixation; also, lateral masking effects were controlled for by the use of the random line pattern prime as a base line.

This appears to throw some light on the mechanisms underlying interference effects under masking conditions. If interference occurred because primes and targets competed for common resources **during their processing** (e.g., in the processes governing the activation of the stored representations of the stimuli), increasing the prime–target separation by moving the target away from fixation should, if anything, magnify the interference effect (because the target will be more data limited); clearly, it should **not** reduce interference. Also, since the categorization of primes was so poor, it is doubtful whether primes ever achieved perceptual identification (presumably because of the masking conditions); this rules out the possibility that interference occurred because primes were perceptually identified before targets. However, the findings are consistent with the proposal that primes and targets competed for specialized resources during the perceptual identification process. If perceptual identification is a resource-limited process, responses to targets would suffer under this circumstance. The suggestion here is that, under some circumstances, masking[5] may prevent the perceptual identification of primes, but it does not prevent primes from engaging some of the resources required for perceptual identification. However, this may only occur when primes and targets are parsed as the same perceptual event. One effect of increasing the prime–target separation may be to in-

[5]In particular, central backward masking (see Marcel, 1983a).

crease the likelihood that the stimuli are parsed as separate events, so reducing the interference effect.[6]

This argument may also account for one of the results of Humphreys *et al.* (1983; see Section III,A,2). They found that identification of a target word was worse when the word was preceded by a row of X's. This result occurred both when the prime was masked to prevent its identification and when it was not masked. The fact that an unmasked prime interfered with the identification of a data-limited target can be attributed to its effect on the report load: during the time taken to report the prime, identity information from the target may have decayed or been lost from memory. However, this cannot have been the case when primes were masked, since no subject correctly identified a prime word and subjects were unable to discriminate whether the prime was a word or a row of X's. This also indicates that interference was not caused by competition for overt word responses. Further, since priming effects based on the procedure used by Humphreys *et al.* (1983) are **independent** of the physical similarity of primes and targets (Evett & Humphreys, 1981), it seems unlikely that interference resulted from differential forward masking. A more subtle possibility, though, is that interference was due to the increased probability of letters from primes being transposed into target reports when the prime was a word relative to when it was a row of X's. To evaluate this, we conducted a detailed analysis of error responses in the word prime condition. The least conservative method of assessing transposition errors, that of counting every prime letter in an erroneous target response irrespective of position, was used. This analysis showed that 11.84% of subjects' errors could have been caused by transposing letters from primes into target responses. To calculate the number of reports of prime letters which can be expected by chance, we matched prime words against a random pool of words drawn from Kucera and Francis (1967). The percentage of chance reports of prime letters was found to be 17.56%. From this, it seems that transpositions of prime letters into target responses are no greater than we would expect by chance. Even this measure fails to show that prime information was available for report. Accordingly, it seems reasonable to claim that interference did not stem either from sensory interaction or from response conflict, and that it resulted from some interaction between primes and targets after the extraction of their visual information but before the achievement of perceptual identification. One candidate process, then, is perceptual identification itself, where fewer

---

[6]This does not mean that when primes and targets are parsed as separate events primes achieve independent perceptual identification; the results demonstrate that this was not the case. It simply means that activation generated by the prime is treated separately from activation generated by the target.

resources may be available for word targets if they have been demanded by word primes.

If the above argument is correct, it is possible that the processing of words prior to their perceptual identification occurs automatically, independent of both resource limitations and the subject's control. However, there are at least two findings which pose problems for this argument. One is that interference from masked letters or digits on target categorization occurs primarily when the stimuli are within a 1° area around fixation (Humphreys, 1979). We have interpreted this finding as suggesting that primes and targets more than 1° apart tend to be parsed as separate perceptual events, reducing competition for the resources involved in the perceptual identification of targets. If stimulus processing prior to perceptual identification is automatic, then the parsing of perceptual events should be determined purely by stimulus factors, independent of the subject's control. What stimulus factors might determine that primes and targets separated by more than 1° are parsed as independent objects? One possibility is that all stimuli (or at least all stimuli of a particular size) falling within the central 1° area around fixation are treated as candidates for a single perceptual event by the visual system, perhaps because these stimuli are less subject to acuity limitations. This seems unlikely, though. Subjects can selectively filter targets from distractors within the central 1° area when they can fixate the target's location (Humphreys, 1981b), suggesting that the parsing process is not hard wired but that it is a flexible operation, dependent on how subjects attend to events in the visual field. When subjects are able to attend to a target within a particular area of visual field, events outside that area may not compete for resources during the perceptual identification of the target. In the data reported by Humphreys (1979), primes and targets may only have competed for resources when they were within the central 1° area because that was the area of field to which subjects were attending (cf. Humphreys, 1981b).

The second finding presenting difficulties for the argument that preperceptual identification processes are automatic comes from the experiments reported by Duncan (1980b). In these experiments subjects searched four-character stimulus arrays for a digit target among letter distractors. There were two main conditions: either all four characters were presented together (the SIM condition) or characters appeared two at a time (the SUCC condition). The SUCC condition provided less of a demand on the ability of subjects to divide their attention between array characters (see also Shiffrin & Gardner, 1972). Subjects either searched for a single target or they searched for two independent targets in the two halves of the array. Arrays were briefly presented and backward pattern masked. The major finding was that when subjects searched for two independent targets performance was considerably better in the SUCC condition than in the SIM condition, particularly when more than one target was presented on a trial. This finding replicates numerous other studies of divided attention showing that subjects are limited in their ability to assign unique discriminatory responses to two simultaneously presented stimuli (e.g., Egeth & Pachella, 1969; Forbes, Taylor & Lindsay, 1967; Moray, 1975; Pohlman & Sorkin, 1976). This limitation may be in the ability to perceptually identify more than one stimulus at a time. However an ancillary finding was that there was a small but consistent advantage for the SUCC condition over the SIM condition both when subjects searched for only one target and when they searched for two targets but only one was present. This consistent advantage suggests that some resources may be demanded by the simultaneous processing of targets and distractors, since it occurred even when distractors did not have to be assigned a unique discriminatory response (i.e., perceptually identified). To be sure this effect is substantially smaller than that found when simultaneous stimuli both require discriminatory responses, and therefore compete for perceptual identification; nevertheless, it appears to be real (Duncan, 1980b).

In summary, a number of experiments have shown that primes masked to prevent their identification can interfere with responses to a target. There is thus a dissociation between the tenets that an automatic process can occur unintentionally and that it does not interfere with other processes: stimuli processed without intention can produce interference effects. Most of these results can be explained if we assume that the perceptual identification process is resource limited and that primes and targets compete for the resources required for this process. This may take place even when the presentation conditions prevent primes from being perceptually identified. Two further results suggest that even some of the processes prior to perceptual identification are nonautomatic, in the sense that they may be affected by how subjects attend to stimuli in the visual field and they may demand processing resources; interference effects from masked primes are greatest when primes and targets fall within an attended region of visual field (Humphreys, 1979), and there are small costs associated with the simultaneous processing of items in the visual field, even when the items fall into distinct, well-practiced categories and only one item must be perceptually identified (Duncan, 1980b). Our conclusions about processes prior to perceptual identification should be guarded, however. It may be that the parsing of perceptual events is not an independent stage preceding perceptual identification; it may be part of the perceptual identification process itself. Further, even though the distractors in Duncan's (1980b) studies did not require perceptual identification, they may nevertheless have competed for perceptual identification resources. The trouble here is that, in any task, measurements are based on responses to some stimulus, and, accordingly, that stimulus requires perceptual identification. Interference effects on processes prior to perceptual identification cannot be assessed in isolation; perceptual identification is always required.

B. Direct Measures of Resource Limitations

1. Letter Processing

In the above studies, the role of control processes in word recognition and identification is implicated indirectly from the dilution and interference effects which occur when more than one stimulus must be processed concurrently. Other studies have attempted to assess the resource demands of letter and word processing more directly by using dual task procedures. In dual task studies, experimenters examine the trade-offs which can occur when subjects perform concurrent primary and secondary tasks. Typically, it is assumed that if a primary task demands processing resources, there will be detrimental effects on secondary task performance when it is carried out concurrently with the primary task, relative to when it is performed alone (Posner & Boies, 1971). On the other hand, if the primary task does not demand processing resources (and is in this sense automatic) performance of the two tasks should be independent. One problem with this argument is that interference between the tasks may only be observed when their **total** demands exceed the resource capacity (Kahneman, 1973; Norman & Bobrow, 1975). Thus, considered alone, the absence of interference between tasks is not diagnostic of automaticity.

Recently, in experiments using a dual task procedure, Ogden, Martin, and Paap (1980) and Paap and Ogden (1981) have argued that the encoding of single letters consumes some resources. Ogden *et al.* (1980) used a primary sequential letter-matching task, in which subjects had to determine whether two letters had the same or different names. Subjects also performed a concurrent secondary task, where they made simple RT responses to auditory probes which could occur at various points in time during the primary task. To assess the resource demanded by letter processing, Ogden *et al.* compared secondary task RT when the probe was presented just after the first letter relative to probe RT when no letter was presented. Such no-letter base line RT's occurred on a small proportion of the trials. Since any expectancies about the first letter should be the same on the letter-present and the letter-absent trials, any difference in probe RT should reflect the resource demanded when subjects have to process the letter. Ogden *et al.* found consistently slower probe RT's when the first letter was present relative to when it was absent.

This work has been extended by Paap and Ogden (1981). In their primary task, subjects categorized target letters as either vowels or consonants. Targets were preceded by prime letters, to which no responses were made. In one condition, there was a high probability that the category of the prime would be the same as that of the target. In another condition, there was no predictive relationship between the stimuli. In the secondary task, subjects again made simple RT responses to auditory probes. Similarly to Ogden *et al.* (1980), the critical test concerned the difference in probe RT's just after the presentation of a prime relative to probe RT's when the prime was absent. Paap and Ogden found that probe RT's were longer when primes were present, with both predictive and unpredictive primes. The effect was larger with predictive primes.

This study is of interest since it investigates secondary task performance when the primary task involved a priming procedure which attempts to separate "automatic" and expectation-dependent priming, using Posner and Snyder's (1975a,b) two-factor account of priming (Section II,B). In fact, the priming task data conformed to the distinction of Posner and Snyder. In the unpredictive prime condition, benefits to target processing from related primes occurred without costs on the unrelated trials. This suggests that subjects did not make intentional use of primes. In the predictive condition, the intentional use of primes was indicated by the presence of costs on trials when primes and targets were unrelated, which accompanied benefits when they were related. Since detriments to probe RT's were found in both cases, it appears that resources are demanded for letter processing even when letter information is not used intentionally. It would seem that "automatic" priming, as defined by Posner and Snyder, is not automatic if we consider all the criteria by which an automatic process may be specified (Section I).

As noted above, in the primary tasks used by Ogden *et al.* and Paap and Ogden, subjects received two sequentially presented letters. In both studies, the first letter was briefly presented. This was done to try and force subjects to encode the first letter immediately, preventing the strategy of delaying the encoding of the first letter to ensure that secondary task probes presented shortly after the letter were responded to quickly. Unfortunately, it is possible that the brief exposure of the first letter encouraged subjects to allocate resources to its processing. This possibility has been examined in a series of experiments by Johnson, Forester, Calderwood, and Weisgerber (1983), whose results suggest that subjects can allocate resources flexibly to primary and secondary tasks. They used a dual task procedure similar to that of Ogden *et al.* except that the first letter in the primary task was left exposed until the presentation of the second letter. They found that secondary task interference occurred when the interval between the letters in the primary task was varied (between 50 and 1000 msec), but not when it

was constant (at 1000 msec). The reason for this difference appears to be
that subjects shifted resources to the secondary task when the first letter in
the primary task was left exposed and there was a relatively long and constant interval between the primary task letters. Johnson *et al.* tested this by
varying the probability that probes were presented shortly after the onset
of the first letter. When early probes were likely, no secondary task interference was found (presumably because subjects allocated resources to the
secondary task). When early probes were unlikely, secondary task interference occurred: RT's to probes were slower when the first letter was presented than when it was not presented. Also, increasing the intensity of the
auditory probes reduced secondary task interference for the low probability
probes, which may be attributable to the tendency for high intensity stimuli
to draw resources (Nissen, 1977). These data indicate that the processing
of the first letter in the primary task did demand resources, producing interference effects on the secondary task. However, the effects of these demands can be masked in dual task procedures when subjects allocate
resources to the secondary task (e.g., when the demands of the primary
task are reduced and there is a high probability of probe occurrence at particular intervals).

Interestingly, Johnson *et al.* also measured probe RT's when subjects
were presented with no primary task letters over a block of trials. Probe
RT's here were faster than in all the other conditions, indicating that there
was some probe-task interference produced simply by incorporating the
probe task in a dual task procedure (dual task interference). However, dual
task interference was independent of the interference produced by the presentation of the first letter in the primary task. This suggests that these two
interference effects are derived from separate sources. It may be that dual
task interference occurs due to demands on an independent set of resources
(Navor & Gopher, 1979; Wickens, 1983), or that it reflects increased response uncertainty (when subjects must make responses to both primary
and the secondary tasks, Duncan, 1980a).

2. The Effects of Practice

To what extent might the resource demands of letter processing change
as a function of practice? It might be that letter processing under the somewhat unusual demands of sequential matching and vowel–consonant discrimination tasks is rendered nonautomatic and resource consuming, though
it may normally proceed automatically in word recognition and reading.
Perhaps secondary task interference might disappear as subjects become
more practiced at the tasks.

The effects of practice on dual task performance have been investigated
by Hoffman, Nelson, and Houck (1983). One of their tasks was similar to

that of Duncan (1980b): subjects searched a four-character array for a target digit among letters. Before each trial, subjects were told either the identity of the digit which could occur or the identities of four digits, one of which could be the target (the memory load). The display was briefly presented and pattern masked. Subjects given practice at this task showed a rapid initial reduction in RT's followed by stable performance (see also Schneider & Shiffrin, 1977). Also, following practice, the slope of the positive RT's (when targets were present) was close to that found on negative trials; quite different to the 1:2 slope differences found when subject search displays serially (Treisman & Gelade, 1980). Further, there was a relatively small effect of memory load. On each of these criteria the processes involved in the search task can be deemed automatic (Shiffrin & Dumais, 1981). In the other task used by Hoffman *et al.*, subjects were given brief exposures of a light which could occur adjacent to one of the locations of the characters in the search task. Subjects had to determine the location of the light (the flicker location task). The light was presented just prior to the onset of the search characters, but subjects responded to its location following their search response. In different conditions subjects were instructed to divide their attention between the tasks in three ways: 90% to the search task, 10% to the flicker location task; 50% search/50% flicker; 10% search/90% flicker. The question of major interest was whether subjects can perform these two tasks independently of each other.

Hoffman *et al.* found that performance on both the search and the flicker location tasks under dual task conditions was worse than when either task was performed alone. Performance on each task was worst when subjects were instructed to pay most attention to the other task. Thus, even after practice sufficient to classify search performance as automatic on the criteria of stable RT's, parallel search, and small memory-load effects, the task remained vulnerable to dual task interference. This strongly suggests that some stages in letter processing are normally subject to resource limitations.

There were a number of other interesting aspects of the Hoffman *et al.* results. One was that the accuracy of flicker location responses was worse when a target was present in the search array than when the target was absent **(the intrusion effect)**. A second was that target detection was more accurate when the flicker occurred in an adjacent location **(the adjacency effect)**. Both of these effects were independent of the instructions to attend one or other task. These results help to locate the stages of processing where the trade-offs occur in dual task performance. Let us consider the adjacency effect first. Here, the flickering light captured attention, and so improved the detection of an adjacent target, irrespective of how subjects allocated resources to the tasks. It appears then that brief light exposures, presented away from the fovea, can cue attention automatically (cf. Posner, 1980). More enlightening for understanding resource limitations in letter processing is the instrusion effect, where digit targets cued attention independently of resource allocation to the tasks. This suggests that alphanumeric characters can be categorized without making resource demands; that is, their categorization may be automatic. In fact, the intrusion effect was relatively independent of whether the target digit was correctly detected on a given trial (Hoffman *et al.*, 1983, Experiment 3). Thus, it appears that letters and digits may be automatically categorized, but that being processed to this level of representation does not ensure correct detection. Earlier, we have used the term perceptual identification to describe the process of translating information into a unique discriminatory response. The findings of Hoffman *et al.* are consistent with the notion that perceptual identification is resource limited and that resources must be allocated to a stimulus for perceptual identification to occur.

There is, however, one result reported by Hoffman *et al.* which is problematical for the argument that preperceptual identification processes are automatic. In their Experiment 2, the lights in the flicker task were presented in a small area around fixation (within a 0.5° × 0.5° square), while the search characters were presented further out (each was 4.27° from fixation). In this case, they found **no** intrusion effects. It may be that presenting the flicker lights in a separate location from the search characters enabled subjects to attend selectively to the light locations. Letters and digits which fall in nonattended spatial regions may not activate their stored representations, preventing categorization from occurring (see Section III,A,2 for a similar argument). This conclusion contradicts the proposal that categorization occurs automatically prior to perceptual identification. Alternatively, it may be that automatic categorization does occur, but that targets in the search task do not interfere with flicker location responses when subjects are fairly certain about the location of information in the two tasks. According to this view, when subjects attended selectively to the flicker lights they were able to control which information influenced responses. This would be consistent with an operation which, via a spatial parsing process, selectively allocated resources for perceptual identification. Letters and digits segmented from the flicker lights would not compete for the same perceptual identification resources.

3. Word Processing

Dual task studies of letter and digit processing clearly show that resources are required when subjects make unique discriminatory responses to the stimuli. It remains possible, though, that processes prior to perceptual identification are automatic.

Unfortunately, relatively few experiments have examined word processing under dual task conditions. One such study was reported by Becker (1976). In this study, two types of secondary task were used: in one, subjects made a simple RT response to the onset of either a high or low frequency auditory tone; in the other, subjects made a choice RT response according to whether the high or the low tone was presented. In the primary task, subjects made lexical decisions to high and to low frequency words. The resource demands of the primary task can be assessed by the difference in RT between the simple and choice RT secondary tasks: in particular, choice RT's should be relatively slower when the primary task is more resource demanding. Becker found that differences in RT's between the two secondary tasks were larger when low rather than high frequency words were presented in the primary lexical decision task. This indicates that the processing of low frequency words demanded more resources than the processing of high frequency words.

According to some theories of word recognition (e.g., the logogen model, Morton, 1969; the lexical search model, Forster, 1976), access to the input lexical representations of words is a frequency-sensitive process. If we interpret the findings of Becker (1976) according to these frameworks, we might suggest that lexical access is resource demanding. However, this is by no means the only interpretation of frequency effects which can be proposed; for instance, it is possible that frequency effects reside in the accessing of semantic information about a word (James, 1975), or in the processes involved in integrating visual information from a word with the products of lexical processing (Becker, 1976; Besner & Swan, 1982). According to the latter two positions, the findings of Becker (1976) confirm that at least some processes *subsequent* to lexical access are resource demanding. One step toward specifying the locus of dual task interference would be to investigate whether it remains when word naming latency is measured, since naming may well be less influenced by semantic information accessed from words than lexical decision (Besner, 1983).

The above studies, which have investigated resource limitations in letter and word processing directly by using dual task procedures, have produced strong evidence for the involvement of at least some resources in the processing of these stimuli. For letters, this evidence obtains even when they are not processed intentionally (Paap & Ogden, 1981), and when performance in the primary letter-processing task is highly practiced and conforms in other respects to criteria defining an automatic process (Hoffman *et al.,* 1983). For words, evidence of resource involvement in lexical decisions has been obtained (Becker, 1976). Though it remains unclear precisely which processes demand resources, it is clear that word identification and recognition are processes which do. A final procedural note must also be made. In cases where no trade-offs occur in dual task performance, a cautious interpretation should be made. This is because trade-offs may occur only when the overall demands of the tasks exceeds capacity, and because trade-offs can be masked when subjects can anticipate and allocate resources to the secondary task (Johnson *et al.,* 1983).

C. Priming, Inhibition, and Resource Capacity

1. Inhibition and Expectation-Dependent Priming

One of the clearest distinctions on which the dichotomy between automatic and control processes is based is that between "automatic" and expectation-dependent priming (Posner & Snyder, 1975a,b). Although the distinction between the two forms of priming effect may not allow us to claim that prime information is processed automatically (Section II,B), it nevertheless appears to be the case that the information accessed by a prime can influence the processing of a subsequent target irrespective of whether subjects use prime information intentionally (Neely, 1977). The distinction between "automatic" and expectation-dependent priming is also important for the automaticity position because one criterion on which it is based is the presence of inhibition effects when incorrect expectation-dependent priming occurs. Such inhibition effects are attributed to the misallocation of resource capacity when subjects generate an incorrect expectation of the target from the prime (Posner & Snyder, 1975a). This account, then, links inhibition effects to the concept of resource capacity and the notion that capacity is required only by control processes (e.g., in generating expectations). It follows that studies showing that inhibitory priming effects are not necessarily caused by the intentional use of prime information or by the misallocation of resource capacity blur the distinction between automatic and control processes.

We have already noted that some studies have shown that responses to targets can be inhibited by the presence of primes masked to prevent their identification (e.g., Humphreys, 1981a; Humphreys *et al.,* 1983). Since such primes cannot be processed intentionally, we can argue that inhibition effects can be separated from the intentional use of prime information. This indicates that there are dissociations between two criteria for defining an automatic process: namely, that it does not interfere with other processes and that it can occur without intention (Section III,A,3).

It may nevertheless be that priming with masked primes demands resource capacity. One possibility is that the perceptual identification of the target is resource demanding (Section III,A,3). Another possibility is that processes up to and including the perceptual identification of clearly presented stimuli are not resource limited, but that the processes involved in the recovery of data-limited information are (see Section II,B for a similar argument regarding dual task interference effects with briefly presented targets). Studies showing inhibition from masked primes have typically used data-limited targets. In order to demonstrate that inhibition effects can be dissociated from resource-dependent processes, we need to study inhibition under conditions where primes and targets are not data limited.

In fact, some indications that inhibitory priming effects are not necessarily related to the misallocation of resource capacity were present in the priming study reported by Posner and Snyder (1975b). As we have already noted, subjects in this study had to match a pair of target letters which could be preceded by a letter prime. The target letters could either be the same or different from the prime letter. When the target letters did not match, Posner and Snyder found that RT's were faster when the prime was a completely different letter relative to when it was one of the nonmatching target letters. This suggests that subjects matched the letter prime against the target letters. When a match was detected, a "yes" response may have been biased; when no match was detected, a "no" response may have been biased. Accordingly, RT's to nonmatching targets will be faster when the prime also does not match either target letter. Posner and Synder obtained this result with both informative primes (in the 80–20 condition) and with noninformative primes (in the 20–80 condition), which illustrates that the process of matching primes to targets may be obligatory. If this process occurred, it is possible that the cost to RT's on trials when the target letters matched and the prime was different was because a "no" response was biased by the mismatch between prime and target letters.

Quite similar effects have also been demonstrated in priming studies with words using the lexical decision task (e.g., de Groot, 1984; de Groot, Thomassen, & Hudson, 1982; Neely, 1976, 1977; Schvaneveldt & McDonald, 1981). In this case, "no" responses to nonwords are facilitated when they are preceded by words rather than by a neutral prime. This may be because subjects perform an obligatory match of primes with targets. When some form of relationship between these stimuli is detected, a "yes" response may be biased, and there may be a corresponding "no" bias when no relationship is detected. This process is termed a coherence check by de Groot et al. (1982; see also Forster, 1979). If this bias has time to operate prior to a response for the target becoming available, it will affect performance. Thus, when a word prime is followed by a nonword target, the bias towards a "no" response from the failure to detect a relationship between the stimuli will facilitate a "no" response in the lexical decision task. Additionally, when two words are presented, the "yes" response required to the target will be facilitated when it is related to the prime and inhibited when the stimuli are unrelated.

One problem with this argument is that inhibitory priming effects have not always been found in studies when primes and targets are unrelated and when primes ought to bias the wrong response to the target, via the matching process. For example, in Posner and Snyder's (1975b) letter-matching study there were no inhibition effects when the prime was unrelated to a pair of matching target letters when the prime was not informative and when there were short prime–target intervals. Similarly, there were no inhibition effects in the RT data with short prime–target intervals in Neely's (1977) study. However, in Neely's study there is some indication of a speed–accuracy trade-off between the conditions with short intervals between the stimuli. For instance, relative to the row of X's prime base line, errors were increased when the prime and target were not semantically related but the prime was predictive (*body–door*), when the prime and target were semantically related but the target was unexpected (*body–arm*), and when the stimuli were unrelated and the target was unexpected (*bird–arm*). It is possible that the costs in the error data masked any effects with RT's. Interestingly, Neely (1976), in an investigation of associative priming between words using a lexical decision task, found inhibitory priming effects between unrelated words separated by short intervals, and that these effects did not vary as a function of the interval.

One further factor that could influence the presence or absence of inhibitory priming effects is the type of neutral prime base line used. In both Neely's (1977) study and that of Posner and Snyder (1975b), a row of X's was used. It has been argued that this tends to be a conservative base line, since in studies of letter and word priming, subjects may tend to respond to the second linguistic event. Accordingly, when the prime is a row of X's, target responses may be delayed artificially because the target is then the first linguistic event. Direct evidence for this has been reported by de Groot *et al.* (1982). They showed that, relative to when a nonpredictive linguistic prime is used (e.g., the word blank, neutral or ready, in word priming studies), lexical decisions are slower when the prime is a row of X's.

Antos (1979) and de Groot (1984) have used a neutral linguistic prime as a base line in studies of word priming using the lexical decision task, and Myers and Lorch (1980) used a similar base line in a study where subjects classified target words as members of particular categories. In each of these studies, inhibitory priming effects from unrelated word primes were established with short intervals between the stimuli. Also, de Groot (1984) found that the predictive utility of the prime did not affect the inhibition effects, and de Groot *et al.* (1982) found that inhibition was present even when word primes were **always** unrelated to targets. In these studies subjects had to classify target information against stored knowledge (to check if the target is a known word or if it is a category member), which may in itself force subjects to use a matching strategy. Nevertheless, the data strongly indicate that, at least with these tasks, the matching of primes against targets is obligatory, as are the inhibition effects which are generated when a match is not detected.

Support for this conclusion can also be drawn from studies investigating the effects of sentence contexts on responses to target words. Fischler and Bloom (1979) presented subjects with incomplete sentence contexts followed by a single target word or nonword, to which subjects made a lexical decision. Target words could either be predictable completions of the sentences (a range of predictability was incorporated, from words which 99% of subjects gave as completions to words which 9% gave as completions), unlikely but semantically and syntactically appropriate completions (these were words which only 3% of subjects gave as completions), or semantically anomalous completions. In a control condition, the words in the sentence context were replaced by rows of X's. Fischler and Bloom found no difference between the predictable completion condition, the unlikely but acceptable completion condition, and the control condition. However, there was a substantial inhibition effect for target words in the anomalous condition relative to the control. Further, this effect still occurred when subjects were instructed to try and ignore the context. This demonstrates that, contrary to Posner and Snyder's (1975b) two-factor account of priming, cost effects can occur in the absence of benefits, and that these effects are not intentional, since they were not eliminated when subjects attempted to ignore the context. In a subsequent study, Fischler and Bloom (1980) presented contexts using a rapid serial visual presentation technique, at rates varying from 4 to 28 words per second. The contexts were followed by a target word or nonword to which subjects made lexical decisions. In a control condition, one group of subjects was presented with sentence contexts which were always completed by an anomalous word. Other subjects were presented with predictable, unlikely but acceptable, and anomalous conditions at random. At the fastest presentation rates (20 and 28 words per second) they again found only an inhibition effect for the anomalous sentences relative to the control condition. This shows that inhibition can occur rapidly following the presentation of a context. The result is more consistent with the view that inhibition stems from the obligatory matching of primes with targets, rather than the misallocation of resource capacity when the stimuli are incongruent.

The hypothesized obligatory matching of primes and targets should affect performance when responses to targets are fairly slow, when a match can be conducted prior to a response being made, and when the matching process can bias a binary response. In tasks which enable faster target responding than in lexical decision tasks, and which do not require a binary response, the effects of the matching process should at least be reduced.

West and Stanovich (1982) tested this proposal in an investigation of sentential context effects on lexical decision and naming performance to target words. Incomplete sentences were presented which could be completed by a congruous or an incongruous target word. In a control condition, the context was the word "the." They showed that naming latencies to targets were faster than lexical decision latencies. More importantly, while RT's to targets preceded by a congruent context were facilitated relative to the control in both tasks, reliable inhibition effects in the incongruent condition were only observed in the lexical decision task. This was not due simply to a shift in the control condition in the two tasks, since the amount of facilitation was approximately the same (the possible reason why West and Stanovich found facilitatory priming effects but Fischler and Bloom did not will be discussed further in Section IV,A). It therefore appears that inhibitory priming effects predominate in lexical decision and similar tasks requiring binary responses because of the bias towards a "no" response when primes do not match targets. The lexical decision task may be particularly prone to such effects because it may also require more postlexical processing of words than does naming (James, 1975; Theios & Muise, 1977). This makes it more likely that a match process will be effected prior to the response being carried out.

Taken together, the data indicate that with tasks where subjects make relatively slow, binary responses to targets, inhibitory priming effects follow from the mandatory matching of primes and targets. Interestingly, it may be that masking primes to prevent their identification prevents this matching process and so minimizes inhibition effects (cf. Marcel, 1980). This is not to state that all inhibition effects reflect an obligatory matching process. The evidence that inhibition tends to increase with longer intervals between primes and targets (de Groot, 1984; Neely, 1977; Posner & Snyder, 1975b), and when primes are informative (de Groot, 1984; Posner & Snyder, 1975b), suggests that inhibition can be associated with the generation of incorrect target expectations by subjects. Also, Becker (this volume) and Underwood and Bargh (1982) have found inhibition effects when skilled readers name target words preceded by unrelated sentence contexts (unlike West & Stanovich, 1978; Section II,D). Such effects cannot be linked with biases on a binary classification mechanism. Becker proposes that they occur when subjects generate a large set of target expectancies from the context and compare each expectancy with the target prior to making a response based on stimulus information alone; when the expectancies are incorrect, performance will be inhibited relative to a neutral context condition where subjects respond from target stimulus information without the prior, exhaustive sampling of the set of expectancies. Nevertheless, even if some inhibition effects are due to the use of incorrect target expectations, it is important to note that the presence of inhibition ought no longer to be considered diagnostic of the involvement of control processes in priming.

2. Inhibition and Resource Capacity

McLean and Shulman (1978) have further attempted to examine directly the relation between inhibitory priming effects with unmasked primes and resource capacity. They used a primed letter-matching task similar to that used by Posner and Snyder (1975b). Primes were presented for 100 msec, and subjects made a response to a visually presented target letter pair. Primes were informative (the probability of a match between the prime and the target letters was .67), and the stimulus onset asynchrony (SOA: the time between onset of the prime and that of the target) was either 100 or 500 msec. However, on half of the trials an auditory probe, rather than the target letter pair, was presented equiprobably to either ear, and subjects had to indicate the ear of presentation. Following the probe response, the target letter pair was presented. Subjects were instructed that the letter-matching task was of primary importance and that choice RT's to the auditory probe constituted the secondary task.

McLean and Shulman found that, in the primary letter-matching task, inhibition on "same" response trials when primes mismatched with targets increased as a function of SOA (see also Posner & Snyder, 1975b). In contrast, choice RT's to auditory probes preceded by letter primes were slower at the short SOA than at the long SOA, relative to when primes were neutral. If inhibition in the primary task reflects the misallocation of resource capacity, costs in the secondary task should show the same trends over time as costs in the primary task. Clearly, this was not the case. The finding demonstrates a dissociation between inhibitory priming effects and the allocation of resource capacity. The high cost to the secondary probe task at the short SOA suggests that resources are required for the processing of the prime; subsequently that demand lessens, and the cost in the secondary task decreases. The increasing cost effects in the primary task at the long SOA may well be related to the generation of incorrect target expectations. Thus it appears that the generation of target expectations is itself divorced from any demands on the resource capacity of the subject.

D. Searching for Words

One of the criteria defining an automatic process is that it can operate in parallel with other processes (Section I). A common way of examining this is to evaluate search times for a target as a function of the number of distractors in a display. Evidence for a positive slope in the RT–display size function is usually thought to indicate the involvement of control processes, either because only one element can be processed at a time or because the elements are processed in parallel but with limited capacity constraints (Shiffrin & Schneider, 1977). On the other hand, evidence for a flat RT–display size function is taken to indicate that the elements are processed in parallel and that this is not subject to capacity constraints: that is, that the target can be processed automatically.

Recent evaluation of search functions for words suggests that word identification is not an automatic process on the basis of the above criterion. Kahneman, Treisman, and Burkell (1983) examined RT's to **name** single words which could be presented in displays including varying numbers of nonsense shapes. The words were three letters in length, high frequency, and were presented in white. They could appear randomly at one of six locations in an approximately circular array. The nonsense shapes were red, they were as tall as the letters in the words, and they were presented in sets with the spacing between the elements in each set matching those between the letters in the words. Words were presented against a background of zero, one, two, or three shape sets. Kahneman *et al.* found that RT's to name the word yielded a positive slope as a function of the number of shape sets in the display (13.6 msec/item). This was not due to sensory interference between the target word and the shapes since RT's to **detect** the presence of the target were much shallower (3.4 msec/item). The fact that detecting the target gave rise to an almost flat RT–display size function is not surprising, given that its presence could be discriminated from its color (cf. Treisman & Gelade, 1980). For instance, the color difference between the target and the homogenous group of distractors may have enabled subjects to respond from a description provided by the whole stimulus array (consistent color vs inconsistent color). On the other hand, it appears that the requirement of having to make a unique discriminatory response (naming) to a member of the array forces subjects to search the array serially.

Other research also suggests that there may be dissociations between the criterion of serial processing and the definition of a control process as only encompassing one operation at a time. For instance, Ryan (quoted in Ryan, 1983) presented subjects with a fixed memory set of between 2 and 16 words to learn. They then undertook a memory search experiment in which they were also given a new (varied) memory set of between 2 and 6 words on each trial. Subjects were required to decide whether a subsequent probe word was a member of either set, or a member of neither. Ryan showed that, for memory sets of up to six elements, there were serial increases in RT's on positive trials for both the fixed and the varied memory sets; and the two functions differed only in their intercept values. That is, subjects were able to perform two serial searches concurrently: one for the fixed and one for the varied memory set. Similar evidence for concurrent serial searches through different types of information has been reported by Burrows and his associates (e.g., see Burrows & Okada, 1973, for searches of semantic and form information; Burrows & Okada, 1974, for searches of physical and categorical information; and Burrows & Solomon, 1975, for searches of auditory and visual information). These results indicate that it may be difficult to sustain a distinction between automatic and control processes on the basis of a set of converging criteria. Nevertheless, even taking serial search functions as one of the criteria for separating these processes, word identification cannot be classed as automatic.

IV. FUNCTIONAL AUTONOMY IN WORD PROCESSING

In Section III, I argued that there is evidence showing that:

1. Effects due apparently to the obligatory processing of words can be diluted by instructing subjects to attend to and process the words in particular ways (Section III,A,1 and III,A,2);

2. Letters and words processed unintentionally can interfere with responses to other stimuli (Section III,A,3);

3. Resources are demanded when subjects must make unique discriminatory responses to letters and words (Section III,B);

4. Inhibitory priming effects between word primes and targets are not necessarily indicative of the intentional use of prime information or of the involvement of resource capacity (Sections III,A,3 and III,C); also, those inhibition effects due to the generation of incorrect target expectations are not related to the misallocation of resource capacity (Section III,C);

5. Subjects required to make a unique discriminatory response to a word cannot process that word in parallel with other objects in the visual field (Section III,D).

This evidence indicates that word processing can be affected by the strategies adopted by subjects, it can be resource demanding, and it may not operate in parallel with other processes. Each of these attributes contradicts the claim for the automaticity of all processes up to and including word recognition and identification responses. It especially seems that the process of forming a unique discriminatory response to a word (or a letter) is not automatic; I have termed this process perceptual identification. There are some indications that processes prior to perceptual identification are also not automatic. For instance, there is evidence suggesting that when subjects do not attend to the area of visual field in which stimuli (words, letters) are presented, the stimuli fail to activate their internal representations fully (e.g., Hoffman et al., 1983; Smith, 1979); also, stimuli which do not require perceptual identification may nevertheless demand resources (Duncan, 1980b). However, this evidence is equivocal because either the experiments have not been sufficiently sensitive to pick up possible consequences of word processing (Section III,A,2), or it remains possible that stimuli which do not require perceptual identification (or even **cannot** be perceptually identified) may still compete for the resources required by this process (Section III,A,3). In fact, it may be that the claim that processes prior to perceptual identification are automatic cannot be refuted, because the perceptual identification of some stimulus is necessary in any experiment, any evidence against automaticity can be attributed to the demands of the perceptual identification process (Section III,A,3). If I am correct in this argument, then the claim for automaticity has no predictive power and, therefore, it may have little useful part to play in understanding the mechanisms of word processing.

The evidence discussed in Section III is also damaging to the automaticity argument in a further respect, because it suggests that the criteria defining automatic processes do not converge. For example, letters and words masked to prevent their identification cannot be processed intentionally yet they still seem to compete for processing resources (Humphreys, 1981a; Humphreys *et al.,* 1983; see Section III,B for similar direct evidence from dual task studies); also, the intentional use of prime information does not necessarily demand resources (Section III,C). Both of these findings indicate a dissociation between the criteria linking intentionality with resource capacity. Other work suggests dissociations between serial processing and the operation of only one process at a time (e.g., Ryan, 1983; Section III,D), and between practiced operations and their vulnerability to interference from other concurrent processes (Hoffman *et al.,* 1983; Section III,B). The criteria outlined in Section I, then, define discrete properties of information-processing functions (e.g., resource demanding or independent; serial or parallel; intentional or unintentional; practiced or novel), but they do not represent a single underlying attribute (namely, whether or not a process is automatic). As far as word processing is concerned, the nearest claim to the automaticity position that we can reliably make is that, under some circumstances (such as when we attend to its full spatial extent), word processing proceeds involuntarily. This, though, is not sufficient to define it as automatic: it is simply a particular property of the information-processing task.

Nevertheless, if word processing does proceed involuntarily on at least some occasions, there are some interesting implications concerning the control of such operations. For instance, one possibility is that control operates locally so that once a set of word-processing procedures is activated, it runs to completion and cannot be amended by other higher order processes (i.e., it is "cognitively inpenetrable"; see Pylyshyn, 1981). Such processes may be termed functionally autonomous (Forster, 1979). An implication of this is that word processing cannot be benefited by other ongoing processes (e.g., see Fodor, 1983). This is a different prediction from that which holds that the effects of word processing cannot be prevented (cf. the argument that processing is involuntary), since it is feasible that subjects are unable to prevent a particular process but they may still supplement it when required.

The degree to which the autonomy argument is interesting probably depends on the level of the processes involved. For instance, it may be of less theoretical interest to suggest that the processing of letter features is autonomous (and therefore cannot be benefited by higher order processes) than to suggest that the processes enabling words to activate their own lexical representations plus those of related words are autonomous. If the latter hypothesis were true then the word recognition system might be thought of as having certain knowledge hard wired into it, a consequence being that the effects of this knowledge will occur, irrespective of the likelihood created by particular sentence contexts, and they will influence a different level of processing to that affected by sentential information. In Section IV,A, some tentative evidence is discussed which suggests that both lexical activation and some context effects occur autonomously. A framework to accommodate both these and the previous results is outlined in Section IV,C.

A. Some Evidence for Functional Autonomy

Perhaps the primary criterion for defining an autonomous process concerns the locus of control; an autonomous process should **not** be controlled by high order processes (Fodor, 1983). Thus, an autonomous process should operate according to its own set of constraints,[7] and it should not be modified by higher order constraints created by novel contexts. Accordingly, one way to investigate whether certain processes in word recognition and identification in skilled readers operate autonomously is to evaluate whether word recognition is affected by novel sentence contexts.

The results of Fischler and Bloom (1979) are relevant here (see Section III,C). In their study of sentential context effects they found no overall facilitative effects on lexical decisions to target words preceded by related contexts, relative to when the context words were replaced by rows of X's. However, in a post hoc analysis they did show that a facilitative priming effect was present, but only with highly predictive sentences (when 91% of

---

[7]If this is the case, then a goal for future research will be to define how constraints come to be "built into" an autonomous process. For the present, I simply assume that this has taken place.

the subjects gave the same completion). It seems likely that such highly predictive sentences will contain words which have pre-established, associative relationships with target words; the facilitative priming effects may reflect these word-level relationships and not the constraints provided by sentence-level representations.

Other evidence from sentential priming studies which is consistent with the above argument has been presented by Stanovich and West (1983; West & Stanovich, 1982). Unlike Fischler and Bloom, Stanovich and West have tended to use related sentences containing words with pre-established relationships to target words (e.g., as assessed by association norms), and they have consistently found small beneficial effects on target responses in the related context condition relative to an unpredictive, neutral sentence context condition (e.g., "They said it was the ——"). These effects have been established with both lexical decision and naming tasks, which suggests that they are localized during the lexical access process[8] (cf. Section III,C).

One prediction from this is that word-level context effects should interact with a variable which affects the rate of lexical access, such as whether or not the target is degraded (cf. Sternberg, 1969). In studies of single word priming effects, the effect of degrading the target by reducing its intensity or by masking is to give rise to larger associative priming effects, consistent with the above argument (Becker & Killion, 1977; Meyer *et al.,* 1975). We may expect, then, word-level effects in studies of sentential priming to interact with target degradation, and degradation and sentence-level effects to be additive. Unfortunately, the data are equivocal on this point. Interactive effects of sentence contexts and target degradation have been reported in some cases (e.g., Stanovich & West, 1983) but not others (Schuberth, Spoehr, & Lane, 1981). It is tempting to speculate that these differences respectively reflect the presence and absence of word-level re-

---

[8]Forster (1981), using the sentences employed by Stanovich and West (1981), has replicated these findings when using a neutral sentence base line, but not when using a base line created by randomly permuting a set of words matched for length to sentence contexts. The choice of an appropriate base line for a cost–benefit analysis of priming is always problematical (see also Becker, this volume). Ideally, the base line should equate for the alerting properties of the context and its processing demands, while remaining unpredictive of the identity of the target (Fischler & Bloom, 1979). In studies of sentential priming, the use of a random word list context may induce a different strategy in subjects from that induced by an unpredictive sentence. For instance, a random word list prevents subjects from integrating the meanings of the context words, which may lessen processing demands. At this stage, it seems most appropriate to use a base line context which balances for as many properties of the related context as possible. It thus seems reasonable to use the unpredictive, neutral sentence context employed by Stanovich and West (1981, 1983).

lationships in the studies (present in Stanovich & West, 1983; but not in Schuberth *et al.*, 1981), but this requires verification.

A further complicating factor is that different effects may occur depending on the **type** of degradation used. For example, Stanovich and West (1983, Experiment 7) slowed target word naming by inserting asterisks between the letters. This increased the size of facilitatory sentential priming, and no inhibition effects were found when targets were unrelated to the sentence. In contrast, in another experiment (Stanovich & West, 1983, Experiment 6), they found that reducing the **contrast** of word targets both increased facilitatory priming effects and gave rise to inhibition effects on target naming when the sentence and target were unrelated. This suggests that different procedures may be invoked under these two forms of degradation. It seems likely that Stanovich and West's asterisk manipulation slowed down lexical access, and so enabled prior lexical activation to have a greater effect, without introducing data limitations. However, contrast reduction may involve data limitations, preventing the activation in lexical representations from reaching criterion levels. This may allow postlexical expectancies to determine responses. It is important to note here that while such expectancies may affect the processes involved in assigning a response to a stimulus (e.g., the order of interrogating candidate lexical information), they do **not** affect the level of lexical activation directly. Such expectancies therefore reflect **postlexical** processes.

Other evidence that postlexical biases affect lexical decisions to degraded targets has been reported by Schvaneveldt and McDonald (1981). They presented subjects with single word primes followed by a target word or nonword, to which a lexical decision was made. Nonwords could be orthographically similar to words associated to primes (e.g., *lion-tigar*). In one experiment, lexical decision latencies were measured and targets remained present until subjects responded. In another experiment, lexical decision accuracy was measured; targets were briefly presented and followed by a pattern mask. Schvaneveldt and McDonald found that, in both experiments, responses to word targets primed by associates were facilitated relative to when primes were neutral (a row of X's) or unrelated. When RT's were measured, there was no effect when primes were followed by nonwords orthographically similar to an associated word (e.g., *lion–tigar*), relative to when the prime was neutral (*xxxxx–tigar*). This suggests that, when targets are clearly presented, primes affect the lexical access of target words without inducing a response bias. On the other hand, evidence for such a bias was present when targets were masked and accuracy measured. Then, there was a tendency to make "word" responses to nonwords orthographically similar to associates of primes. For skilled readers, contexts can be effective by influencing the likelihood that partially activated lexical informaton will determine a response; however, this effect is separate from the word-level effects which occur with undegraded stimuli. Interestingly, it is possible that, in less skilled readers, lexical access is not stable enough for particular word representations to be activated consistently to criteria. Consequently, context effects may be highly dependent on postlexical strategies in such readers. This could account for why these readers show both large facilitatory and inhibitory sentence context effects (see Section II,D).

I have argued, then, that two forms of sentence context effect can be distinguished, and that effects on target lexical access are confined to when a pre-established relationship exists between the target and other words in the sentence. Postlexical effects may be introduced by degrading the target.[9] However, this distinction is to a large extent built on post hoc analysis of those sentence contexts which have facilitated target responses and those which have been ineffective. More direct evidence would be to show that word-level effects in sentence priming are not influenced by higher order determinants. In line with this argument, Stanovich and West (1983) showed that their sentence priming effects on target word naming were not affected by varying the predictive utility of the sentences (i.e., the likelihood that the sentences would be related to the target). Unfortunately, the interpretation of this result again rests on the inference that Stanovich and West manipulated word-level effects in their study; also, Becker (this volume) has found that sentence context effects on word naming can be influenced by instructing subjects to use contexts in particular ways, suggesting that some higher order effects may influence lexical access. To resolve these contradictions, converging evidence is needed to verify the particular process involved when sentence context effects occur (e.g., would Becker's effects be additive with different forms of target degradation?), and to manipulate sentence-level and word-level relationships directly.

One interesting study which has taken the latter step has been reported by Kleiman (1980). He presented subjects with incomplete sentences followed by a target word or nonword to which subjects made a lexical decision. Target words were either the standard completion given to the sentence, a word associated with the standard completion, or an unrelated word. In the associated and the unrelated condition, targets could also be either acceptable completions of the sentences (i.e., appropriate) or they could be anomalous completions (i.e., semantically and syntactically inappropriate). Table II contains examples of the type of stimuli used.

---

[9]The important factor seems to be whether or not data limitations are present, not the time available for postlexical effects to become effective (contrary to Posner & Snyder, 1975a), since Stanovich and West's (1983) asterisk manipulation slowed target naming down without apparently introducing bias effects.

TABLE II

Examples of the Conditions in Kleiman (1980)

1. **Acceptable completions**
   The cup was placed on the table (standard completion)
                        chair (associated with standard)
                        floor (unrelated to standard)
2. **Standard sentence control for anomalous sentences**
   The king of the beasts is the lion (standard completion)
3. **Derived anomalous sentences**
   The king of the beasts is the roar (associated with standard)
                        work (unrelated to standard)

Kleiman found that RT's to words which were standard completions of the sentences were faster than to words which were associated with these completions or which were unrelated. RT's to targets associated with the standard completions were also facilitated relative to the unrelated condition. Presumably, this is because any completions activated by words in the sentence further activate the representations of words to which they are associated. Importantly, the difference between the associated and the unrelated conditions was **additive** with the effects of sentence acceptability. That is, targets associated with standard completions were facilitated irrespective of whether they were an acceptable or an anomalous completion of the sentence. Another dissociation between sentence-level and word-level effects, but this time based on the influence of auditory sentences on visual word naming, has been reported by Seidenberg, Tanenhaus, Leiman, and Bienkowski (1982). Both studies illustrate that the constraints of novel sentential contexts can be independent of word-level priming effects. It remains possible that the results of Seidenberg *et al.* are specific to auditory sentence processing, and that Kleiman's results reflect postlexical involvements in the lexical decision task; nevertheless, the findings are consistent with the argument that both lexical access and the activation of the lexical representations of related words are functionally autonomous in skilled readers.

B. Autonomy and Automaticity

The concepts of autonomy and automaticity overlap to the extent that both autonomous and automatic processes should occur involuntarily given the appropriate conditions, and that both must develop through extensive practice. However, while the term automatic implies that a process operates in parallel with other concurrent processes and that it does not demand resource capacity (Section I), the concept of autonomy does not encompass these broader issues. It is quite possible that an autonomous process may not operate in parallel with other processes and that it does demand resource capacity. In the final section, I outline a framework for word processing which holds that lexical access, and the activation of related representations, are autonomous, though both may involve the use of some resources.

C. A Two-Level Framework for Word Processing

Recently, a number of theorists have suggested that visual information processing can be categorized into two broad stages (Duncan, 1980b; Hoffman, 1979; Hoffman *et al.,* 1983; Kahneman & Treisman, 1983). Although proposals differ about the type of information represented at these stages, the common suggestion is that the first stage makes available data-driven representations, and that these representations may subsequently be translated into an episodic representation (the second stage), which can form the basis of a unique discriminatory response. The transition between these stages involves a limited-capacity process which operates serially on the data-driven representations.

1. Level One

At the first level, words are processed sufficiently to activate their lexical representations plus the representations of other words with which they share a well-learned relationship. These processes may demand some resources, as suggested by the interference effects which occur when stimuli do not need to be (Duncan, 1980b) or cannot be perceptually identified (Humphreys *et al.,* 1983). Representation at this level occurs autonomously in skilled readers; that is, it operates independently of higher order constraints and pragmatic knowledge (Section IV,B). One implication of this is that we need to distinguish between different forms of stored knowledge and their operation in reading. According to the evidence of a dissociation between word-level associative priming effects and sentence-level effects (Kleiman, 1980), associative knowledge is represented independently of pragmatic knowledge. In terms of the present framework, associative relations are represented at the first level while pragmatic knowledge is represented at the second. Also represented at the first level are the stored abstract orthographic description appropriate to a particular word (Evett & Humphreys, 1981) and the stored phonological description (Humphreys *et al.,* 1982).

Importantly, although words contact their stored representations at the first level, this information is not available for a unique discriminatory response; representation at the second level must be achieved before this is possible (see also Duncan, 1980b). Also, the activation present in first-level representations may decay very rapidly and/or it may be overridden by activation from other subsequent stimuli; consequently, priming based on such activation may only occur when the stimuli are presented in rapid succession (Humphreys *et al.*, 1983). Because of the above constraints, the recovery of first-level information is time limited, making it vulnerable to masking. This accounts for reports that associative, orthographic, and phonological priming effects can occur even when subjects fail to recover sufficient prime information to make a unique discriminatory response, due to masking conditions (Evett & Humphreys, 1981; Humphreys *et al.*, 1982).

2. Level Two

Representation at the second level is based upon the formation of an episodic representation of a word. Second-level representations can be stored, rehearsed, and translated to provide a unique discriminatory response. At this level, word meaning may be integrated into higher order descriptions operating above the single-word level (Forster, 1979). Accordingly, second-level representations are affected by the congruity of words with higher order textual and pragmatic knowledge (Kleiman, 1980), and they are affected by depth-of-processing manipulations (Jacoby & Dallas, 1981). However, nonelaborated episodic representations may also persist for considerable time periods, forming the basis for long-lasting repetition priming effects (Humphreys *et al.*, 1983; Jacoby, 1983).

As with first-level representations, there are probably resource constraints involved in the construction and maintenance of second-level representations (e.g., Baddeley, 1979; Britton, Westbrook & Holdredge, 1978; Daneman & Carpenter, 1980); however, first- and second-level resource constraints are independent (Johnson *et al.*, 1983).

3. Perceptual Identification

The processes governing the translation of tacit, first-level representations into explicit, second-level representations, termed perceptual identification here, appear limited to operating on only one stimulus at a time. Thus, subjects produce serial search functions when given the task of naming a word presented in a random array of shapes, even when the word and the shapes differ in color (Kahneman *et al.*, 1983); the detection of two data-limited targets is superior when they are presented successively relative to when they occur simultaneously (Duncan, 1980b); and Stroop interference is diluted when subjects perceptually identify a neutral stimulus rather than the interfering color word (Kahneman & Chajczyk, 1983).

However, the parameters determining how perceptual identification occurs remain obscure (Marcel, 1983b; Turvey, 1974). Some insights here may come from the study of event perception. In order for the perceptual identification of a word to occur, the word must be segmented as an event separate from extraneous background stimuli. To understand perceptual identification we need to specify which cues determine the segmentation process.

To illustrate this, consider another result from the experiment of Humphreys *et al.* (1983) reported in Section III,A,2: namely, the finding that the identification of a data-limited, upper case target word was very poor when it was preceded by a relatively long exposure of the same word in lower case (the immediate repeat condition with an unmasked prime). In this condition subjects typically reported that they found it difficult to discriminate whether any target had been presented, and they made a written response to only the lower case prime. This result may have occurred because letter case was difficult to identify under the data-limited conditions (Adams, 1979; Coltheart & Freeman, 1974; Friedman, 1981; Pillsbury, 1897), and, consequently, there were few cues available to segment primes and targets.

To test whether the poor performance was due to poor segmentation, we conducted a further experiment in which unmasked primes were presented for 200 msec and followed by a pattern mask for 100 msec. Targets were briefly presented and backward pattern-masked immediately following the offset of the first (100-msec) mask. Primes were again in lower case and targets were in upper case. These presentation conditions differ from the earlier presentation conditions only in that there is a mask interposed between the prime and the target, though the interval between the onsets of the prime and the target are the same. If the difficulty in target identification in the immediate repeat condition occurred because subjects found primes and targets difficult to segment, the interposition of a mask between the stimuli might facilitate target identification. There were three priming conditions: primes and targets were the same word (immediate repeat); primes and targets were orthographically similar words (one letter change); and primes and targets were unrelated.[10] Subjects were asked to write down both words on a trial in the case the words were presented in.

Table III shows the percentage correct target identifications in the three priming conditions. Primes were always correctly identified.

The results are quite clear. Target identification was facilitated in the immediate repeat condition relative to the orthographically similar and unrelated word conditions, which did not differ. Thus, interposing a mask between the prime and target reinstated the immediate repetition effect. This demonstrates that the segmentation of stimuli is critical to their per-

---

[10]The condition with orthographically similar primes and targets was introduced to try and minimize the strategy of guessing that primes and targets were identical following the detection that there was at least one letter in common.

TABLE III

Percentage Correct Target Identifications with *Unmasked* Prime and Interpolated Mask, in Humphreys *et al.* (1983)

Condition	Percentage correct
1. Immediate repeat e.g., *bent–BENT*	76.04
2. Orthographically similar word prime e.g., *beat–BENT*	59.79
3. Unrelated word prime e.g., *dark–BENT*	60.42

ceptual identification; accordingly, the presentation of an extraneous stimulus may facilitate performance if it provides further cues to segment the target from its background.

Interestingly, if the prime preactivates the input lexical representation of the target in the immediate repeat condition, the result also demonstrates that this activation is not sufficient to facilitate performance; there must also be cues to suggest the presence of the target event. From the resultant facilitation when the stimuli are repeats, we may suspect that the episodic representation achieved by the prime influences the perceptual identification of the data-limited target. For instance, it may affect the response assigned to the partial information offered up by first-level representations (see also Section IV,B for a similar argument). It is also possible that perceptual identification is influenced by second-level representations even when targets are not degraded. Under circumstances where subjects generate expectancies of targets they may attempt to match the expectancies with first-level representations of targets prior to perceptually identifying them solely from stimulus information (Section III,C; Becker, this volume). Thus it is suggested that perceptual identification can be influenced either by stimulus factors alone (e.g., intensity, affecting first-level representations) or by an interaction between stimulus and higher order information (expectancies determined by second-level representations).

Of course the cues governing the segmentation of words in briefly presented visual displays will differ radically from the segmentation cues available for readers processing a page of printed text. Nevertheless, many of the lessons may be the same: segmentation may determine perceptual identification, and when segmentation cues are reduced, higher order information may guide the segmentation process (Fisher & Lefton, 1976; Hochberg, 1970).

Perceptual identification may also operate at different levels of structural description. Subjects may perceptually identify the features in letters, the letters in words, whole words, or even larger structures. The crucial point is that second-level representations are achieved only at the level of the perceptually identified structural descriptions. Thus a description of a visual array in which a target word is a component will allow subjects to assign a discriminatory response to the array but not the word; this would enable a response to be made from the global array description (e.g., color change or not), but not to the word's identity. When perceptual identification of the word is required each array element must be treated as a separate perceptual object (cf. Kahneman *et al.,* 1983). Also, when subjects search for letters in words, perceptual identification of component letters will preclude the simultaneous achievement of second-level representation for the word, particularly when subjects know the location of the target letter. The extent to which this would influence performance will be determined by whether performance is primarily affected by first- or second-level representations. For instance, consider the word superiority effect (the superior identification of letters in words compared to nonwords) which occurs when subjects have to identify a letter in a briefly presented word or nonword. This may depend on the achievement of a second-level representation of a word based on partially activated first-level representations, and on the use of this second-level representation in the perceptual identification of the target letter. Prespecifying the location of the target letter may limit the second-level representation of the word, eliminating the effect (Johnston & McClelland, 1974).

The evidence on the dilution of word priming effects under letter search conditions further suggests that the perceptual identification of letters in words may prohibit the activation of whole word first-level representations (Section III,A,2). However, as noted earlier, this evidence may have been obtained using conditions only sensitive to second-level representations, so it remains feasible that first-level representations are immune to the influence of higher order processes on perceptual identification. Clearly, though, this position would have to be amended if it turns out that word priming is eliminated under letter search instructions even with very short prime–target intervals. We may, for instance, need to distinguish between the effects of instructions to attend to particular spatial regions, which might affect first-level representations, and the effects of higher order contextual knowledge, which affects only perceptual identification and first-level representations.[11]

[11]Interestingly, Allport, Tipper, and Chmiel (1985) and Hoffman and MacMillan (1985) have both recently presented data suggesting that access to what I have termed first level representations is not constrained by higher level processes. Thus priming effects from one stimulus on another can occur even when subjects do not attend to the spatial region where primes are presented. These priming effects can be indicated by slow responding to subsequent stimuli which are related to to-be-ignored primes. The results are consistent with the idea that perceptually identifying another stimulus and ignoring the prime is resource limited (at least in the sense that it can take place for only one stimulus at a time), with the result that the representations of stimuli competing for perceptual identification are in some way temporarily suppressed.

D. Some Concluding Remarks

In the above section, I outlined a broad framework to accommodate the major effects due to manipulations of subject strategies or resources on visual word processing. The levels of representation distinguished by this framework are not meant to be thought of as irreducible modules, but rather as incorporating a range of processes which can be distinguished in terms of the factors controlling their operation. The operation of first-level representations is controlled by data-driven constraints[12]; the operation of second-level representations can be controlled by higher order constraints (pragmatic knowledge, instructions, etc.). It is almost certain that processes within these levels will fractionate (as evidenced by the effects of brain damage on performance; Coltheart, 1981; Patterson, 1981, 1982); this, though, need not invalidate the distinction.

Whether or not this framework proves to be correct, my suggestion is that word processing is better conceptualized as **autonomous** rather than automatic, since the autonomy argument provides both a better account of the data and a better heuristic for research. This is because the specification of an autonomous process demands the detailing of a processing mechanism (e.g., one which operates using local control), whereas automatic process can be specified by default (i.e., not a control process). The detailing of such processing mechanisms is necessary if we are to make progress.

ACKNOWLEDGMENTS

This article was supported by a grant from the Social Science Research Council. It was, in part, prepared while the author was visiting Waterloo University, Ontario, with aid of grants from the Natural Sciences and Engineering Research Council of Canada to Derek Besner and Philip Merikle. I would like to thank the Department of Psychology, Waterloo University, for their facilities. Derek Besner, Philip Quinlan, and Jane Riddoch provided helpful discussion and comments on the article.

REFERENCES

Adams, M. J. (1979). Models of word recognition. *Cognitive Psychology,* **11,** 133–176.
Allport, D. A. (1977). On knowing the meaning of words we are unable to report: The effects of visual masking. In S. Dornic (Ed.), *Attention and performance VI.* Potomac, Md: Erlbaum.
Allport, D. A. (1980). Attention and performance. In G. Claxton (Ed.), *Cognitive psychology: New Directions.* London: Routledge & Kegan Paul.
Allport, D. A., Tipper, S. P., & Chmiel, N. R. J. (1985). Perceptual integration and post-

[12]Though individuals will differ in the types of stored knowledge which can be represented at this level, the factors controlling the operation of first-level processes will be the same.

categorical filtering. In M. I. Posner & O. S. M. Marin (Eds.), *Attention and performance XI*. Hillsdale, NJ: Lawrence Erlbaum Associates.

Antos, S. J. (1979). Processing facilitation in a lexical decision task. *Journal of Experimental Psychology: Human Perception and Performance, 5,* 572-545.

Baddeley, A. D. (1979). Working memory and reading. In P. A. Kolers, M. E. Wrolstad, & H. Bouma (Eds.), *Processing of visible language* (Vol 1). New York: Plenum.

Balota, D. A. (1983). Automatic semantic activation and episodic memory encoding. *Journal of Verbal Learning and Verbal Behavior, 22,* 88-104.

Becker, C. A. (1976). Allocation of attention during word recognition. *Journal of Experimental Psychology: Human Perception and Performance, 2,* 556-566.

Becker, C. A. (1985). What do we really know about context effects? In D. Besner, T. G. Waller, & G. E. MacKinnon (Eds.), *Reading research: Advances in theory and practice* (Vol 5). New York: Academic Press.

Becker, C. A., & Killion, T. H. (1977). Interaction of visual and cognitive effects in word recognition. *Journal of Experimental Psychology: Human Perception and Performance, 3,* 389-401.

Besner, D. (1983). Basic decoding processes in reading: Two dissociable feature extraction processes. *Canadian Journal of Psychology, 37,* 429-438.

Besner, D., & Swan, M. (1982). Models of lexical access in visual word recognition. *Quarterly Journal of Experimental Psychology, 34A,* 313-325.

Britton, B. K., Westbrook, R. D., & Holdredge, T. S. (1978). Reading and cognitive capacity usage: Effects of text difficulty. *Journal of Experimental Psychology: Human Learning and Memory, 4,* 583-591.

Broadbent, D. E. (1982). Task combination and selective intake of information. *Acta Psychologia, 50,* 253-290.

Burrows, D., & Okada, R. (1973). Parallel scanning of semantic and formal information. *Journal of Experimental Psychology, 97,* 254-257.

Burrows, D., & Okada, R. (1974). Scanning temporarily structured lists: Evidence for dual retrieval processes. *Memory & Cognition, 2,* 441-446.

Burrows, D., & Solomon, B. A. (1975). Parallel scanning of visual and auditory information. *Memory & Cognition, 3,* 416-420.

Coltheart, M. (1981). Disorders of reading and their implications for models of normal reading. *Visible Language, 15,* 245-286.

Coltheart, M., & Freeman, R. (1974). Case alternation impairs word identification. *Bulletin of the Psychonomic Society, 3,* 102-104.

Daneman, M., & Carpenter, P. A. (1980). Individual differences in working memory and reading. *Journal of Verbal Learning and Verbal Behavior, 19,* 450-466.

De Groot, A. M. B. (1984). Primed lexical decision: Combined effects of the proportion of related prime-target pairs and the stimulus onset asynchrony of prime and target. *Quarterly Journal of Experimental Psychology, 36A,* 253-280.

De Groot, A. M. B., Thomassen, A. J. W. M., & Hudson, P. T. W. (1982). Associative facilitation of word recognition as measured from a neutral prime. *Memory & Cognition, 10,* 358-370.

Duncan, J. (1980a). The demonstration of capacity limitation. *Cognitive Psychology, 12,* 75-96.

Duncan, J. (1980b). The locus of interference in the perception of simultaneous stimuli. *Psychological Review, 87,* 272-300.

Dyer, F. H. (1973). The Stroop phenomenon and its use in the study of perceptual, cognitive and response processes. *Memory & Cognition, 1,* 106-120.

Egeth, H., & Pachella, R. (1969). Multidimensional stimulus identification. *Perception & Psychophysics*, **5**, 341–346.

Eriksen, C. W., & Hoffman, J. E. (1972). Temporal and spatial characteristics of selective encoding from visual displays. *Perception & Psychophysics*, **12**, 201–204.

Evett, L. J. & Humphreys, G. W. (1981). The use of abstract graphemic information in lexical access. *Quarterly Journal of Experimental Psychology*, **33A**, 325–350.

Evett, L. J., Humphreys, G. W., & Quinlan, P. T. (1984). *Orthographic segmentation processes in visual word identification*. Paper presented to the Experimental Psychology Society, Amsterdam.

Fischler, I., & Bloom, P. A. (1979). Automatic and attentional processes in the effects of sentence contexts on word recognition. *Journal of Verbal Learning and Verbal Behavior*, **18**, 1–20.

Fischler, I., & Bloom, P. A. (1980). Rapid processing of the meaning of sentences. *Memory & Cognition*, **8**, 216–225.

Fischler, I., & Goodman, G. O. (1978). Latency of facilitation in memory, *Journal of Experimental Psychology: Human Perception and Performance*, **4**, 455–470.

Fisher, D. F., & Lefton, L. A. (1976). Peripheral information extraction: A developmental examination of reading processes. *Journal of Experimental Child Psychology*, **21**, 77–93.

Flom, M. C., Weymouth, F. W., & Kahneman, D. (1963). Visual resolution and contour interaction. *Journal of the Optical Society of America*, **53**, 1026–1032.

Fodor, J. A. (1983). *The modularity of mind: An essay on faculty psychology*. Cambridge, Mass.: MIT Press.

Forbes, S. M., Taylor, M. M., & Lindsay, P. H. (1967). Cue timing in a multi-dimensional detection task. *Perceptual and Motor Skills*, **25**, 113–120.

Forster, K. I. (1976). Accessing the internal lexicon. In R. J. Wales & E. C. T. Walker (Eds.), *New approches to language mechanisms*. Amsterdam: North Holland Publ.

Forster, I. I. (1979). Levels of processing and the structure of the language processor. In W. E. Cooper & E. Walker (Eds.), *Sentence processing; Psycholinguistic studies presented to Merrill Garrett*. Hillsdale, N.J.: Erlbaum.

Forster, K. I. (1981). Priming and the effects of sentence and lexical contexts on naming time: Evidence for autonomous lexical processing. *Quarterly Journal of Experimental Psychology*, **33A**, 465–495.

Fowler, C. A., Wolford, G., Slade, R., & Tassinary, L. (1981). Lexical access with and without awareness. *Journal of Experimental Psychology: General*, **110**, 341–362.

Friedman, R. B. (1980). Identification without form: Abstract representations of letters. *Perception & Psychophysics*, **28**, 53–60.

Gatti, S. V., & Egeth, H. E. (1978). Failure of spatial selectivity in vision. *Bulletin of the Psychonomic Society*, **11**, 181–184.

Gough, P. B., Alford, J. A., & Holley-Wilcox, P. (1981). Words and contexts. In O. J. L. Tzeng & H. Singer (Eds.), *Perception of print: Reading research in experimental psychology*. Hillsdale, N.J.: Erlbaum.

Hasher, L., & Zacks, R. T. (1979). Automatic and effortful processes in memory. *Journal of Experimental Psychology: General*, **108**, 356–388.

Hillinger, M. L. (1980). Priming effects with phonemically similar words: The encoding-bias hypothesis reconsidered. *Memory & Cognition*, **8**, 115–123.

Hirst, E. S., Spelke, C. C., Reaves, G., Caharack, G., & Neisser, U. (1980). Dividing attention without alternation or automaticity. *Journal of Experimental Psychology: General*, **109**, 98–117.

Hochberg, J. (1970). Components of literacy: Speculation and exploratory research. In H. Levin & J. P. Williams (Eds.), *Basic studies on reading.* New York: Basic Books.

Hoffman, J. E. (1979). A two-stage model of visual search. *Perception & Psychophysics, 29,* 319–327.

Hoffman, J. E., & MacMillan, F. W. III (1985). Is semantic priming automatic? In M. I. Posner & O. S. M. Marin (Eds.), *Attention and performance XI.* Hillsdale, NJ: Lawrence Erlbaum Associates.

Hoffman, J. E., Nelson, B., & Houck, M. R. (1983). The role of attentional resources in automatic detection. *Cognitive Psychology, 51,* 379–410.

Humphreys, G. W. (1978). The use of category information in perception. *Perception, 7,* 589–604.

Humphreys, G. W. (1979). *Conscious and unconscious priming: Facilitation and inhibition in the recognition of alphanumeric stimuli.* Unpublished doctoral dissertation, Bristol University.

Humphreys, G. W. (1981a). Direct vs indirect tests of the information available from masked displays: What visual masking does and does not prevent. *British Journal of Psychology, 72,* 323–330.

Humphreys, G. W. (1981b). On varying the span of visual attention: Evidence for two modes of spatial attention. *Quarterly Journal of Experimental Psychology, 33A,* 17–30.

Humphreys, G. W., Evett, L. J., & Taylor, D. E. (1982). Automatic phonological priming in visual word recognition. *Memory & Cognition, 10,* 576–590.

Humphreys, G. W., Quinlan, P. T., & Besner, D. (1983). *Word repetition effects with masked and unmasked primes.* Paper presented to the Experimental Psychology Society, Oxford.

Jacoby, L. L. (1983). Perceptual enhancement: Persistent effects of an experience. *Journal of Experimental Psychology: Learning, Memory and Cognition, 9,* 21–38.

Jacoby, L. L., & Dallas, M. (1981). On the relationship between autobiographical memory and perceptual learning. *Journal of Experimental Psychology: General, 110,* 306–340.

James, C. T. (1975). The role of semantic information in lexical decision. *Journal of Experimental Psychology: Human Perception and Performance, 1,* 130–136.

Johnson, P. J., Forester, J. A., Calderwood, R., & Weisgerber, S. A. (1983). Resource allocation and the attentional demands of letter encoding. *Journal of Experimental Psychology: General, 112,* 616–638.

Johnston, J. C., & McClelland, J. L. (1974). Perception of letters in words: Seek not and ye shall find. *Science, 184,* 1192–1194.

Kahneman, D. (1973). *Attention and effort.* New York: Prentice-Hall.

Kahneman, D., & Chajczyk, D. (1983). Tests of the automaticity of reading: Dilution of Stroop effects by color-irrelevant stimuli. *Journal of Experimental Psychology: Human Perception and Performance, 9,* 497–509.

Kahneman, D., & Henik, A. (1981). Perceptual organization and attention. In M. Kubovy & J. R. Pomerantz (Eds.), *Perceptual organization.* Hillsdale, N.J.: Erlbaum.

Kahneman, D., & Treisman, A. (1983). Changing views of attention and automaticity. In R. Parasuraman, R. Davies, & J. Beatty (Eds.), *Varieties of attention,* New York: Academic Press.

Kahneman, D., Treisman, A., & Burkell, J. (1983). The cost of visual filtering. *Journal of Experimental Psychology: Human Perception and Performance, 9,* 510–522.

Keele, S. W. (1972). Attention demands of memory retrieval. *Journal of Experimental Psychology, 93,* 245–248.

Kleiman, G. M. (1980). Sentence frame contexts and lexical decisions: Sentence-acceptability and word-relatedness effects. *Memory & Cognition, 8,* 336, 344.

Klein, G. S. (1964). Semantic power measured through the interference of words with color-naming. *American Journal of Psychology, 77,* 576–588.

Krueger, L. E., & Weiss, M. E. (1976). Letter search through words and nonwords: The effect of fixed, absent or mutilated targets. *Memory & Cognition, 4,* 200–206.

Kucera, H., & Francis, W. M. (1967). *Computational analysis of present-day American English.* Providence, R.I.: Brown Univ. Press.

Laberge, D. (1973). Attention and the measurement of perceptual learning. *Memory & Cognition, 1,* 268–276.

Laberge, D., & Samuels, S. J. (1974). Toward a theory of automatic information processing in reading. *Cognitive Psychology, 6,* 293–323.

Logan, G. D. (1979). On the use of a concurrent memory load to measure attention and automaticity. *Journal of Experimental Psychology: Human Perception and Performance, 5,* 189–207.

Lowe, D. G., & Mitterer, J. O. (1982). Selective divided attention in a Stroop task. *Canadian Journal of Psychology, 36,* 684–700.

McLean, J. P., & Shulman, G. L. (1978). On the construction and maintenance of expectancies. *Quarterly Journal of Experimental Psychology, 30,* 441–454.

Marcel, A. J. (1980). Conscious and preconscious recognition of polysemous words: Locating the selective effects of prior verbal context. In R. S. Nickerson (Ed.), *Attention and performance VIII.* Hillsdale, N.J.: Erlbaum.

Marcel, A. J. (1983a). Conscious and unconscious perception: Experiments on visual masking and word recognition. *Cognitive Psychology, 15,* 197–237.

Marcel, A. J. (1983b). Conscious and unconscious perception: An approach to the relations between phenomenal experience and perceptual processes. *Cognitive Psychology, 15,* 238–300.

Merikle, P. M. (1982). Unconscious perception revisited. *Perception & Psychophysics, 31,* 298–301.

Meyer, D. E., Schvaneveldt, R. W., & Ruddy, M. G. (1975). Loci of contextual effects on visual word recognition. In P. M. A. Rabbitt & S. Dornic (Eds.), *Attention and Performance, V.* New York: Academic Press.

Moray, N. (1975). A data base for theories of selective listening. In P. M. A. Rabbitt & S. Dornic (Eds.), *Attention and Performance, V.* New York: Academic Press.

Morton, J. (1969). Interaction of information in word recognition. *Psychological Review, 76,* 165–178.

Myers, J. L., & Lorch, R. F., Jr. (1980). Interference and facilitation effects of primes upon verification processes, *Memory & Cognition, 8,* 405–414.

Navon, D., & Gopher, D. (1979). On the economy of the human processing system. *Psychological Review, 86,* 214–255.

Neely, J. H. (1976). Semantic priming and retrieval from lexical memory: Evidence for facilitatory and inhibitory processes. *Memory & Cognition, 4,* 648–654.

Neely, J. H. (1977). Semantic priming and retrieval from lexical memory: The roles of inhibitionless spreading activation and limited-capacity attention. *Journal of Experimental Psychology: General, 106,* 226–254.

Nissen, M. J. (1977). Stimulus intensity and information processing. *Perception & Psychophysics, 22,* 338–352.

Norman, D. A., & Bobrow, D. G. (1975). On data-limited and resource-limited processes. *Cognitive Psychology, 7,* 44–64.

Ogden, W. C., Martin, D. W., & Paap, K. R. (1980). Processing demands of encoding; What does secondary task performance reflect? *Journal of Experimental Psychology: Human Perception and Performance, 6,* 355–367.

Paap, K. R., & Ogden, W. C. (1981). Letter encoding is an obligatory but capacity-demanding operation. *Journal of Experimental Psychology: Human Perception and Performance, 7,* 518–527.

Parkin, A. J. (1979). Specifying levels of processing. *Quarterly Journal of Experimental Psychology.* **31,** 179–195.

Patterson, K. E. (1981). Neuropsychological approaches to the study of reading. *British Journal of Psychology,* **72,** 151–174.

Patterson, K. E. (1982). The relation between reading and phonological coding: Further neuropsychological observations. In A. W. Ellis (Ed.), *Normality and pathology in cognitive functioning.* New York: Academic Press.

Perfetti, C. A., Goldman, S. R., & Hogaboam, T. W. (1979). Reading skill and the identification of words in discourse context. *Memory & Cognition,* **7,** 273–282.

Perfetti, C. A., & Roth, S. (1981). Some of the interactive processes in reading and their role in reading skill. In A. M. Lesgold & C. A. Perfetti (Eds.), *Interactive processes in reading.* Hillsdale, N.J.: Erlbaum.

Pillsbury, W. B. (1897). A study in apperception. *American Journal of Psychology,* **8,** 315–393.

Pohlman, L. D., & Sorkin, R. D. (1976). Simultaneous three-channel signal detection: Performance and criterion as a function of order of report. *Perception & Psychophysics,* **20,** 179–186.

Posner, M. I. (1978). *Chronometric explorations of mind.* Hillsdale, N.J.: Erlbaum.

Posner, M. I. (1980). Orienting of attention. *Quarterly Journal of Experimental Psychology,* **32,** 3–25.

Posner, M. I., & Boies, S. J. (1971). Components of attention. *Psychological Review,* **78,** 391–408.

Posner, M. I., & Snyder, C. R. R. (1975a). Attention and cognitive control. In R. L. Solso (Ed.), *Information processing and cognition: The Loyola symposium.* Hillsdale, N.J.: Erlbaum.

Posner, M. I., & Snyder, C. R. R. (1975b). Facilitation and inhibition in the processing of signals. In P. M. A. Rabbitt & S. Dornic (Eds.), *Attention and performance V.* New York: Academic Press.

Purcell, D. G., & Stewart, A. L. (1974). Backward masking by pattern mask: Effect of adaptation and target energy. *Bulletin of the Psychonomic Society,* **3,** 137–138.

Purcell, D. G., Stewart, A. L., & Stanovich, K. E. (1983). Another look at semantic priming without awareness. *Perception & Psychophysics,* **34,** 65–71.

Pylyshyn, Z. W. (1981). The imagery debate: Analogue media versus tacit knowledge. *Psychological Review,* **88,** 16–45.

Ryan, C. (1983). Reassessing the automaticity–control distinction: Item recognition as a paradigm case. *Psychological Review,* **90,** 171–178.

Scarborough, D. L., Cortese, C., & Scarborough, H. S. (1977). Frequency and repetition effects in lexical memory. *Journal of Experimental Psychology: Human Perception and Performance,* **3,** 1–17.

Scarborough, D. L., Gerard, L., & Cortese, C. (1979). Accessing lexical memory: The transfer of word repetition effects across task and modality. *Memory & Cognition,* **7,** 3–12.

Schneider, W., & Shiffrin, R. M. (1977). Controlled and automatic human information processing: I. Detection, search and attention. *Psychological Review,* **84,** 1, 66.

Schuberth, R. E., Spoehr, K. T., & Lane, D. M. (1981). Effects of stimulus and contextual information on the lexical decison process. *Memory & Cognition,* **9,** 68–77.

Schvaneveldt, R. W., & McDonald, J. E. (1981). Semantic context and the encoding of words: Evidence for two modes of stimulus analysis. *Journal of Experimental Psychology: Human Perception and Performance,* **7,** 673–687.

Schvaneveldt, R. W., Meyer, D. E., & Becker, C. A. (1976). Lexical ambiguity, semantic context and visual word recognition. *Journal of Experimental Psychology,* **2,** 243–256.

Seidenberg, M. S., Tanenhaus, M. K., Leiman, J. M., & Bienkowski, M. (1982). Automatic access of the meaning of ambiguous words in context: Some limitations of knowledge-based processing. *Cognitive Psychology, 14,* 489–537.

Seymour, P. H. K. (1977). Conceptual encoding and locus of the Stroop effect. *Quarterly Journal of Experimental Psychology, 29,* 245–265.

Shiffrin, R. M., & Dumais, S. T. (1981). The development of automatism. In J. R. Anderson (Ed.), *Cognitive skills and their acquisition.* Hillsdale, N.J.: Erlbaum.

Shiffrin, R. M., & Gardner, G. T. (1972). Visual processing capacity and attentional control. *Journal of Experimental Psychology, 93,* 72–83.

Shiffrin, R. M., & Schneider, W. (1977). Controlled and automatic human information processing: II. Perceptual learning, automatic attending and a general theory. *Psychological Review, 84,* 127–190.

Shulman, H. G., & Davison, T. C. B. (1977). Control properties of semantic coding in a lexical decision task. *Journal of Verbal Learning and Verbal Behavior, 16,* 91–98.

Shulman, H. G., Hornak, R., & Sanders, E. (1978). The effects of graphemic, phonetic, and semantic relationships on access to lexical structures. *Memory & Cognition, 6,* 115–123.

Smith, M. C. (1979). Contextual facilitation in a letter search task depends on how the prime is processed. *Journal of Experimental Psychology: Human Perception and Performance, 5,* 239–251.

Smith, M. C., Theodor, L., & Franklin, P. E. (1983). The relationship between contextual facilitation and depth of processing. *Journal of Experimental Psychology: Learning, Memory and Cognition, 9,* 697–712.

Stanovich, K. E. (1980). Toward an interactive-compensatory model of individual differences in the development of reading fluency. *Reading Research Quarterly, 16,* 32–71.

Stanovich, K. E., & West, R. F. (1981). The effect of sentence context on ongoing word recognition: Tests of a two-process theory. *Journal of Experimental Psychology: Human Perception and Performance, 7,* 658–672.

Stanovich, K. E., & West, R. F. (1983). On priming a sentence context. *Journal of Experimental Psychology: General, 112,* 1–36.

Sternberg, S. (1969). The discovery of processing stages: Extensions of Donder's method. In W. G. Koster (Ed.), *Attention and performance, II.* Amsterdam: North Holland Publ.

Sternberg, S. (1969). The discovery of processing stages: Extensions of Donder's method. In W. G. Koster (Ed.), *Attention and performance, II.* Amsterdam: North Holland Publ.

Stroop, J. R. (1935). Studies of interference in serial verbal reactions. *Journal of Experimental Psychology, 18,* 643–661.

Taylor, D. E. (1982). *Automatic processes in word recognition.* Unpublished doctoral dissertation, Bristol University.

Theios, J., & Muise, J. G. (1977). The word identification process in reading. In N. J. Castellan, D. B. Pisoni, & G. R. Potts (Eds.), *Cognitive theory* (Vol 2). Hillsdale, N.J.: Erlbaum.

Treisman, A. (1969). Strategies and models of selective attention. *Psychological Review, 76,* 282–289.

Treisman, A., & Gelade, G. (1980). A feature-integration theory of attention. *Cognitive Psychology, 12,* 197–236.

Turvey, M. T. (1974). Constructive theory, perceptual systems and tacit knowledge. In W. B. Weimer & D. S. Palermo (Eds.), *Perceiving, acting and knowing: Toward an ecological psychology.* Hillsdale, N.J.: Erlbaum.

Underwood, G., & Bargh, K. (1982). Word shape, orthographic regularity, and contextual interactions in a reading task. *Cognition, 12,* 197–209.

Warren, R. E. (1974). Association, directionality and stimulus encoding. *Journal of Experimental Psychology, 102,* 151–158.

West, R. F., & Stanovich, K. E. (1978). Automatic contextual facilitation in readers of three ages. *Child Development,* **49,** 717-727.

West, R. F., & Stanovich, K. E. (1982). Source of inhibition in experiments on the effect of sentence context on word recognition. *Journal of Experimental Psychology: Learning, Memory and Cognition,* **8,** 385-399.

Wickens, C. D. (1983). Processing resources in attention. In R. Parasuraman, R. Davies, & J. Beatty (Eds.), *Varieties of attention.* New York: Academic Press.

WORD RECOGNITION
AND CONSCIOUSNESS

JIM CHEESMAN* AND PHILIP M. MERIKLE

Department of Psychology
University of Waterloo
Waterloo, Ontario, Canada

I. OVERVIEW

In this article, we evaluate recent evidence presumed to demonstrate that word recognition does not require conscious perceptual processing. Many recent studies involving masked visual stimuli appear to indicate that awareness is not necessary for word recognition. Given the theoretical importance of these findings, a critical evaluation of the studies is warranted. Our review of the available evidence leads to the conclusion that all studies reported to date can be criticized because the methodology does not allow

*Present address: Department of Psychology, University of Saskatchewan, Saskatoon, Saskatchewan, Canada S7N 0W0.

Copyright © 1985 by Academic Press, Inc.
All rights of reproduction in any form reserved.

firm conclusions concerning the detectability of the presumed unconscious words. Since word detection, as indicated by the presence of discriminated, forced choice responses, is the assumed definition of awareness, the success or failure of most studies in demonstrating perception without awareness depends critically upon the adequacy of the detectability measures.

Following a discussion of the methodological problems in previous studies, we present the results of several of our studies involving Stroop color-word priming. The results of these studies, which involved reliable estimates of word detectability, indicate that discriminated reports accurately reflect perceptual processing. In other words, when discriminated, forced choice responses concerning the words are at a chance level, **no other evidence for perceptual processing is found.** However, as the level of word detectability increases, other measures of perceptual processing, such as priming, also indicate that the words are being recognized.

The apparent discrepancy between our findings and the many reported demonstrations of perception without awareness can be resolved by adopting a revised definition of awareness. We suggest that awareness should be defined in terms of a subjective threshold, the level of detectability where an observer **claims** not to be able to discriminate perceptual information at better than a chance level, rather than an objective threshold, the level of detectability where perceptual information is actually discriminated at a chance level. We argue that subjective rather than objective thresholds are in fact the thresholds that were actually measured in many of the previous studies which appear to demonstrate perception without awareness. However, we also argue that a revised definition of awareness by itself is an insufficient criterion for demonstrating perception without awareness. In addition, it is necessary to demonstrate that words presented below a subjectively defined awareness threshold have qualitatively different effects upon behavior than words presented above this threshold. The success of our twofold approach is demonstrated experimentally.

Finally we examine the implications of our approach and how it is related to several recent models of perceptual processing that emphasize phenomenal awareness. It appears that our approach based on subjective thresholds provides a more reasonable account of phenomenal awareness.

II. INTRODUCTION AND REVIEW

The relationship between word recognition and consciousness has been the subject of considerable controversy for over 30 years. Over this period of time, the pivotal question has concerned whether or not word recognition occurs in the absence of conscious perceptual processing, or to state the question somewhat differently, are words perceived without awareness? In spite of extensive research directed at answering this question (see Dixon, 1971, 1981 for reviews), there is still no general agreement as to the necessity of conscious perceptual processing for word recognition. However, several recent theoretical accounts of word recognition explicitly state that words can be recognized without conscious perceptual processing (e.g., Allport, 1977; Henderson, 1982; Marcel, 1983b). Given this state of affairs, it is important to evaluate critically the empirical basis for the assumption that word recognition, at least under certain conditions, can occur solely on the basis of unconscious perceptual processes. If word recognition can be shown to occur on the basis of unconscious perceptual processes, then theoretical accounts of word recognition will obviously follow considerably different lines of development than if word recognition occurs only following conscious processing.

The most convincing evidence to date favoring the hypothesis that words are unconsciously perceived comes from studies involving backward visual masking. The reason the results of these studies are so compelling is that awareness has been assessed **directly** by presenting words in isolation prior to the beginning of the experimental task and degrading the visibility of these otherwise clear stimuli through the presentation of a pattern-masking stimulus. This direct measurement of awareness stands in sharp contrast to the approach adopted in other types of studies, such as those based on selective attention or parafoveal priming. In these studies, awareness for words presented in conjunction with an experimental task has been measured either concurrently with performance of the experimental task or subsequent to the completion of the task. Thus statements concerning awareness are equivocal because alternative explanations based on dual task interference or memory loss can always be invoked (cf. Holender, 1985). Given that direct assessment of awareness eliminates these alternative interpretations, the recent studies involving backward visual masking are considered to provide the strongest evidence favoring unconscious word recognition. It is for this reason that the recent backward masking studies are the major focus of this review.

Any discussion of unconscious perceptual processes must necessarily begin with a consideration of how best to define consciousness or awareness. In fact, the success or failure of any attempt to distinguish conscious from unconscious perceptual processes depends critically on the manner in which consciousness is defined and measured. In general, two different approaches to the definitional problem have been adopted. One approach advocated by Dixon and his colleagues (e.g., Dixon, 1971, 1981; Henley, 1984), measures awareness by asking observers whether or not they are "consciously aware" of a stimulus. If an observer reports no awareness of a stimulus, then, by definition, the observer is not conscious of the stimulus. In contrast to this subjective approach, the objective approach, advocated by Eriksen (1960) in his classic critique of subception research, defines awareness as the ability to make a discriminated response. Thus, according to the objective approach, if an observer cannot discriminate among several possible stimulus states in a forced choice task, then the observer is not conscious or aware of the stimuli.[1]

The relative merits of these two approaches are fairly obvious. Since the subjective approach simply defines awareness in terms of observers' self-reports of their conscious experiences, this approach transfers the responsibility for operationally defining awareness from the investigator to the observer, and any experimenter who uses this approach is, in effect, asking each observer to provide his or her own definition of awareness. Awareness thresholds, as measured by self-reports, will vary tremendously depending upon the demand characteristics in a particular experimental situation, and the same criticisms can be directed at the subjective approach as can be directed at any study of perceptual processes based solely on observers' introspective reports. On the other hand, an objective approach based on forced choice decisions among stimulus states has the obvious advantage of providing a method for assessing perceptual sensitivity independent of an observer's biases in a particular situation. Thus, the objective approach places the responsibility for defining awareness clearly with the experimenter, as the experimenter has a method for distinguishing response patterns attributable to biased responding from those due to true perceptual sensitivity.

Fortunately, an examination of the methodology used to determine awareness thresholds in recent backward masking studies indicates that there is general agreement as to what constitutes strong evidence for unconscious perception. Consistent with Eriksen's (1960) earlier position, awareness or consciousness has been defined in terms of an observer's ability to discriminate among several possible stimulus alternatives in a forced choice task. When the correlation between an objectively specified stimulus state (e.g., the presence or absence of a stimulus) and an objectively specified response (e.g., the verbal response "present" or "absent") approximates zero, it has been assumed that observers are unaware of the stimuli. Conversely, when the correlations are greater than zero, it has been assumed that observers are aware of the stimuli. With this approach, evidence for perception with-

---

[1]No distinction is made in this article between the terms "discriminated report" and "discriminated verbal report." Both terms refer to performance on n-alternative forced choice tasks. Although tasks involving verbal, forced choice responses are typically used to measure awareness, any task based on observable forced choice responses emitted by an observer (e.g., button pressing, toe tapping, ear twitching, etc.) may be used.

out awareness consists of demonstrating that perceptual processing occurs even when observers cannot discriminate among alternative stimulus states. Thus, for example, if it is demonstrated that observers cannot detect the presence of a stimulus but that this same stimulus nevertheless affects behavior as indicated by some other dependent measure, then this pattern of results would provide strong evidence for perception without awareness.

In the immediately following sections, these criteria for demonstrating perception without awareness provide the context for our review of the masking studies commonly cited as providing evidence for unconscious word recognition. To date, three different approaches have been used to assess the perceptual processing of masked words. One approach is to require observers to make various types of decisions concerning masked words (e.g., detection, semantic, or graphic) and then to ascertain if certain types of information are more readily available for these decisions (e.g., Marcel, 1983a). Another approach, exemplified by the work of Allport (1977), involves presenting masked words which observers attempt to identify and then assessing subsequent identification errors to determine if they are semantically related to the original words. The third approach involves using masked words, which are presented below a previously established awareness threshold, to prime subsequent responses to target stimuli (e.g., Balota, 1983; Fowler, Wolford, Slade, & Tassinary, 1981; Marcel, 1983a).

In general, our review of the evidence from these approaches indicates that, even though awareness was measured directly, the associated methodologies were inadequate (cf. Merikle, 1982; Purcell, Stewart, & Stanovich, 1983). Each study can be criticized either because the awareness threshold was established by an inappropriate procedure (e.g., Balota, 1983; Fowler *et al.,* 1981; Marcel, 1983a) or because an inappropriate estimate of chance detection performance was used (e.g., Allport, 1977; Marcel, 1983a). Without exception, there are simply no guarantees in these studies that the presumed unconscious stimuli were in fact undetectable, as indicated by a properly implemented forced choice task. Given these methodological inadequacies, any conclusions favoring unconscious word recognition based on the results of these studies are completely unwarranted.

A. Decisions concerning Masked Words

Marcel (1983a) has reported results which appear to indicate that semantic and graphic information are available following the presentation of a masked word even when observers cannot detect the presence of the word. In his experiment, observers were required to make one of three decisions following the presentation of each masked word: (1) decide which of two alternative words was more similar in meaning to the masked word,

(2) decide which of two alternative words was more similar graphically to the masked word, or (3) decide whether a word or a blank field preceded the masking stimulus. Accuracy for each type of decision was examined at six different word–mask stimulus onset asynchronies (SOAs), which were individually determined to ensure that the range of SOAs allowed each observer's performance on each task to vary from a high level to a chance level. The counterintuitive findings reported by Marcel indicate that presence/absence decisions were **less** accurate than either graphic or semantic decisions. Furthermore, at the word–mask SOA where presence/absence decisions reached a chance level of performance, both semantic and graphic decisions were above a chance level, and with a continued decrease in the word–mask SOA, the graphic decisions reached a chance level of accuracy before the semantic decisions.

Marcel's findings are intriguing because they suggest that the perceptual processes responsible for graphic and semantic decisions do not provide adequate information to indicate that a visual event has even occurred. Thus, his results seem to provide strong support for unconscious word recognition. Furthermore, these results also challenge more traditional views of perceptual processing which imply either that lower level information (e.g., the presence of a stimulus) is perceived prior to higher level information (e.g., the meaning of a stimulus) or that sufficient information for many types of perceptual decisions is perceived simultaneously (cf. Eriksen, 1960).

Two methodological considerations, however, suggest that it may be premature to abandon more traditional views of perceptual processing on the basis of Marcel's results. First, Fowler et al. (1981) demonstrated that response strategies, independent of perceptual experiences, play an important role in experiments such as the one reported by Marcel. Following a successful replication of Marcel's findings, these investigators conducted a pseudoexperiment where no words were presented prior to the masking stimulus, but observers were still required to choose between response alternatives. Surprisingly, the results of this pseudoexperiment indicated that the observers' semantic and graphic decisions were still at a better than chance level of performance when they were evaluated against the actual stimulus words that should have been presented prior to each set of response alternatives. Thus, as noted by Fowler et al., similar patterns of results are found in this type of experiment independent of whether or not stimulus words are presented. On the other hand, Fowler et al. also found that semantic decisions were more accurate when the words were actually presented (63%) than when no words were presented (57%). Therefore, response strategies cannot account for the entire semantic decision effect. However, until the problems associated with response strategies are eliminated, no firm conclusions can be made as to the implications of any results that may be obtained using this approach.

An equally serious problem with Marcel's experiment concerns the definition he adopted for chance detection performance. Marcel defined chance performance for presence/absence decisions as less than 60% correct. This is a most unusual definition of chance performance for a two-choice task since, without a strong theoretical rational to the contrary, it is logical to assume that chance performance should be 50% correct. In fact, when Nolan and Caramazza (1982) conducted a similar experiment but defined chance performance as 50% correct, they found that both semantic and visual similarity judgments fell to a chance level of performance when presence/absence decisions were also at a chance level. Thus, Nolan and Caramazza's results suggest that Marcel's findings may be due entirely to the inappropriate definition of chance performance he adopted.

These criticisms of Marcel's experiment indicate that his results do not support the claim that semantic and graphic information are perceived even when it is impossible to detect the presence of a word. Rather, on the basis of Nolan and Caramazza's results, it appears that the same threshold is applicable for detection, graphic, and semantic decisions. Thus, in agreement with Eriksen's (1960) earlier position, no evidence for perception without awareness is found when awareness is measured in terms of forced choice decisions concerning the presence of a word and a proper definition of chance performance is adopted. On the other hand, it is possible that once the threshold for detecting a word is exceeded, the information needed for semantic and graphic decisions is more readily perceived than the information needed for presence/absence decisions. This would account for the somewhat greater accuracy for semantic and graphic decisions than for detection decisions reported by both Marcel and Fowler *et al*. However, a final decision concerning this question must await the results of experiments which solve the response–strategy problem documented in the pseudo-experiment reported by Fowler *et al*. (1981).

B. Guesses concerning Masked Words

Allport (1977) has reported another type of evidence that is often cited as support for the proposition that the meaning of a word may be perceived without conscious perceptual processing. In his experiments, Allport induced observers to make whole word errors by presenting displays containing either two or four words and masking these displays so that observers could only report a small proportion of the words correctly. The interesting result obtained in these experiments is that a significant proportion of the errors was semantically, but neither visually nor phonologically, related to one of the nonreported words in the displays. For example, if one of the words in a display was "blues," an observer may have given the word "jazz" as a response. Allport found that 6–8% of the errors could be classified as being semantically related to one of the nonreported words. On the basis of these results, Allport argued that the effects of a pattern-masking stimulus are quite selective. A mask does not interfere with the perceptual processing required to extract semantic information from a visual stimulus. Rather, its primary effect is to disrupt the recovery of the visual code that leads to awareness, or in Allport's words, the phenomenal experience of "seeing" a word.

A major problem with Allport's studies is that no attempt was made to estimate the proportion of semantic errors expected on the basis of chance correlations between stimuli and responses. The implicit assumption underlying Allport's experiments is that no semantic errors should occur on the basis of chance guesses. However, the results of several later experiments clearly demonstrate that this assumption is incorrect (Ellis & Marshall, 1978; Fowler et al., 1981; Williams & Parkin, 1980). For example, Ellis and Marshall (1978) replicated Allport's experiment involving four-word displays and found, as reported by Allport, that approximately 9% of the errors could be classified as semantic errors. However, when the error responses were randomly reassigned to the stimulus displays to obtain an estimate of chance performance, Ellis and Marshall found that the proportion of semantic errors remained approximately 9%. Thus, on the basis of these results, it appears that the proportion of semantic errors observed by Allport was no greater than would be expected to occur on the basis of chance guesses.

Additional evidence indicating that the semantic errors which occur as responses to masked words are actually due to guessing strategies has been reported by Williams and Parkin (1980). In their experiment, half of the displays contained four words and the remaining displays contained four nonwords. To establish a base line for chance performance, the responses to the nonword displays were randomly assigned to the word displays, and independent judges rated the semantic relatedness between the responses and the words in the displays. The results were quite straightforward. The judges' ratings indicated that the proportion of semantic errors among the randomly assigned responses to nonwords (11.5%) was approximately the same as the proportion of semantic errors for the actual responses to these displays. These findings, as well as the results of a related experiment reported by Fowler et al. (1981), clearly indicate that the "semantic errors" which occur following the presentation of masked words are simply due to chance guesses.

Given that all attempted replications of Allport's original finding indicate that the observed proportion of semantic errors does not differ from the proportion of semantic errors expected on the basis of chance guesses, the occurrence of semantic errors to masked words provides no support whatsoever for the hypothesis that word meaning is perceived without awareness. Rather, the only conclusion supported by the results of these experiments is that the meaning of masked words is perceived only when the perceptual processing is sufficient to permit correct report of the words.

C. Priming by Masked Words

Recent studies in which priming tasks are used in conjunction with backward visual masking provide what appears to be the strongest evidence for unconscious perceptual processing (Balota, 1983; Fowler *et al.,* 1981; Marcel, 1983a). In these studies, the presentation of a clearly visible target stimulus is preceded by the presentation of a priming stimulus which is centrally masked so as to preclude it from awareness. The surprising result found in these studies is that the associative relationship between a prime and a target affects the reaction time to the target stimulus, even though the masking stimulus presumably eliminates all awareness of the prime. Thus, masked primes appear to produce effects similar to those observed when priming stimuli are clearly visible (cf. Meyer, Schvaneveldt, & Ruddy, 1975; Neely, 1976, 1977; Stanovich & West, 1983).

Given that the awareness thresholds in these studies were established on the basis of forced choice tasks administered prior to the beginning of the priming trials, and the perception of the primes was measured indirectly through their effects on the perception of clearly visible target stimuli, the results of these studies appear to provide compelling evidence for perceptual processing in the absence of awareness. However, whether or not the results of these studies actually demonstrate perception without awareness depends entirely upon the adequacy of the procedures used to establish the awareness thresholds. If these procedures are inadequate, then it is premature to conclude that the results of these studies provide evidence for unconscious perceptual processes.

Marcel (1974) was the first to report evidence indicating unconscious priming. Although Marcel published two early reports describing some of his experiments (Marcel, 1980; Marcel & Patterson, 1978), complete details of his methodology only became available recently (Marcel, 1983a). In this recent article, Marcel describes two different types of priming experiments which produce unconscious priming, and it is these priming studies that are the major focus of our review of Marcel's work.

One priming experiment reported by Marcel (1983a) was based on a modified version of the Stroop (1935) color–word interference task. In this experiment, relatively large color patches with a smaller word superimposed in the center were presented to observers who identified the colors by pressing an appropriate button. Consistent with previous research (cf. Dyer, 1973), Marcel found that clearly visible words produced increased response latencies when the words and the color patches were incongruent (e.g., word = *blue,* color patch = green) and decreased response latencies when the words and the color patches were congruent (e.g., word = *blue,* color patch = blue).

The important results reported by Marcel concern what happened when the color words were masked so that the observers were unaware of their presence. Under these conditions, Marcel found that both congruent and incongruent words affected the reaction times to the color patches. When the onsets of the color patches and the color words were simultaneous, the difference in reaction time between congruent and incongruent conditions was approximately the same under conditions where the color words were masked (46 msec) as under conditions where the color words were clearly visible (52 msec). Thus, under these conditions, it appears that the presentation of the mask had absolutely no effect on the magnitude of the Stroop effect, even though the observers were presumably unaware of the masked color words.

In addition to conditions where the onsets of the color words and color patches were simultaneous, Marcel also included a condition in this experiment where the onset of each color word preceded the onset of a color patch by 400 msec. Under these conditions, the difference in reaction time between congruent and incongruent conditions was considerably smaller when the color words were masked (54 msec) than when the color words were clearly visible (108 msec). It is unclear exactly why the magnitudes of priming differed, but one possibility is that the relatively long prime–color SOA allowed for the initiation of conscious strategies in the unmasked condition (cf. Posner & Snyder, 1975a). Nevertheless, the important finding from this condition in Marcel's experiment is that the masked primes had a considerable impact which was approximately equal in magnitude to the effect of a masked prime presented simultaneously with the onset of a color patch (54 msec versus 46 msec). Thus, the results from both prime–color SOA conditions in Marcel's experiment suggest that masked primes which observers are unable to see, as indicated by a forced choice detection task, produce a considerable amount of priming.

The second type of priming experiment reported by Marcel (1983a) involved a lexical decision task, where observers classified letter strings as either words or nonwords and the presentation of these letter strings was preceded by priming stimuli which were either clearly visible or masked to preclude them from awareness. As in the Stroop experiment, awareness thresholds for the primes were established on the basis of a forced choice task administered prior to the lexical decision task, and each observer's awareness threshold was defined in terms of the prime–mask SOA where detection of the primes approximated a chance level of performance. In addition, all primes, whether masked or unmasked, were presented 2000 msec prior to the onset of the target letter strings.

The critical trials in the experiment involved word targets that were preceded by either semantically related or unrelated words, and the measure of semantic activation was the difference in reaction time on these two types of trials. The intriguing result found in the experiment is that both masked and unmasked semantically related primes facilitated the reaction times to the target words, relative to the reaction times observed when the target words were preceded by semantically unrelated primes. Furthermore, Marcel also found approximately the same magnitude of facilitation for both masked (56 msec) and unmasked (62 msec) primes. These results based on a lexical decision task lead to the same inferences as the results obtained with the Stroop task when the onsets of the color patches and color words were simultaneous. The results of both experiments suggest that a pattern masking stimulus presented so as to make prime detection impossible has virtually no effect on the perceptual processing of a prime's semantic content. Thus, the results of both studies support the conclusion that the perceptual processing necessary for complete semantic activation can occur without observers having any awareness of this processing.

Whether or not these results reported by Marcel actually provide evidence for unconscious perceptual processes depends entirely upon the adequacy of the procedures he used to establish awareness thresholds. The critical assumption underlying his experiments is that when the observers were unaware of the primes, they could not make presence/absence decisions concerning the primes at a better than chance level of performance. Thus, Marcel, in a manner consistent with the earlier position put forth by Eriksen (1960), assumed that awareness was indicated by above-chance discriminated verbal reports concerning the primes and, conversely, that nonawareness was indicated by chance level discriminated verbal reports. Therefore, if there are reasons to question either Marcel's definition of chance performance or his methods for establishing detection thresholds, then his results may not necessarily provide compelling evidence for unconscious perceptual processing as assumed by many people.

Unfortunately, both Marcel's definition of chance performance and his methodology for establishing detection thresholds are questionable. In these studies, Marcel equated nonawareness of the primes with less than 60%

correct detection on a two-choice task. As stated previously, when discussing Marcel's experiments involving decisions concerning masked words, this is an inappropriate definition of chance performance, and in fact, this level of performance on a two-choice task suggests that the primes could be detected. Thus, by equating nonawareness with less then 60% correct detection performance, Marcel ensured that the observers were actually aware of the presence of the primes, contrary to his critical assumption.

An even more serious problem with the methodology used by Marcel to establish awareness thresholds concerns the fact that the overall percent correct detection performance for each observer was based on only 40 presence/absence trials. With such a small number of trials, any measurement error would seriously influence the observed detection performance, as each response would account for 2.5% of the overall performance. More importantly, even if one makes the unlikely assumption that no measurement error occurred, it is impossible to interpret the overall detection performance without additional information concerning the relative frequency of the two possible responses. According to signal detection theory, if both responses were used equally often, then 60% correct detection performance would indicate a relatively modest level of perceptual sensitivity. However, if there was a bias to use one response alternative more frequently than the other, then 60% overall correct detection performance would indicate a higher level of perceptual sensitivity, since, in general, with a constant percent correct performance, the greater the bias to use one of two possible response alternatives, the greater is the perceptual sensitivity. In fact, if the response bias was fairly extreme, as has been suggested previously (Merikle, 1982), 60% correct performance would indicate a very high level of perceptual sensitivity for the primes. Although it is not possible to determine exactly how well the masked primes may have been detected by the subjects in Marcel's experiments, the one conclusion that can be made on the basis of his data is that the subjects were able to detect the primes at a considerably better than chance level of performance.

In addition to Marcel's experiments, other investigators have also reported studies which appear to indicate that words are unconsciously perceived. In one such study, Fowler et al. (1981) studied primed lexical decisions using nearly identical procedures to the ones used by Marcel and found that the magnitude of priming was similar for both masked (29 msec) and unmasked (38 msec) primes. Although Fowler et al. claim that their subjects were unaware of the masked primes, the procedures they used to establish awareness thresholds, like Marcel's procedures, were inadequate. As noted previously (Merikle, 1982), Fowler et al. established awareness thresholds solely on the basis of percent correct detection performance across a trial block consisting of just five trials. With such a small number of trials, it is not possible to establish reliable estimates of response probabilities. Thus, it is impossible to determine if the observed detection performance actually approximated a chance level of performance, as demanded by the perception-without-awareness hypothesis, or if observed detection performance indicated a considerable perceptual sensitivity for the primes. Given the extremely small number of detection trials used by Fowler *et al.*, it is simply impossible to reach any conclusions on the basis of their data concerning whether or not words are unconsciously perceived.

Balota (1983) has also reported the results of a priming study which appear to indicate that unconsciously perceived primes affect subsequent lexical decisions. In this experiment, Balota defined the awareness threshold as less than 60% correct performance on a two-choice detection task, and he established each observer's awareness threshold solely on the basis of a single block of 26 trials. Given that Balota's methodology for establishing awareness thresholds is very similar to the methodology used by both Marcel and Fowler *et al.*, his study is subject to many of the same criticisms that have been directed at these studies. Thus, the significant priming that Balota reports for masked primes certainly does not provide critical evidence either for or against the hypothesis that words are perceived without awareness. On the other hand, the fact that Balota found significantly less priming for masked (35 msec) than unmasked (51 msec) primes suggests that the major effect of the masking stimulus in his study was to degrade the primes so that they were somewhat less effective than the unmasked primes.

In summary, each of the recent studies involving masked priming stimuli can be criticized on methodological grounds. Thus, the results of these studies are equivocal concerning whether or not words are unconsciously perceived. Since awareness was defined in these studies as the ability to make discriminated verbal reports concerning the presence or absence of the primes, it is critical for the success of these studies to demonstrate conclusively that the masked primes were detected at a chance level of performance. However, given the procedures used in these studies, there are simply no guarantees that the primes could not be detected, or in other words, that the detection of the primes approximated a chance level of performance. In fact, our review of the methodology employed in these studies indicates either that the observers could probably detect the masked primes (Balota, 1983; Marcel, 1983a) or that it is impossible to interpret the observed detection performance because so few trials were administered to establish the awareness thresholds (Fowler *et al.*, 1981). Given these considerations, the only reasonable conclusion that can be made on the basis of the results of these studies is that fairly wide variations in stimulus visibility have relatively little influence upon the efficacy of priming stimuli.

III. MEASUREMENT OF AWARENESS
BY DISCRIMINATED REPORTS

Previously, we noted that there is fairly general agreement that awareness is best defined in terms of an observer's ability to discriminate among stimulus states, as indicated by verbal reports in a forced choice task. However, as our review indicates, all studies reported to date can be criticized on the basis of methodological inadequacies which raise serious questions as to whether the observers were actually unable to make discriminated reports concerning the presumed unconscious stimuli. Thus, as long as it is assumed that awareness is reflected by the ability to make correct discriminated reports and that nonawareness is the absence of such an ability, the results obtained in these studies simply do not provide any strong evidence against the view that discriminated reports accurately reflect perceptual processing.

Defining awareness in terms of discriminated reports is completely consistent with the position put forward by Eriksen (1960) in his influential paper concerning methodological considerations underlying subception research. Eriksen's main concern was to establish an appropriate empirical measure of awareness, and for this reason, he proposed that awareness is best defined in terms of forced choice decisions concerning stimuli. A definition of awareness based on forced choice decisions has several distinct advantages: (1) it is objective, (2) it is readily implemented in different laboratories, and (3) it provides a method for assessing perceptual sensitivity independent of response bias. The third advantage is particularly important because observers are frequently very reluctant to make decisions concerning difficult-to-perceive stimuli, and in any study involving the presentation of highly degraded stimuli, it must be possible to distinguish extreme response biases from a true absence of perceptual sensitivity.

On the basis of his review of the evidence available at that time, Eriksen (1960) reached the important conclusion that discriminated reports are as sensitive an indicator of perceptual processing as any response that has been studied. Thus, according to Eriksen, if observers cannot discriminate among alternative stimulus events, as indicated by directly measured forced choice decisions (e.g., discriminated verbal responses), then all other measures of perceptual processing (e.g., priming) will also indicate an absence of perceptual sensitivity. Eriksen's conclusion applied to the recent studies involving masked priming stimuli implies that the expected pattern of results should be similar to the one depicted by the solid line in Fig. 1. This view of perceptual processing has two important implications. First, no priming should occur when observers are unable to discriminate among alternative stimulus states at a better than chance level of performance, and second, the magnitude of priming should increase monotonically as an observer's

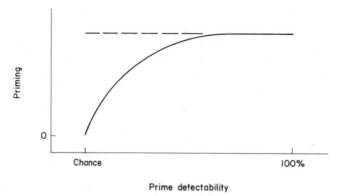

Fig. 1. Relationship between priming and detectability as predicted by the positions of Eriksen (——) and Marcel (---).

ability to discriminate among the stimulus alternatives improves with increased stimulus visibility.

These implications of Eriksen's conclusion obviously contradict the more recent conclusions made by several investigators (e.g., Balota, 1983; Fowler *et al.,* 1981; Marcel, 1983a) who claim, on the basis of the results from studies involving masked priming stimuli, that indirect measures (i.e., priming) are more sensitive indicators of perceptual processing than direct measures (i.e., discriminated verbal reports). In fact, on the basis of results which appear to indicate that equivalent priming effects are produced by stimuli presented above or below the awareness threshold, it has even been argued that complete semantic processing may occur in the absence of conscious perceptual processing (e.g., Fowler *et al.,* 1981; Marcel, 1983a). These conclusions imply that the relationship between priming and discriminated reports should be similar to the one depicted by the broken line in Fig. 1, which shows no variation in the magnitude of priming as a function of the level of detection performance on a forced choice task. Clearly, the implications of the conclusions made on the basis of the results obtained in the recent masked prime studies completely contradict the implications of the position originally put forward by Eriksen (1960).

Fortunately, there is a very straightforward empirical method for determining which of the two positions depicted in Fig. 1 is more correct. The assumption that discriminated reports are a completely adequate indicator of perceptual processing can be easily falsified by demonstrating that priming occurs even when observers cannot discriminate among several possible stimulus states. Such a pattern of results would clearly contradict any position which implies that direct and indirect measures provide equally sensitive indicators of perceptual processing. Furthermore, given that both positions assume that an absence of discriminated reports indicates an absence of awareness, any demonstration that priming occurs when discriminated reports are not possible would provide strong evidence favoring the hypothesis that words may be unconsciously perceived.

Although the recent masked prime studies appear to indicate that priming occurs in the absence of discriminated reports, weaknesses in the procedures employed in these studies to determine awareness thresholds preclude any conclusion implying that the reported results support the perception-without-awareness hypothesis. As noted previously (Merikle, 1982), a major problem with these studies is that the presumed awareness thresholds were based on such a small number of trials that it is impossible to determine exactly how well the observers may have been able to discriminate among the alternative stimulus states. Furthermore, as indicated in our review of the masked prime studies, inappropriate criteria for nonawareness have been adopted in many of these studies so that nonawareness has actually been equated with slightly better than chance discriminative responding. Thus, on the basis of the reported results, it is not possible to conclude that the observers were unable to discriminate among the alternative stimulus states, and therefore, the data obtained in these studies provide no evidence to contradict the position based on Eriksen's conclusion.

Failure to establish that discriminative responding actually approximates a chance level of performance means that any priming observed in a masked prime experiment is actually consistent with the view of perceptual processing represented by the solid line in Fig. 1. The assumption that discriminated reports provide an adequate indicator of perceptual processing implies that priming should occur whenever discriminated reports exceed a chance level of performance. Therefore, a demonstration of priming by degraded stimuli does not provide any evidence against this assumption, unless it is also demonstrates that observers cannot discriminate among the possible alternative stimulus states. Furthermore, even demonstrations of equivalent priming by masked and unmasked primes, such as those reported by both Fowler et al. (1981) and Marcel (1983a), do not provide any strong support for the perception-without-awareness hypothesis. Eriksen's view that perceptual processing is adequately indicated by discriminated reports predicts, as indicated by the solid line in Fig. 1, only that the relative magnitudes of priming produced by degraded and clearly visible stimuli should become approximately equivalent at some **undefined** level of discriminated report accuracy. If the critical level of report accuracy correlated with maximal priming is relatively low, then the priming effects produced by degraded and clearly visible stimuli may be equivalent even when it is impossible to discriminate among the degraded stimuli with complete accuracy. Thus, equivalent priming effects, by themselves, do not provide any compelling evidence either to support the view that indirect measures are more sensitive indicators of perceptual processing than direct measures (Balota, 1983; Fowler *et al.,* 1981; Marcel, 1983a,b) or to contradict the view that indirect and direct measures are equally sensitive indicators of perceptual processing (Eriksen, 1960).

Given the assumption that chance-level discrimination performance defines the boundary between conscious and unconscious perceptual processes, it is only possible to establish the relationship between word recognition and consciousness when procedures are used which ensure that nonawareness, as indicated by the absence of discriminated reports, has been measured adequately. There is simply no substitute for accurate measurement of discriminative responding. If discriminative responding is not measured accurately, Eriksen's view that directly measured discriminated reports provide an adequate indicator of perceptual processing cannot be falsified. If Eriksen's view cannot be falsified, then it is impossible to provide evidence for unconscious perceptual processing, given that consciousness is equated with accurate discriminative responding.

IV. PRIMING WITHOUT AWARENESS: A PROPER EXPERIMENTAL EVALUATION

Given that serious questions can be raised concerning the procedures used to establish awareness thresholds in previous masked prime studies, we conducted two experiments in which a considerably better methodology was used to establish each observer's awareness threshold. Our approach differed from previous studies in three major respects. First, each observer's ability to detect the primes was measured using a four-alternative, forced choice discrimination procedure. This method was chosen because it has the advantage of removing the "no" or negative responses from the set of possible answers. Individual differences in the willingness to guess a response were thus avoided. Second, thresholds were based on a sufficient number of trials to obtain reliable estimates of each observer's response distributions. Third, rather than simply measuring priming under a mask or threshold condition and a no-mask condition, priming was measured at several levels of prime detectability. In this manner, the functional relationship between priming and level of awareness could be established.

Following Marcel (1983a), a variant of the Stroop (1935) color–word interference task was used. The task involved naming a color that was immediately preceded by the presentation of a congruent color word, an incongruent color word, or a control letter string. Previous research indicates that color-naming latencies in this task increase when a color is preceded by an incongruent color word (e.g., Dyer & Severance, 1973) and decrease when the word prime and the color target are congruent (e.g., Dalrymple-Alford, 1972). Thus, this variant of the Stroop task was used to investigate both facilitation and inhibition at various levels of prime detectability.

The method used to establish detection thresholds for the color words used as the primes is described in Cheesman and Merikle (1984). Briefly, each subject's forced choice threshold for discriminating among four possible color words (*blue, green, yellow,* and *orange*) was established during a series of trials involving systematic decreases in the exposure duration for each word. The presentation of each word was followed immediately by the presentation of a pattern-masking stimulus consisting of letter pieces. The words were presented to the nondominant eye and the masking stimulus was presented to the dominant eye. The observers' task was simply to indicate on each trial which of the four possible color words had been presented.

Two critical differences distinguish our studies from previous studies. First, the observers were forced to choose one of the four color words as a response on each trial. Thus, it was possible to establish that the observers distributed their responses across the four possible alternatives. Second, a minimum of 120 trials was presented at the threshold exposure duration. While this number of trials may not satisfy a good psychophysicist, it is a considerably greater number of trials than used in previous studies of unconscious priming effects (cf. Balota, 1983; Fowler *et al.,* 1981; Marcel, 1983a), and it was a sufficient number of trials to establish that each subject's performance was at a chance level.

A. Experiment 1

In this study, two intermediate levels of detectability were established in addition to the forced choice discrimination threshold. In this way, the functional relationship between prime detectability and the magnitude of priming could be investigated. Both a 55 and a 90% level of detectability were established for each subject by presenting the color words for the exposure duration used on the threshold trials and systematically increasing the duration of a blank field presented between the offset of the word and the onset of the masking stimulus. As for the threshold trials, a minimum of 120 trials was used to establish both the 55 and the 90% levels of detection performance.

Four levels of prime detectability were evaluated on the experimental trials: threshold or 25% detection, 55% detection, 90% detection, and a no-mask condition. It was assumed that prime detectability would have been

100% in the no-mask condition if detection performance had actually been measured. Each level of prime detectability was evaluated in a separate block of 216 trials, and in each block of trials, the three types of prime–target relationships—congruent, incongruent, and control—were randomly intermixed.

An example of the masked stimulus displays is shown in Fig. 2, and the sequence of events for each prime detectability condition is illustrated in Fig. 3. Initially, a color word, or a control letter string consisting of five X's, was presented either above or below the fixation rectangle to the nondominant eye for the threshold exposure duration. Upon offset of the word, a color patch (blue, green, yellow, or orange) that filled the fixation rectangle was presented for 300 msec to the dominant eye. The masking stimulus was then presented to the dominant eye at the predetermined prime-mask interstimulus interval (ISI) corresponding to the particular detection condition. Of course, the masking stimulus was not presented in the no-mask condition. The task for the subject was simply to name the color patch as quickly as possible.

The predictions for this study were quite straightforward. If, contrary to our criticisms, detection thresholds have been measured adequately in previous masked prime studies, then significant facilitation and inhibition should be observed at all levels of prime detectability. On the other hand, if detection thresholds have not been measured accurately in previous studies, then no priming should occur at the detection threshold and both facilitation and inhibition should increase with increased prime detectability.

The results of the experiment are shown in Fig. 4, where the mean facilitation and inhibition, relative to the control trials, is presented for each

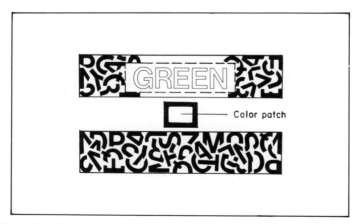

Fig. 2. Spatial arrangement of the masked stimulus displays in Experiment 1.

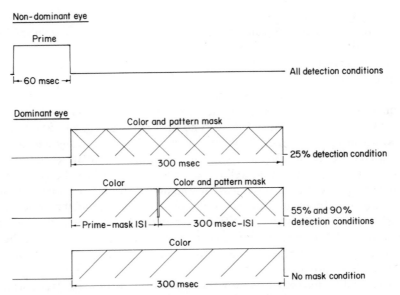

Fig. 3. Sequence of events for each detectability condition in Experiment 1.

level of detectability. The data show a very clear pattern. At the detection threshold (25% prime detectability), no facilitation or inhibition was observed. Thus, there was no evidence for any priming effects when the primes were presented at the detection threshold. This result stands in sharp con-

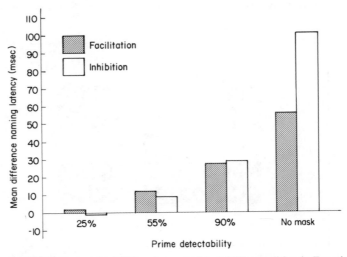

Fig. 4. Mean facilitation and inhibition for each detectability condition in Experiment 1.

trast to other reported findings which suggest that priming effects are observed even when the primes are presented at the detection threshold (e.g., Balota, 1983; Fowler *et al.*, 1981; Marcel, 1983a). On the other hand, the data presented in Fig. 4 indicate that both facilitation and inhibition increase systematically with increases in prime detectability. This result is entirely consistent with the hypothesis that discriminated verbal reports accurately reflect perceptual processing (e.g., Eriksen, 1960), and it provides support for our claim that the inadequate procedures used in previous studies gave unreliable estimates of the detection thresholds which led to spurious observations indicating perception without awareness.

The results of this experiment thus provide no evidence whatsoever indicating perception without awareness. Since no priming was observed at the detection threshold and the magnitude of priming increased systematically with increases in the accuracy of the discriminated verbal reports concerning the primes, the results are completely inconsistent with any interpretation favoring perception without awareness. Minimal support for perception without awareness requires, at the very least, significant priming at the detection threshold, and strong support for perception without awareness, such as reported by Fowler *et al.* (1981) and Marcel (1983a), requires equal magnitudes of priming across all levels of detectability. Clearly, the results shown in Fig. 4 satisfy neither of these conditions.

Although the results shown in Fig. 4 indicate that no evidence for unconscious perceptual processing is obtained in a masked prime paradigm when precautions are taken to insure that detection thresholds have been measured accurately, there is one possible counterargument that can be raised by strong supporters of the perception-without-awareness hypothesis. Both Balota (1983) and Fowler *et al.* (1981) failed to obtain evidence for unconscious priming when the prime–target SOA was relatively short (e.g., 200–300 msec). However, in both studies, priming was observed when the prime–target SOA was 2000 msec. Balota (1983) has suggested that semantic activation may be slowed considerably when a word is severely degraded. Given that the prime–target SOA in the present study averaged 60 msec, it is possible that this aspect of the procedure accounts for the absence of evidence consistent with the perception-without-awareness hypothesis.

B. Experiment 2

In order to establish if our failure to find priming at the detection threshold was due to the short SOAs separating the primes and the targets, we conducted a second experiment which involved an evaluation of priming at several prime–target SOAs (Cheesman & Merikle, 1984). The three prime-target SOAs chosen for evaluation were 50, 550, and 1050 msec. If the proponents of the perception-without-awareness hypothesis are correct, then priming at the detection threshold should increase as the SOA separating the primes and the targets is increased.

As in the previous experiment, the Stroop-priming paradigm was used. Since we were primarily interested in establishing whether or not the overall magnitude of priming changed as a function of the prime–target SOA, only congruent and incongruent trials were used. Detection thresholds were established in the same manner as in the previous experiment, and detection threshold performance was compared to performance in a suprathreshold condition where the prime–mask SOA was a constant 300 msec. The relatively long prime–mask SOA used in the suprathreshold condition ensured that all subjects could easily identify the primes.

The results obtained in the experiment are shown in Table I. The critical finding is that the overall magnitude of priming did not change across the three prime–target SOAs for either the detection threshold or the suprathreshold conditions. Thus, this experiment provides no evidence whatsoever to support the suggestion made by both Balota (1983) and Fowler *et al.* (1981) that unconscious priming is more likely to be observed at relatively long prime–target SOAs. If this suggestion were correct, then a systematic increase in the magnitude of priming should have been observed when the prime–target SOA was increased in the detection threshold condition of this study.

The implications of the results from these two experiments are clear. When primes are centrally masked and steps are taken to insure that detection performance actually approximates a chance level of accuracy, no

TABLE I

Median Naming Latencies and Percentage Errors for Each Prime–Target SOA under Detection Threshold and Suprathreshold Conditions

Prime detectability	Prime–target relationship	Prime-target SOA (msec)					
		50		550		1050	
		RT	%E	RT	%E	RT	%E
Detection threshold (27%)	Incongruent	510	5.5	487	3.8	485	4.2
	Congruent	496	3.9	482	1.7	482	0.8
	Priming	14		5		3	
Supra-threshold	Incongruent	555	20.5	513	3.9	489	2.5
	Congruent	456	2.9	421	1.7	395	2.5
	Priming	99		92		94	

evidence for priming without awareness is found. Rather, the results of both experiments indicate that there is a positive relationship between the magnitude of priming and prime detectability. Thus, the data support both Eriksen's (1960) contention that discriminated reports are an accurate indicator of perceptual processing and Merikle's (1982) criticisms of the threshold procedures used in previous masked prime studies. These conclusions imply that no evidence for unconscious priming will ever be found when precautions are taken to measure detection thresholds accurately and that previously reported evidence must be rejected because of the inappropriate procedures used to measure detection thresholds.

V. SUBJECTIVE VERSUS OBJECTIVE THRESHOLDS: A POSSIBLE RESOLUTION

There are two possible approaches that can be taken to resolve the discrepancy between our findings and the results of previous studies that appear to demonstrate perception without awareness. First, it can be assumed that all past research is flawed because detection thresholds were determined by inappropriate procedures. This assumption leads to the conclusion that perception without awareness is a bogus phenomenon since, as indicated by our studies, evidence supporting the phenomenon disappears when appropriate threshold procedures are used. While our results certainly support such a conclusion, this is not the conclusion that we would like to make. Rather, we have adopted a second position which assumes that perception without awareness is a real phenomenon. However, we also take the position that previous investigators, in addition to measuring detection thresholds inappropriately, have also adopted an inappropriate definition of awareness. In our opinion, awareness should be defined in terms of a **subjective threshold,** the detection level where subjects claim not to be able to discriminate perceptual information at better than a chance level, rather than an **objective threshold,** the level of detectability where perceptual information is actually discriminated at a chance level. If the subjective threshold is accepted as the proper definition of awareness, then it is possible to relate our findings to previously reported results, since it is very probable that previous investigators, because of the poor procedures used to establish detection thresholds, have inadvertently measured the subjective rather than the objective detection threshold.

All masked prime studies reported to date have equated awareness with the objective threshold. It has been assumed, either implicitly or explicitly, that a subject is aware of a stimulus any time an accurate report concerning the stimulus is made and that a subject is unaware of a stimulus whenever an accurate report is not possible. However, as we have demonstrated, no evidence for perception without awareness is found when the detection threshold is measured accurately. Thus, if the objective detection threshold is assumed to be the appropriate definition of awareness, then the only possible conclusion is that perception without awareness does not occur.

On the other hand, several observations suggest to us that the subjective threshold is a much more appropriate definition of awareness. In our first experiment, we asked subjects after every block of trials to estimate how often they noticed the primes. As expected, we found that all subjects claimed to have absolutely no awareness of the primes in the threshold condition. Surprisingly, all subjects also reported that they rarely, if ever, noticed the primes in either the 55 or the 90% detection conditions. In these conditions, subjects simply did not have any confidence that a prime may have preceded the presentation of a color target, even though the objective detection measure, administered immediately prior to these trials, indicated that the subjects could perform a forced choice discrimination task with a relatively high level of accuracy.

These observations suggest that a major effect of the mask was to reduce confidence that a stimulus had been presented. If a mask reduces confidence, then it is very possible that observers may claim consistently that no stimulus has been presented even when discriminative behavior can be demonstrated in a properly controlled forced choice detection situation. This speculation is consistent with previous criticisms that have been directed at masked prime studies (Merikle, 1982) and suggests that previous investigators may have inadvertently measured a subjective rather than an objective threshold (e.g., Balota, 1983; Fowler et al., 1981; Marcel, 1983a).

In order to test this speculation, we measured priming under conditions where subjects expressed no confidence in their ability to perform a forced choice discrimination task (Cheesman & Merikle, 1984). These subjective thresholds were established by using a procedure similar to the one used in our other studies. The thresholds were determined over a series of trials which involved systematic decreases in the SOA separating the color words from the mask, and subjects were given no feedback concerning their performance. The novel aspect of our approach is that after every block of 48 trials, subjects were required to provide an estimate of their detection performance. In this way, we determined when subjects thought that their detection performance was at a chance level, and thus we were able to establish a subjective threshold for each subject. At the same time, since we also measured detection performance, we were able to establish the actual level of detection performance that subjects obtained when they claimed to be detecting the four color words at no better than a chance level.

Table II shows the magnitude of priming obtained at each of three prime–target SOAs when subjects claimed not to be able to discriminate among

TABLE II

Median Naming Latencies and Percentage Errors for Each Prime–Target SOA under the Subjective Threshold Condition

Prime detectability	Prime–target relationship	Prime–target SOA (msec)					
		50		550		1050	
		RT	%E	RT	%E	RT	%E
Subjective threshold (67%)	Incongruent	516	4.3	491	5.1	487	3.9
	Congruent	486	4.6	448	2.5	449	1.7
	Priming	30		43		38	

the primes. It is clear from an inspection of this table that a relatively large priming effect occurred at each SOA and that the magnitude of priming did not change significantly across the three SOAs. A consideration of the objective level of detection performance reveals why priming effects were observed in this situation. The average objective detection performance was 67% correct, which is considerably above the chance detection level of 25% correct. Thus, even though subjects claimed not to be able to see the primes, their objective detection performance indicated a considerable ability to discriminate among the primes. Therefore, it is not surprising that priming occurred in this situation, since subjects were able to detect the primes, contrary to their professed claims.

These results are consistent with our suggestion that subjective rather than objective thresholds may have been established inadvertently in previous masked prime studies because inappropriate psychophysical techniques were used. Two other observations are consistent with this conclusion. First, as previously noted, Marcel (1983a) defined awareness thresholds in his experiments as the point where presence/absence decisions were less than 60% correct in a two-choice task. Thus, some detection of the primes occurred. The second observation supporting this conclusion is found in the Fowler *et al.* (1981) article. They admit that the awareness thresholds in their studies may have been established so that they were somewhat above the objective threshold. Nonetheless, they argue that the important point concerning their experiments is that the subjects **claimed** that their decisions about the primes were always based upon movement or changes in brightness rather than the identity of the primes per se. What Fowler *et al.* appear to be stating is that their psychophysical technique may have established a subjective threshold rather than an objective threshold. This is precisely the conclusion that we wish to make.

It is possible to argue that our criticisms of both the Marcel and the Fowler *et al.* experiments are mere nit-picking with no real substance. Surely, one may question, isn't the important observation in these experiments the fact that significant priming occurred even when the primes were **barely** visible? We do not think that this is the case. If priming only occurs when the primes are visible, as indicated by discriminated verbal reports, then there is no basis for arguing either against Eriksen's (1960) position that verbal reports accurately reflect perceptual processing or in favor of Marcel's (1983b) position that lexical access occurs when detection performance is at a chance level.

Actually, priming appears to occur whenever detection performance deviates slightly above the objective threshold. The results from our second experiment support this conclusion. The data presented in Table I indicate that we were not completely successful in establishing the objective threshold in that the actual detection performance in the threshold condition was 27% correct. While no significant priming was observed in this condition, the data presented in the table suggest that a small amount of priming may have occurred across the three prime–target SOAs. When each subject's actual detection performance in this condition was correlated with the average magnitude of priming across the three SOAs, a significant correlation was obtained [$r(8) = .71$] and the intercept for zero priming was 25% correct. Thus, the small amount of priming that did occur in the threshold condition appears attributable to those subjects whose detection performance was slightly above chance, and the greater the deviation from chance, the greater was the observed priming.

A distinction between objective and subjective thresholds appears to be a critical consideration for all studies investigating perception without awareness. Our data suggest that evidence for perception without awareness will never be found when awareness is equated with the objective threshold and this threshold is established by proper psychophysical methods. On the other hand, our data also indicate that a considerable amount of perceptual processing occurs when information is presented at the subjective threshold. Unfortunately, this distinction between objective and subjective thresholds has not been acknowledged in any of the recent studies presumed to demonstrate unconscious perceptual processing of words. In fact, recent theoretical interpretation of these data implies that these two types of threshold are equivalent (e.g., Balota, 1983; Fowler *et al.,* 1981; Marcel, 1983a,b). It is very probable, however, that subjective rather than objective thresholds were established in these previous studies. Therefore, a distinction must be made between subjective and objective thresholds, and, in our opinion, the subjective threshold is the more appropriate definition of awareness. If it is assumed that the subjective threshold is the appropriate definition of awareness, then our results become entirely consistent with previous findings indicating that words may be unconsciously perceived.

VI. DISTINGUISHING CONSCIOUS
FROM UNCONSCIOUS PROCESSES

Our research suggests that a subjective rather than an objective threshold provides the better definition of awareness. We take the position that the subjective threshold captures the "aware–unaware" distinction at the phenomenological level (cf. Bowers, 1984) and thus defines the boundary between conscious and unconscious processes. On the other hand, our research also implies that discriminated verbal reports are as sensitive an indicator of perceptual processing as any other possible response (cf. Eriksen, 1960). The apparent contradiction between these two conclusions is resolved when it is recognized, as demonstrated in numerous signal detection experiments, that correct forced choice responses can be made even when observers lack any confidence that their responses accurately reflect their perceptual experiences (e.g., Rollman & Nachmias, 1972; Parasuraman, Reicher, & Beatty, 1982). Thus, forced choice responses provide an accurate description of perceptual processing and subjective confidence indicates the point on the perceptual sensitivity function where perceptual processing changes from unconscious to conscious. It is important to emphasize that our position implies that even unconscious processes require perceptual processing, as indicated by discriminated reports. Therefore, if discriminated verbal reports indicate a complete absence of perceptual processing, it will not be possible to demonstrate either conscious or unconscious perceptual processes.

Unfortunately, the empirical problem of distinguishing conscious from unconscious processes is not solved by simply changing the definition of awareness. As we have noted previously, many criticisms can be directed at any approach that equates awareness solely with a subjective threshold. The most obvious criticism is that any measure of awareness based on subjective confidence alone allows each observer to establish his or her own criteria for awareness (cf. Merikle, 1983, 1984). Furthermore, as noted by Eriksen (1960), there can never be any empirical validation of the measure itself, since differences in subjective confidence cannot be distinguished empirically from differences in bias on a verbal report task. Thus, if the awareness threshold is simply equated with the subjective threshold, disagreements concerning the perception-without-awareness hypothesis will not be resolved because of the impossibility of establishing the validity of the subjective threshold as an adequate measure of awareness.

Given these problems with defining awareness solely in terms of the subjective threshold, at least one additional criterion must be used to distinguish conscious from unconscious processes. Fortunately, the solution to this definitional problem has been expressed several times (Dixon, 1971, 1981; Shevrin & Dickman, 1980), although the proposed solution has had surprising little empirical impact. Simply stated, the additional criterion needed to distinguish conscious and unconscious perceptual processes is a demonstration that a particular independent variable has a qualitatively different effect when information is presented at an unconscious level than when the same information is presented at a conscious level. The demonstration of qualitative differences provides much stronger support for the distinction between conscious and unconscious processes than is provided by any approach based solely on evidence indicating that perceptual information is processed both above and below a particular threshold. In fact, if qualitative differences cannot be established, then it is probably impossible to reach general agreement as to the most appropriate definition of awareness.

The need to establish qualitative differences between the effects of conscious and unconscious perceptual information is entirely consistent with recent discussions of unconscious perceptual processes. Marcel (1983b), for example, states that the single most important distinction between conscious and unconscious processes is that they reflect qualitatively different representational codes. According to Marcel, conscious processing is not merely a stronger version of unconscious processing, but conscious processing imposes a different structure and interpretation on the perceptual information which leads to qualitatively different behavioral effects. Furthermore, if behavioral differences cannot be demonstrated between conscious and unconscious perceptual processes, it is even reasonable to question the need for a distinction between these two presumed types of perceptual processes in the first place.

A major weakness in the approach exemplified by many of the recent studies presumed to provide evidence for unconscious perceptual processes is that the experimental data are based entirely upon demonstrating that the magnitude of semantic priming is the same regardless of an observer's level of awareness (Balota, 1983; Fowler *et al.*, 1981; Marcel, 1983a; Marcel & Patterson, 1978). Thus, the conclusiveness of the reported data depends entirely upon the adequacy with which the awareness thresholds in these studies was defined and measured, and it is the absence of any general consensus concerning the adequacy of the threshold measures used in these studies that has led to the disagreements concerning the importance of the reported findings for the perception-without-awareness hypothesis (Henley, 1984; Merikle, 1982, 1984; Purcell *et al.*, 1983).

To avoid the problems associated with these other recent approaches to the study of unconscious perceptual processes, we have adopted an approach where we first define the awareness threshold in terms of an observer's subjective threshold and then attempt to establish that similar perceptual information presented above or below this threshold has qualitatively different behavioral effects. Our approach implies that perceptual information presented below the subjective threshold but above the objective threshold is unconsciously perceived and that perceptual information presented above the subjective threshold is consciously perceived. If it can be demonstrated that perceptual information presented below the subjective threshold has a qualitatively different behavioral effect from perceptual information presented above the subjective threshold, then strong support would be provided for our claim that the subjective threshold defines the transition between two different perceptual states which may be equated with conscious and unconscious perceptual processing.

To date, our experimental attempts to distinguish conscious from unconscious processes have relied on the Stroop color–word priming paradigm. We have exploited the fact that the relative magnitudes of facilitation and inhibition in a Stroop task vary as a function of the proportion of congruent trials (e.g., Lowe & Mitterer, 1982; Taylor, 1977). For example, in a Stroop task involving the presentation of congruent, incongruent, and control trials, the usual procedure is to administer a series of trials where each of the three types of trials is presented equally often (i.e., 33.3% of the trials). This is precisely what we did in the first experiment reported in this article. However, it has been demonstrated that both inhibition and facilitation **increase** when the proportion of congruent trials is increased. Thus, if congruent color–word combinations occur on 66.7% of the trials and incongruent and neutral combinations each occur on 16.7% of the trials, both facilitation and inhibition are greater than is found when each trial type occurs equally often.

Probability effects, such as the one described above, have been interpreted to indicate that observers adopt a strategy on any particular task to maximize performance (e.g., Logan, Zbrodoff, & Williamson, 1984; Neely, 1977; Posner & Snyder, 1975a; Taylor, 1977). According to this view, the increased facilitation and inhibition that occur when congruent color–word combinations occur on 66.7% of the trials are due to the fact that the observers adopt a strategy whereby they assume that the word predicts the color response. This is a reasonable strategy for the task, given that it should facilitate performance on 66.7% of the trials and possibly only disrupt performance on the small proportion of trials which involve incongruent color–word combinations.

Another reasonable assumption is that observers can only initiate a particular strategy when they are consciously aware of a stimulus. This assumption is consistent with views such as those expressed by Posner and Snyder (1975a,b) and Underwood (1982), who equate attentional processes with consciousness. If this assumption is correct, then the probability effect in the Stroop task should only occur when observers are aware of the words.

On the other hand, when observers claim to have no awareness of the words, then it should be impossible for them to implement any strategy which predicts a future event such as the presentation of a particular color. A demonstration that the probability effect is limited to situations where observers are consciously aware of the color words, as defined by the subjective threshold, would indicate that conscious and unconscious perceptual processes are qualitatively different, and it is this type of a finding that is needed to support the distinction between conscious and unconscious perceptual processes.

A. Experiment 3

The purpose of this study was to establish if an increased proportion of congruent trials increases the relative magnitudes of facilitation and inhibition in a Stroop priming task, as has been found in other reported studies involving the Stroop effect. The general methodology was similar to that used in Experiments 1 and 2, and complete details are available in Cheesman and Merikle (1985). Given that we were only interested, initially, in establishing that changes in the proportion of congruent trials increase the relative magnitudes of facilitation and inhibition, the prime-mask SOA was set at 250 msec so that all words were clearly visible. Each observer received two blocks of 144 experimental trials. In one block of trials, congruent, incongruent, and control trials were presented equally often, or in other words, each condition occurred on 33.3% of the trials. In the other block of trials, congruent color-word combinations were presented on 66.7% of the trials and incongruent and neutral combinations were each presented on 16.7% of the trials. Prior to the presentation of each block of experimental trials, each observer received a block of 48 practice trials where the proportion of congruent trials was the same as was to occur on the immediately following block of experimental trials. If changes in the proportion of congruent trials change the strategy that observers adopt in our version of a Stroop priming task, then greater facilitation and inhibition should occur in the block of trials where congruent color-word combinations are presented on 66.7% of the trials.

The results of the experiment are presented in Table III, where the mean performance on the three types of trials is shown for the two probability conditions. The important aspect of the data shown in the table is that both facilitation and inhibition increased when the proportion of congruent trials within a trial block increased to 66.7%. Thus, the observers responded more rapidly on the congruent trials and more slowly on the incongruent trials when the congruent trials occurred on 66.7% of the trials than they did when only 33.3% of the trials involved congruent color-word combina-

TABLE III

**Mean Naming Latencies and Percentage Errors for Each Level
of Congruent Trial Probability**

Prime–target relationship	Congruent trial probability			
	33.3%		66.7%	
	RT	%E	RT	%E
Congruent	454	.4	441	0.4
Control	494	2.0	500	2.4
Incongruent	576	13.0	602	19.0

tions. This pattern of results indicates that we were successful in replicating the probability effect reported by other investigators (e.g., Lowe & Mitterer, 1982; Taylor, 1977). More importantly, given that we were able to replicate the probability effect in our version of a Stroop priming task, it was possible to use this task to establish if strategy changes induced by variations in the proportion of congruent trials are limited to conditions where observers are aware of the presence of the primes.

B. Experiment 4

The question of primary interest in this experiment concerned whether or not the strategy changes observed in the previous experiment also occur when observers claim to have no awareness of the color–word primes. As discussed previously, it is reasonable to expect that observers can only implement a strategy based upon an expectation of a future event when they "consciously see" a prime. If this assumption is correct, then the probability effect should not be observed when the color–word primes are presented below the awareness threshold. On the other hand, given that the awareness threshold is defined in terms of the subjective threshold, both facilitation and inhibition should occur even when observers claim they cannot "see" the primes, since these primes are presented at an energy level which exceeds the objective threshold. Thus, when the primes are presented below the awareness threshold, both facilitation and inhibition should be observed across all probability conditions, but the relative magnitudes of facilitation and inhibition should not vary with changes in the proportion of congruent trials, as occurs when the primes are presented above the awareness threshold.

The general methodology for this experiment was much the same as followed in the previous experiment. However, there were two important exceptions. First, prior to the beginning of the experiment proper, each observer's subjective threshold was established. Several blocks of 48 trials were presented, and after each block of trials, the SOA separating the color words from the mask was systematically decreased until the observers estimated that their detection performance approximated a chance level. It was found that the objective detection performance approximated 66% correct when the observers claimed that they were unable to detect the color words. This finding is entirely consistent with our previous results.

The second procedural change introduced in the present study was that each block of experimental trials contained primes presented at both subjective threshold and suprathreshold (i.e., 250-msec) prime–mask SOAs. Thus, there were two blocks of 288 experimental trials which were differentiated by whether the proportion of congruent trials was 33.3 or 66.7%, and within each trial block, presentations of the subjective threshold and suprathreshold primes were randomly intermixed. By randomizing the presentation of the two threshold conditions within each trial block, it was possible to ensure that any observed strategy differences across the two threshold conditions were induced on a trial-by-trial basis and did not result from a general strategy applicable only to a particular threshold condition.

The results of this experiment are shown in Table IV. The data presented in the table indicate that both facilitation and inhibition occurred in both threshold conditions. Although the Stroop effects were somewhat smaller in the subjective threshold than the suprathreshold condition, the presence of both facilitation and inhibition in the subjective threshold condition clearly indicates that the primes were being detected. However, in spite of the fact that the primes were detected in the subjective threshold condition, the data presented in Table IV show that no probability effect was observed. That is to say, the relative magnitudes of facilitation and inhibition

TABLE IV

Mean Naming Latencies and Percentage Errors for Each Level of Congruent Trial Probability under Subjective Threshold and Suprathreshold Conditions

Prime detectability	Prime–target relationship	Congruent trial probability			
		33.3%		66.7%	
		RT	%E	RT	%E
Subjective threshold	Congruent	446	2.1	439	1.7
	Control	464	2.1	470	3.4
	Incongruent	488	3.8	487	4.2
Suprathreshold	Congruent	424	0.8	412	0.4
	Control	464	1.1	469	2.1
	Incongruent	550	9.4	584	13.8

were the same irrespective of whether the congruent color–word combinations were presented on 33.3 or 66.7% of the trials within a block.

In contrast to the effects observed for the subjective threshold condition, the data presented in Table IV for the suprathreshold condition indicate that we were able to replicate successfully the results obtained in Experiment 3. Thus, in the suprathreshold condition, both facilitation and inhibition increased when the proportion of congruent trials was increased from 33.3 to 66.7%.

The different patterns of results observed in the two threshold conditions become even clearer when only the results from the congruent and incongruent conditions are considered.[2] The results for these two conditions are presented in Fig. 5, where it can be seen that the proportion of congruent trials had virtually no effect in the subjective threshold condition but a relatively large effect in the suprathreshold condition. These different patterns of results indicate that the primes had qualitatively different effects in the

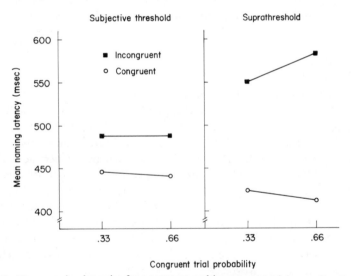

Fig. 5. Mean naming latencies for congruent and incongruent trials as a function of congruent trial probability under subjective and suprathreshold conditions in Experiment 4.

[2]Given that the critical comparisons only involved the congruent and incongruent trials, the results from the control trials are not essential. Furthermore, in the subjective threshold condition, the control trials may not have been completely comparable to the other two types of trials. For the congruent and incongruent trials, separate prime–mask SOAs were determined for each color word. However, on the control trials each observer's prime–mask SOA for the neutral stimulus was based on the average prime–mask SOA for the color words. Thus, the neutral stimulus may have been more discriminable than the color words.

two threshold conditions, and therefore, they are consistent with our hypothesis that strategy effects can be induced only when observers are aware of the primes, as they were in the suprathreshold condition.

The results obtained in this experiment provide strong support for the two-fold approach we advocate for distinguishing conscious from unconscious processes. Given the assumption that the subjective threshold identifies the transition between conscious and unconscious perceptual processes, then the fact that the probability effect only occurs when perceptual information is presented at an energy level which exceeds the subjective threshold provides additional support for this assumption. Furthermore, the demonstration of qualitative differences also provides an indication of how unconscious and conscious perceptual processes differ, and it is only by establishing qualitative differences that it will ever be possible to specify the critical differences which distinguish conscious from unconscious processes. Finally, it is important to emphasize once again that the only way to avoid endless controversy over the proper definition of awareness is to demonstrate that conscious and unconscious perceptual processes produce qualitatively different behavioral effects.

C. Other Experimental Evidence

Previously, we criticized the procedures used by Marcel (1980; 1983a) to establish awareness thresholds and argued that it is very probable that he established subjective rather than objective thresholds in his studies. If our arguments are accepted and it is assumed that Marcel did inadvertently establish subjective thresholds in his studies, then one experiment reported by Marcel (1980) actually provides strong support for unconscious perceptual processes, as the reported data are consistent with the twofold approach we advocate. In particular, Marcel (1980) found that polysemous or ambiguous words are differentially processed depending upon the level of awareness. Thus, Marcel appears to have demonstrated that unconsciously perceived words have a qualitatively different behavioral effect than consciously perceived words.

In this important experiment, Marcel (1980) presented three successive letter strings and required subjects to make word–nonword decisions to the first and third letter strings. On critical trials, the second letter string was a polysemous word (e.g., *palm*), which was either masked or not masked, and as an index of the particular meaning accessed by a polysemous word, Marcel used the reaction time for the lexical decision to the third word presented in the series. The results of the experiment indicated that, on unmasked trials where all three words were clearly visible, lexical decisions to the third words in triads such as *tree-palm-wrist* were considerably slower than decisions to the third words in triads such as *clock–race–wrist* which contained three unrelated words. On the other hand, the fastest lexical decisions were made to the third words in series such as *hand–palm–wrist*. This pattern of results indicates that the initial word in a triad biased the interpretation of the second word so that the only meaning of the second word available to influence the lexical decision to the third word was the one associated with the meaning of the first word.

In contrast to the results observed when the second word in a triad was clearly visible, Marcel found a completely different pattern of results when the second word was centrally masked so that observers claimed to have no awareness of its presence. With central masking of the second words, lexical decisions to the third words in triads such as *tree–palm–wrist* and *hand–palm–wrist* were both facilitated relative to lexical decisions to the third words in trials containing three unrelated words (e.g., *clock–race–wrist*). This result suggests that **both** meanings of the second words were activated when these words were centrally masked, as the initial word in each triad had relatively little influence on the time needed to make a lexical decision to the third word.

Marcel's results, if replicable, provide strong support for unconscious word recognition. His results indicate that the particular perceptual processes initiated by the presentation of a polysemous word (e.g., *palm*) are dependent upon whether or not the word is consciously or unconsciously perceived. When the polysemous word is clearly visible and therefore consciously perceived, the meaning activated by its presentation is selectively biased by a previously presented word (e.g., *tree* or *hand*). On the other hand, when observers claim that they cannot "see" the polysemous word, no selective bias is induced by the presentation of a previous word. These differential effects, which depend upon the level of awareness for the polysemous words, suggest that consciously perceived words initiate qualitatively different cognitive processes from unconsciously perceived words. Thus, Marcel's (1980) results are completely consistent with the twofold approach we advocate for distinguishing conscious from unconscious processes, as long as one accepts the assumption that he inadvertently defined awareness in terms of the subjective threshold.

VII. IMPLICATIONS AND CONCLUSIONS

Taken together, the experimental findings reported in this article indicate that an explicit distinction must be made between objective and subjective thresholds in order to account for the relationship between word recognition and consciousness. Given that evidence for both conscious and unconscious perceptual processing was found only when visual information was presented at an energy level which exceeded the objective threshold, our research demonstrates that the objective threshold, defined in terms of discriminated verbal reports, provides a completely adequate indicator of perceptual processing (cf. Eriksen, 1960). On the other hand, our research also indicates that observers may **claim** to have no awareness for stimuli which are presented at an energy level that exceeds the one associated with the objective threshold. It is this observation that led us to consider the subjective threshold as an indicator of awareness. The subjective threshold, defined in terms of self-reports of awareness, is assumed to reflect the transition between unconscious and conscious perceptual processing, and its use as an indicator of awareness is supported by the demonstration in Experiment 4 that perceptual information presented above or below this threshold has qualitatively different consequences.

This distinction between subjective and objective thresholds has important implications for recent models of perceptual processing proposed to account for the unconscious perception of masked words (Allport, 1977; Marcel, 1983b). These models are based on the assumption that the objective threshold provides an adequate measure of awareness. However, if the proposed distinction between subjective and objective thresholds is accepted, then these models must be revised before they can provide an adequate account of the findings reported in this article.

A. Models of Unconscious Word Recognition

Both Allport (1977) and Marcel (1983b) have proposed models of perceptual processing in which consciousness or phenomenal awareness is equated with the ability to provide a verbal report concerning a visual stimulus. According to these models, the visual presentation of a word activates functionally independent processing modules which collect evidence concerning the specific attributes of the word. It is assumed that there are independent modules corresponding to the semantic, phonemic, graphemic, and visual information contained in a word and that these modules operate automatically and **unconsciously** to produce perceptual records. Stable percepts of stimuli, however, are produced only through the subsequent integration of these individual perceptual records, and verbal reports can be based only on these integrated percepts. Thus, if the perceptual integration of the individual records is disrupted for any reason, then an observer will not be conscious of a visual stimulus, since, by definition, a verbal report concerning the stimulus will be impossible.

The models proposed by Allport and Marcel can account for the apparent independence between verbal reports and semantic priming observed in the recent masked prime studies if two additional assumptions are made. These assumptions are that (1) central pattern masking **only** disrupts the processing necessary to form visual records and (2) the visual record is the critical record required for perceptual integration. Taken together, these assumptions imply that central masking, through its selective effect on visual processing, prevents perceptual integration. Thus, the stable percepts necessary for phenomenal awareness are never formed, and observers are unable to provide verbal reports describing their perceptual experiences. However, since a central mask only disrupts visual processing, all other perceptual records are presumed to proceed to the highest possible level of unconscious representation, and it is these records that are presumed to provide the basis for priming effects. Given that the models proposed by Allport and Marcel provide an account of why priming appears to occur in the absence of verbal reports, these models, or very close variants, have been used to explain the results obtained in all recent masked prime studies (e.g., Balota, 1983; Fowler *et al.*, 1981; Marcel, 1980, 1983a,b).

One implication that may be derived from these models of perceptual processing is that a centrally masked word should always produce a complete semantic record. This implication follows from the fact that no process exists in these models to interrupt the accumulation of semantic information. The strong prediction that follows from this implication is that centrally masked primes, no matter how short the prime–mask SOA, should always produce maximal semantic priming. Although this prediction is consistent with the results reported by both Fowler *et al.* (1981) and Marcel (1983a), who found approximately equal magnitudes of priming following the presentation of either masked or unmasked primes, other investigators (e.g., Balota, 1983) have reported that less priming is produced by masked primes than by unmasked primes. Thus, it appears that evidence favoring this strong prediction is not always found, and perhaps a weaker prediction is more realistic.

A weaker, and probably more reasonable, prediction based on these models of perceptual processing is that maximal semantic priming should **always** occur whenever discriminated verbal reports concerning masked words exceed a chance level of performance. This prediction follows from the assumption that verbal reports indicate successful perceptual integration. Given that perceptual integration requires a complete visual record and that a mask only interferes with the formation of visual records, then complete semantic processing should always accompany perceptual integration, as indicated by verbal reports.

Even this weaker prediction derived from these models is not supported by the results of our experiments. In particular, the results of Experiments 1 and 2 clearly show that the magnitude of priming is positively correlated with forced choice discrimination performance. Thus, our results suggest, at the very least, that a central mask limits the accumulation of **both** semantic and visual information. This finding indicates that certain assumptions contained in these models must be incorrect, since the models clearly predict that the magnitude of priming should remain constant once discriminated verbal reports exceed a chance level of performance. Given these contradictory findings, it appears that these models, at least in their present form, do not provide an adequate account of the relationship between word recognition and consciousness.

B. A Revised Model of Unconscious Word Recognition

It is possible to revise the models of perceptual processing proposed by Allport (1977) and Marcel (1983b) so that they can account for both our results and the results obtained in previous masked prime studies. Such a revision is based on the assumption that phenomenal awareness or consciousness is indexed by the subjective threshold rather than by the objective threshold. Given the relationship between subjective and objective thresholds established in our studies, it follows from this assumption that discriminated verbal reports not only indicate conscious perceptual processing, as assumed in the Allport and Marcel models, but also serve as an indicator of when a stimulus may have initiated unconscious perceptual processes. It is important to note that this revised assumption does not contradict the original assumption made by both Allport and Marcel suggesting that phenomenal awareness is based on stable percepts produced through the integration of individual perceptual records. This revised assumption implies only that the subjective threshold rather than the objective threshold indicates when a stable integrated percept of a stimulus has been formed.

Before the Allport and Marcel models can account for our findings, a second revision is also required. This revision concerns the assumption in these models which specifies that a central mask has a very selective effect. Rather than assuming that a central mask only disrupts visual processing, a more reasonable assumption is that a central mask disrupts *all* perceptual processing. This revised assumption is more consistent with previous interpretations of central masking (cf. Turvey, 1973), and it is also consistent with our results indicating that a central mask disrupts both semantic and visual processing.

With these two revisions, the original models proposed by Allport and Marcel lead to the following account of perceptual processing. The presentation of any visual stimulus will activate the various processing modules corresponding to the different attributes of the stimulus. Normally, these modules will operate automatically and unconsciously until sufficient information is processed so that individual records can be integrated to form stable percepts. These stable percepts will then form the basis for phenomenal awareness or consciousness. However, whenever the stimulus energy is insufficient or a central mask disrupts perceptual processing, perceptual integration will not occur, and observers will claim not to be aware or conscious of a stimulus.

According to this revised account of perceptual processing, an absence of phenomenal awareness following the presentation of a stimulus can occur for two different reasons. If the stimulus information was insufficient for the formation of any perceptual records, then no evidence for perceptual processing will be revealed by either direct or indirect measures of perception. On the other hand, if the stimulus information was sufficient to permit the formation of at least a limited number of perceptual records, then all measures of perceptual processing, including discriminated verbal reports, will indicate that some perceptual processing has occurred. In both cases, however, there will be no phenomenal awareness, since the perceptual records would be insufficient to allow the formation of stable integrated percepts.

It is our view that the objective threshold defines the point on the detectability continuum where sufficient information has been accumulated to permit the formation of at least a limited number of perceptual records and that the subjective threshold defines the point on this continuum where sufficient information has been accumulated to form stable integrated percepts. This view implies that both discriminated verbal reports and indirect measures of perception such as priming can be based on unconscious perceptual records. In fact, whenever stimulus information is presented at an energy level that is both below the subjective threshold and above the objective threshold, all measures of perceptual processing should indicate a sensitivity to the presence of this information, even though the observers may claim not to be aware of the stimulus.

This revised account of perceptual processing leads to a model of unconscious word recognition that has one major advantage over the earlier models proposed by Allport and Marcel. The revised model can account for both the correlation we found between indirect and direct measures of perceptual processing and the independence previous investigators found between indirect measures of semantic processing and direct measures of claimed awareness (Balota, 1983; Fowler *et al.,* 1981; Marcel, 1980, 1983a). Thus, by distinguishing between subjective and objective thresholds, it is possible to integrate apparently contradictory results within a common theoretical framework.

ACKNOWLEDGMENTS

The preparation of this manuscript was supported by a Natural Sciences and Engineering Research Council of Canada Postgraduate Scholarship to the first author and by Grant APA-231 from the Natural Sciences and Engineering Research Council of Canada to the second author.

REFERENCES

Allport, D. A. (1977). On knowing the meaning of words we are unable to report: The effects of visual masking. In S. Dornic (Ed.), *Attention and performance VI* (pp. 505–533). Hillsdale, NJ: Erlbaum.

Balota, D. A. (1983). Automatic semantic activation and episodic memory encoding. *Journal of Verbal Learning and Verbal Behavior,* **22,** 88–104.

Bowers, K. S. (1984). On being unconsciously influenced and informed. In K. S. Bowers & D. Meichenbaum (Eds.), *The unconscious reconsidered* (pp. 227–272). New York: Wiley.

Cheesman, J., & Merikle, P. M. (1984). Priming with and without awareness. *Perception & Psychophysics,* **36,** 387–395.

Cheesman, J., & Merikle, P. M. (1985). *Distinguishing conscious from unconscious perceptual processes.* Submitted.

Dalrymple-Alford, E. C. (1972). Associative facilitation and interference in the Stroop color-word task. *Perception & Psychophysics,* **11,** 274–276.

Dixon, N. F. (1971). *Subliminal perception: The nature of a controversy.* New York: McGraw-Hill.

Dixon, N. F. (1981). *Preconscious processing.* New York: Wiley.

Dyer, F. N. (1973). The Stroop phenomenon and its use in the study of perceptual, cognitive, and response processes. *Memory & Cognition,* **1,** 106–120.

Dyer, F. N., & Severance, L. J. (1973). Stroop interference with successive presentations of separate incongruent words and colors. *Journal of Experimental Psychology,* **98,** 438–439.

Ellis, A. W., & Marshall, J. C. (1978). Semantic errors or statistical flukes? A note on Allport's "On knowing the meaning of words we are unable to report." *Quarterly Journal of Experimental Psychology,* **30,** 569–575.

Eriksen, C. W. (1960). Discrimination and learning without awareness: A methodological survey and evaluation. *Psychological Review,* **67,** 279–300.

Fowler, C. A., Wolford, G., Slade, R., & Tassinary, L. (1981). Lexical access with and without awareness. *Journal of Experimental Psychology: General,* **110,** 341–362.

Henderson, L. (1982). *Orthography and word recognition in reading.* New York: Academic Press.

Henley, S. H. A. (1984). Unconscious perception re-revisited: A comment on Merikle's (1982) paper. *Bulletin of the Psychonomic Society,* **22,** 121–124.

Holender, D. (1985). Semantic activation without conscious identification in dichotic listening, parafoveal vision, and visual masking: A survey and appraisal. *Behavioral and Brain Sciences,* in press.

Logan, G. D., Zbrodoff, N. J., & Williamson, J. (1984). Strategies in the color–word Stroop task. *Bulletin of the Psychonomic Society,* **22,** 135–138.

Lowe, D. G., & Mitterer, J. O. (1982). Selective and divided attention in a Stroop task. *Canadian Journal of Psychology,* **36,** 684–700.

Marcel, A. J. (1974). *Perception with and without awareness.* Paper presented at the July meeting of the Experimental Psychology Society, Stirling, Scotland.

Marcel, A. J. (1980). Conscious and preconscious recognition of polysemous words: Locating the selective effects of prior verbal context. In R. S. Nickerson (Ed.), *Attention and performance VIII* (pp. 435–457). Hillsdale: NJ: Erlbaum.

Marcel, A. J. (1983a). Conscious and unconscious perception: Experiments on visual masking and word recognition. *Cognitive Psychology, 15,* 197–237.

Marcel, A. J. (1983b). Conscious and unconscious perception: An appoach to the relations between phenomenal experience and perceptual processes. *Cognitive Psychology, 15,* 238–300.

Marcel, A. J., & Patterson, K. E. (1978). Word recognition and production: Reciprocity in clinical and normal studies. In J. Requin (Ed.), *Attention and performance VII* (pp. 209–226). Hillsdale, NJ: Erlbaum.

Merikle, P. M. (1982). Unconscious perception revisited. *Perception & Psychophysics, 31,* 298–301.

Merikle, P. M. (1983). Subliminal perception reaffirmed (Review of *Preconscious processing*). *Canadian Journal of Psychology, 37,* 324–326.

Merikle, P. M. (1984). Toward a definition of awareness. *Bulletin of the Psychonomic Society, 22,* 449–450.

Meyer, D. E., Schvaneveldt, R. W., & Ruddy, M. G. (1975). Loci of contextual effects on visual word-recognition. In P. M. A. Rabbitt & S. Dornic (Eds.), *Attention and performance V* (pp. 98–118). New York: Academic Press.

Neely, J. H. (1976). Semantic priming and retrieval from lexical memory: Evidence for facilitory and inhibitory processes. *Memory & Cognition, 4,* 648–654.

Neely, J. H. (1977). Semantic priming and retrieval from lexical memory: Roles of inhibitionless spreading activation and limited-capacity attention. *Journal of Experimental Psychology: General, 106,* 226–254.

Nolan, K. A., & Caramazza, A. (1982). Unconscious perception of meaning: A failure to replicate. *Bulletin of the Psychonomic Society, 20,* 23–26.

Parasuraman, R., Richer, F., & Beatty, J. (1982). Detection and recognition: Concurrent processes in perception. *Perception & Psychophysics, 31,* 1–12.

Posner, M. I., & Snyder, C. R. R. (1975a). Attention and cognitive control. In R. L. Solso (Ed.), *Information processing and cognition: The Loyola symposium* (pp. 55–85). Hillsdale, NJ: Erlbaum.

Posner, M. I., & Snyder, C. R. R. (1975b). Facilitation and inhibition in the processing of signals. In P. M. A. Rabbitt & S. Dornic (Eds.), *Attention and performance V* (pp. 669–682). New York: Academic Press.

Purcell, D. G., Stewart, A. L., & Stanovich, K. E. (1983). Another look at semantic priming without awareness. *Perception & Psychophysics, 34,* 65–71.

Rollman, G. E., & Nachmias, J. (1972). Simultaneous detection and recognition of chromatic flashes. *Perception & Psychophysics, 12,* 309–314.

Shevrin, H., & Dickman, S. (1980). The psychological unconscious: A necessary assumption for all psychological theory? *American Psychologist, 35,* 421–434.

Stanovich, K. E., & West, R. F. (1983). On priming by a sentence context. *Journal of Experimental Psychology: General, 112,* 1–36.

Stroop, J. R. (1935). Studies of interference in serial verbal reactions. *Journal of Experimental Psychology, 18,* 643–661.

Taylor, D. A. (1977). Time course of context effects. *Journal of Experimental Psychology: General, 106,* 404–426.

Turvey, M. T. (1973). On peripheral and central processes in vision: Inferences from an in-

formation-processing analysis of masking with patterned stimuli. *Psychological Review,*
    80, 1–52.

Underwood, G. (1982). Attention and awareness in cognitive and motor skills. In G. Under-
    wood (Ed.), *Aspects of consciousness: Vol. 3. Awareness and self-awareness* (pp. 111–
    145). New York: Academic Press.

Williams, P. C., & Parkin, A. J. (1980). On knowing the meaning of words we are unable to
    report: Confirmation of a guessing explanation. *Quarterly Journal of Experimental Psy-
    chology,* **32,** 101–107.

INDEX